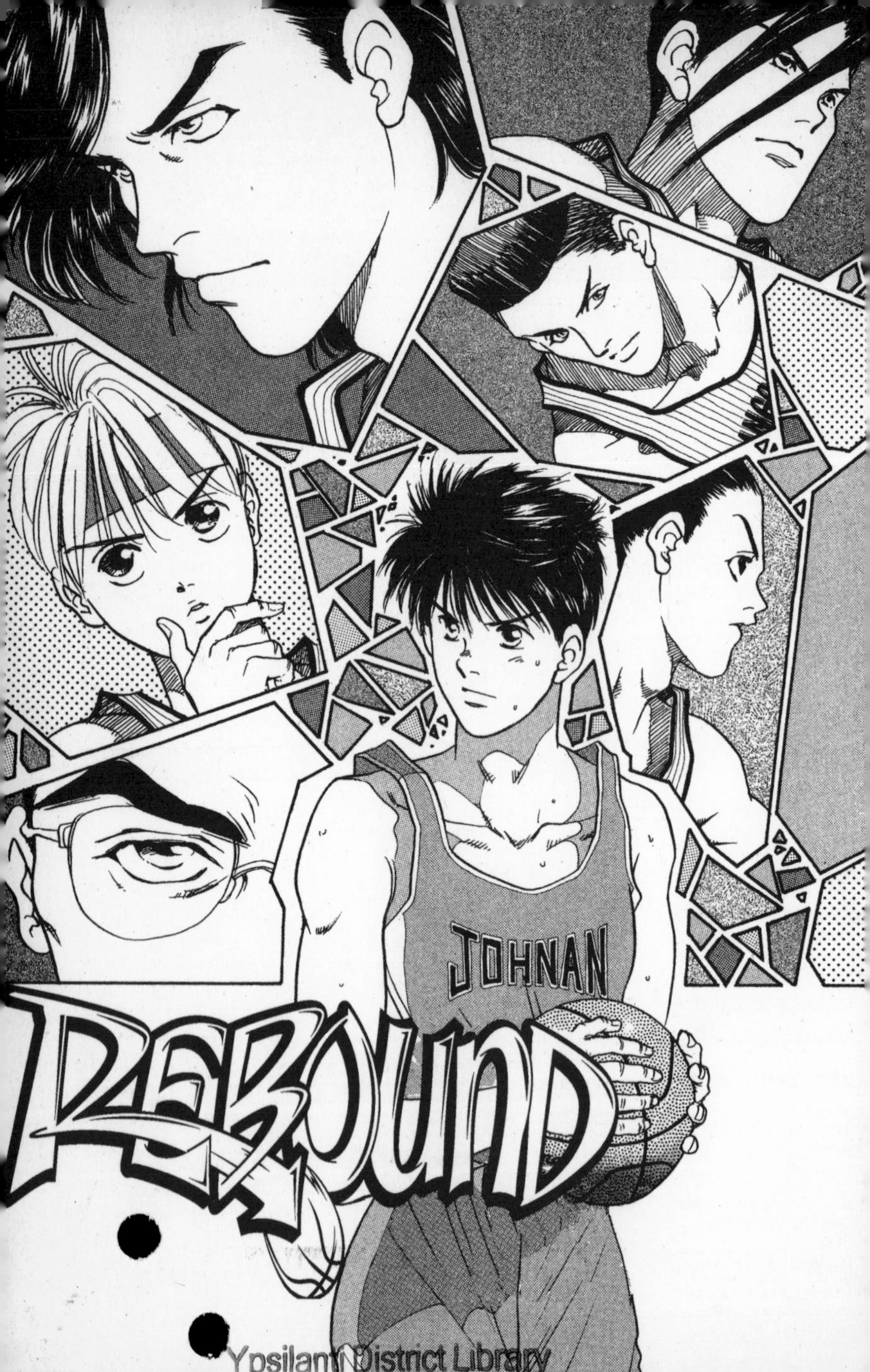
JOHNAN
REBOUND

ALSO AVAILABLE FROM TOKYOPOP®

MANGA

HACK//LEGEND OF THE TWILIGHT*
@LARGE (December 2003)
ANGELIC LAYER*
BABY BIRTH*
BATTLE ROYALE*
BRAIN POWERED*
BRIGADOON*
CARDCAPTOR SAKURA
CARDCAPTOR SAKURA: MASTER OF THE CLOW*
CHOBITS*
CHRONICLES OF THE CURSED SWORD
CLAMP SCHOOL DETECTIVES*
CLOVER
CONFIDENTIAL CONFESSIONS*
CORRECTOR YUI
COWBOY BEBOP*
COWBOY BEBOP: SHOOTING STAR*
CYBORG 009*
DEMON DIARY
DIGIMON*
DRAGON HUNTER
DRAGON KNIGHTS*
DUKLYON: CLAMP SCHOOL DEFENDERS*
ERICA SAKURAZAWA*
FAKE*
FLCL*
FORBIDDEN DANCE*
GATE KEEPERS*
G GUNDAM*
GRAVITATION*
GTO*
GUNDAM WING
GUNDAM WING: BATTLEFIELD OF PACIFISTS
GUNDAM WING: ENDLESS WALTZ*
GUNDAM WING: THE LAST OUTPOST*
HAPPY MANIA*
HARLEM BEAT
I.N.V.U.
INITIAL D*
ISLAND
JING: KING OF BANDITS*
JULINE
KARE KANO*
KINDAICHI CASE FILES, THE*
KING OF HELL
KODOCHA: SANA'S STAGE*
LOVE HINA*
LUPIN III*
MAGIC KNIGHT RAYEARTH*

MAGIC KNIGHT RAYEARTH II* (COMING SOON)
MAN OF MANY FACES*
MARMALADE BOY*
MARS*
MIRACLE GIRLS
MIYUKI-CHAN IN WONDERLAND*
MONSTERS, INC.
PARADISE KISS*
PARASYTE
PEACH GIRL
PEACH GIRL: CHANGE OF HEART*
PET SHOP OF HORRORS*
PLANET LADDER*
PLANETES*
PRIEST
RAGNAROK
RAVE MASTER*
REALITY CHECK
REBIRTH
REBOUND*
RISING STARS OF MANGA
SABER MARIONETTE J*
SAILOR MOON
SAINT TAIL
SAMURAI DEEPER KYO*
SAMURAI GIRL: REAL BOUT HIGH SCHOOL*
SCRYED*
SHAOLIN SISTERS*
SHIRAHIME-SYO: SNOW GODDESS TALES* (Dec. 2003)
SHUTTERBOX
SORCERER HUNTERS
THE SKULL MAN*
THE VISION OF ESCAFLOWNE*
TOKYO MEW MEW*
UNDER THE GLASS MOON
VAMPIRE GAME*
WILD ACT*
WISH*
WORLD OF HARTZ (November 2003)
X-DAY*
ZODIAC P.I. *

For more information visit www.TOKYOPOP.com

*INDICATES 100% AUTHENTIC MANGA (RIGHT-TO-LEFT FORMAT)

CINE-MANGA™

CARDCAPTORS
JACKIE CHAN ADVENTURES (November 2003)
JIMMY NEUTRON
KIM POSSIBLE
LIZZIE MCGUIRE
POWER RANGERS: NINJA STORM
SPONGEBOB SQUAREPANTS
SPY KIDS 2

NOVELS

KARMA CLUB (April 2004)
SAILOR MOON

TOKYOPOP KIDS

STRAY SHEEP

ART BOOKS

CARDCAPTOR SAKURA*
MAGIC KNIGHT RAYEARTH*

ANIME GUIDES

COWBOY BEBOP ANIME GUIDES
GUNDAM TECHNICAL MANUALS
SAILOR MOON SCOUT GUIDES

080503

By Yuriko Nishiyama

Volume 4

TOKYOPOP

Los Angeles • Tokyo • London

Translator - Shirley Kubo
English Adaption - Jordan Capell
Retouch and Lettering - Deron Bennett
Cover Layout - Patrick Hook

Editor - Luis Reyes
Managing Editor - Jill Freshney
Production Coordinator - Antonio DePietro
Production Manager - Jennifer Miller
Art Director - Matt Alford
Editorial Director - Jeremy Ross
VP of Production - Ron Klamert
President & C.O.O. - John Parker
Publisher & C.E.O. - Stuart Levy

Email: editor@TOKYOPOP.com
Come visit us online at www.TOKYOPOP.com

A  Manga

TOKYOPOP Inc.
5900 Wilshire Blvd. Suite 2000
Los Angeles, CA 90036

ISBN: 1-59182-222-X

First TOKYOPOP® printing: October 2003

10 9 8 7 6 5 4 3 2 1
Printed in the USA

4-28-03

-Play by Play-
The Season So Far...

The Johnan High basketball team has
worked hard all year and has finally gotten
to the national championships in Sapporo.
However, if the team loses just one game,
they're on the first plane back to Tokyo.
Hopes are high after winning their first game
against Okinawa Kyan Marine Industry High
School. But now Johnan has to face Tsukuba
High School, the very team that knocked them
out of the finals last year... Which wouldn't be so bad
if most of the team hadn't stayed out all night partying,
Shurman's feet didn't hurt, and Sawamura didn't
just bail to confront his estranged father.

Today on  REBOUND

VIER

REBOUND

GIANNI VALE

You're reading...

REBOUND

Episode 28: Trust and Parts

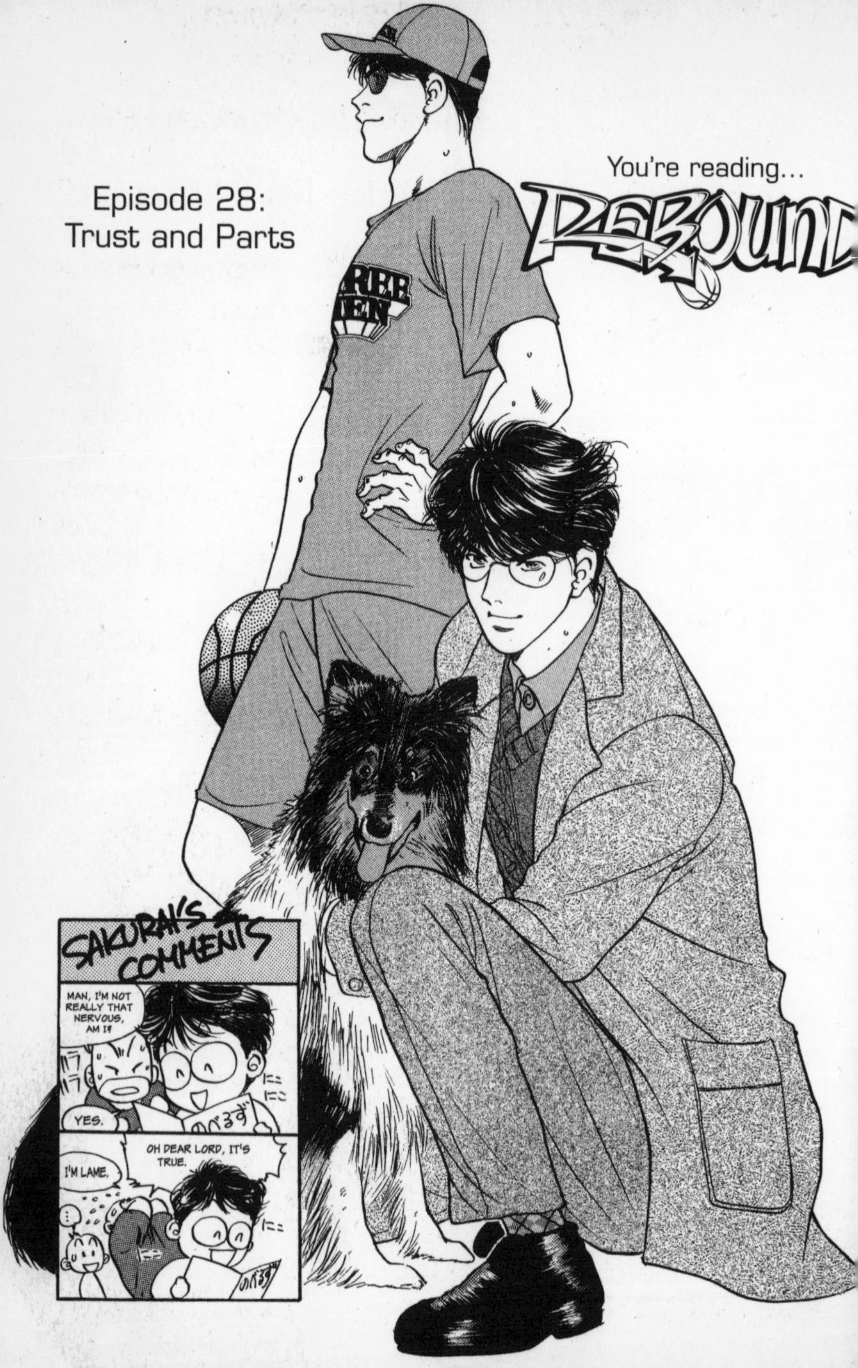
SAKURAI'S COMMENTS
MAN, I'M NOT REALLY THAT NERVOUS, AM I?
YES.
OH DEAR LORD, IT'S TRUE.
I'M LAME.
…

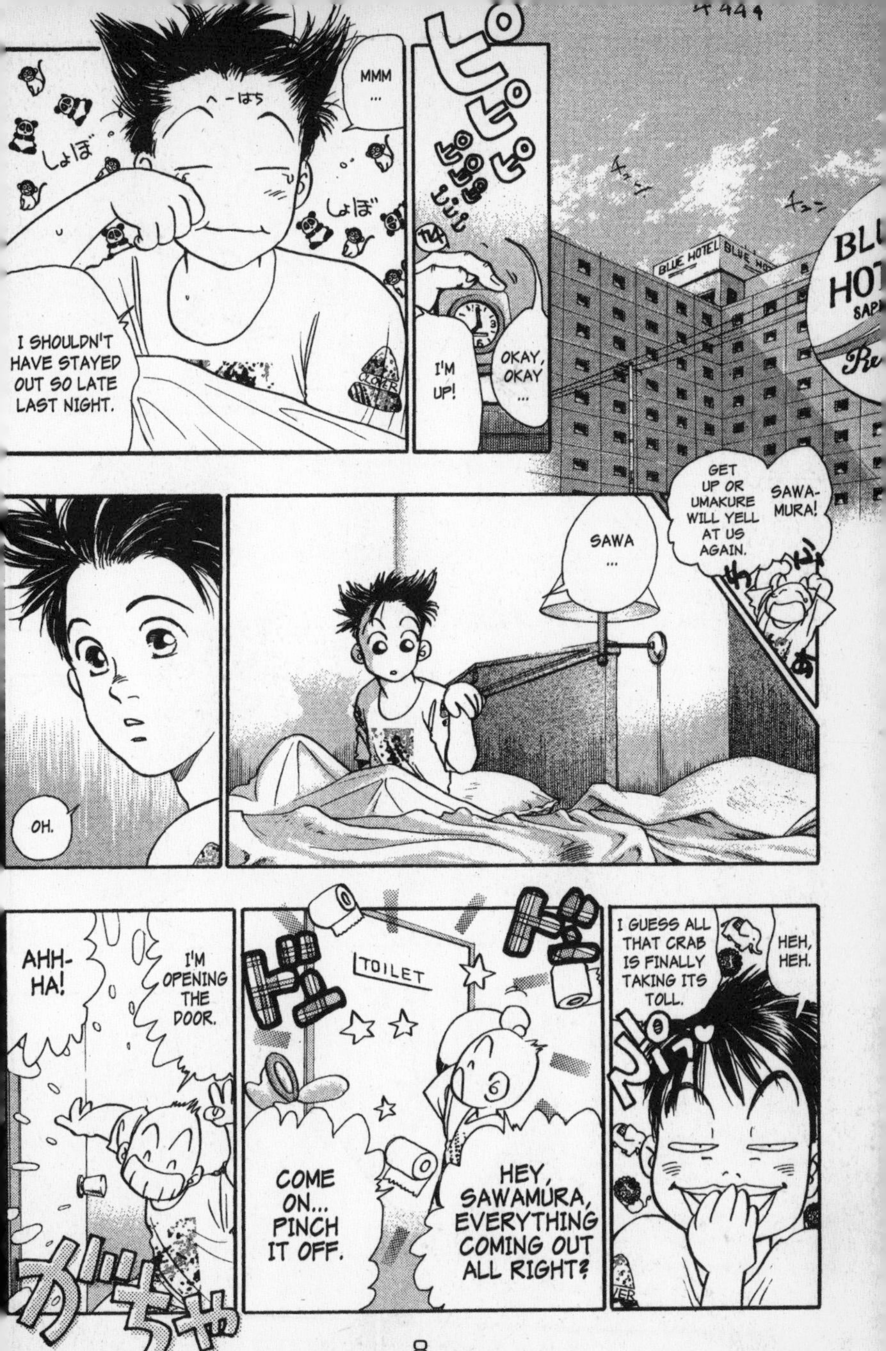

BLUE HOTEL
SAWAMURA!
GET UP OR UMAKURE WILL YELL AT US AGAIN.
ピピピ
OKAY, OKAY ...
I'M UP!
MMM ...
しょぼ
しょぼ
I SHOULDN'T HAVE STAYED OUT SO LATE LAST NIGHT.
SAWA ...
OH.
HEH, HEH.
I GUESS ALL THAT CRAB IS FINALLY TAKING ITS TOLL.
TOILET
HEY, SAWAMURA, EVERYTHING COMING OUT ALL RIGHT?
COME ON... PINCH IT OFF.
I'M OPENING THE DOOR.
AHH-HA!
がちゃ

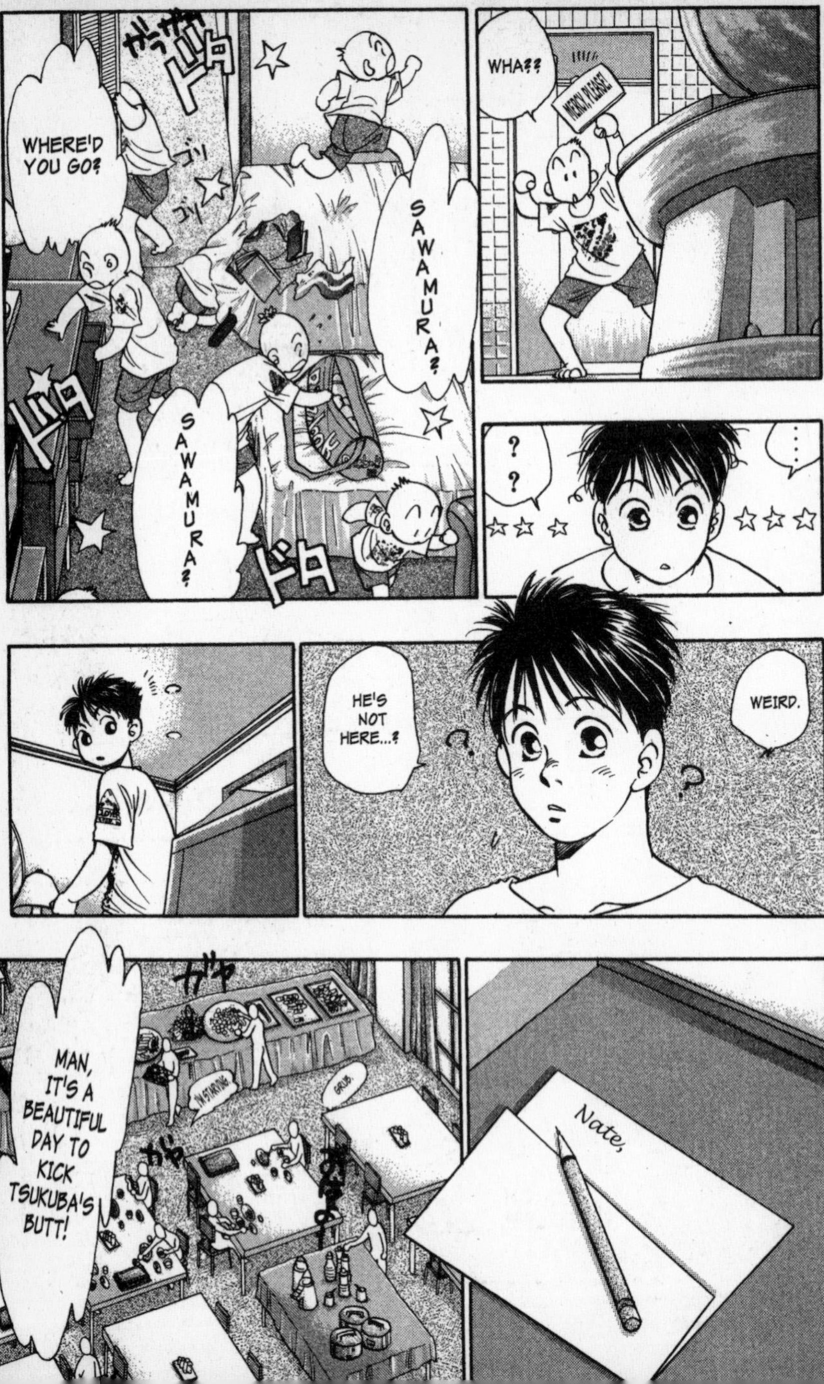
WHA??
MERCY, PLEASE!
? ?
...
SAWAMURA?
WHERE'D YOU GO?
SAWAMURA?
HE'S NOT HERE...?
WEIRD.
Nate,
MAN, IT'S A BEAUTIFUL DAY TO KICK TSUKUBA'S BUTT!
I'M STARVING.
GRUB.

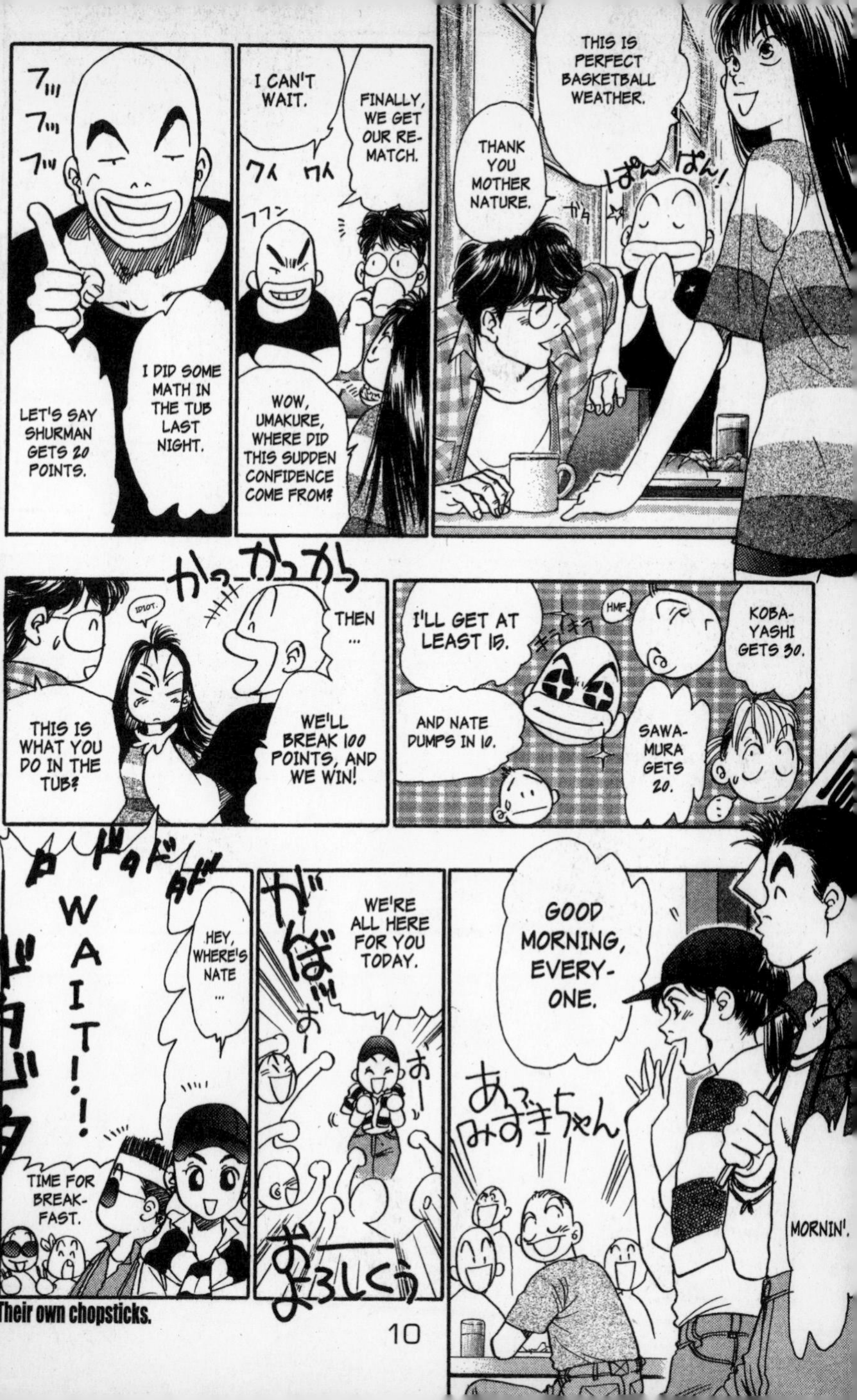
THIS IS PERFECT BASKETBALL WEATHER.
ぱん ぱん!
THANK YOU MOTHER NATURE.
FINALLY, WE GET OUR RE-MATCH.
I CAN'T WAIT.
ワイ ワイ
フフン
WOW, UMAKURE, WHERE DID THIS SUDDEN CONFIDENCE COME FROM?
I DID SOME MATH IN THE TUB LAST NIGHT.
フッ フッ フッ
LET'S SAY SHURMAN GETS 20 POINTS.
KOBA-YASHI GETS 30.
HMF.
SAWA-MURA GETS 20.
I'LL GET AT LEAST 15.
AND NATE DUMPS IN 10.
かっ かっ から
THEN ...
WE'LL BREAK 100 POINTS, AND WE WIN!
IDIOT.
THIS IS WHAT YOU DO IN THE TUB?
GOOD MORNING, EVERY-ONE.
MORNIN'.
あっ みずきちゃん
WE'RE ALL HERE FOR YOU TODAY.
おーよろしくぅ
HEY, WHERE'S NATE ...
WAIT!!
TIME FOR BREAK-FAST.

Their own chopsticks.

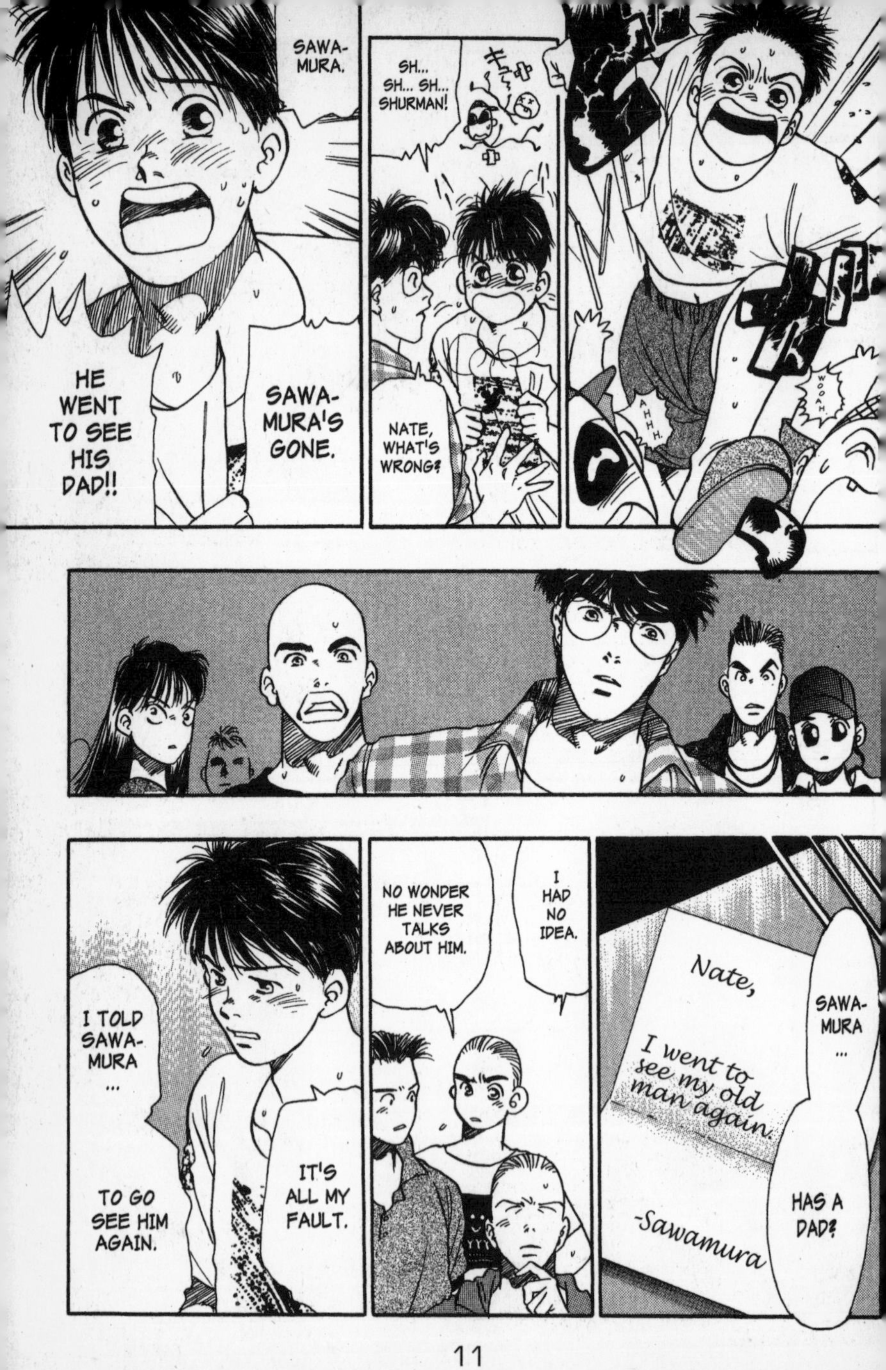
WOOAH.
AHHH.
SH... SH... SH... SHURMAN!
NATE, WHAT'S WRONG?
SAWAMURA.
SAWAMURA'S GONE.
HE WENT TO SEE HIS DAD!!
Nate,
I went to see my old man again.
-Sawamura
SAWAMURA ...
HAS A DAD?
I HAD NO IDEA.
NO WONDER HE NEVER TALKS ABOUT HIM.
IT'S ALL MY FAULT.
I TOLD SAWAMURA ...
TO GO SEE HIM AGAIN.

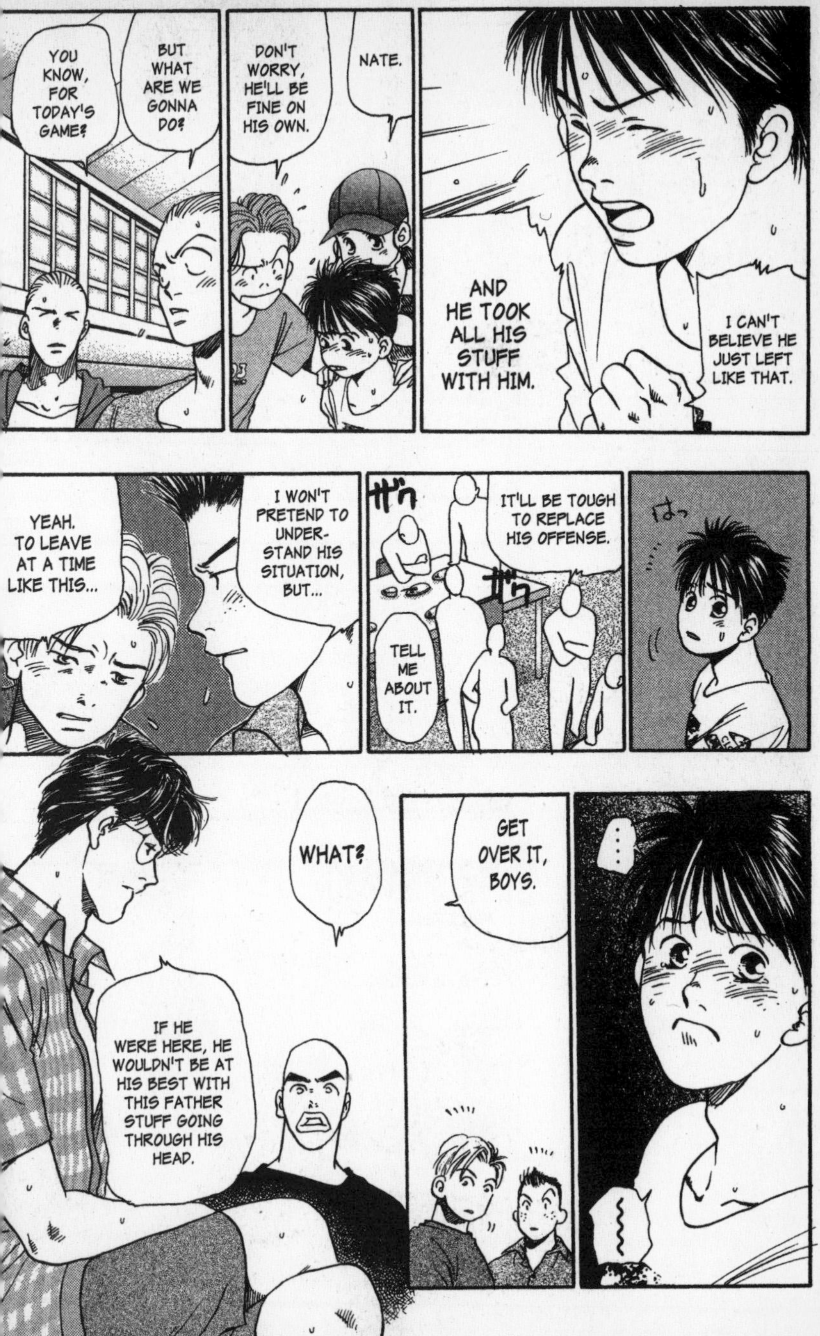
I CAN'T BELIEVE HE JUST LEFT LIKE THAT.
AND HE TOOK ALL HIS STUFF WITH HIM.
NATE.
DON'T WORRY, HE'LL BE FINE ON HIS OWN.
BUT WHAT ARE WE GONNA DO?
YOU KNOW, FOR TODAY'S GAME?
はっ
...
ザワ
IT'LL BE TOUGH TO REPLACE HIS OFFENSE.
ザワ
TELL ME ABOUT IT.
I WON'T PRETEND TO UNDER-STAND HIS SITUATION, BUT...
YEAH. TO LEAVE AT A TIME LIKE THIS...
...
GET OVER IT, BOYS.
WHAT?
IF HE WERE HERE, HE WOULDN'T BE AT HIS BEST WITH THIS FATHER STUFF GOING THROUGH HIS HEAD.

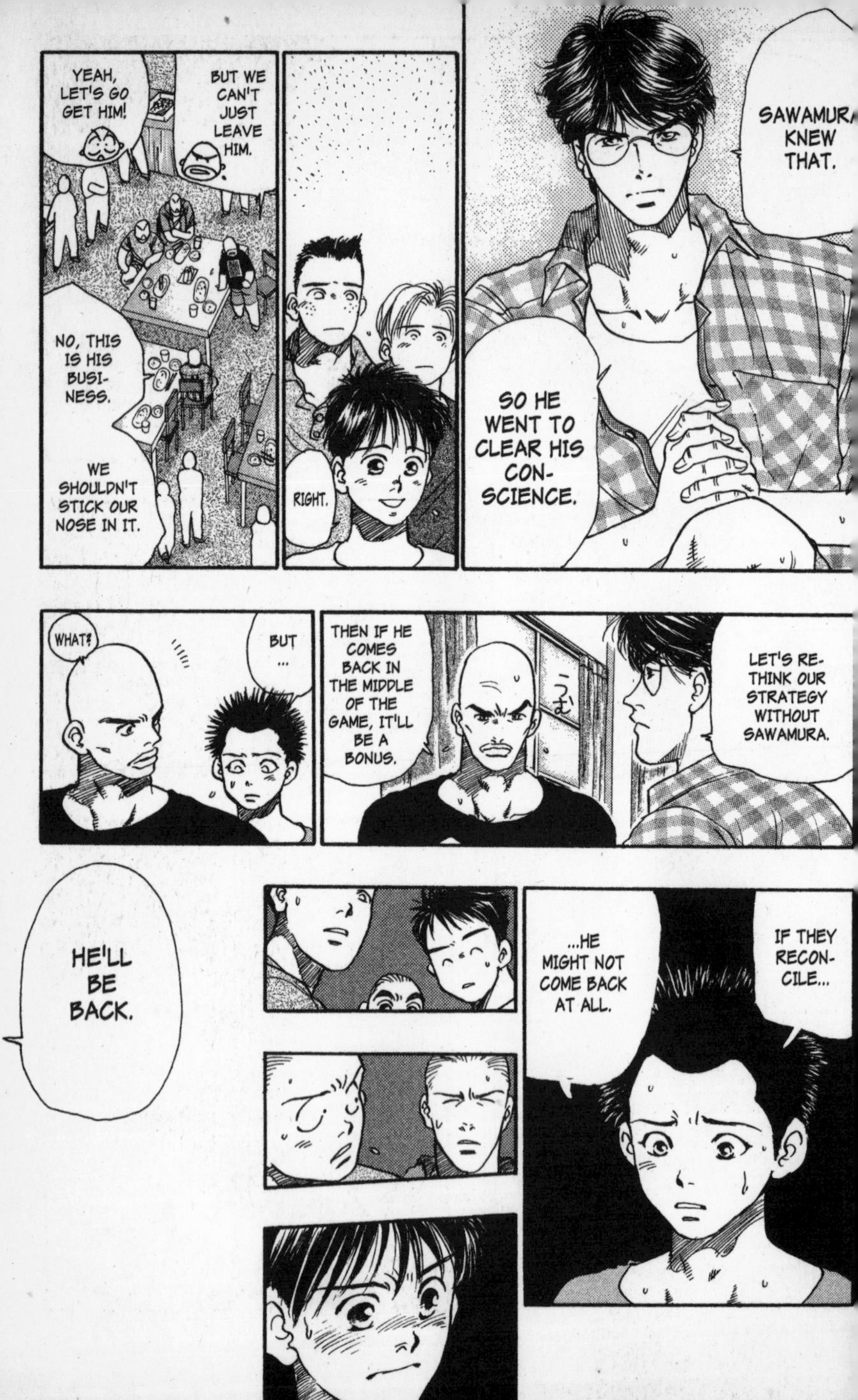
SAWAMURA KNEW THAT.
SO HE WENT TO CLEAR HIS CON-SCIENCE.
RIGHT.
BUT WE CAN'T JUST LEAVE HIM.
YEAH, LET'S GO GET HIM!
NO, THIS IS HIS BUSI-NESS.
WE SHOULDN'T STICK OUR NOSE IN IT.
LET'S RE-THINK OUR STRATEGY WITHOUT SAWAMURA.
うむ
THEN IF HE COMES BACK IN THE MIDDLE OF THE GAME, IT'LL BE A BONUS.
BUT ...
WHAT?
IF THEY RECON-CILE...
...HE MIGHT NOT COME BACK AT ALL.
HE'LL BE BACK.

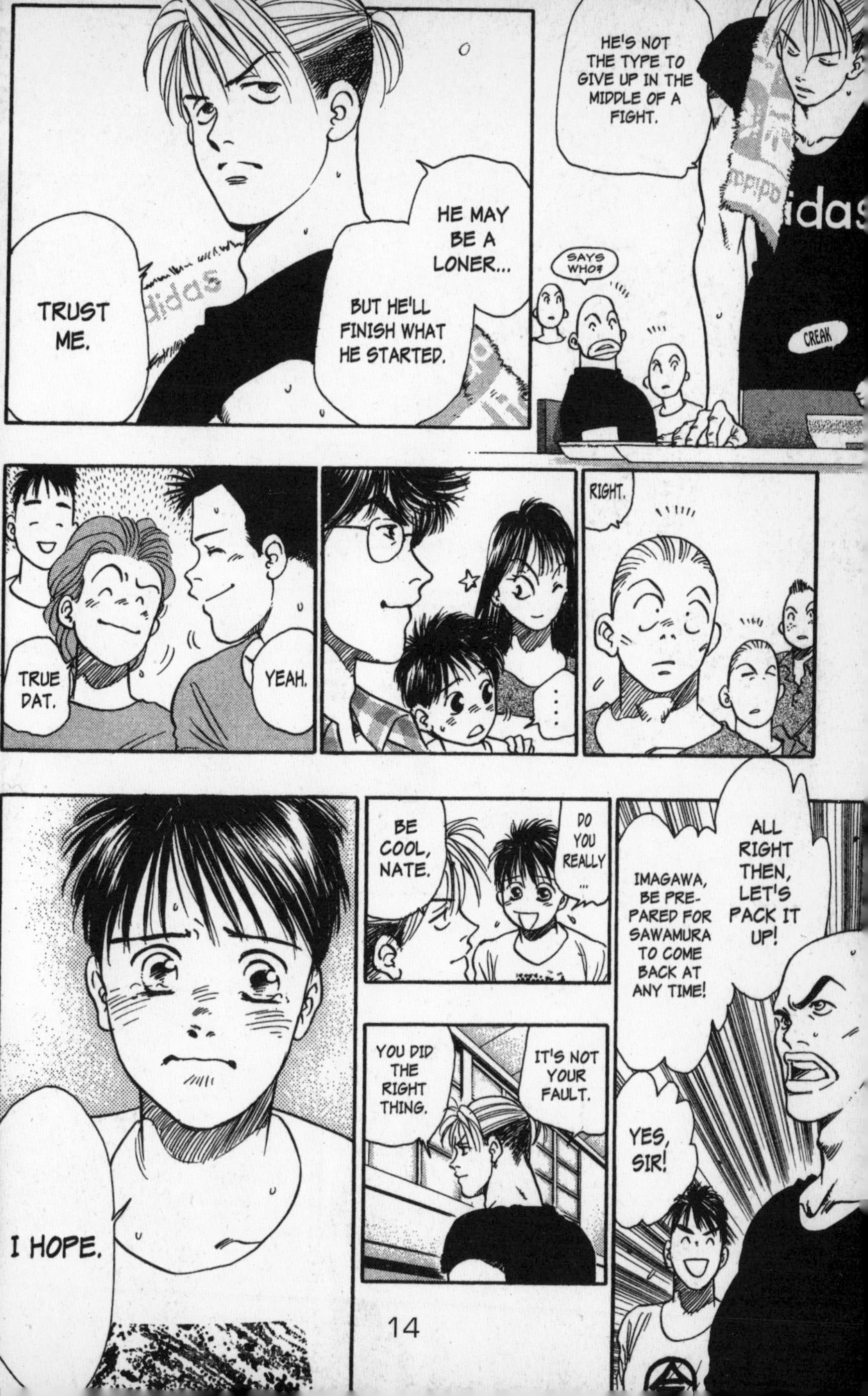
HE'S NOT THE TYPE TO GIVE UP IN THE MIDDLE OF A FIGHT.
SAYS WHO?
CREAK
HE MAY BE A LONER...
BUT HE'LL FINISH WHAT HE STARTED.
TRUST ME.
RIGHT.
....
YEAH.
TRUE DAT.
ALL RIGHT THEN, LET'S PACK IT UP!
IMAGAWA, BE PREPARED FOR SAWAMURA TO COME BACK AT ANY TIME!
YES, SIR!
DO YOU REALLY...
BE COOL, NATE.
IT'S NOT YOUR FAULT.
YOU DID THE RIGHT THING.
I HOPE.

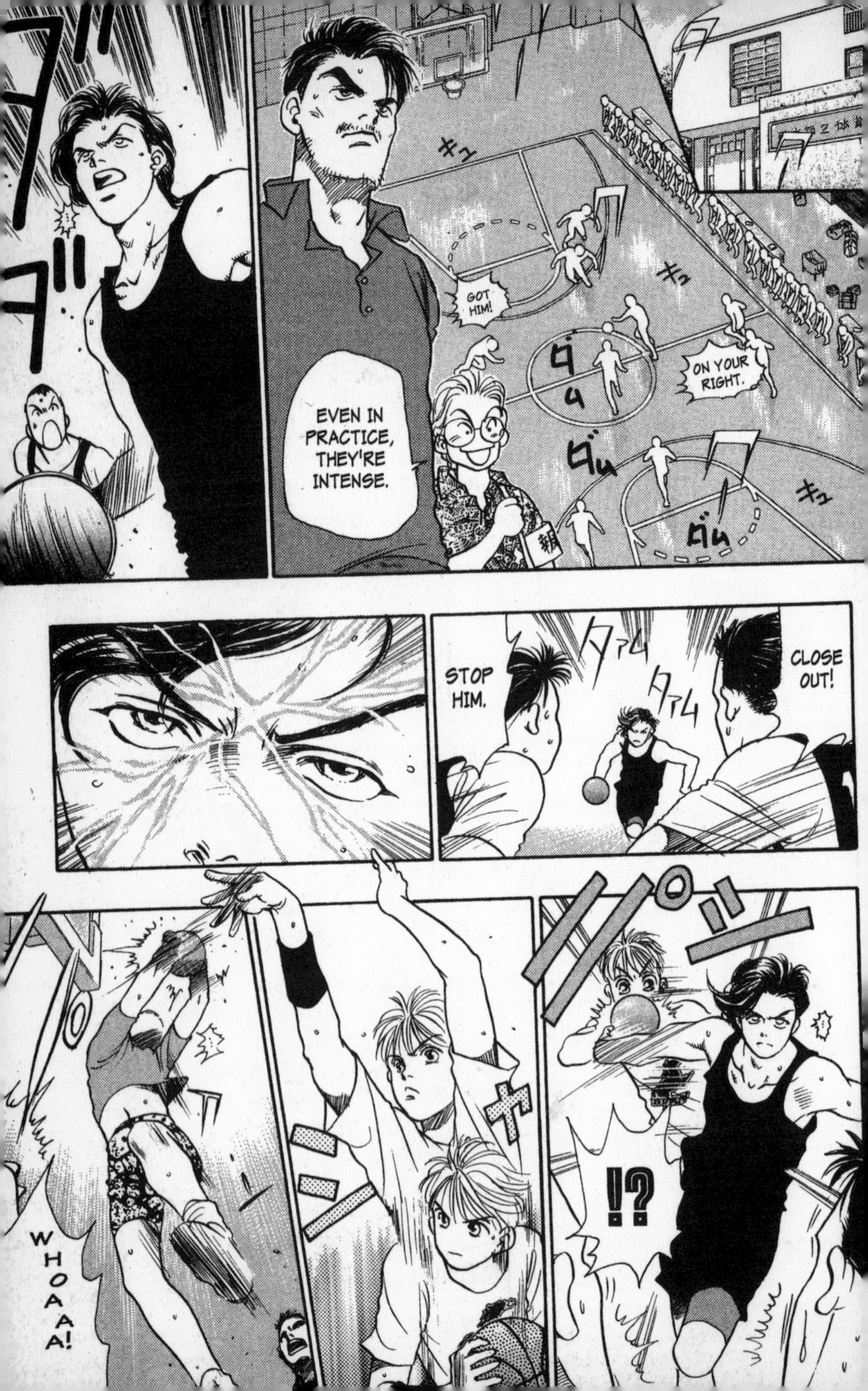
GOT HIM!
ON YOUR RIGHT.
EVEN IN PRACTICE, THEY'RE INTENSE.
CLOSE OUT!
STOP HIM.
!?
WHOAAA!

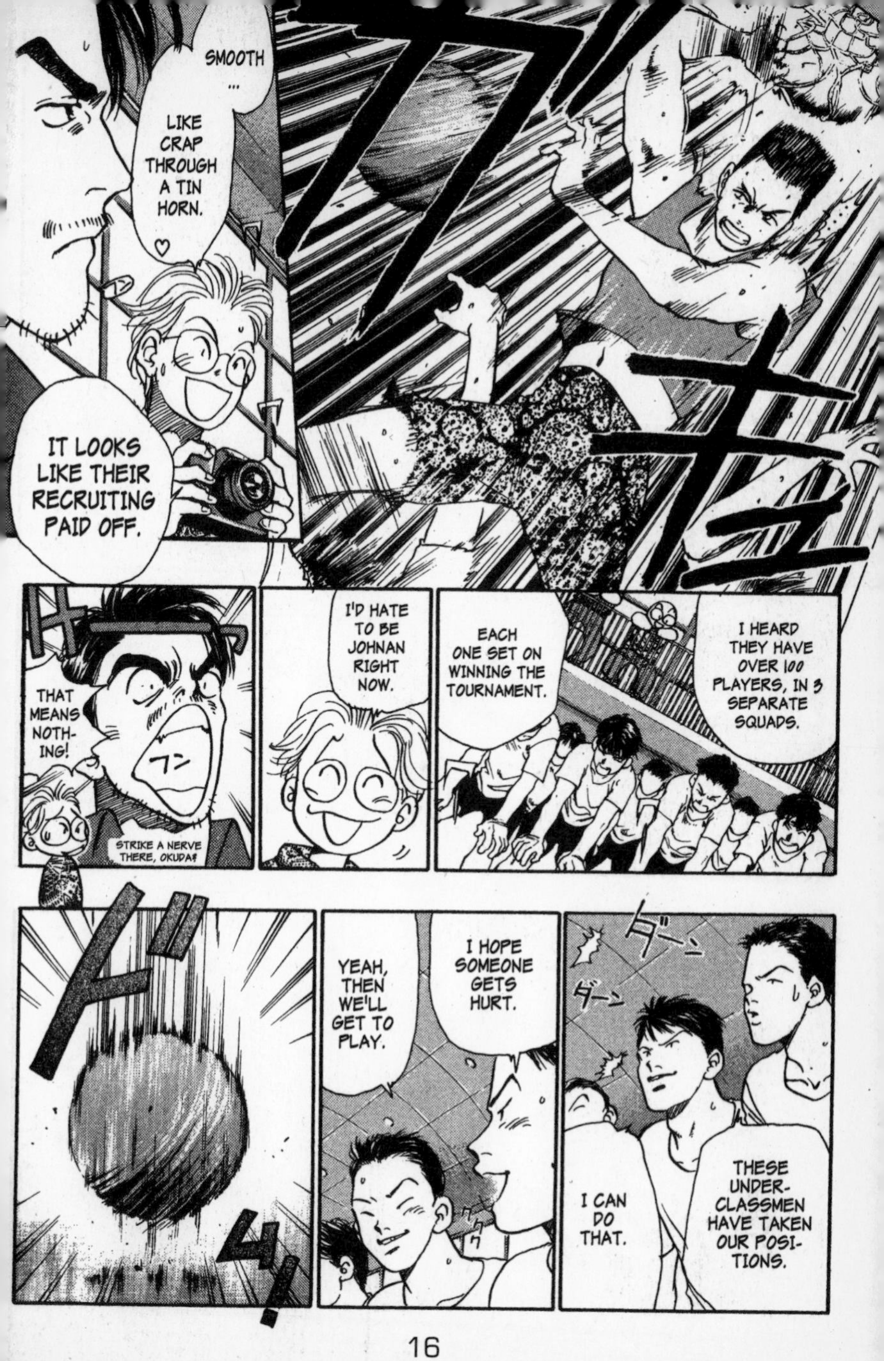
SMOOTH ... LIKE CRAP THROUGH A TIN HORN. ♡
IT LOOKS LIKE THEIR RECRUITING PAID OFF.
I HEARD THEY HAVE OVER 100 PLAYERS, IN 3 SEPARATE SQUADS.
EACH ONE SET ON WINNING THE TOURNAMENT.
I'D HATE TO BE JOHNAN RIGHT NOW.
THAT MEANS NOTHING!
STRIKE A NERVE THERE, OKUDA?
THESE UNDER-CLASSMEN HAVE TAKEN OUR POSI-TIONS.
I CAN DO THAT.
I HOPE SOMEONE GETS HURT.
YEAH, THEN WE'LL GET TO PLAY.

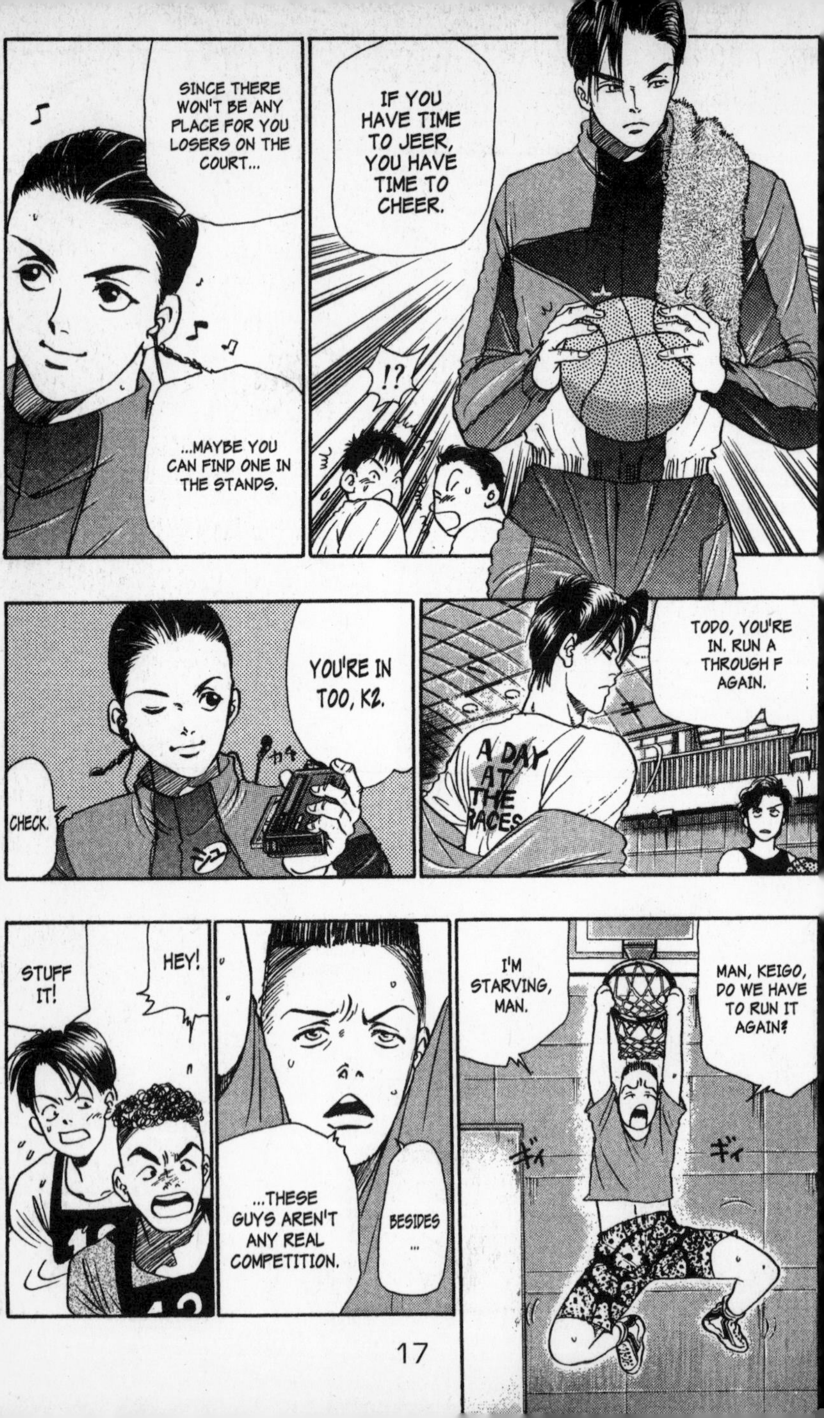
IF YOU HAVE TIME TO JEER, YOU HAVE TIME TO CHEER.
!?
SINCE THERE WON'T BE ANY PLACE FOR YOU LOSERS ON THE COURT...
...MAYBE YOU CAN FIND ONE IN THE STANDS.
TODO, YOU'RE IN. RUN A THROUGH F AGAIN.
A DAY AT THE RACES
YOU'RE IN TOO, K2.
CHECK.
MAN, KEIGO, DO WE HAVE TO RUN IT AGAIN?
I'M STARVING, MAN.
BESIDES...
...THESE GUYS AREN'T ANY REAL COMPETITION.
HEY!
STUFF IT!

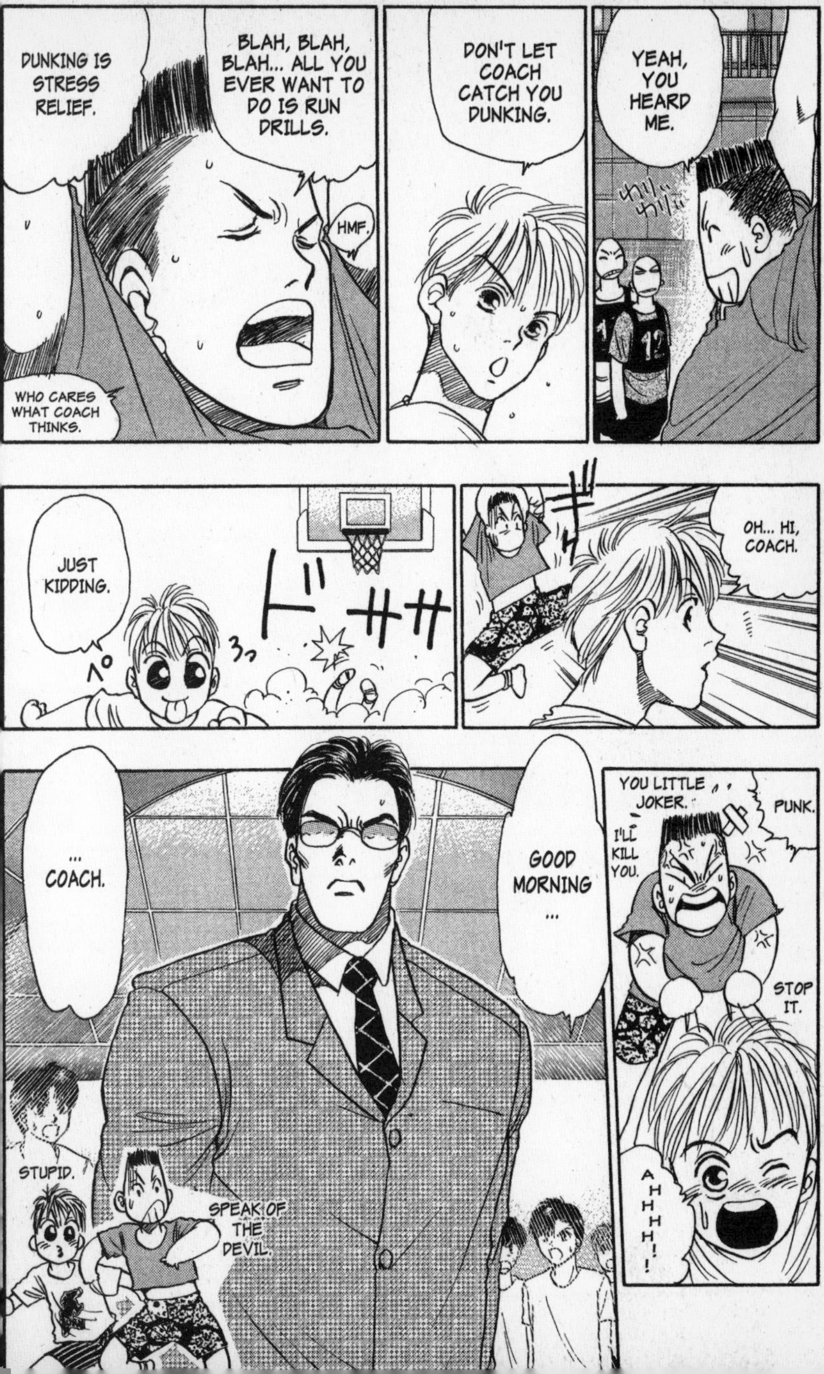
YEAH, YOU HEARD ME.
DON'T LET COACH CATCH YOU DUNKING.
BLAH, BLAH, BLAH... ALL YOU EVER WANT TO DO IS RUN DRILLS.
HMF.
DUNKING IS STRESS RELIEF.
WHO CARES WHAT COACH THINKS.
OH... HI, COACH.
JUST KIDDING.
YOU LITTLE JOKER.
PUNK.
I'LL KILL YOU.
STOP IT.
AHHHH!
GOOD MORNING ...
... COACH.
SPEAK OF THE DEVIL.
STUPID.

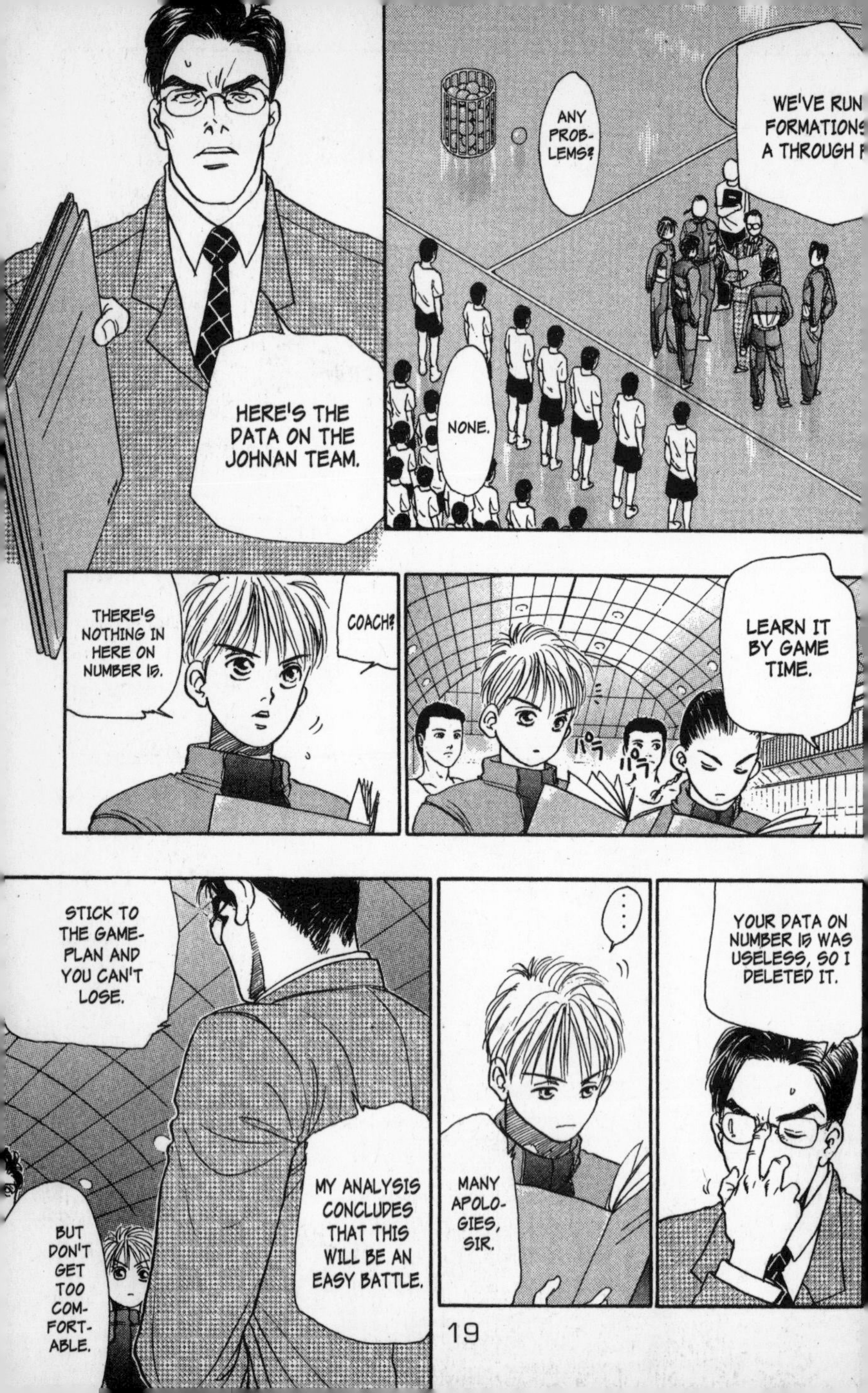

WE'VE RUN FORMATIONS A THROUGH
ANY PROB-LEMS?
NONE.
HERE'S THE DATA ON THE JOHNAN TEAM.
LEARN IT BY GAME TIME.
パラ
パラ
COACH?
THERE'S NOTHING IN HERE ON NUMBER 15.
YOUR DATA ON NUMBER 15 WAS USELESS, SO I DELETED IT.
...
MANY APOLOGIES, SIR.
STICK TO THE GAME-PLAN AND YOU CAN'T LOSE.
MY ANALYSIS CONCLUDES THAT THIS WILL BE AN EASY BATTLE.
BUT DON'T GET TOO COM-FORT-ABLE.

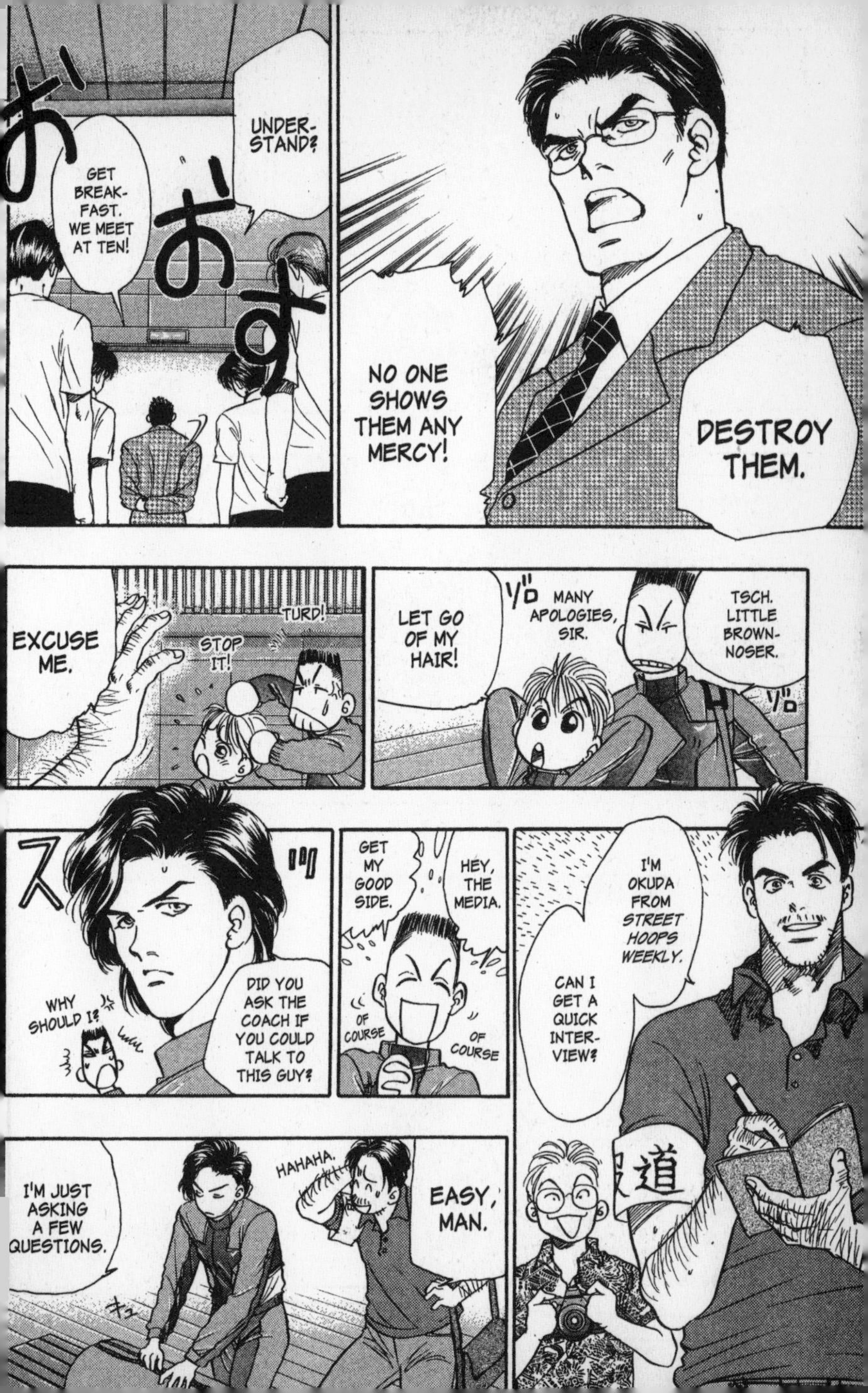
DESTROY THEM.
NO ONE SHOWS THEM ANY MERCY!
UNDER-STAND?
GET BREAK-FAST. WE MEET AT TEN!
おおす
TSCH. LITTLE BROWN-NOSER.
MANY APOLOGIES, SIR.
LET GO OF MY HAIR!
TURD!
STOP IT!
EXCUSE ME.
I'M OKUDA FROM STREET HOOPS WEEKLY.
CAN I GET A QUICK INTER-VIEW?
HEY, THE MEDIA.
GET MY GOOD SIDE.
OF COURSE
OF COURSE
DID YOU ASK THE COACH IF YOU COULD TALK TO THIS GUY?
WHY SHOULD I?
EASY, MAN.
HAHAHA.
I'M JUST ASKING A FEW QUESTIONS.

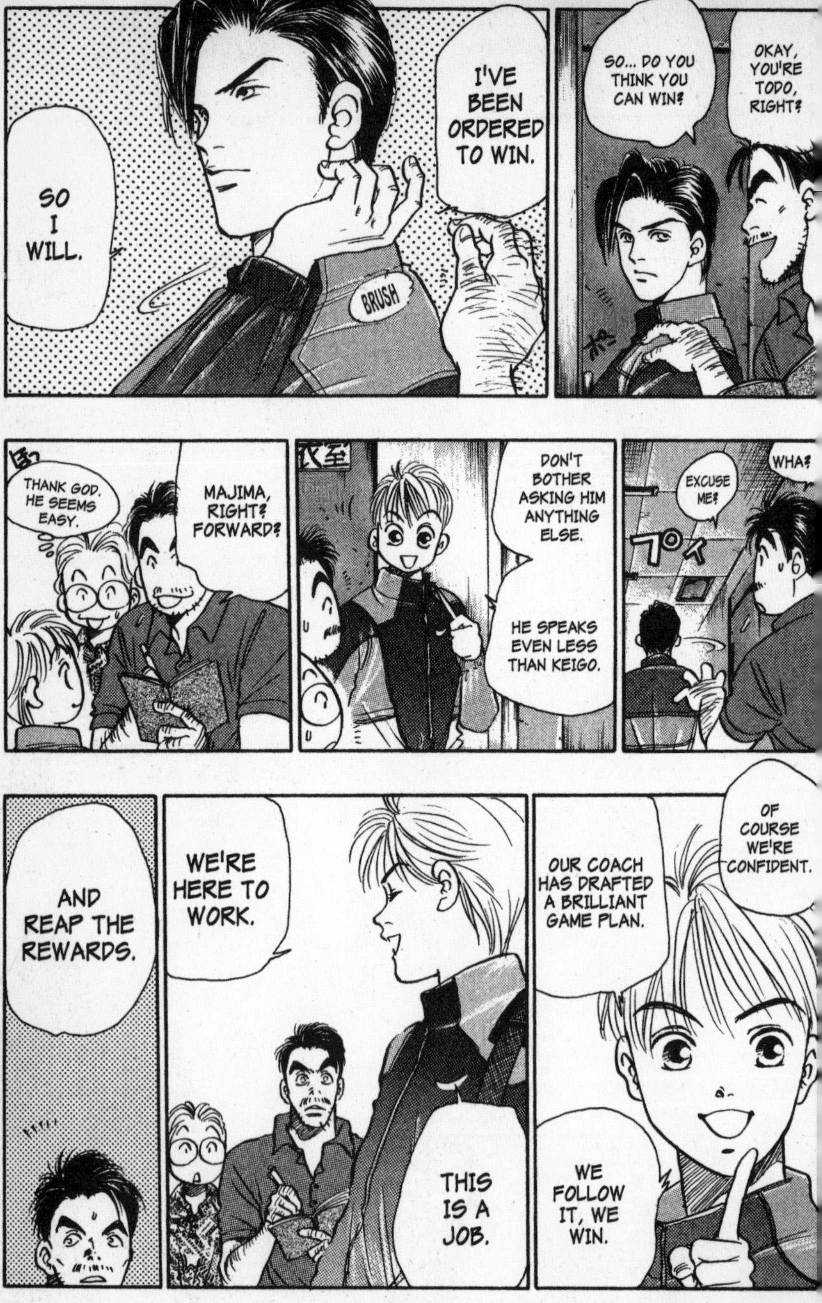
OKAY, YOU'RE TODO, RIGHT?
SO... DO YOU THINK YOU CAN WIN?
I'VE BEEN ORDERED TO WIN.
BRUSH
SO I WILL.
WHA?
EXCUSE ME?
プイ
DON'T BOTHER ASKING HIM ANYTHING ELSE.
HE SPEAKS EVEN LESS THAN KEIGO.
MAJIMA, RIGHT? FORWARD?
THANK GOD. HE SEEMS EASY.
OF COURSE WE'RE CONFIDENT.
OUR COACH HAS DRAFTED A BRILLIANT GAME PLAN.
WE FOLLOW IT, WE WIN.
WE'RE HERE TO WORK.
THIS IS A JOB.
AND REAP THE REWARDS.

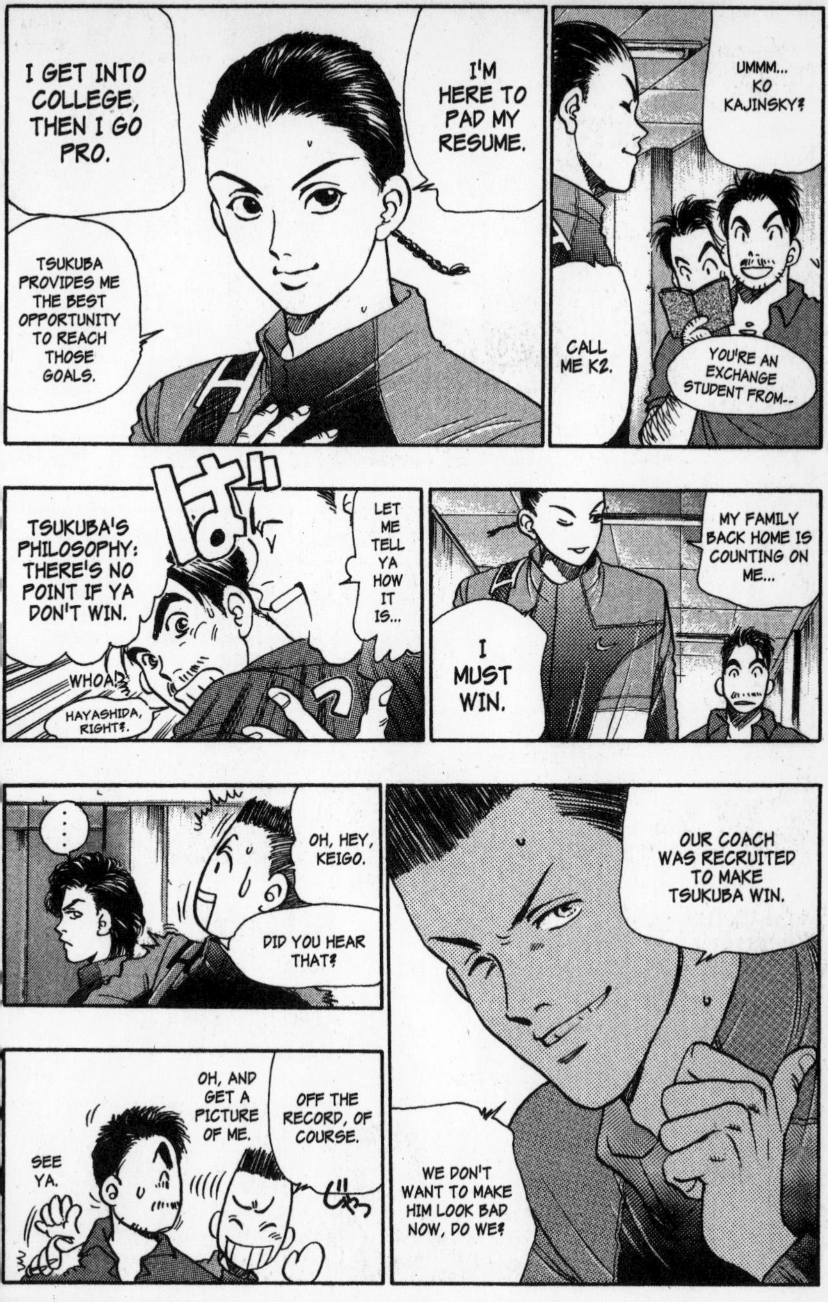
UMMM... KO KAJINSKY?
CALL ME K2.
YOU'RE AN EXCHANGE STUDENT FROM--
I'M HERE TO PAD MY RESUME.
I GET INTO COLLEGE, THEN I GO PRO.
TSUKUBA PROVIDES ME THE BEST OPPORTUNITY TO REACH THOSE GOALS.
MY FAMILY BACK HOME IS COUNTING ON ME...
I MUST WIN.
LET ME TELL YA HOW IT IS...
ば
TSUKUBA'S PHILOSOPHY: THERE'S NO POINT IF YA DON'T WIN.
WHOA!?
HAYASHIDA, RIGHT?.
OUR COACH WAS RECRUITED TO MAKE TSUKUBA WIN.
WE DON'T WANT TO MAKE HIM LOOK BAD NOW, DO WE?
OH, HEY, KEIGO.
DID YOU HEAR THAT?
...
OFF THE RECORD, OF COURSE.
OH, AND GET A PICTURE OF ME.
SEE YA.

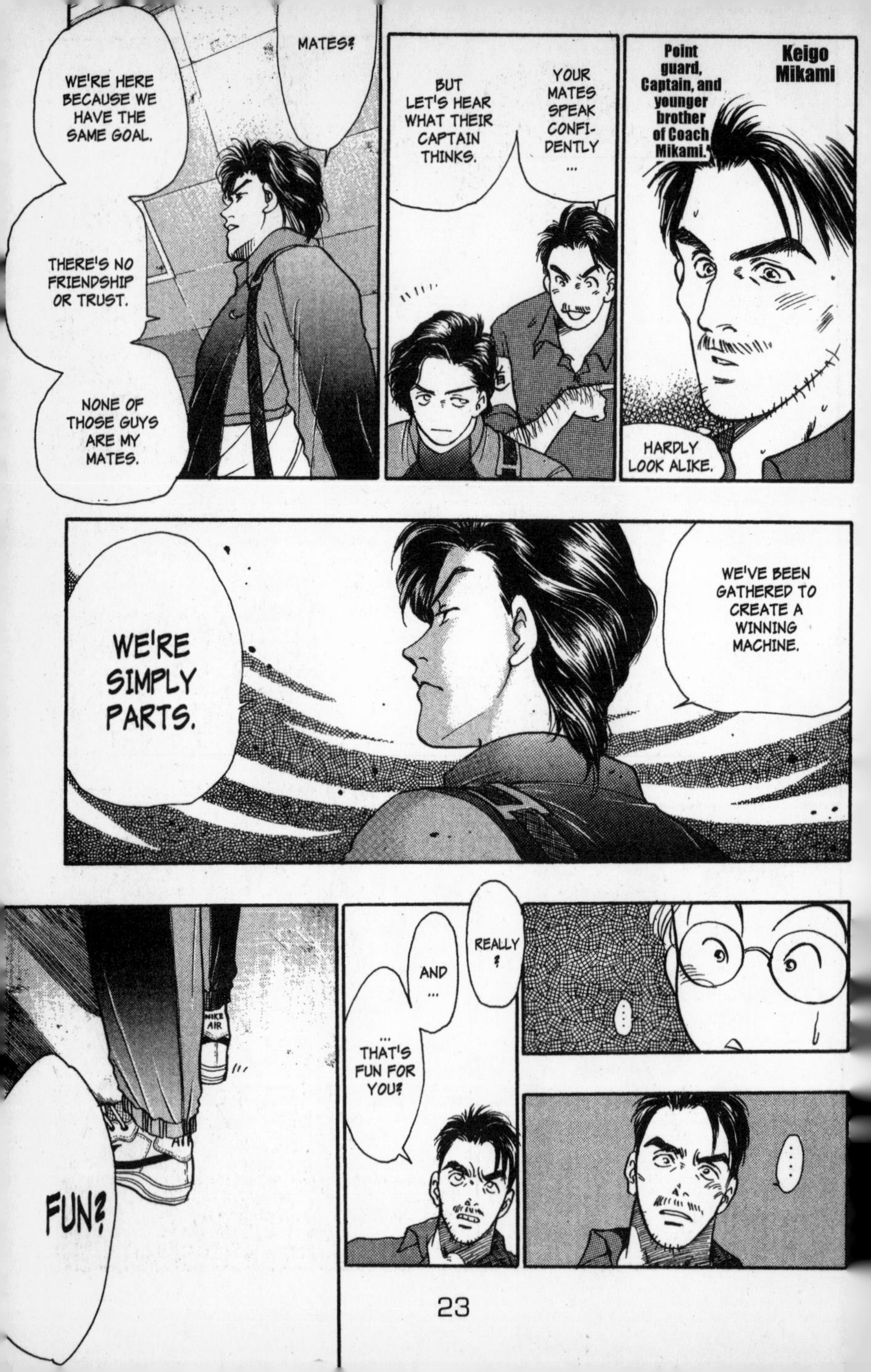
Keigo Mikami
Point guard, Captain, and younger brother of Coach Mikami.
HARDLY LOOK ALIKE.
YOUR MATES SPEAK CONFIDENTLY ...
BUT LET'S HEAR WHAT THEIR CAPTAIN THINKS.
MATES?
WE'RE HERE BECAUSE WE HAVE THE SAME GOAL.
THERE'S NO FRIENDSHIP OR TRUST.
NONE OF THOSE GUYS ARE MY MATES.
WE'VE BEEN GATHERED TO CREATE A WINNING MACHINE.
WE'RE SIMPLY PARTS.
...
...
REALLY?
AND ...
... THAT'S FUN FOR YOU?
FUN?

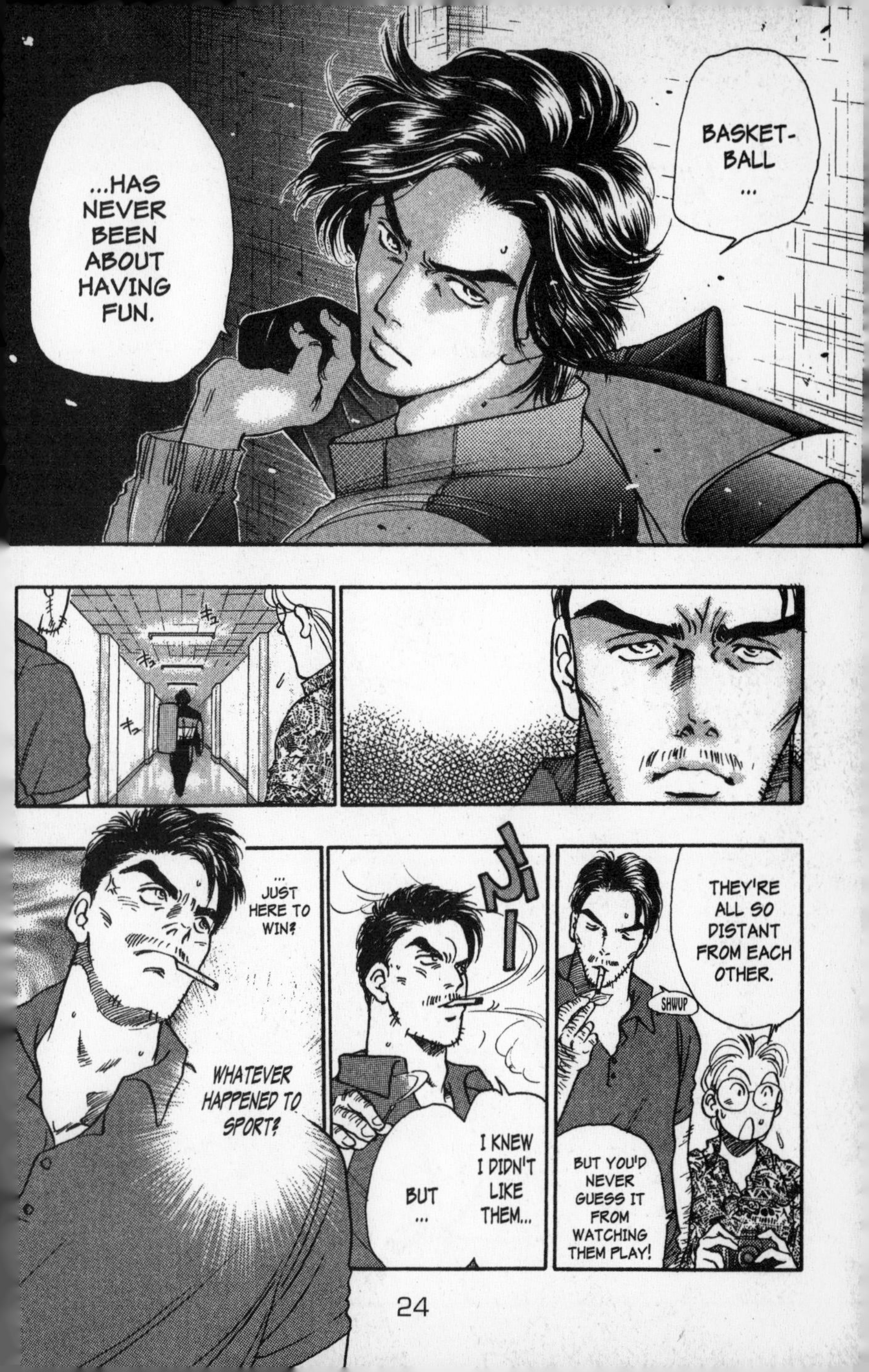
BASKET-BALL ...
...HAS NEVER BEEN ABOUT HAVING FUN.
THEY'RE ALL SO DISTANT FROM EACH OTHER.
SHWUP
BUT YOU'D NEVER GUESS IT FROM WATCHING THEM PLAY!
I KNEW I DIDN'T LIKE THEM...
BUT ...
... JUST HERE TO WIN?
WHATEVER HAPPENED TO SPORT?

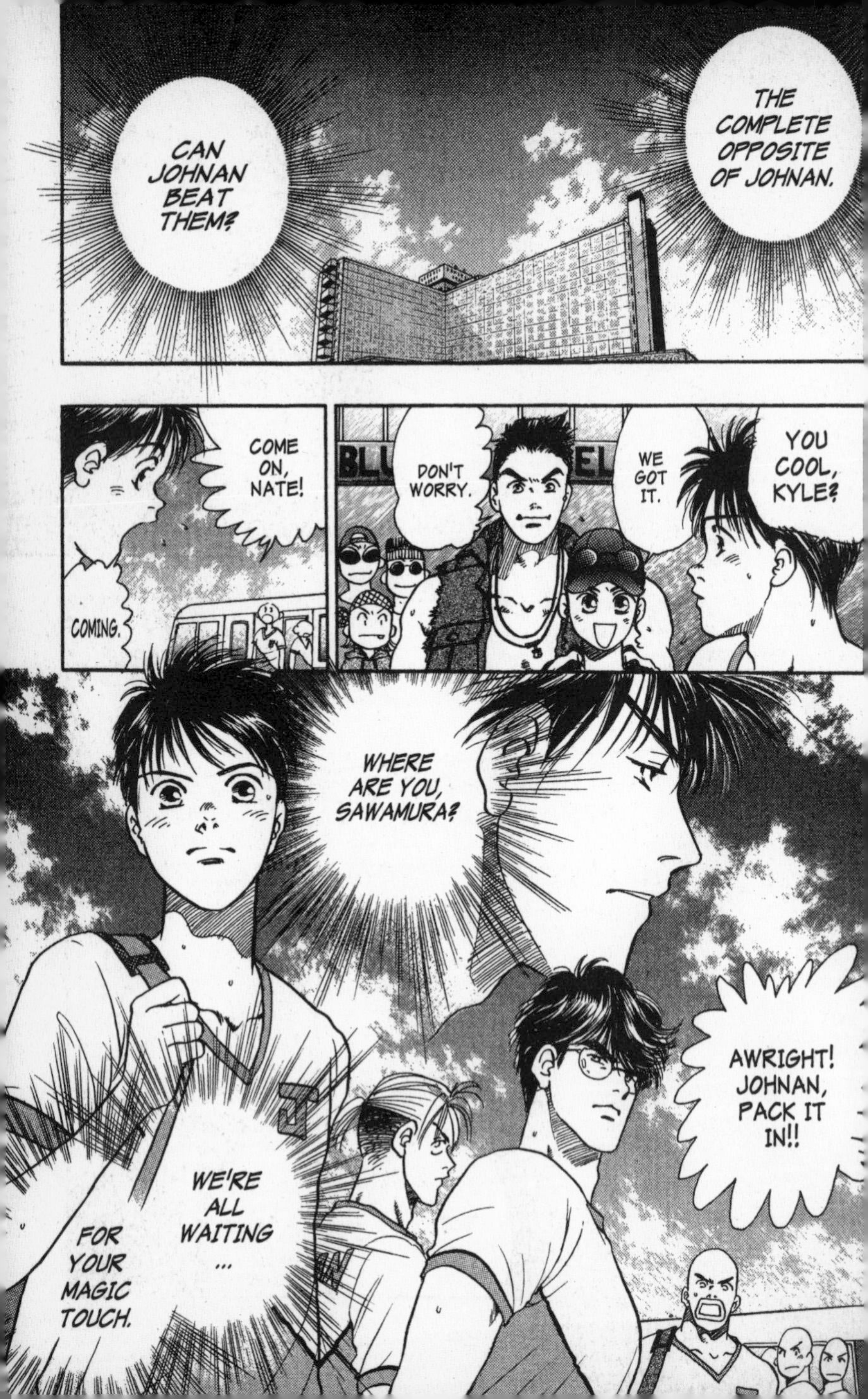
THE COMPLETE OPPOSITE OF JOHNAN.
CAN JOHNAN BEAT THEM?
YOU COOL, KYLE?
WE GOT IT.
DON'T WORRY.
COME ON, NATE!
COMING.
WHERE ARE YOU, SAWAMURA?
AWRIGHT! JOHNAN, PACK IT IN!!
WE'RE ALL WAITING ...
FOR YOUR MAGIC TOUCH.

We're taking this pagination break to remind our readers that we hope you're enjoying this thrilling installment of...

Brought to you by TOKYOPOP Babylon, an all-inclusive vacation resort in the middle of beautiful Miracle Mile Long Island.

And now, back to the manga...

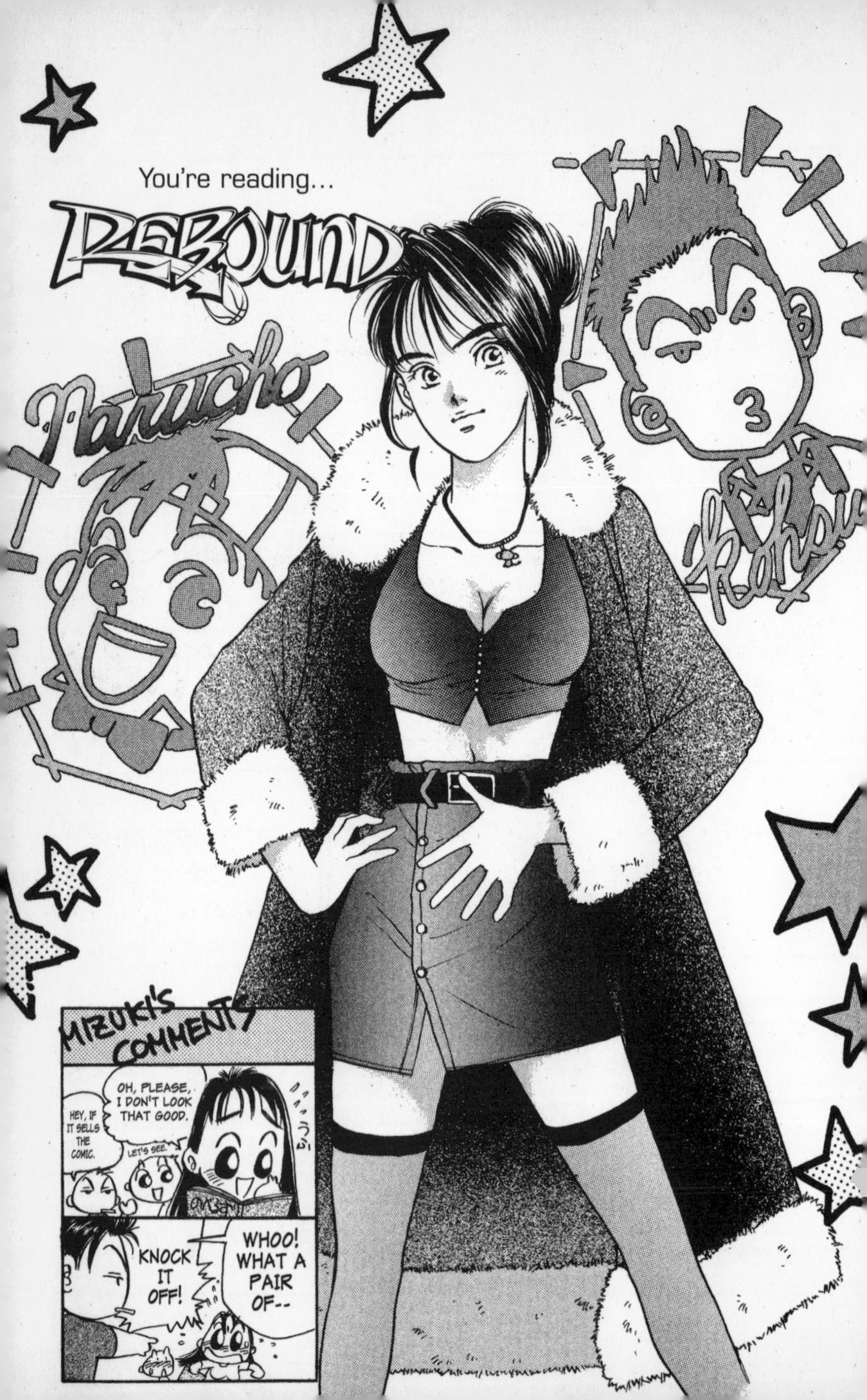
You're reading...
REBOUND
MIZUKI'S COMMENTS
OH, PLEASE, I DON'T LOOK THAT GOOD.
HEY, IF IT SELLS THE COMIC.
LET'S SEE.
WHOO! WHAT A PAIR OF--
KNOCK IT OFF!

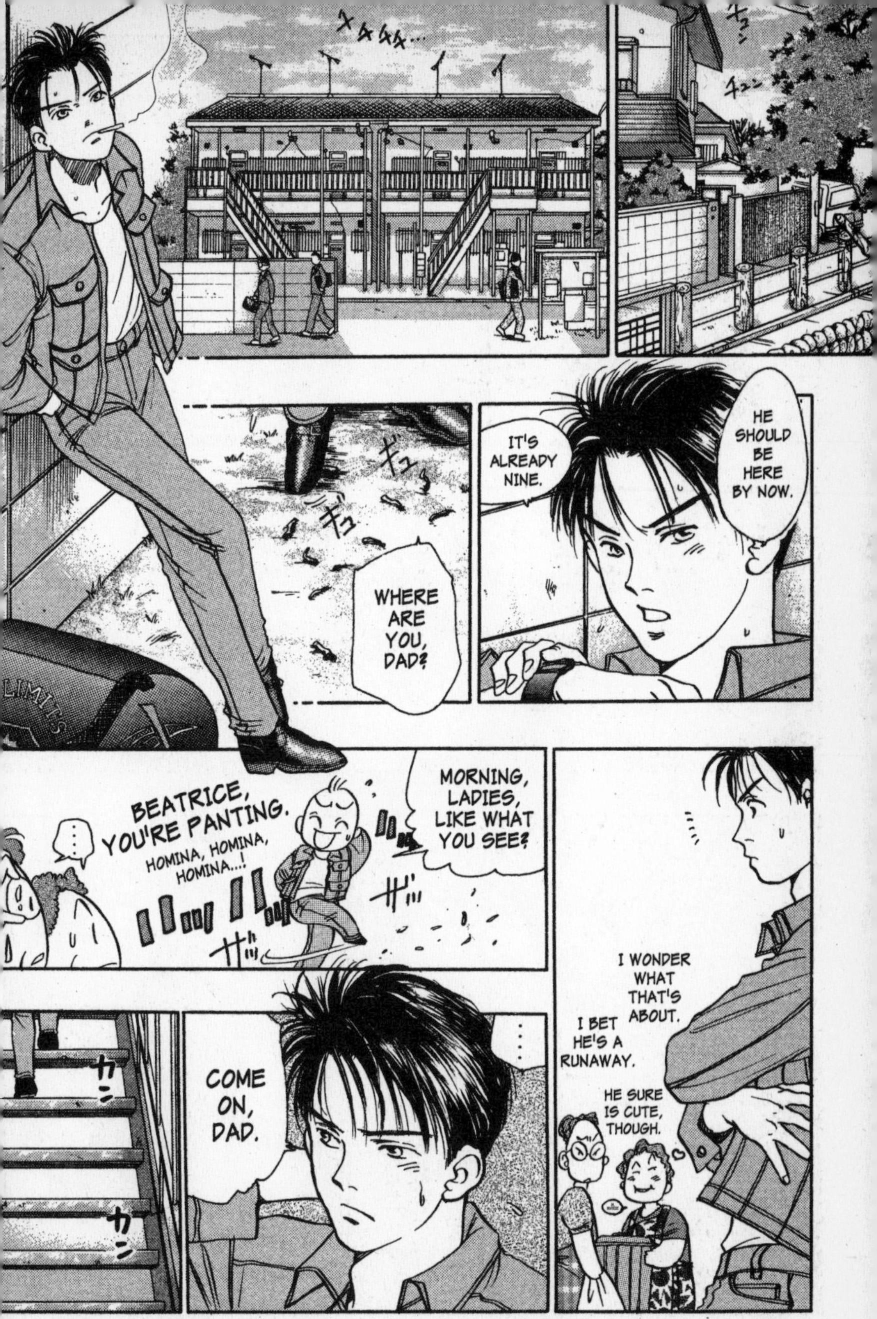
HE SHOULD BE HERE BY NOW.
IT'S ALREADY NINE.
WHERE ARE YOU, DAD?
I WONDER WHAT THAT'S ABOUT.
I BET HE'S A RUNAWAY.
HE SURE IS CUTE, THOUGH.
MORNING, LADIES, LIKE WHAT YOU SEE?
BEATRICE, YOU'RE PANTING.
HOMINA, HOMINA, HOMINA...!
...
....
COME ON, DAD.

Episode 29: Do You Know How Much I Love You?

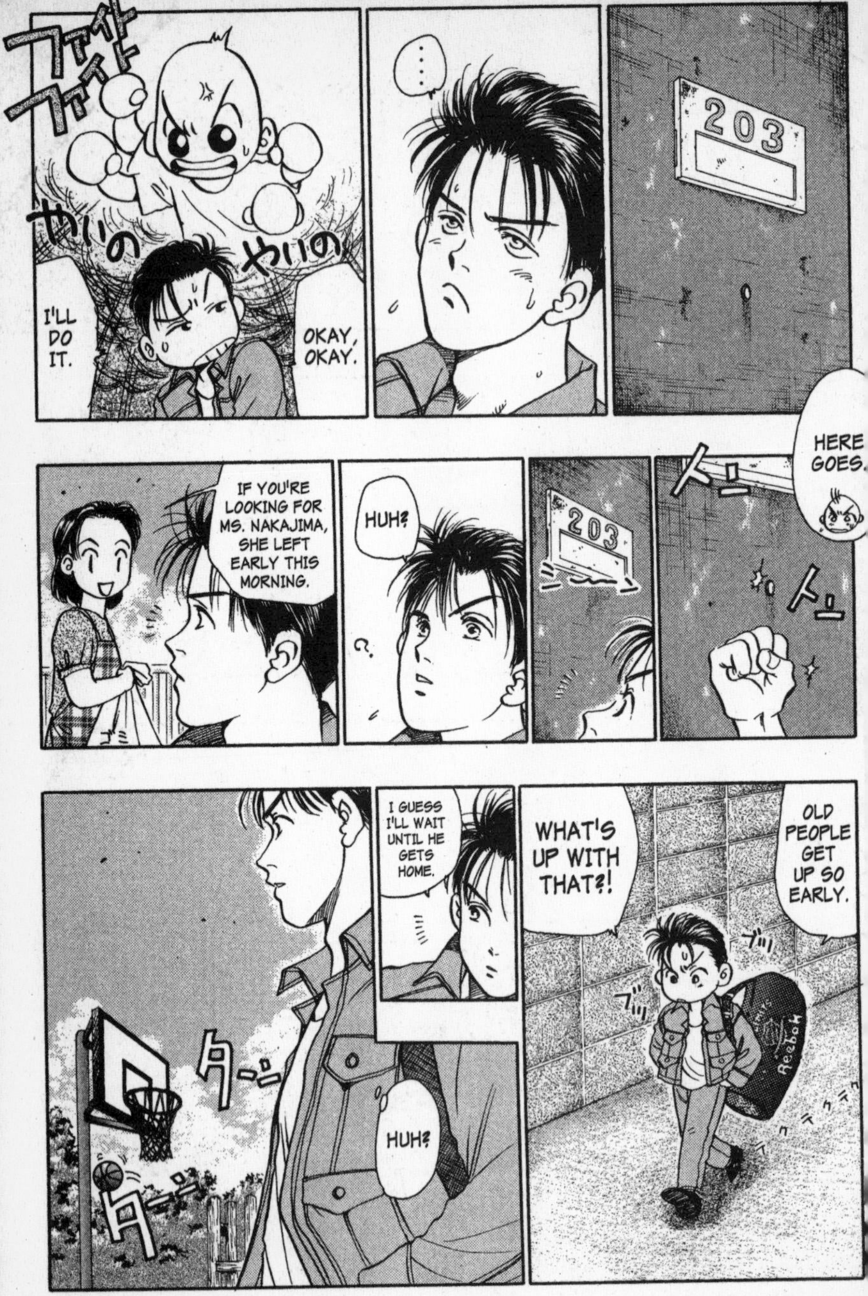

…
ファイト ファイト
やいの やいの
OKAY, OKAY.
I'LL DO IT.
HERE GOES.
トン トン
HUH?
IF YOU'RE LOOKING FOR MS. NAKAJIMA, SHE LEFT EARLY THIS MORNING.
OLD PEOPLE GET UP SO EARLY.
WHAT'S UP WITH THAT?!
ブツ ブツ
I GUESS I'LL WAIT UNTIL HE GETS HOME.
HUH?
ターン ターン

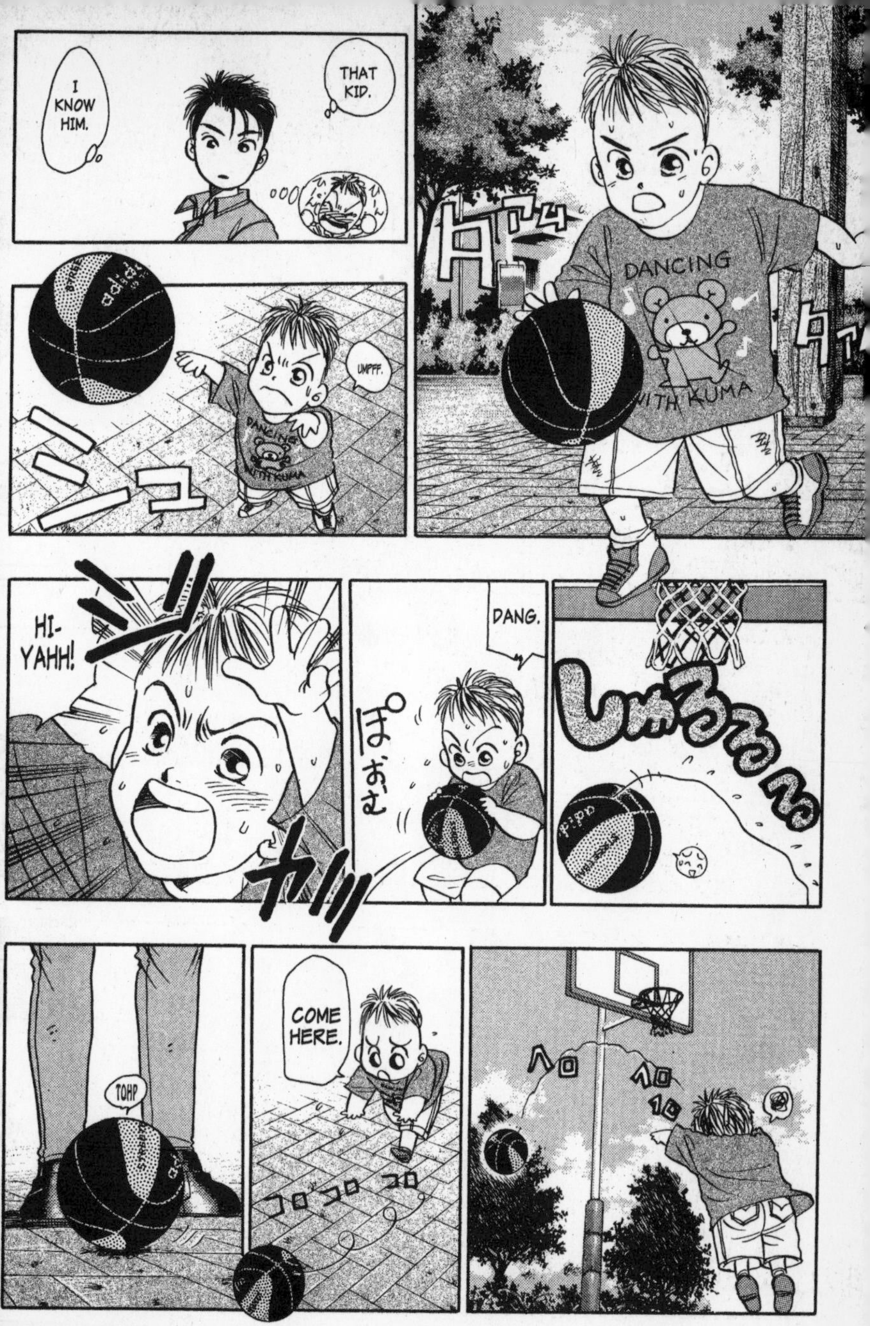
DANCING WITH KUMA
THAT KID.
I KNOW HIM.
DANCING WITH KUMA
UMPFF.
しゅるるる〜
DANG.
ぽおむ
HI-YAHH!
ヘロ ヘロ
COME HERE.
コロコロ コロ
TOHP

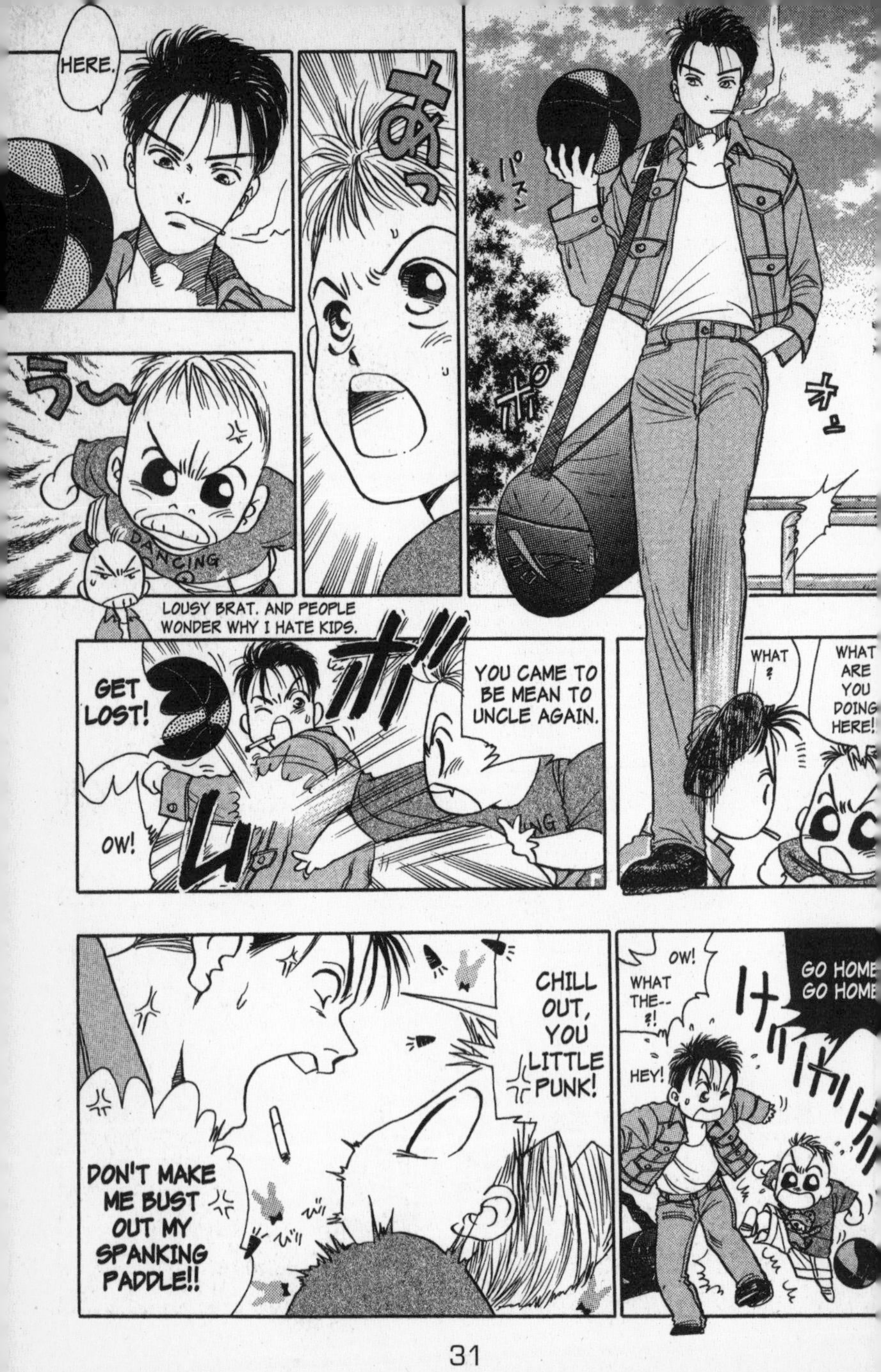

パスン
ポ
あっ
HERE.
う〜
DANCING
LOUSY BRAT. AND PEOPLE WONDER WHY I HATE KIDS.
WHAT?
WHAT ARE YOU DOING HERE!
YOU CAME TO BE MEAN TO UNCLE AGAIN.
GET LOST!
OW!
GO HOME GO HOME
OW!
WHAT THE--?!
HEY!
CHILL OUT, YOU LITTLE PUNK!
DON'T MAKE ME BUST OUT MY SPANKING PADDLE!!

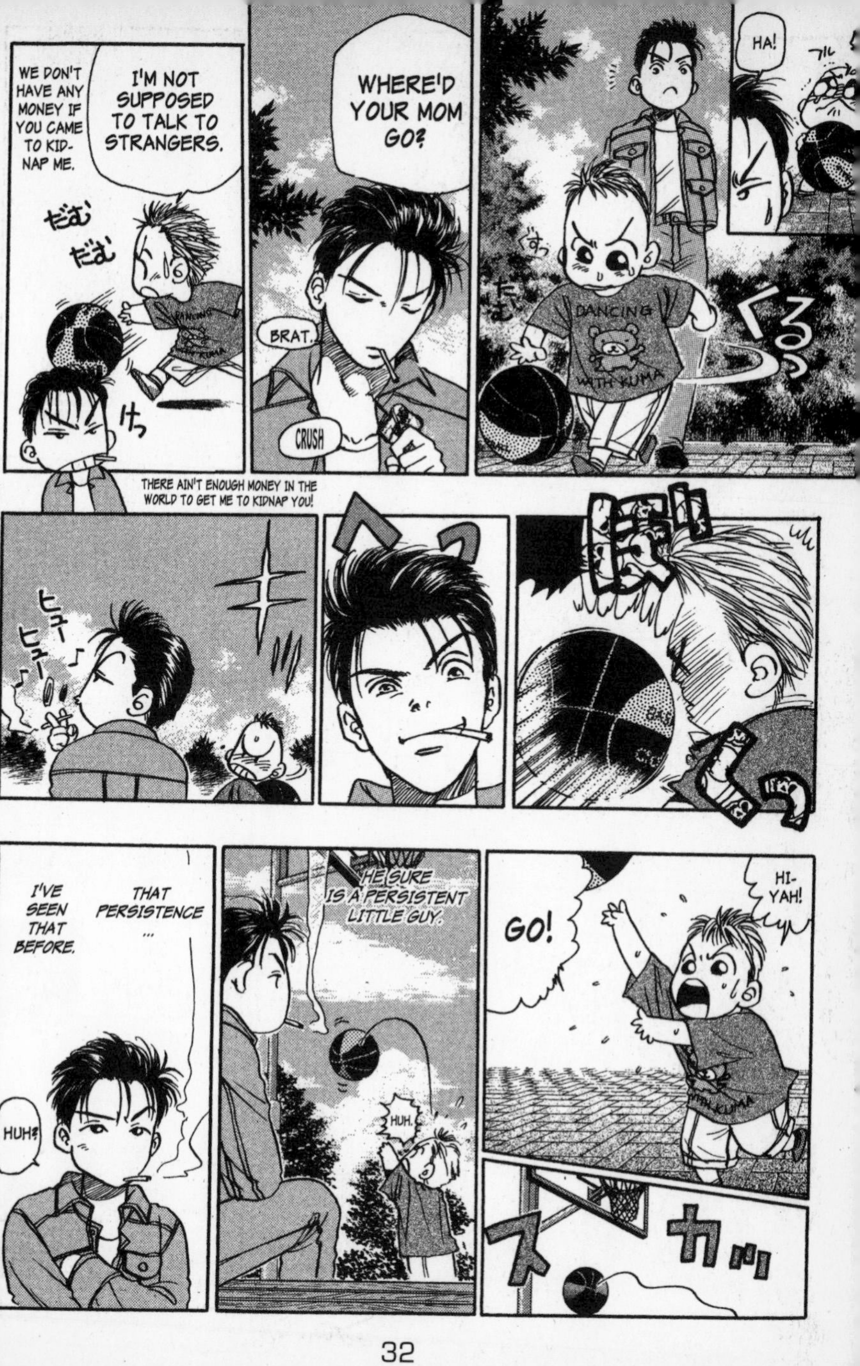
HA!
WHERE'D YOUR MOM GO?
BRAT.
CRUSH
I'M NOT SUPPOSED TO TALK TO STRANGERS.
WE DON'T HAVE ANY MONEY IF YOU CAME TO KID-NAP ME.
だむ
だむ
けっ
THERE AIN'T ENOUGH MONEY IN THE WORLD TO GET ME TO KIDNAP YOU!
HI-YAH!
GO!
スカッ
HE SURE IS A PERSISTENT LITTLE GUY.
HUH.
THAT PERSISTENCE ...
I'VE SEEN THAT BEFORE.
HUH?

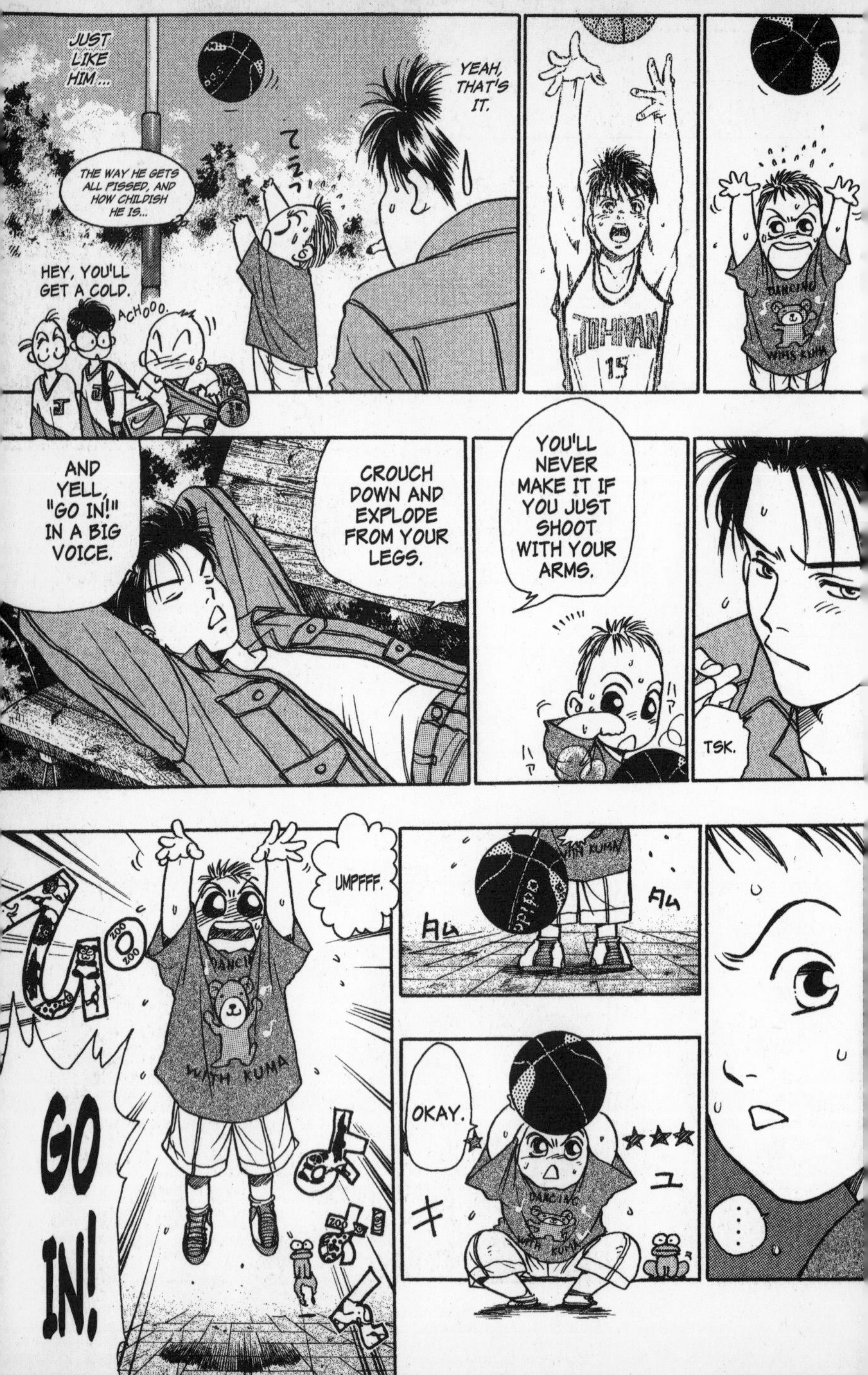
YEAH, THAT'S IT.
JUST LIKE HIM...
THE WAY HE GETS ALL PISSED, AND HOW CHILDISH HE IS...
HEY, YOU'LL GET A COLD.
ACHOOO.
TSK.
YOU'LL NEVER MAKE IT IF YOU JUST SHOOT WITH YOUR ARMS.
CROUCH DOWN AND EXPLODE FROM YOUR LEGS.
AND YELL, "GO IN!" IN A BIG VOICE.
OKAY.
UMPFFF.
GO IN!

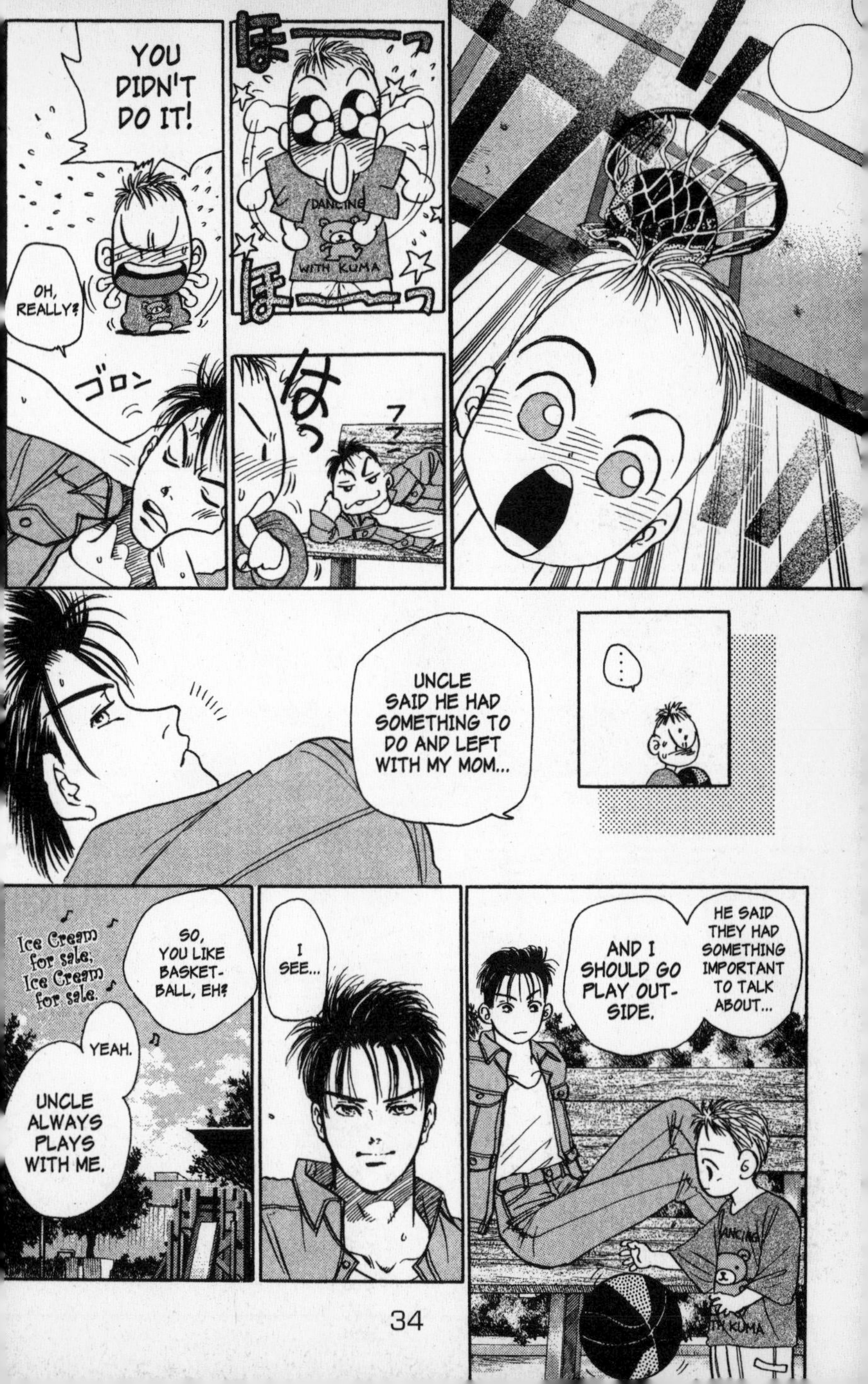
ほーっ
DANCING WITH KUMA
ほーっ
はっ
YOU DIDN'T DO IT!
OH, REALLY?
ゴロン
...
UNCLE SAID HE HAD SOMETHING TO DO AND LEFT WITH MY MOM...
HE SAID THEY HAD SOMETHING IMPORTANT TO TALK ABOUT...
AND I SHOULD GO PLAY OUT-SIDE.
DANCING WITH KUMA
I SEE...
SO, YOU LIKE BASKET-BALL, EH?
Ice Cream for sale, Ice Cream for sale.
YEAH.
UNCLE ALWAYS PLAYS WITH ME.

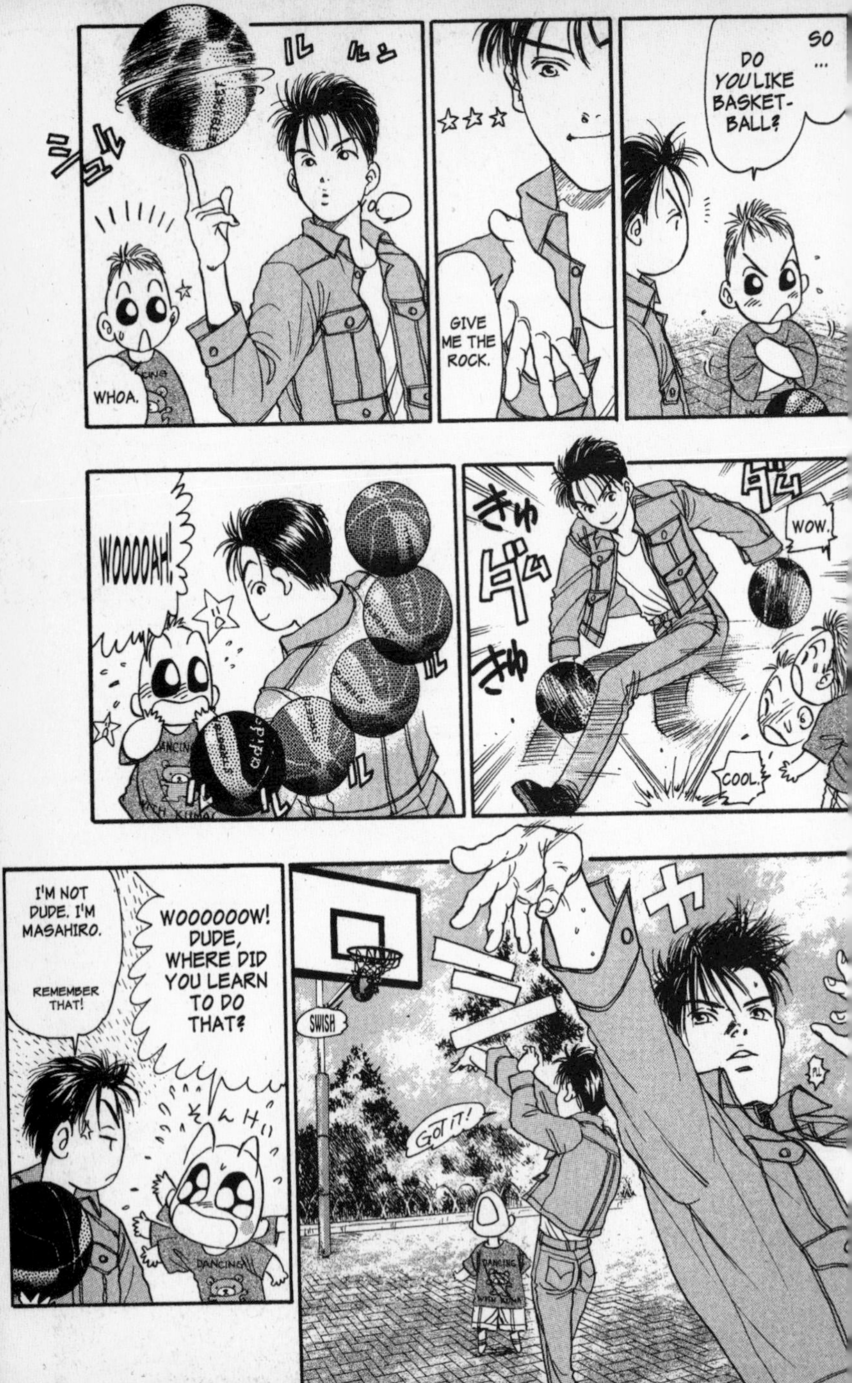
SO ...
DO YOU LIKE BASKET-BALL?
GIVE ME THE ROCK.
WHOA.
WOW.
COOL.
WOOOOAH!
GOT IT!
SWISH
WOOOOOOW! DUDE, WHERE DID YOU LEARN TO DO THAT?
I'M NOT DUDE. I'M MASAHIRO.
REMEMBER THAT!

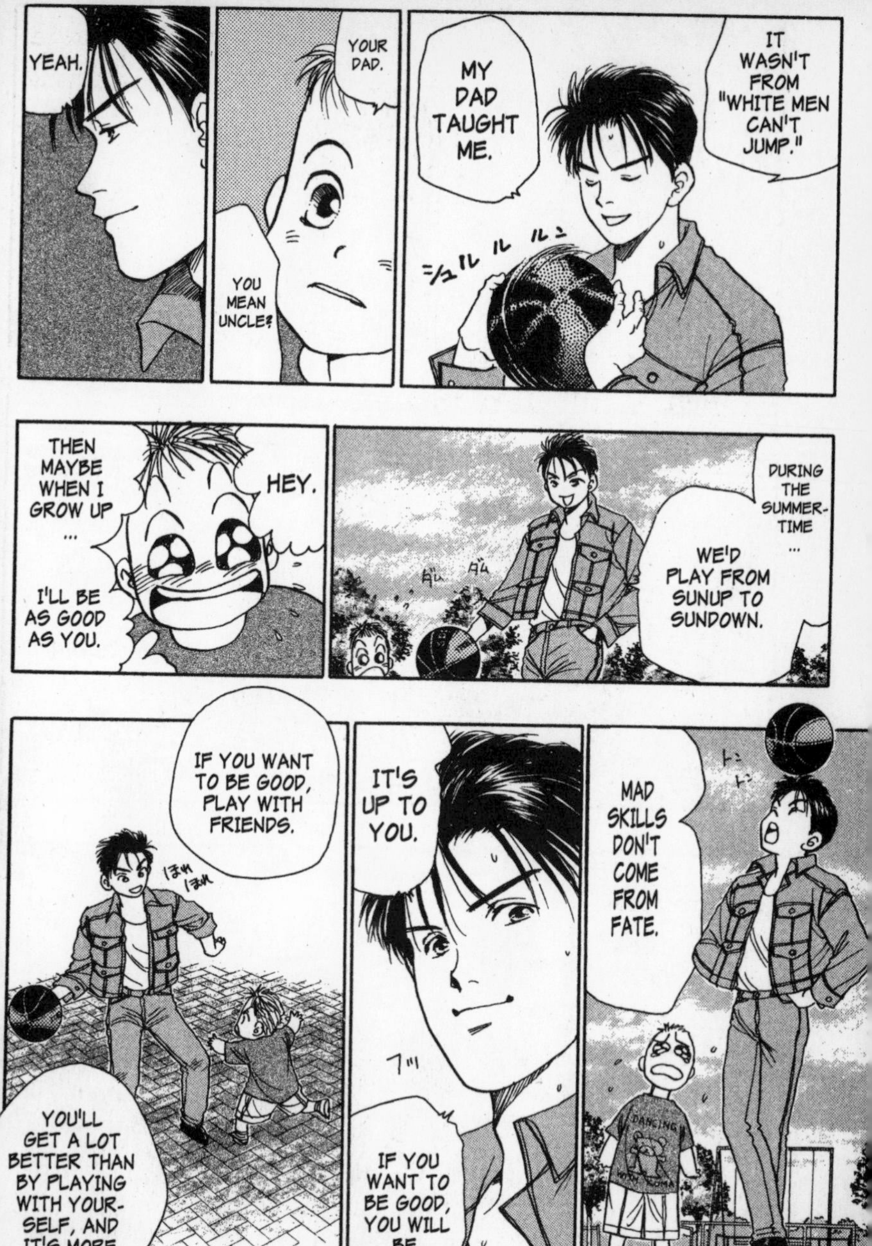
IT WASN'T FROM "WHITE MEN CAN'T JUMP."
MY DAD TAUGHT ME.
シュルルルン
YOUR DAD.
YOU MEAN UNCLE?
YEAH.
DURING THE SUMMER-TIME ...
WE'D PLAY FROM SUNUP TO SUNDOWN.
ダム
ダム
HEY.
THEN MAYBE WHEN I GROW UP ...
I'LL BE AS GOOD AS YOU.
MAD SKILLS DON'T COME FROM FATE.
IT'S UP TO YOU.
フッ
IF YOU WANT TO BE GOOD, YOU WILL BE.
IF YOU WANT TO BE GOOD, PLAY WITH FRIENDS.
ほれ ほれ
YOU'LL GET A LOT BETTER THAN BY PLAYING WITH YOUR-SELF, AND IT'S MORE FUN.

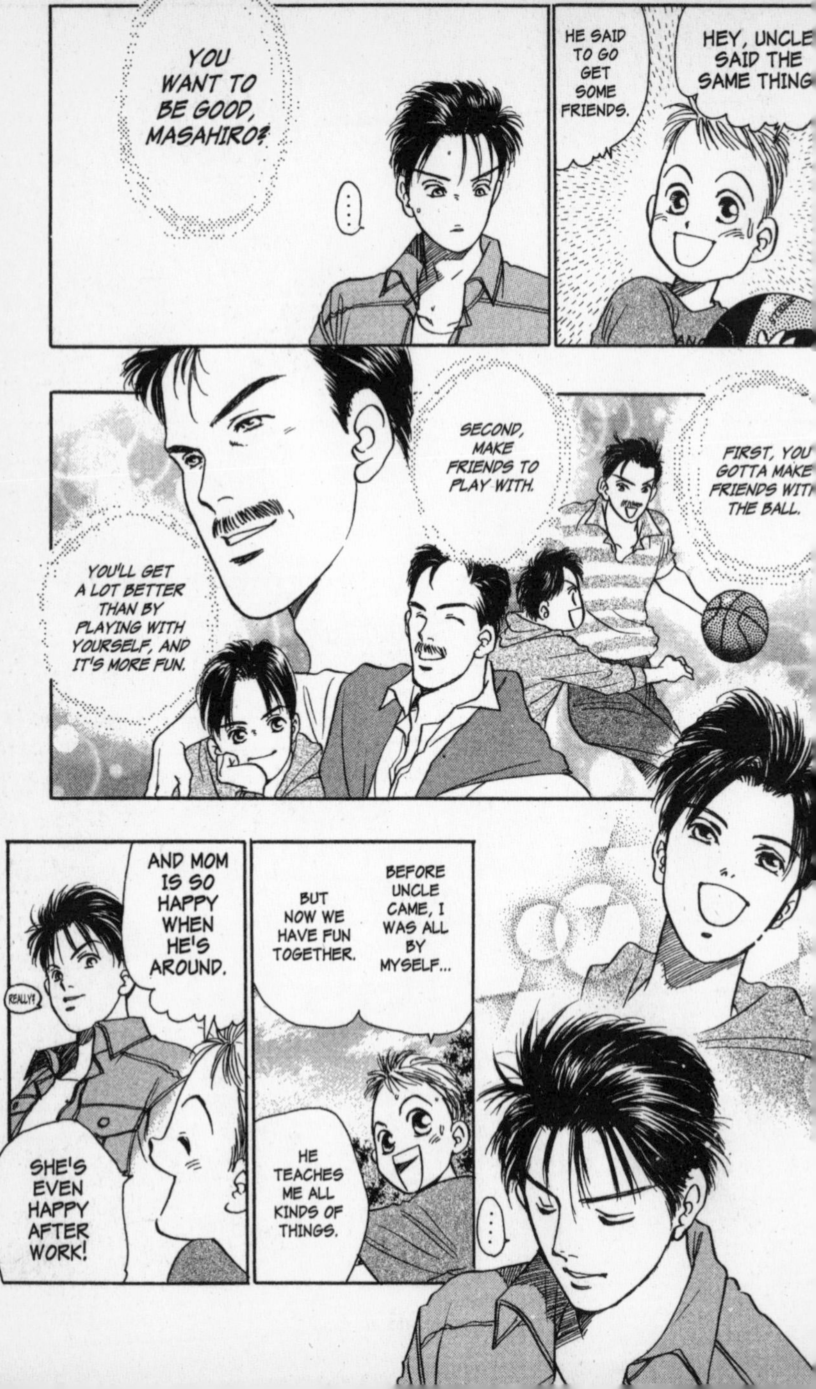
HEY, UNCLE SAID THE SAME THING
HE SAID TO GO GET SOME FRIENDS.
YOU WANT TO BE GOOD, MASAHIRO?
...
FIRST, YOU GOTTA MAKE FRIENDS WIT THE BALL.
SECOND, MAKE FRIENDS TO PLAY WITH.
YOU'LL GET A LOT BETTER THAN BY PLAYING WITH YOURSELF, AND IT'S MORE FUN.
BEFORE UNCLE CAME, I WAS ALL BY MYSELF...
BUT NOW WE HAVE FUN TOGETHER.
HE TEACHES ME ALL KINDS OF THINGS.
AND MOM IS SO HAPPY WHEN HE'S AROUND.
REALLY?
SHE'S EVEN HAPPY AFTER WORK!
...

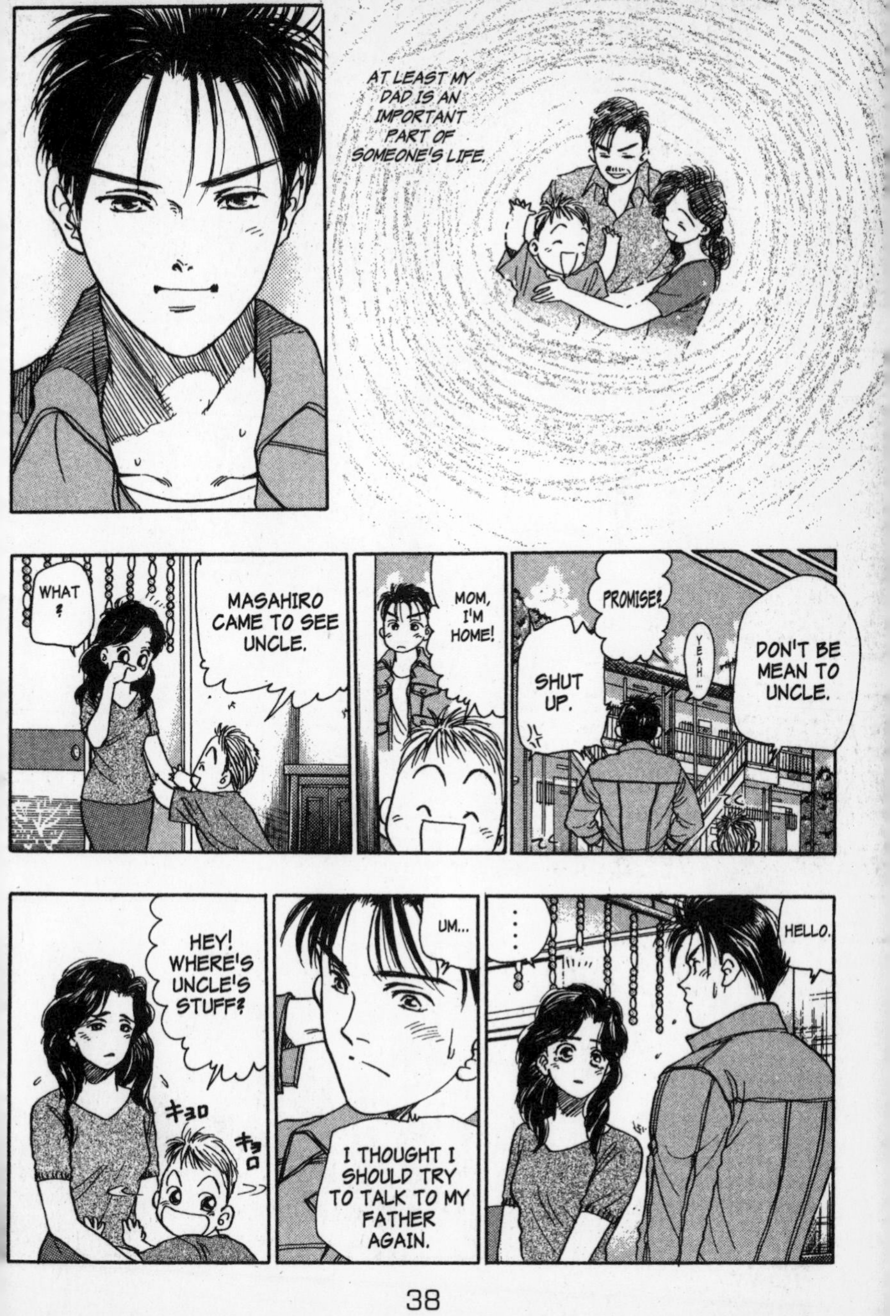

AT LEAST MY DAD IS AN IMPORTANT PART OF SOMEONE'S LIFE.
DON'T BE MEAN TO UNCLE.
PROMISE?
YEAH...
SHUT UP.
MOM, I'M HOME!
MASAHIRO CAME TO SEE UNCLE.
WHAT?
HELLO.
...
UM...
I THOUGHT I SHOULD TRY TO TALK TO MY FATHER AGAIN.
HEY! WHERE'S UNCLE'S STUFF?
キョロ
キョロ

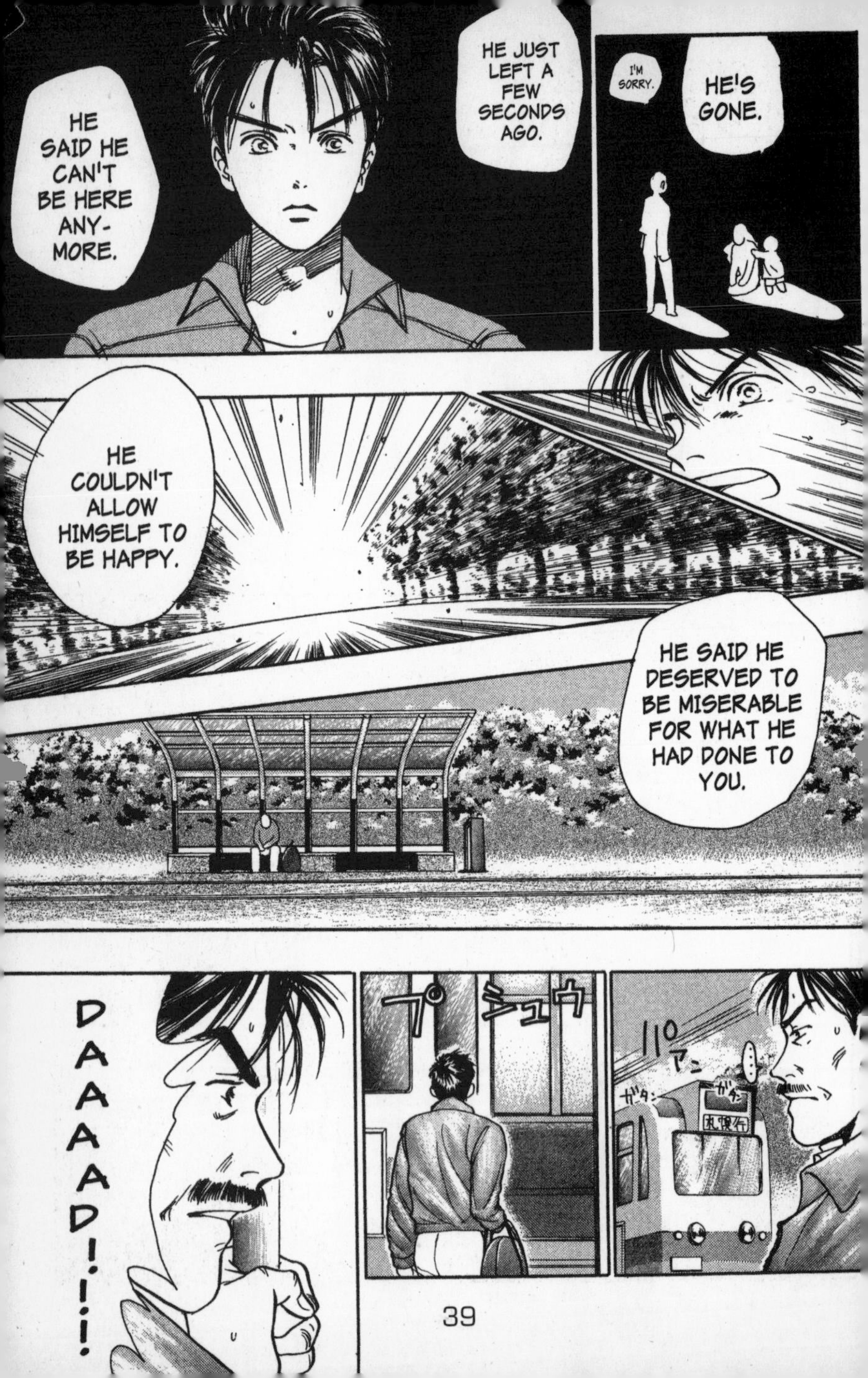
I'M SORRY.
HE'S GONE.
HE JUST LEFT A FEW SECONDS AGO.
HE SAID HE CAN'T BE HERE ANY-MORE.
HE COULDN'T ALLOW HIMSELF TO BE HAPPY.
HE SAID HE DESERVED TO BE MISERABLE FOR WHAT HE HAD DONE TO YOU.
プシュウ
DAAAAD!!!

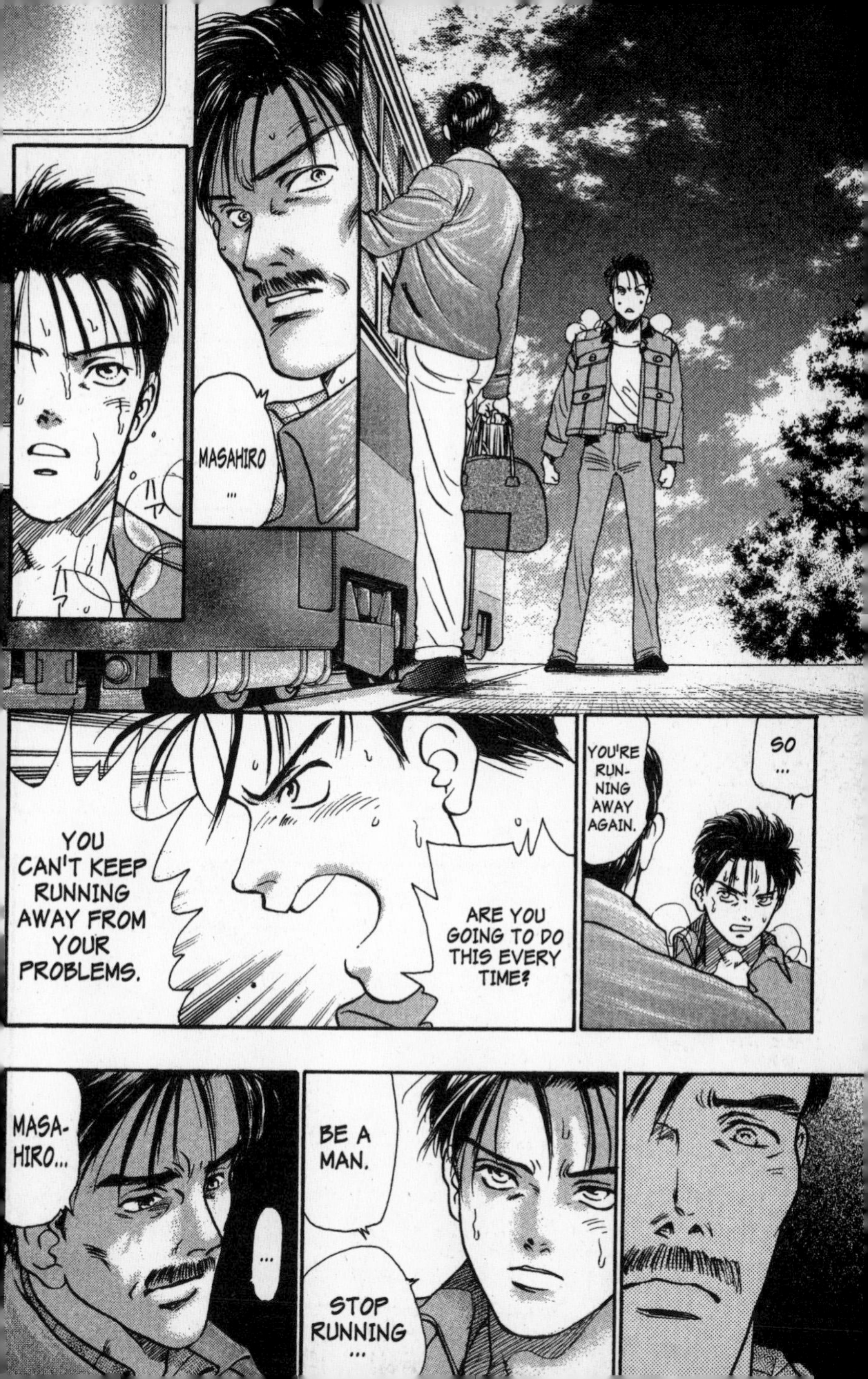
MASAHIRO ...
SO ...
YOU'RE RUNNING AWAY AGAIN.
ARE YOU GOING TO DO THIS EVERY TIME?
YOU CAN'T KEEP RUNNING AWAY FROM YOUR PROBLEMS.
BE A MAN.
STOP RUNNING ...
MASA-HIRO...
...

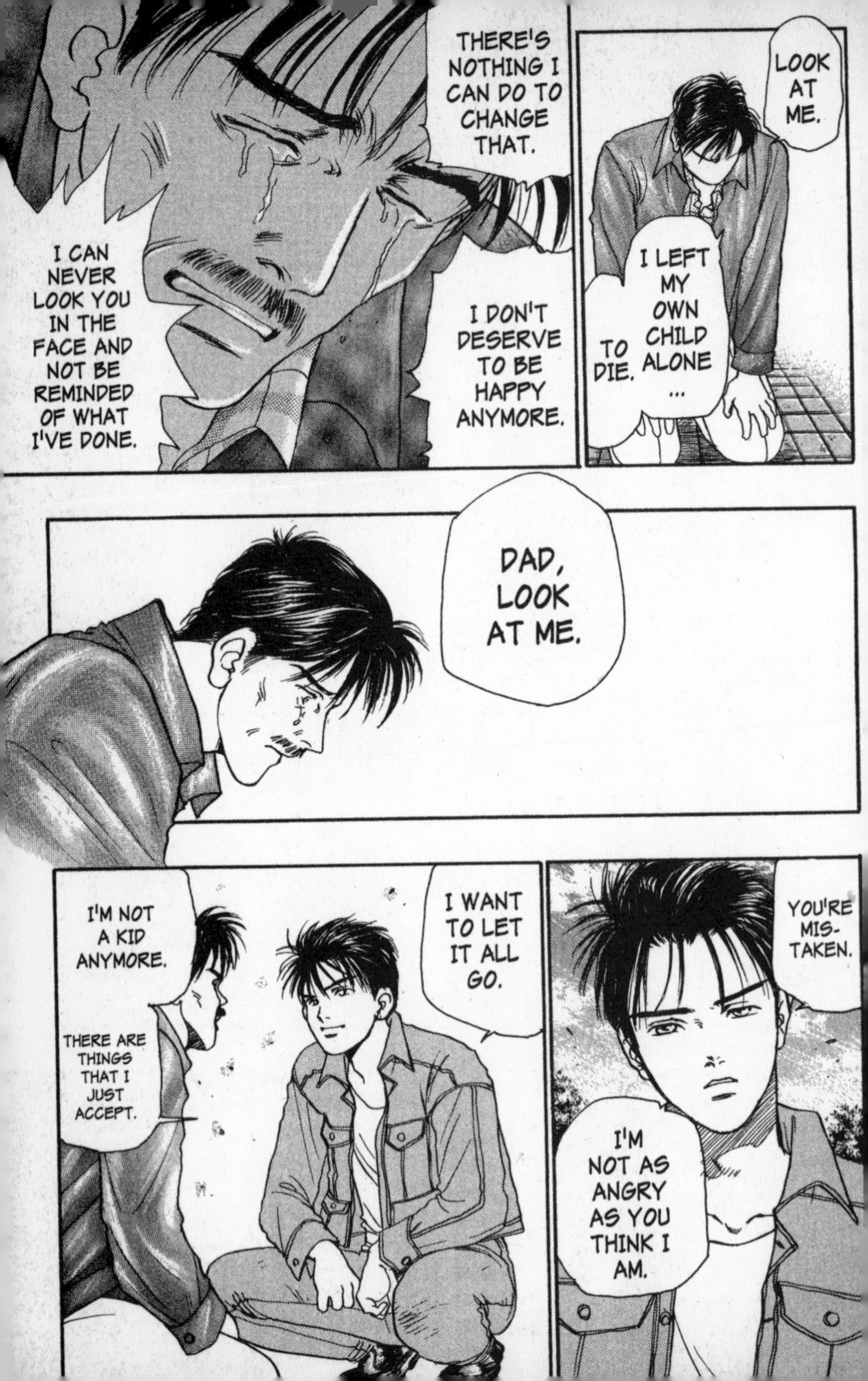
LOOK AT ME.
I LEFT MY OWN CHILD ALONE ...
TO DIE.
THERE'S NOTHING I CAN DO TO CHANGE THAT.
I DON'T DESERVE TO BE HAPPY ANYMORE.
I CAN NEVER LOOK YOU IN THE FACE AND NOT BE REMINDED OF WHAT I'VE DONE.
DAD, LOOK AT ME.
YOU'RE MIS-TAKEN.
I'M NOT AS ANGRY AS YOU THINK I AM.
I WANT TO LET IT ALL GO.
I'M NOT A KID ANYMORE.
THERE ARE THINGS THAT I JUST ACCEPT.

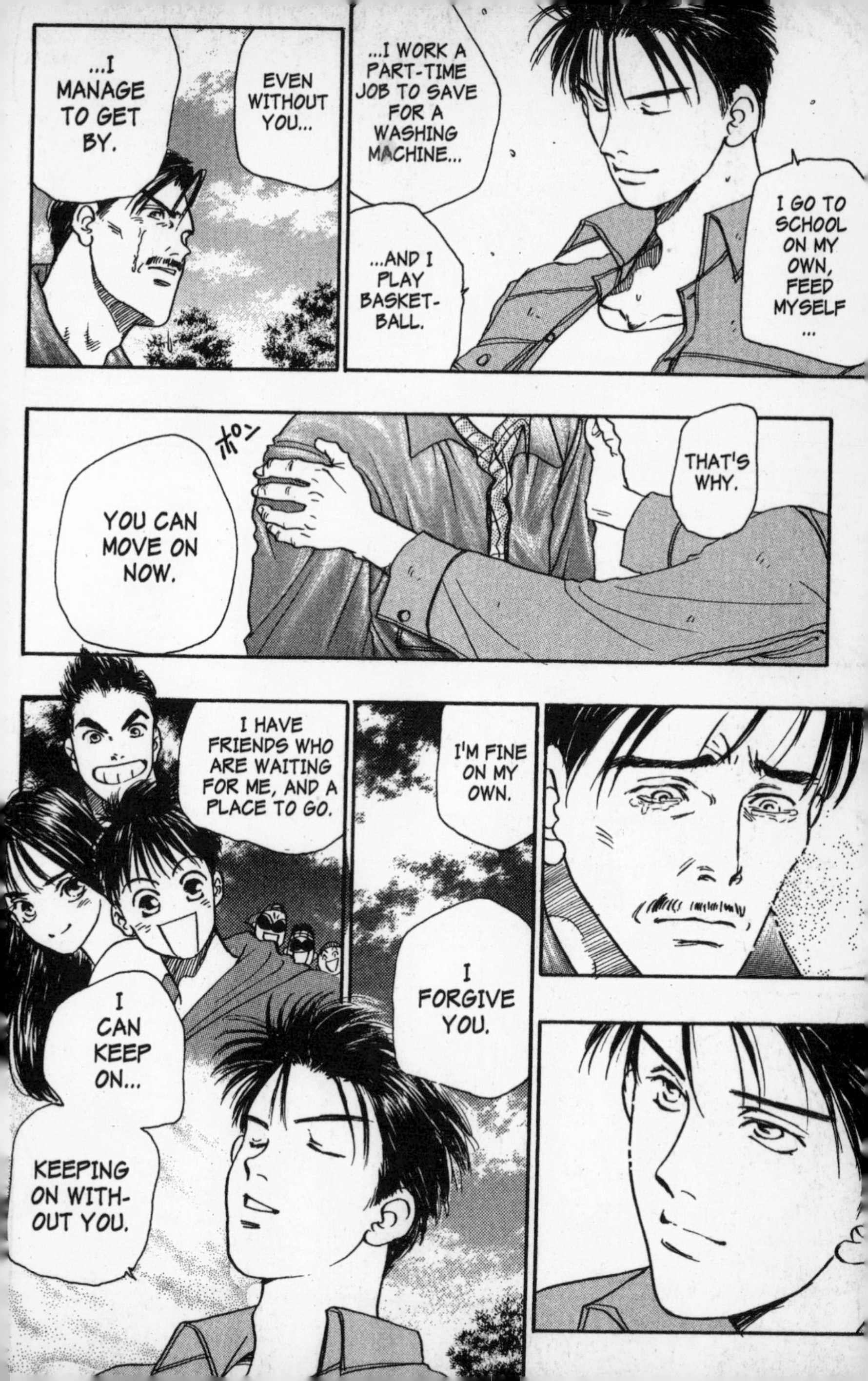
I GO TO SCHOOL ON MY OWN, FEED MYSELF ...
...I WORK A PART-TIME JOB TO SAVE FOR A WASHING MACHINE...
...AND I PLAY BASKET-BALL.
EVEN WITHOUT YOU...
...I MANAGE TO GET BY.
THAT'S WHY.
ポン
YOU CAN MOVE ON NOW.
I'M FINE ON MY OWN.
I HAVE FRIENDS WHO ARE WAITING FOR ME, AND A PLACE TO GO.
I CAN KEEP ON...
KEEPING ON WITH-OUT YOU.
I FORGIVE YOU.

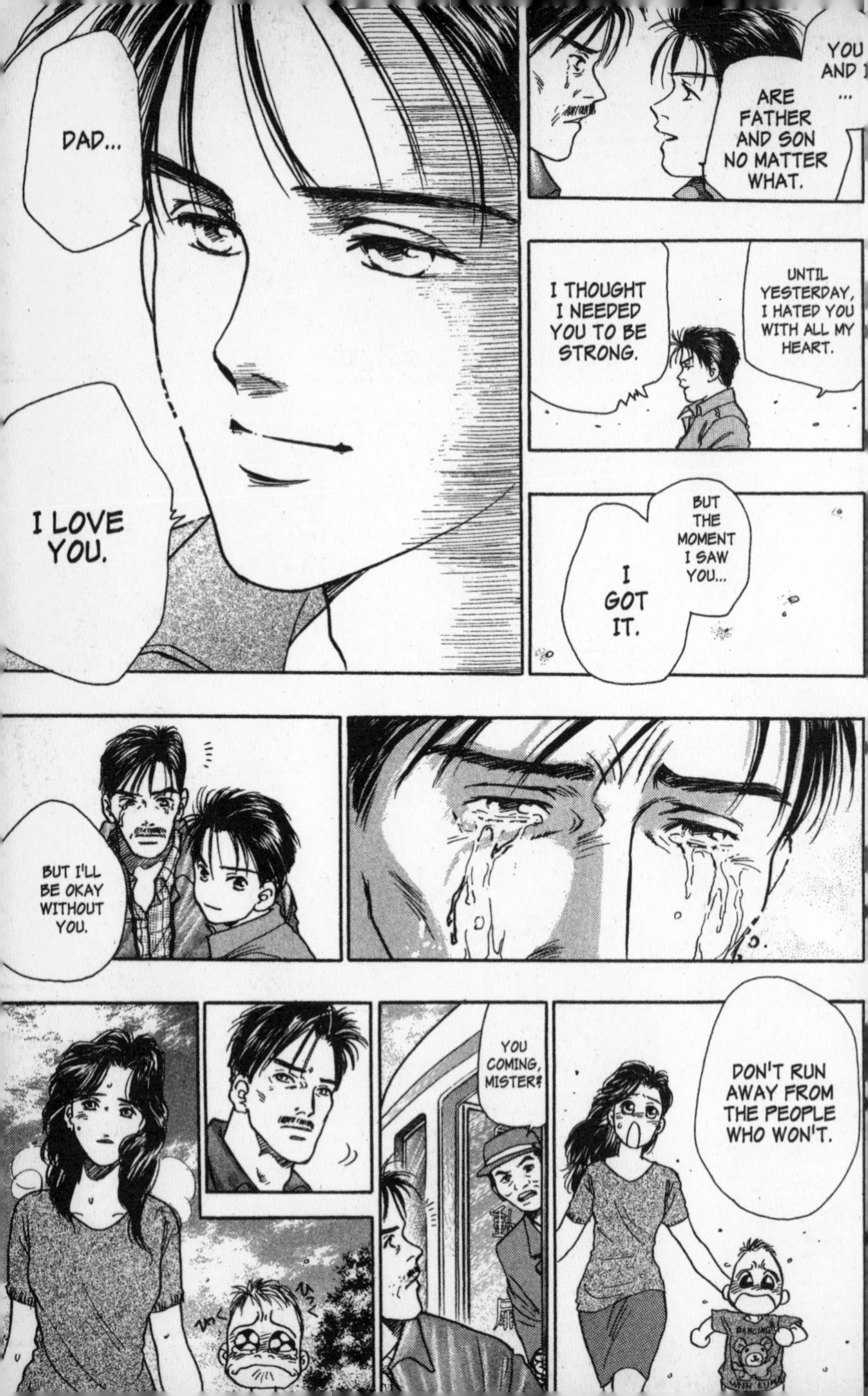
YOU AND I ...
ARE FATHER AND SON NO MATTER WHAT.
UNTIL YESTERDAY, I HATED YOU WITH ALL MY HEART.
I THOUGHT I NEEDED YOU TO BE STRONG.
BUT THE MOMENT I SAW YOU...
I GOT IT.
DAD...
I LOVE YOU.
BUT I'LL BE OKAY WITHOUT YOU.
DON'T RUN AWAY FROM THE PEOPLE WHO WON'T.
YOU COMING, MISTER?

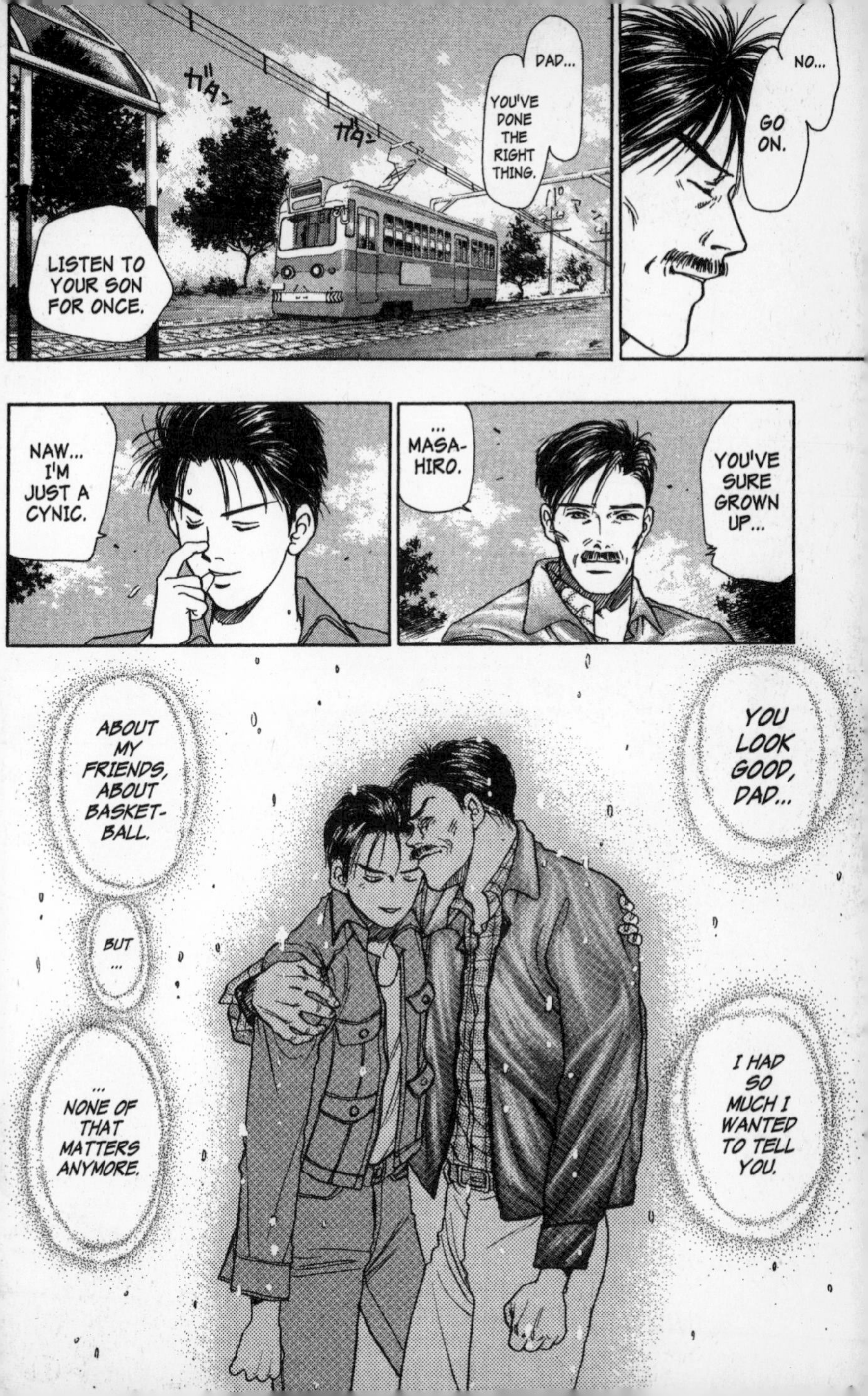
NO...
GO ON.
DAD...
YOU'VE DONE THE RIGHT THING.
LISTEN TO YOUR SON FOR ONCE.
YOU'VE SURE GROWN UP...
... MASA-HIRO.
NAW... I'M JUST A CYNIC.
YOU LOOK GOOD, DAD...
I HAD SO MUCH I WANTED TO TELL YOU.
ABOUT MY FRIENDS, ABOUT BASKET-BALL.
BUT ...
... NONE OF THAT MATTERS ANYMORE.

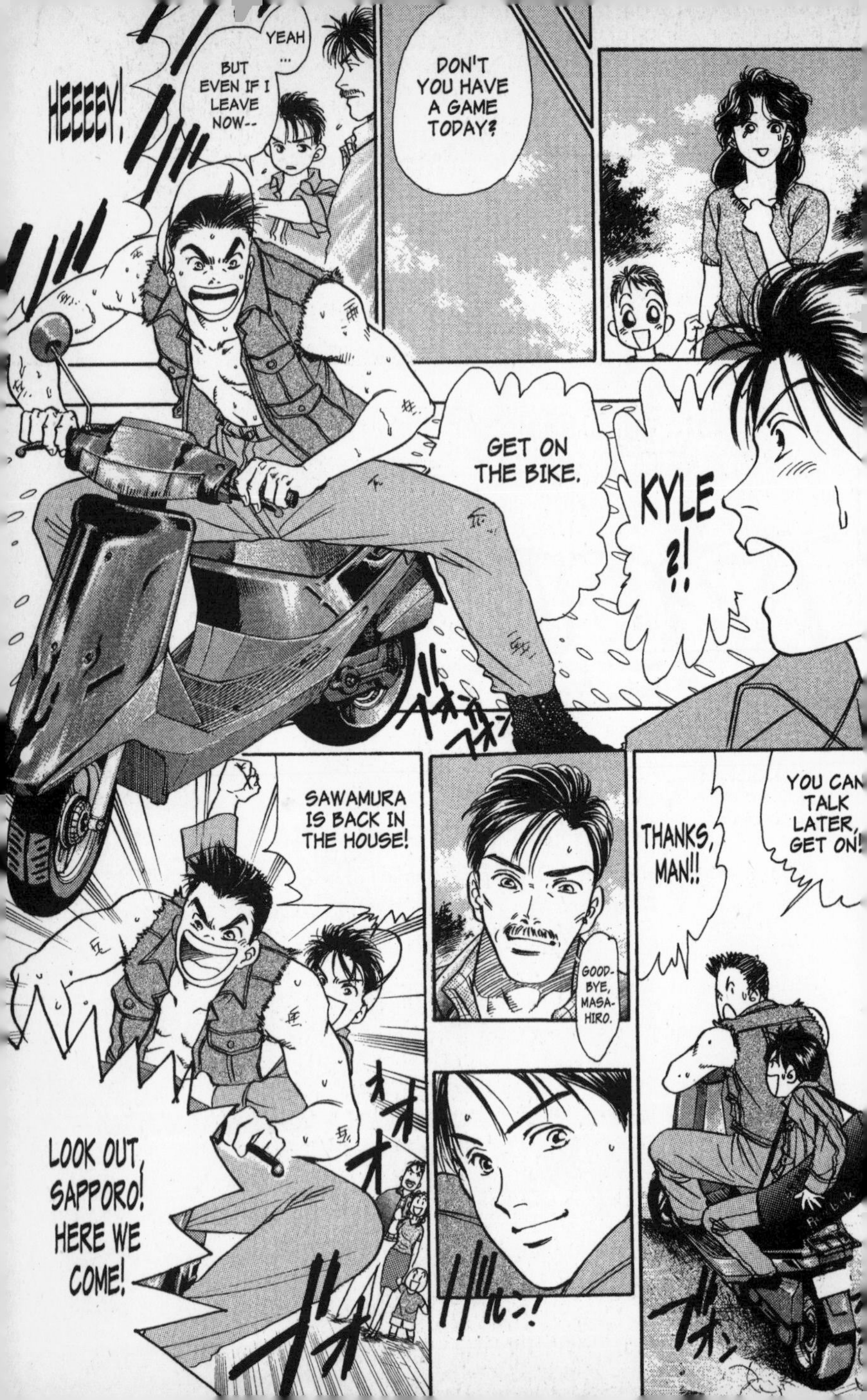
DON'T YOU HAVE A GAME TODAY?
YEAH ...
BUT EVEN IF I LEAVE NOW--
HEEEEY!
KYLE ?!
GET ON THE BIKE.
YOU CAN TALK LATER, GET ON!
THANKS, MAN!!
GOOD-BYE, MASA-HIRO.
SAWAMURA IS BACK IN THE HOUSE!
LOOK OUT, SAPPORO! HERE WE COME!

And once again, all you manga fans,
TOKYOPOP Soda Pop proudly presents...

in brilliant black and white.
And remember, pop a top on TOKYOPOP Soda
Pop, and the fun don't stop.

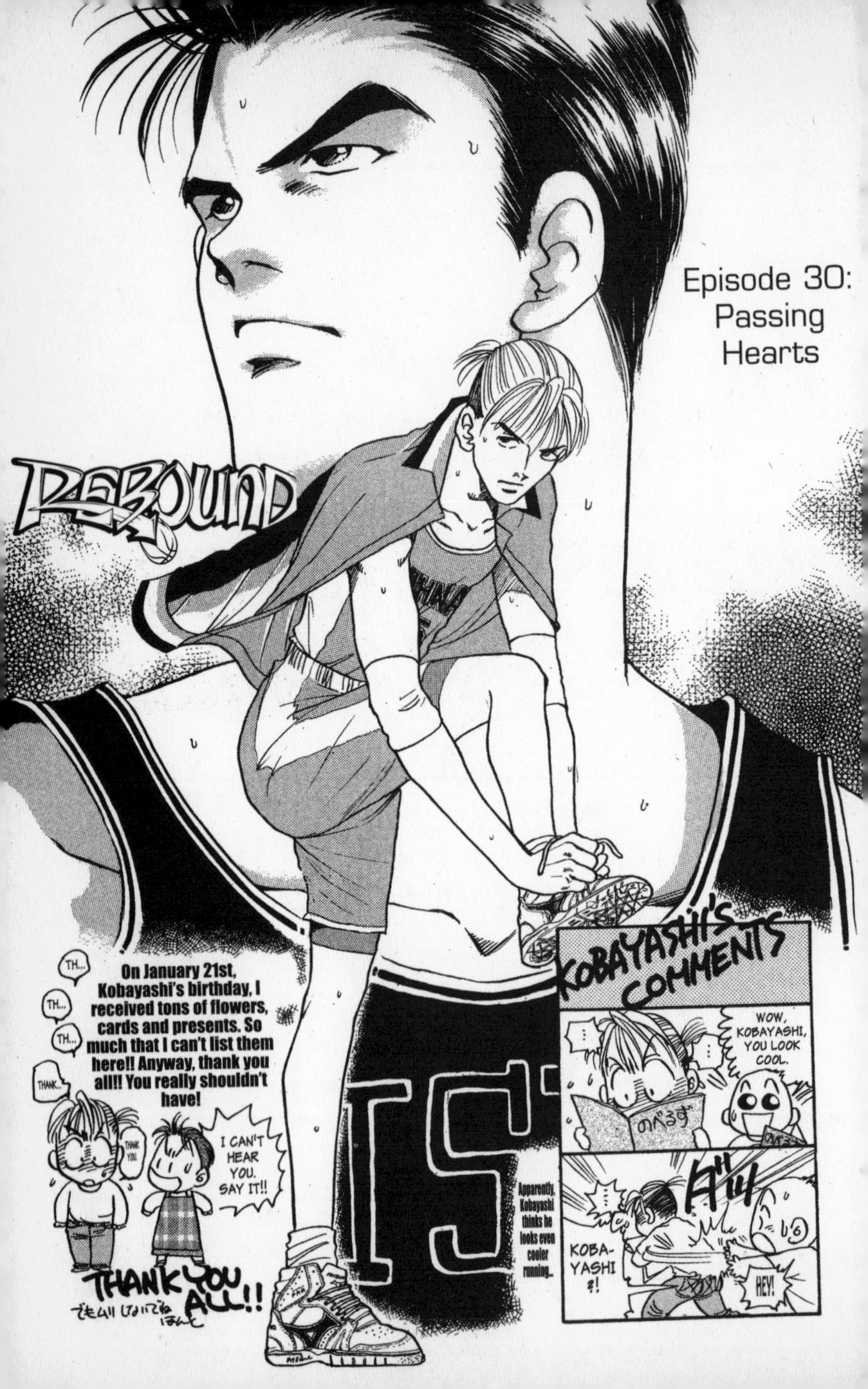
Episode 30: Passing Hearts
REBOUND
KOBAYASHI'S COMMENTS
WOW, KOBAYASHI, YOU LOOK COOL.
...
...
のべるず
ガッ
...
KOBA-YASHI ?!
HEY!
Apparently, Kobayashi thinks he looks even cooler running...
On January 21st, Kobayashi's birthday, I received tons of flowers, cards and presents. So much that I can't list them here!! Anyway, thank you all!! You really shouldn't have!
TH...
TH...
TH...
THANK...
I CAN'T HEAR YOU. SAY IT!!
THANK YOU.
THANK YOU ALL!!
でもムリしないでね ほんと

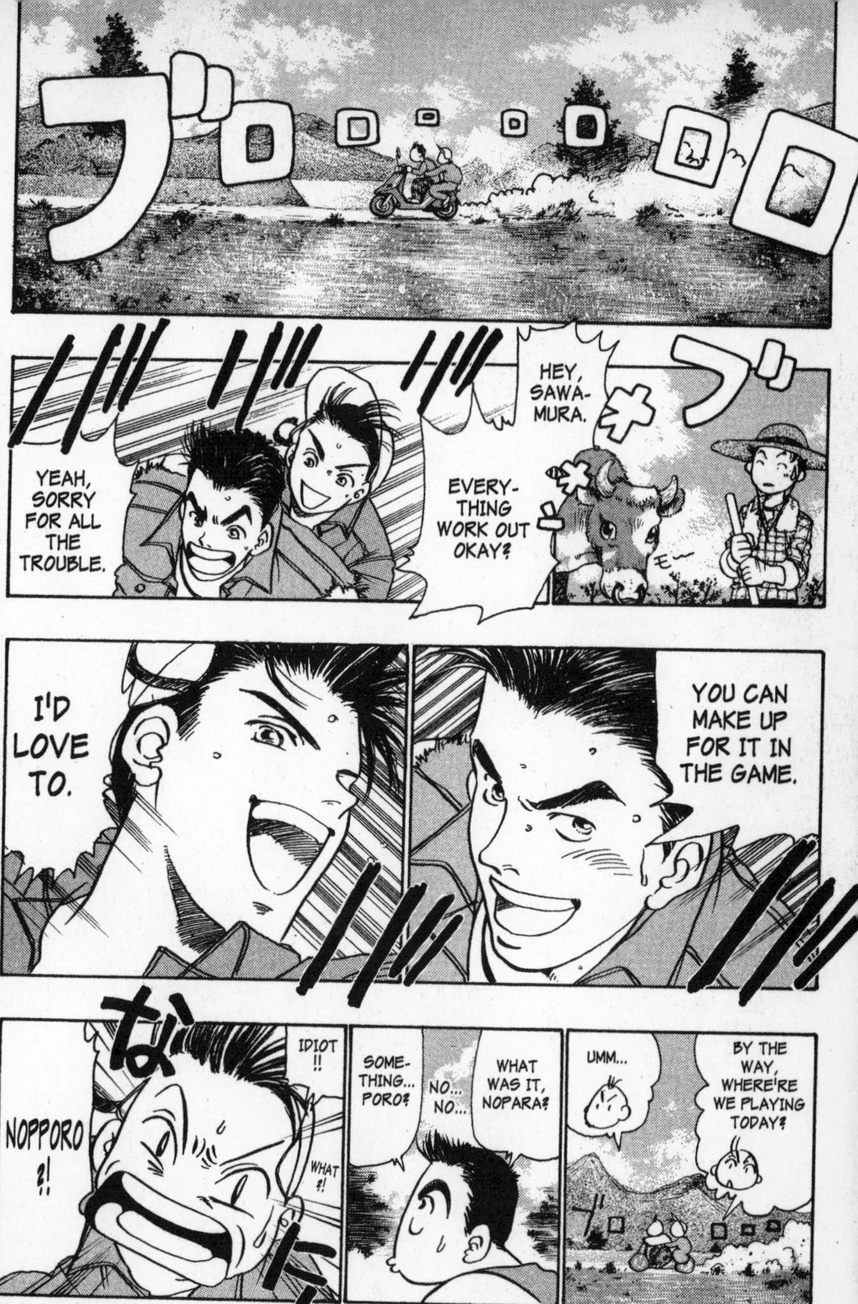
HEY, SAWAMURA.
EVERYTHING WORK OUT OKAY?
YEAH, SORRY FOR ALL THE TROUBLE.
YOU CAN MAKE UP FOR IT IN THE GAME.
I'D LOVE TO.
BY THE WAY, WHERE'RE WE PLAYING TODAY?
UMM...
WHAT WAS IT, NOPARA?
NO... NO...
SOMETHING... PORO?
IDIOT!!
NOPPORO?!
WHAT?!
な

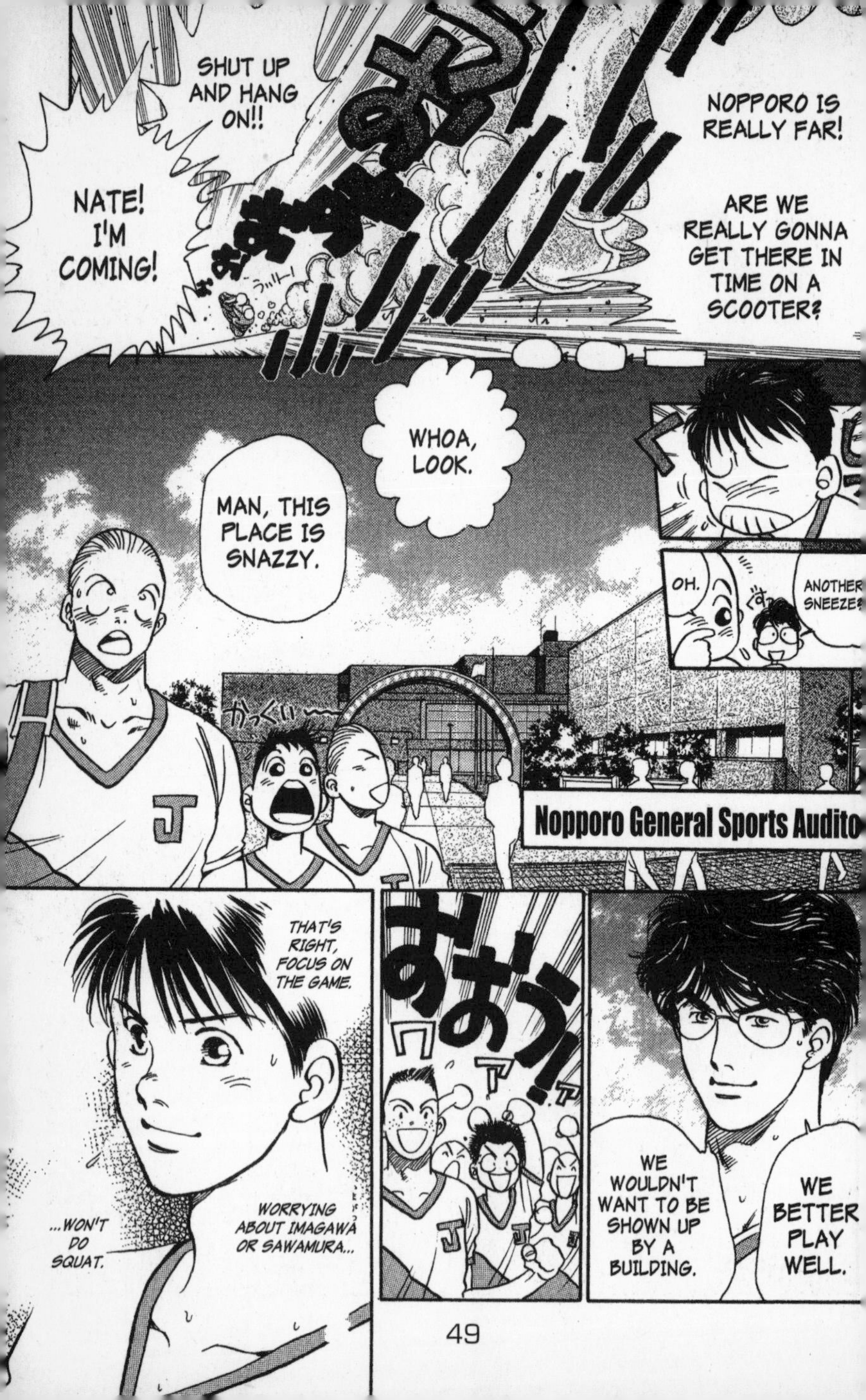
NOPPORO IS REALLY FAR!
ARE WE REALLY GONNA GET THERE IN TIME ON A SCOOTER?
SHUT UP AND HANG ON!!
NATE! I'M COMING!
ANOTHER SNEEZE?
OH.
WHOA, LOOK.
MAN, THIS PLACE IS SNAZZY.
Nopporo General Sports Audito
WE BETTER PLAY WELL.
WE WOULDN'T WANT TO BE SHOWN UP BY A BUILDING.
おおう!!
THAT'S RIGHT, FOCUS ON THE GAME.
WORRYING ABOUT IMAGAWA OR SAWAMURA...
...WON'T DO SQUAT.

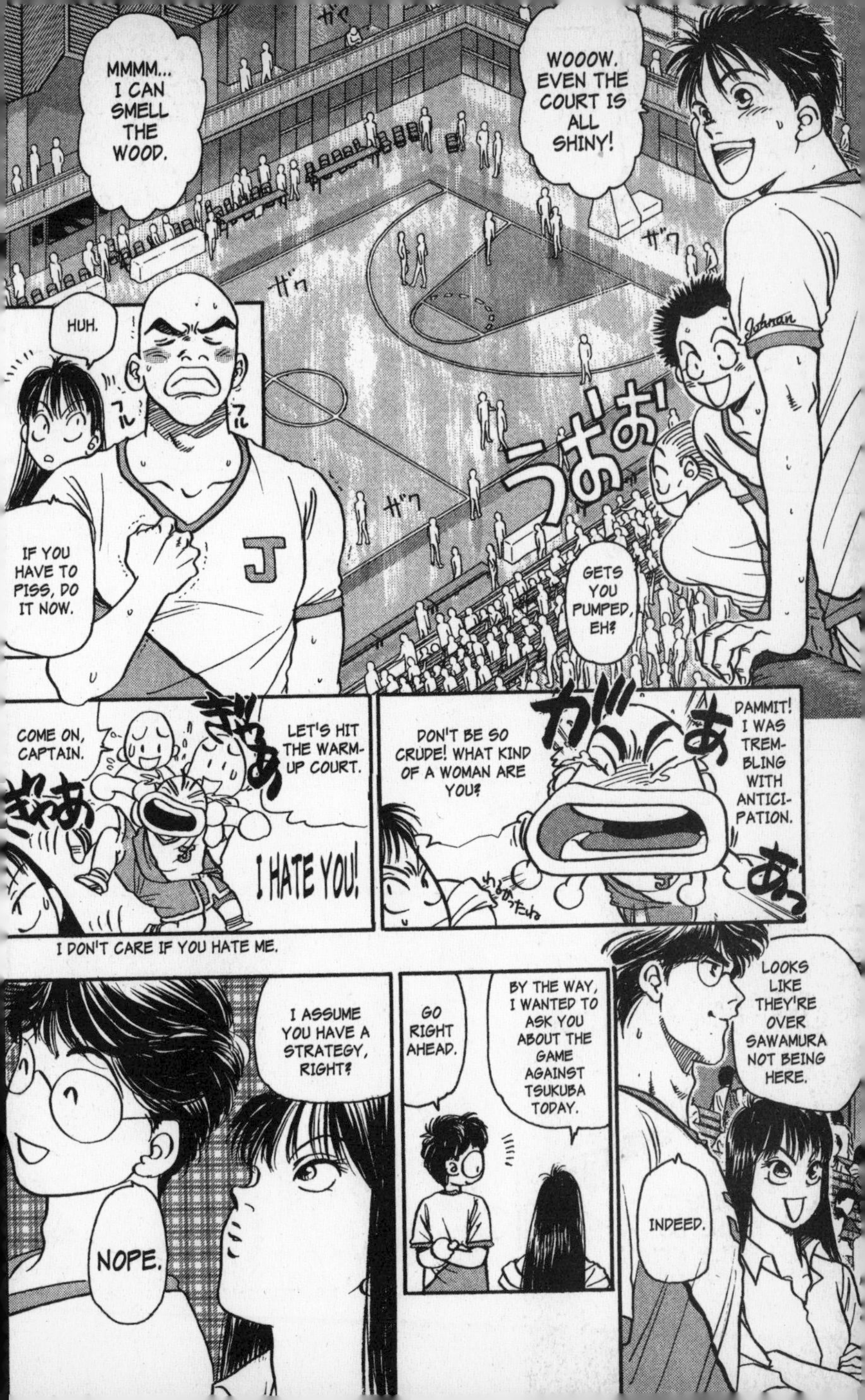
WOOOW. EVEN THE COURT IS ALL SHINY!
MMMM... I CAN SMELL THE WOOD.
GETS YOU PUMPED, EH?
HUH.
IF YOU HAVE TO PISS, DO IT NOW.
DAMMIT! I WAS TREMBLING WITH ANTICIPATION.
DON'T BE SO CRUDE! WHAT KIND OF A WOMAN ARE YOU?
LET'S HIT THE WARM-UP COURT.
COME ON, CAPTAIN.
I HATE YOU!
I DON'T CARE IF YOU HATE ME.
LOOKS LIKE THEY'RE OVER SAWAMURA NOT BEING HERE.
INDEED.
BY THE WAY, I WANTED TO ASK YOU ABOUT THE GAME AGAINST TSUKUBA TODAY.
GO RIGHT AHEAD.
I ASSUME YOU HAVE A STRATEGY, RIGHT?
NOPE.

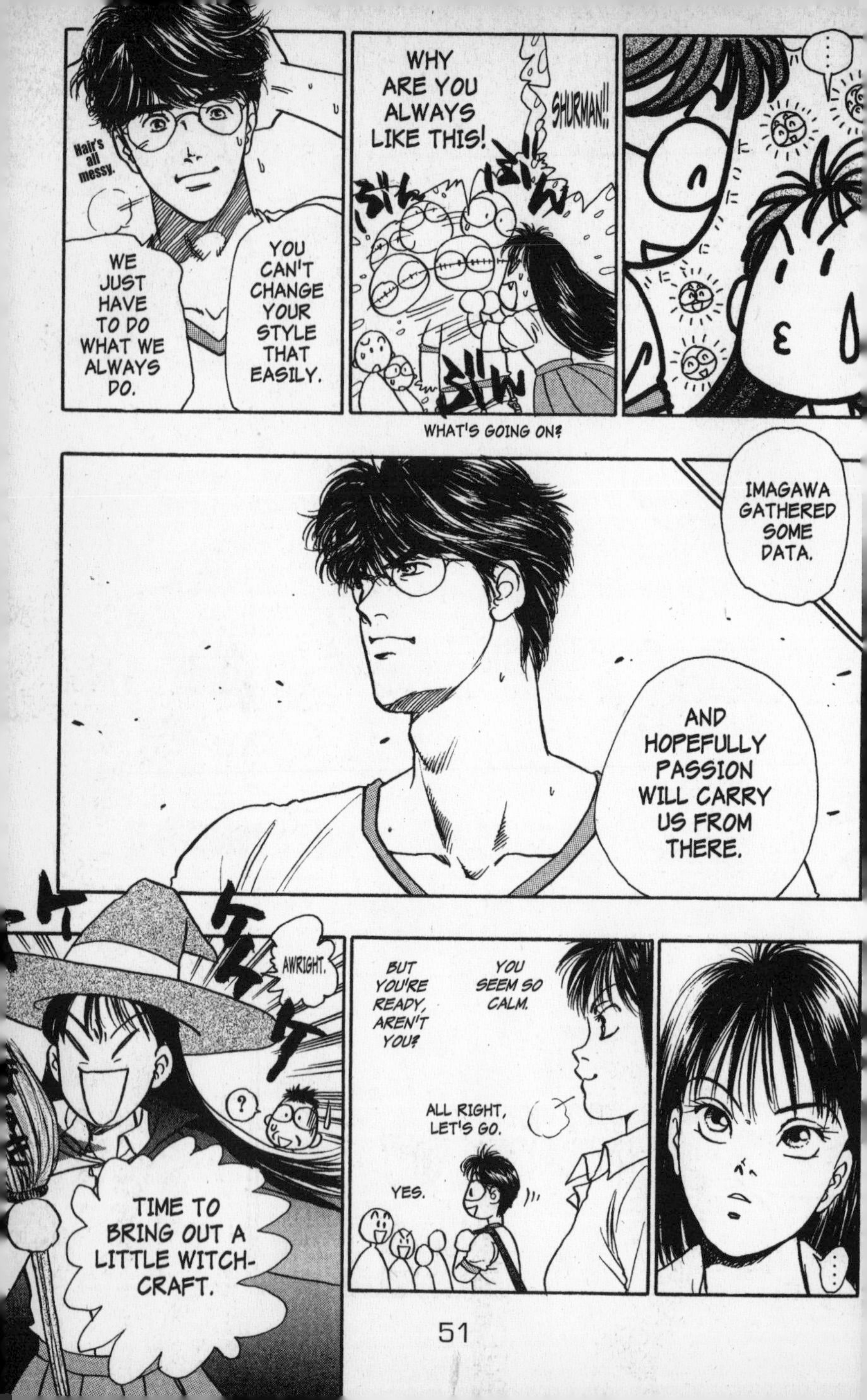
WHY ARE YOU ALWAYS LIKE THIS!
SHURMAN!!
Hair's all messy.
YOU CAN'T CHANGE YOUR STYLE THAT EASILY.
WE JUST HAVE TO DO WHAT WE ALWAYS DO.
WHAT'S GOING ON?
IMAGAWA GATHERED SOME DATA.
AND HOPEFULLY PASSION WILL CARRY US FROM THERE.
YOU SEEM SO CALM.
BUT YOU'RE READY, AREN'T YOU?
ALL RIGHT, LET'S GO.
YES.
AWRIGHT.
TIME TO BRING OUT A LITTLE WITCH-CRAFT.

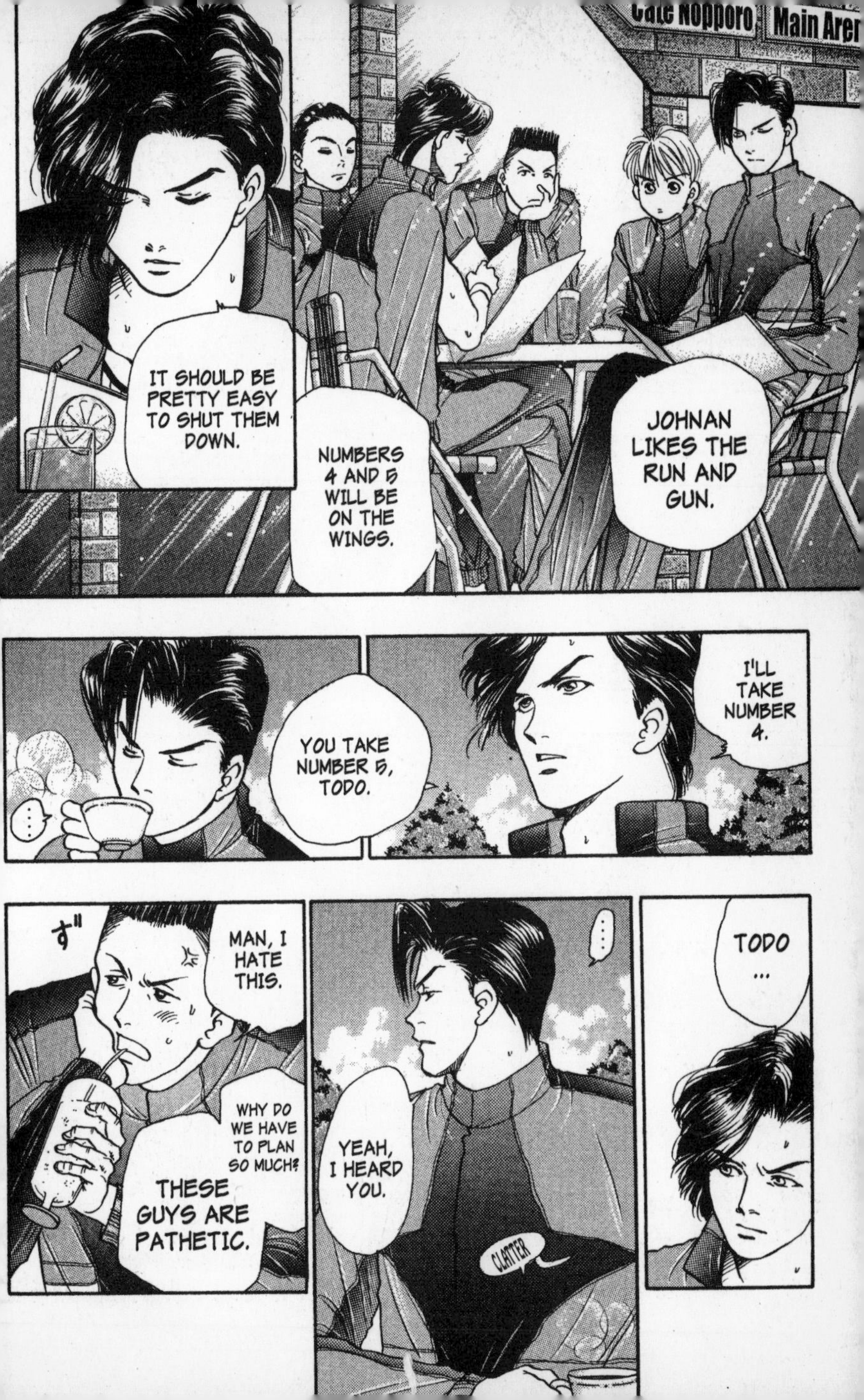
JOHNAN LIKES THE RUN AND GUN.
NUMBERS 4 AND 5 WILL BE ON THE WINGS.
IT SHOULD BE PRETTY EASY TO SHUT THEM DOWN.
I'LL TAKE NUMBER 4.
YOU TAKE NUMBER 5, TODO.
...
TODO ...
...
YEAH, I HEARD YOU.
CLATTER
MAN, I HATE THIS.
ず"
WHY DO WE HAVE TO PLAN SO MUCH?
THESE GUYS ARE PATHETIC.

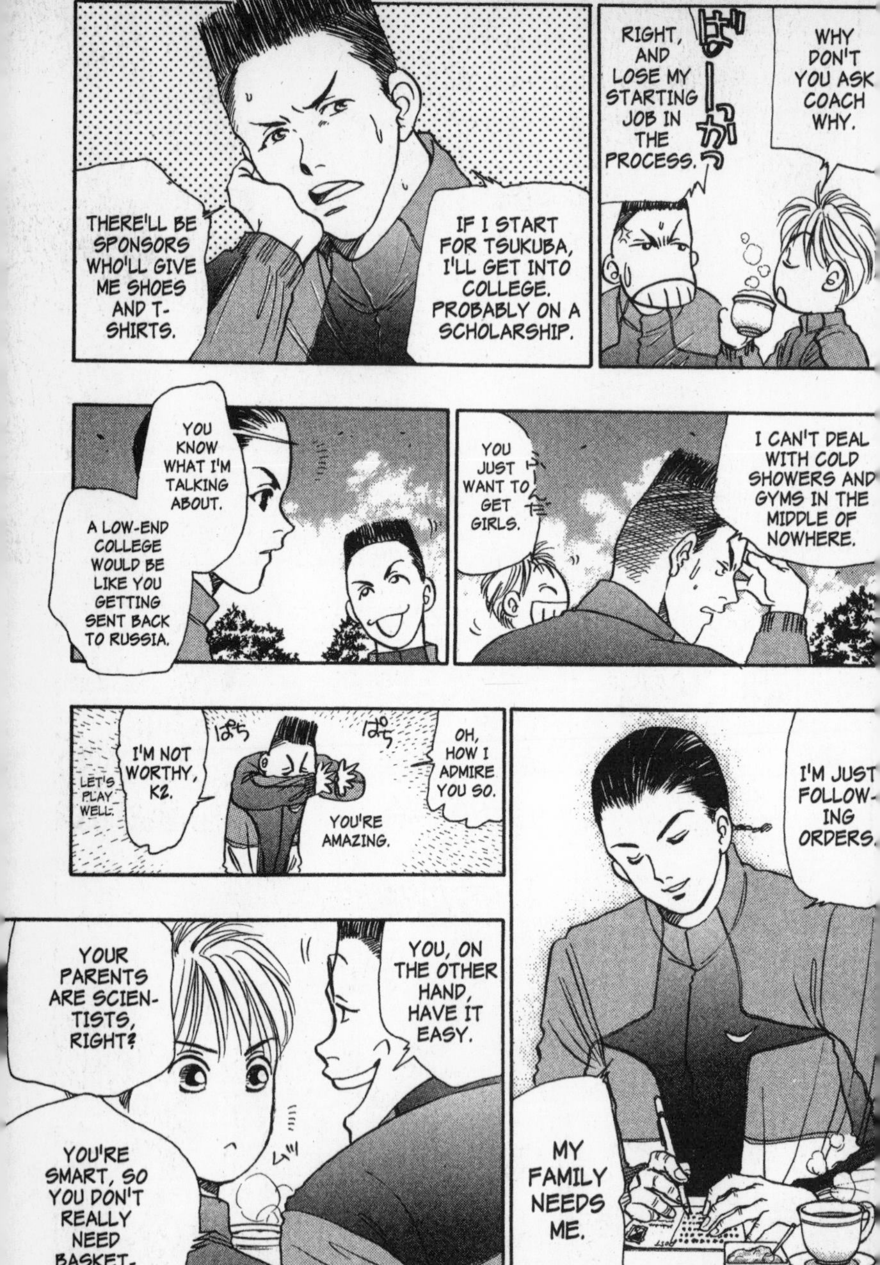
WHY DON'T YOU ASK COACH WHY.
RIGHT, AND LOSE MY STARTING JOB IN THE PROCESS.
IF I START FOR TSUKUBA, I'LL GET INTO COLLEGE. PROBABLY ON A SCHOLARSHIP.
THERE'LL BE SPONSORS WHO'LL GIVE ME SHOES AND T-SHIRTS.
I CAN'T DEAL WITH COLD SHOWERS AND GYMS IN THE MIDDLE OF NOWHERE.
YOU JUST WANT TO GET GIRLS.
YOU KNOW WHAT I'M TALKING ABOUT.
A LOW-END COLLEGE WOULD BE LIKE YOU GETTING SENT BACK TO RUSSIA.
I'M JUST FOLLOWING ORDERS.
MY FAMILY NEEDS ME.
ぱち
ぱち
OH, HOW I ADMIRE YOU SO.
YOU'RE AMAZING.
I'M NOT WORTHY, K2.
LET'S PLAY WELL.
YOU, ON THE OTHER HAND, HAVE IT EASY.
YOUR PARENTS ARE SCIENTISTS, RIGHT?
YOU'RE SMART, SO YOU DON'T REALLY NEED BASKETBALL, DO YOU?

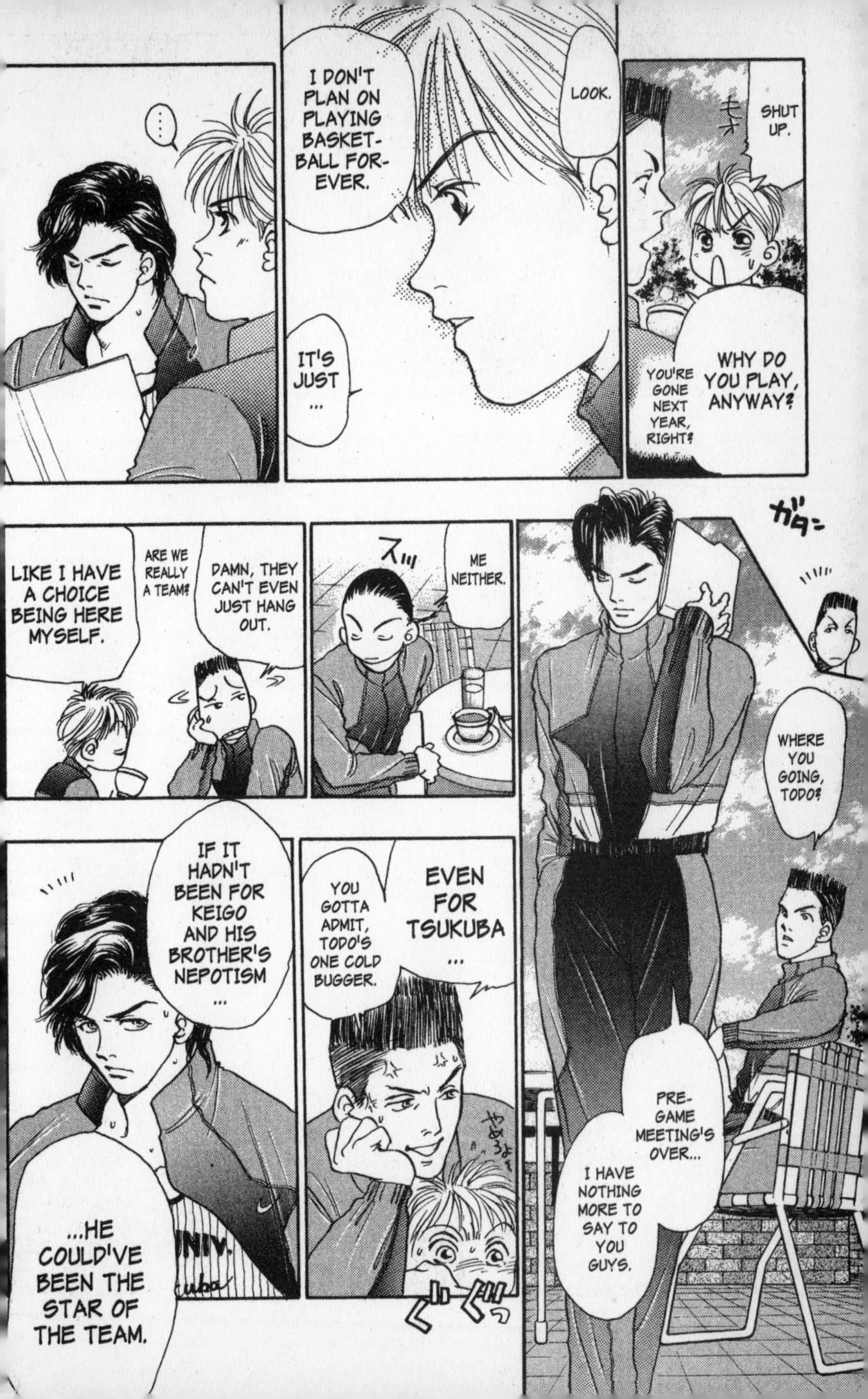
SHUT UP.
WHY DO YOU PLAY, ANYWAY?
YOU'RE GONE NEXT YEAR, RIGHT?
LOOK.
I DON'T PLAN ON PLAYING BASKETBALL FOREVER.
IT'S JUST ...
...
WHERE YOU GOING, TODO?
PRE-GAME MEETING'S OVER...
I HAVE NOTHING MORE TO SAY TO YOU GUYS.
スッ
ME NEITHER.
DAMN, THEY CAN'T EVEN JUST HANG OUT.
ARE WE REALLY A TEAM?
LIKE I HAVE A CHOICE BEING HERE MYSELF.
EVEN FOR TSUKUBA ...
YOU GOTTA ADMIT, TODO'S ONE COLD BUGGER.
IF IT HADN'T BEEN FOR KEIGO AND HIS BROTHER'S NEPOTISM ...
...HE COULD'VE BEEN THE STAR OF THE TEAM.

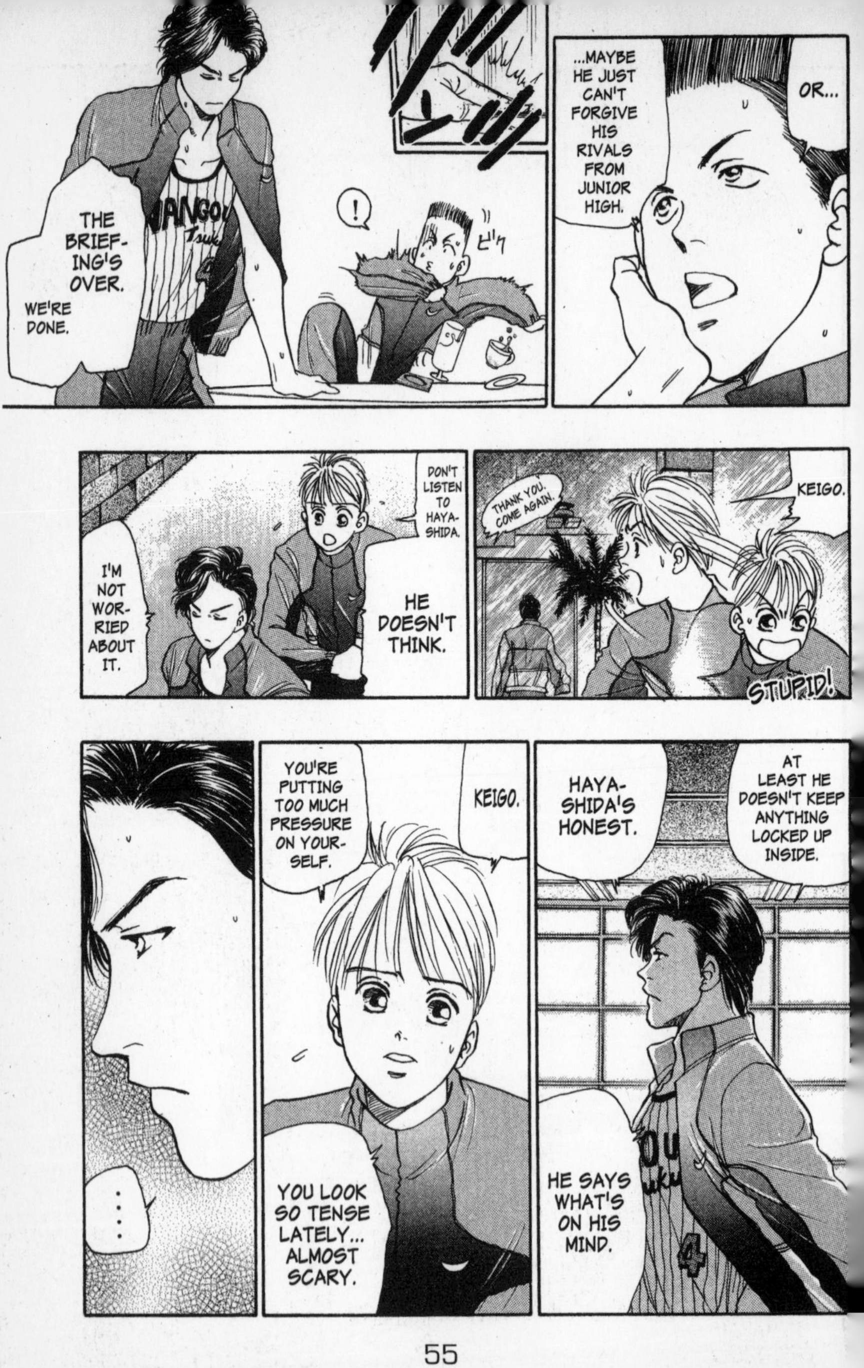
OR...
...MAYBE HE JUST CAN'T FORGIVE HIS RIVALS FROM JUNIOR HIGH.
!
ビク
THE BRIEFING'S OVER.
WE'RE DONE.
KEIGO.
THANK YOU. COME AGAIN.
STUPID!
DON'T LISTEN TO HAYASHIDA.
HE DOESN'T THINK.
I'M NOT WORRIED ABOUT IT.
AT LEAST HE DOESN'T KEEP ANYTHING LOCKED UP INSIDE.
HAYASHIDA'S HONEST.
HE SAYS WHAT'S ON HIS MIND.
KEIGO.
YOU'RE PUTTING TOO MUCH PRESSURE ON YOURSELF.
YOU LOOK SO TENSE LATELY... ALMOST SCARY.
....

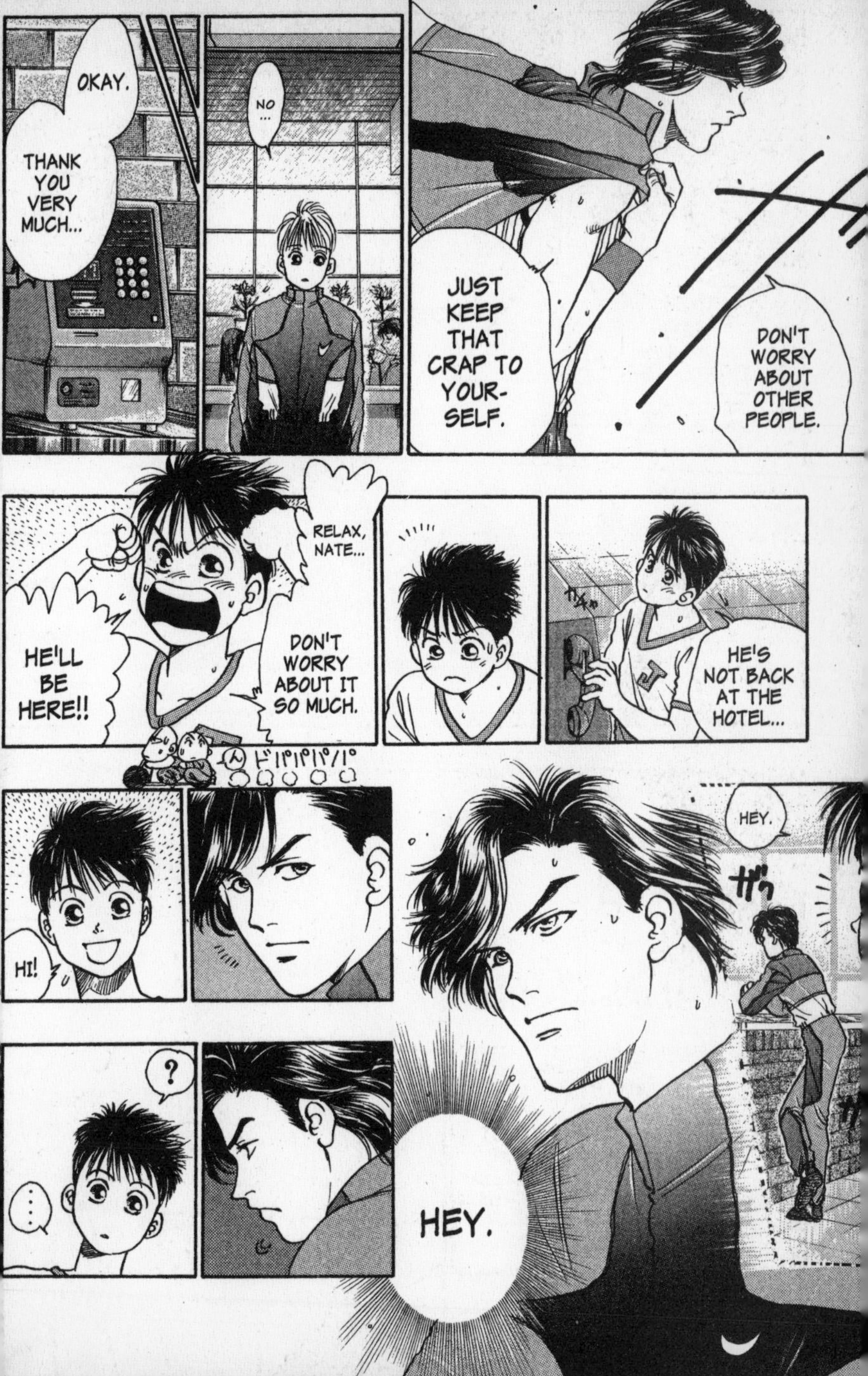
DON'T WORRY ABOUT OTHER PEOPLE.
JUST KEEP THAT CRAP TO YOUR-SELF.
NO ...
OKAY.
THANK YOU VERY MUCH...
HE'S NOT BACK AT THE HOTEL...
RELAX, NATE...
DON'T WORRY ABOUT IT SO MUCH.
HE'LL BE HERE!!
HEY.
HEY.
HI!
?
...

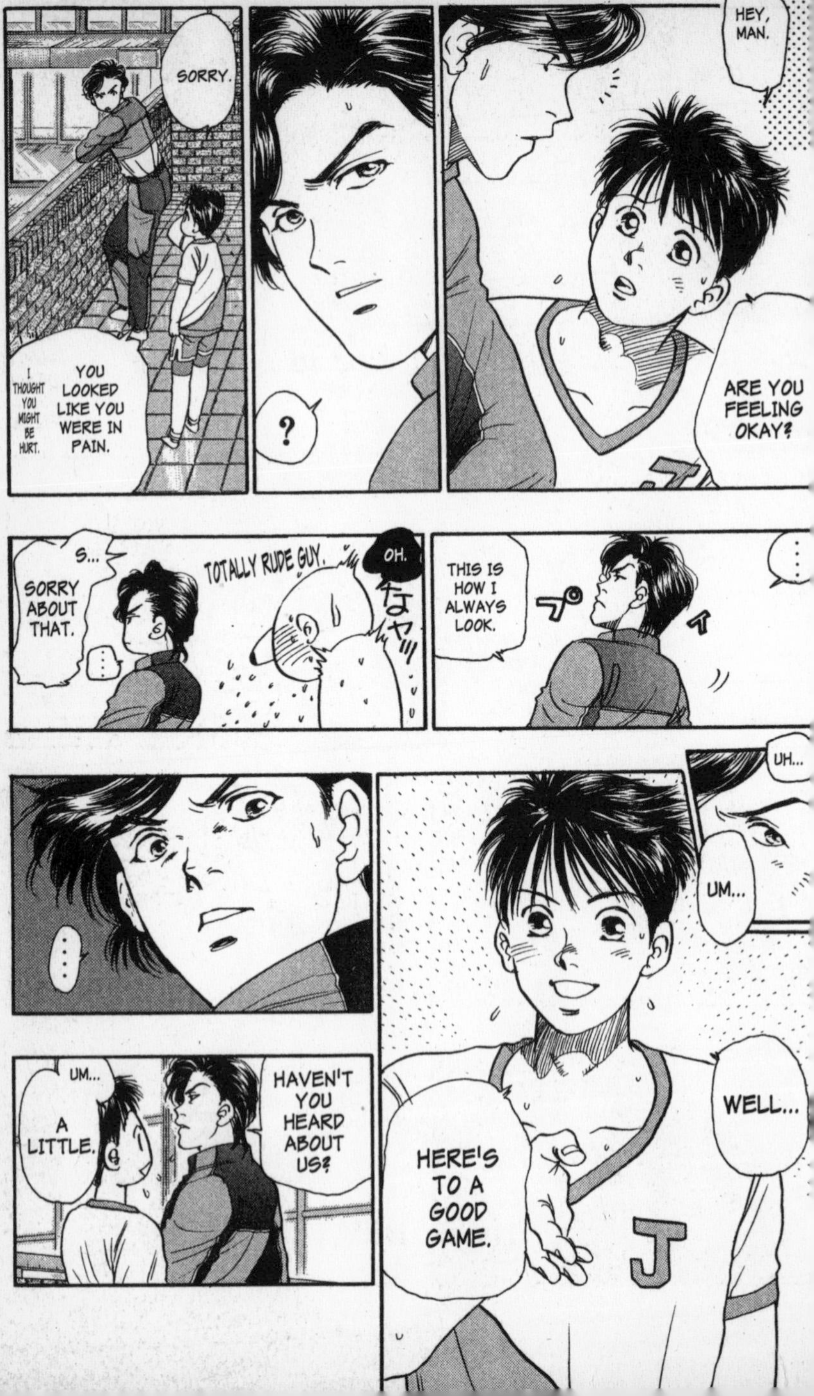
HEY, MAN.
ARE YOU FEELING OKAY?
?
SORRY.
YOU LOOKED LIKE YOU WERE IN PAIN.
I THOUGHT YOU MIGHT BE HURT.
...
THIS IS HOW I ALWAYS LOOK.
OH.
TOTALLY RUDE GUY.
なヤッ
S... SORRY ABOUT THAT.
...
UH...
UM...
WELL...
HERE'S TO A GOOD GAME.
...
HAVEN'T YOU HEARD ABOUT US?
UM... A LITTLE.

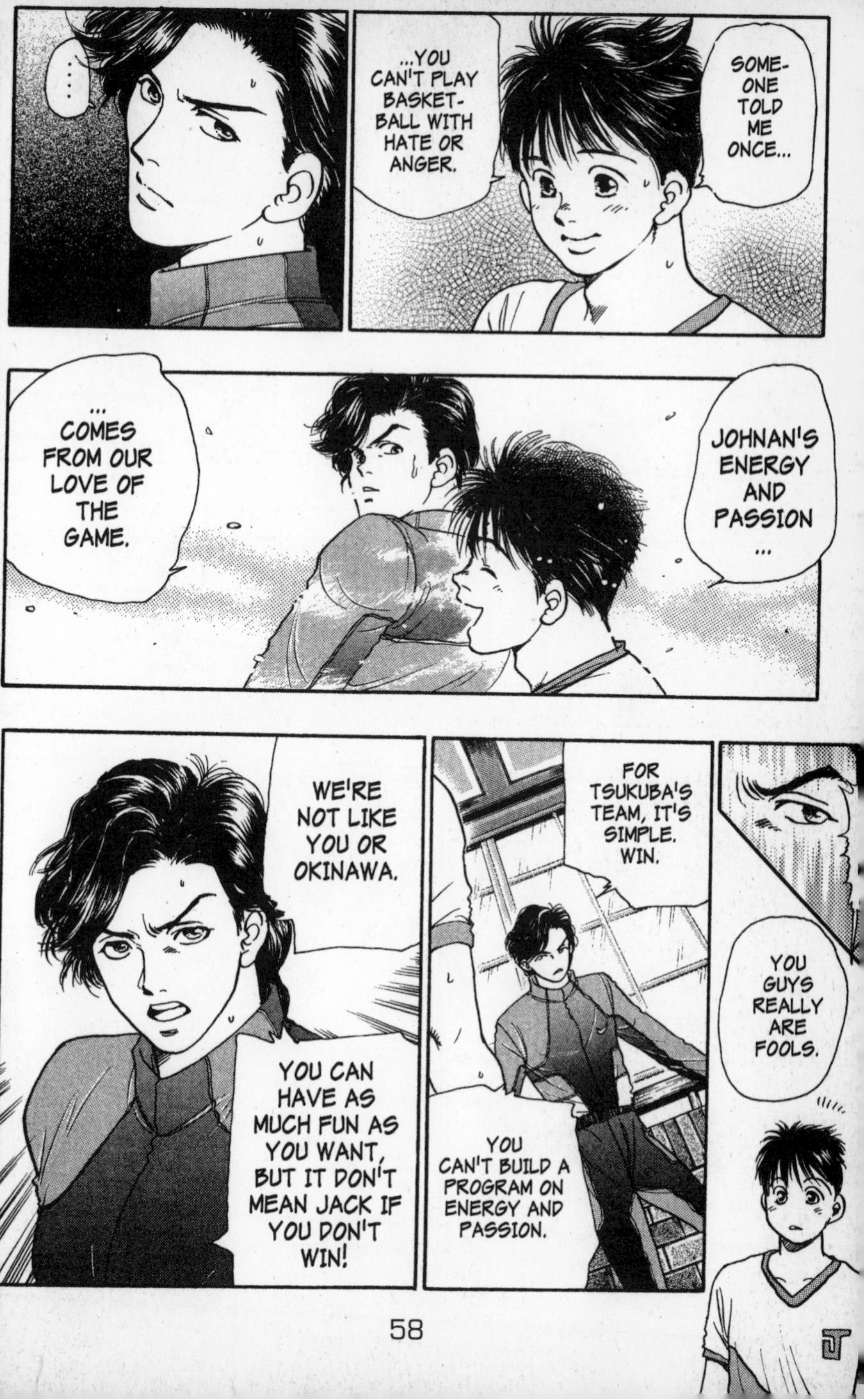
SOME-ONE TOLD ME ONCE...
...YOU CAN'T PLAY BASKET-BALL WITH HATE OR ANGER.
...
JOHNAN'S ENERGY AND PASSION ...
... COMES FROM OUR LOVE OF THE GAME.
YOU GUYS REALLY ARE FOOLS.
FOR TSUKUBA'S TEAM, IT'S SIMPLE. WIN.
YOU CAN'T BUILD A PROGRAM ON ENERGY AND PASSION.
WE'RE NOT LIKE YOU OR OKINAWA.
YOU CAN HAVE AS MUCH FUN AS YOU WANT, BUT IT DON'T MEAN JACK IF YOU DON'T WIN!

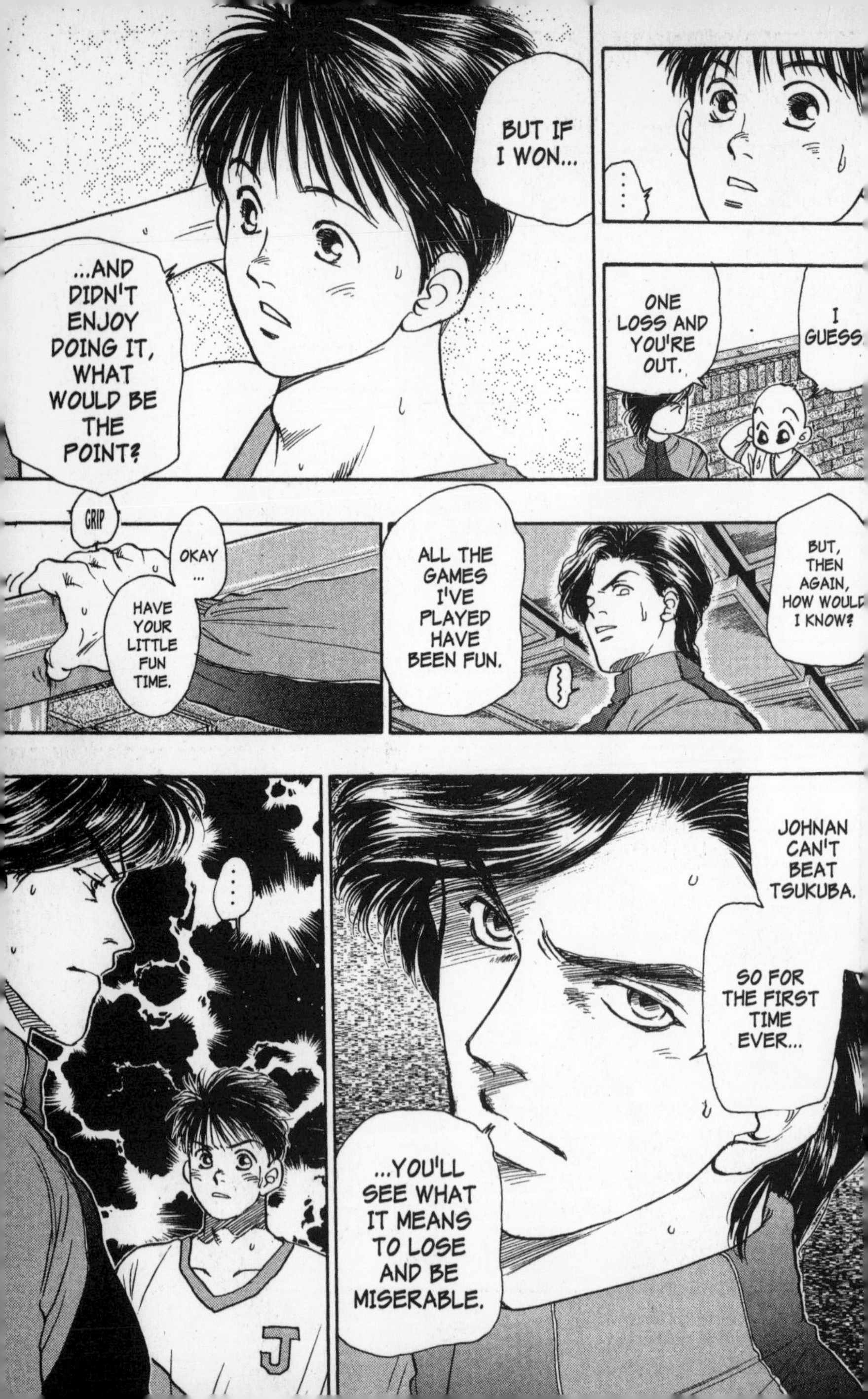
. . .
I GUESS.
ONE LOSS AND YOU'RE OUT.
BUT IF I WON...
...AND DIDN'T ENJOY DOING IT, WHAT WOULD BE THE POINT?
BUT, THEN AGAIN, HOW WOULD I KNOW?
ALL THE GAMES I'VE PLAYED HAVE BEEN FUN.
GRIP
OKAY ...
HAVE YOUR LITTLE FUN TIME.
JOHNAN CAN'T BEAT TSUKUBA.
SO FOR THE FIRST TIME EVER...
...YOU'LL SEE WHAT IT MEANS TO LOSE AND BE MISERABLE.
. . .

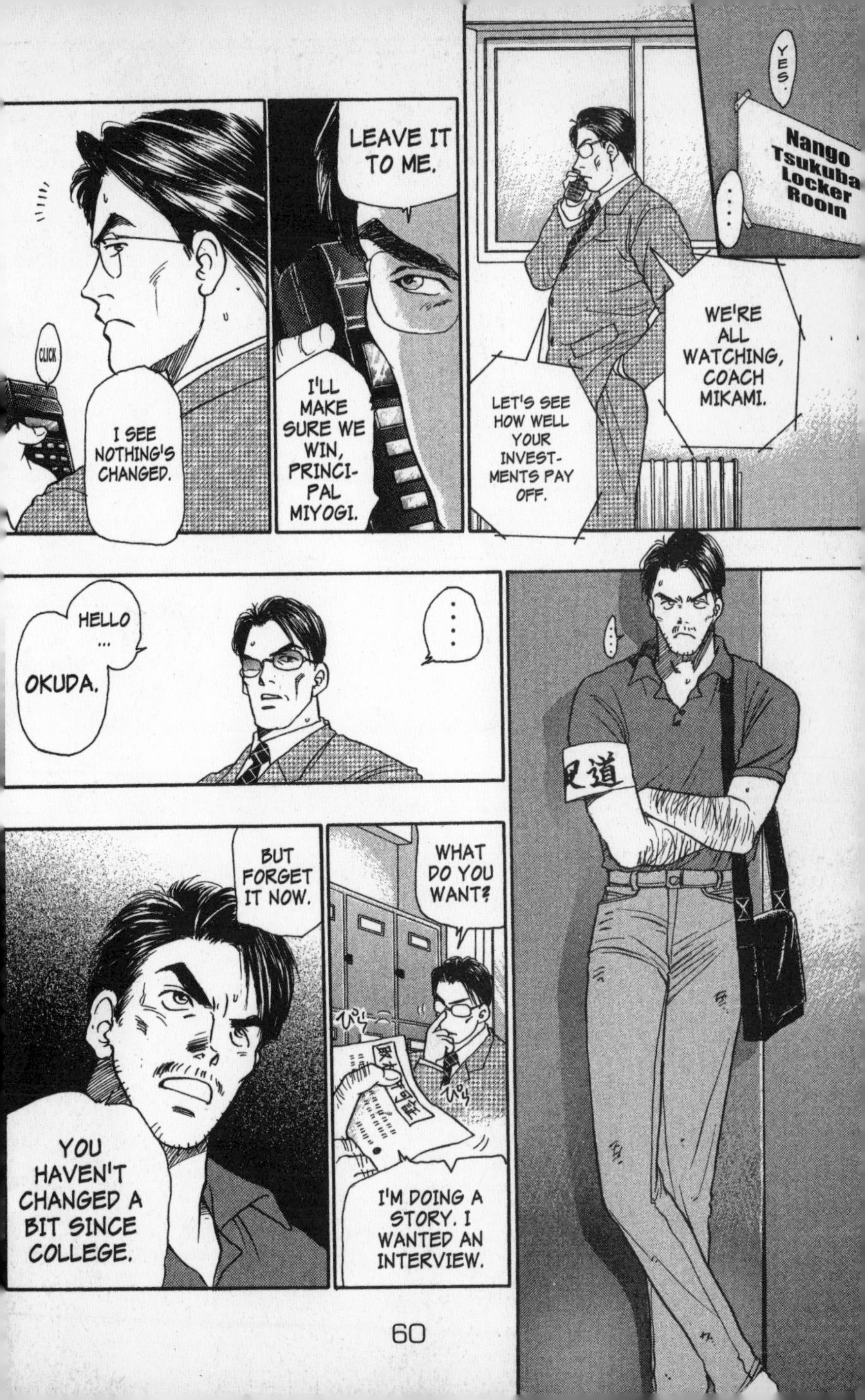
YES.
Nango Tsukuba Locker Rooin
....
WE'RE ALL WATCHING, COACH MIKAMI.
LET'S SEE HOW WELL YOUR INVEST-MENTS PAY OFF.
LEAVE IT TO ME.
I'LL MAKE SURE WE WIN, PRINCI-PAL MIYOGI.
CLICK
I SEE NOTHING'S CHANGED.
...
....
HELLO ... OKUDA.
WHAT DO YOU WANT?
I'M DOING A STORY. I WANTED AN INTERVIEW.
BUT FORGET IT NOW.
YOU HAVEN'T CHANGED A BIT SINCE COLLEGE.

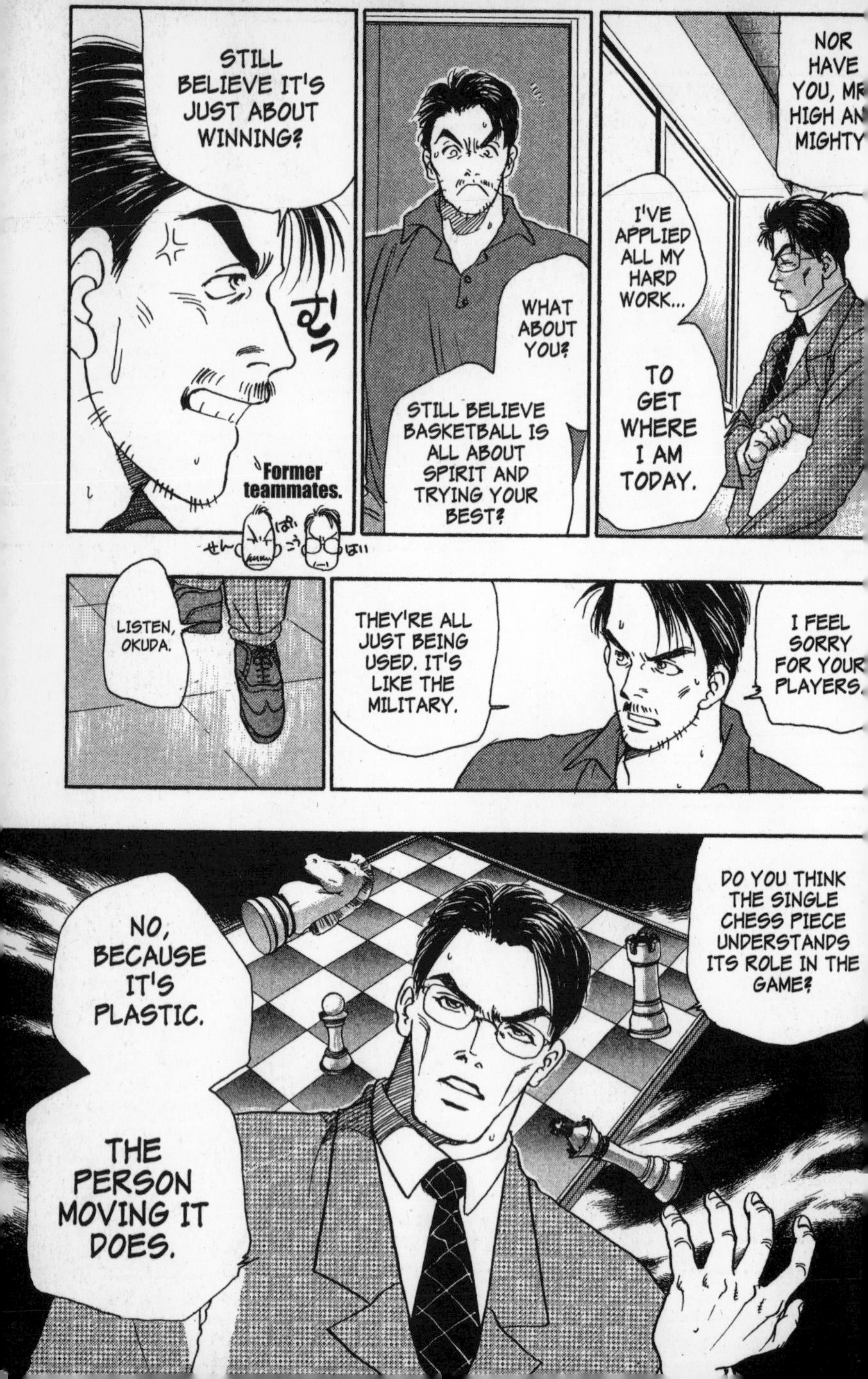
NOR HAVE YOU, MR HIGH AN MIGHTY
I'VE APPLIED ALL MY HARD WORK...
TO GET WHERE I AM TODAY.
WHAT ABOUT YOU?
STILL BELIEVE BASKETBALL IS ALL ABOUT SPIRIT AND TRYING YOUR BEST?
STILL BELIEVE IT'S JUST ABOUT WINNING?
むっ
Former teammates.
I FEEL SORRY FOR YOUR PLAYERS.
THEY'RE ALL JUST BEING USED. IT'S LIKE THE MILITARY.
LISTEN, OKUDA.
DO YOU THINK THE SINGLE CHESS PIECE UNDERSTANDS ITS ROLE IN THE GAME?
NO, BECAUSE IT'S PLASTIC.
THE PERSON MOVING IT DOES.

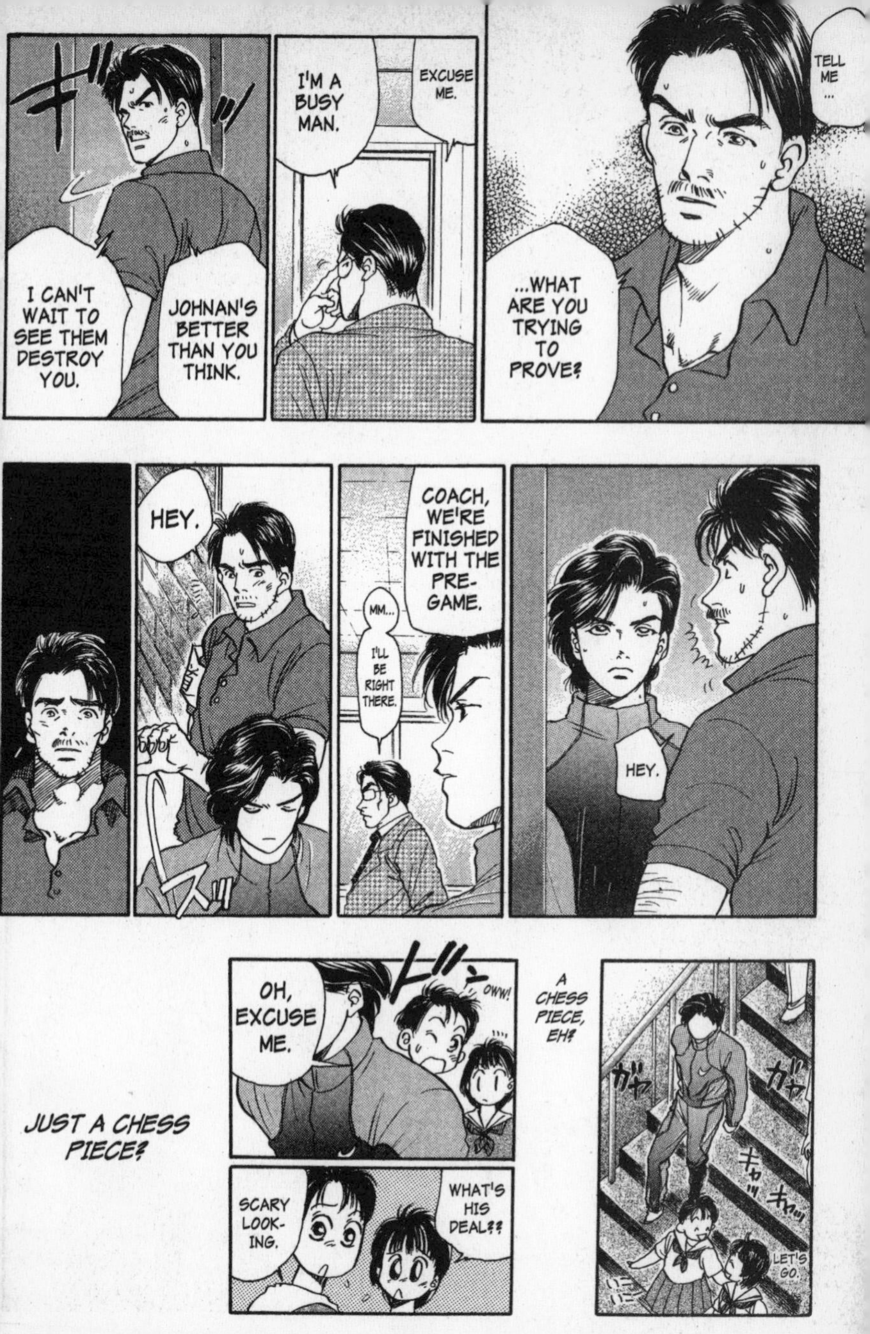
TELL ME ...
...WHAT ARE YOU TRYING TO PROVE?
EXCUSE ME.
I'M A BUSY MAN.
JOHNAN'S BETTER THAN YOU THINK.
I CAN'T WAIT TO SEE THEM DESTROY YOU.
HEY.
COACH, WE'RE FINISHED WITH THE PRE-GAME.
MM... I'LL BE RIGHT THERE.
HEY.
LET'S GO.
A CHESS PIECE, EH?
OH, EXCUSE ME.
OWW!
WHAT'S HIS DEAL??
SCARY LOOK-ING.
JUST A CHESS PIECE?

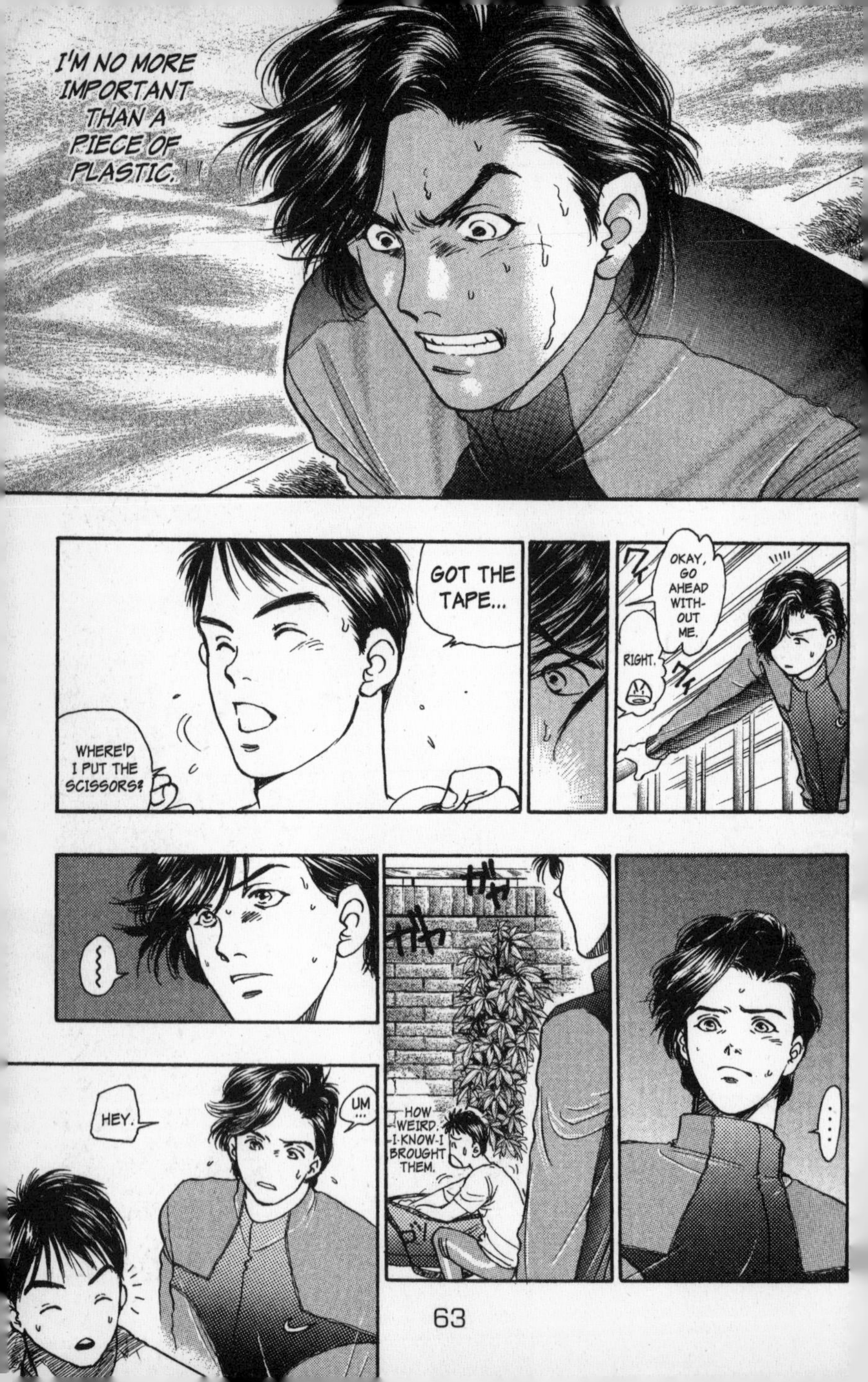
I'M NO MORE IMPORTANT THAN A PIECE OF PLASTIC.
OKAY, GO AHEAD WITH-OUT ME.
RIGHT.
GOT THE TAPE...
WHERE'D I PUT THE SCISSORS?
...
HOW WEIRD. I KNOW I BROUGHT THEM.
...
UM...
HEY.

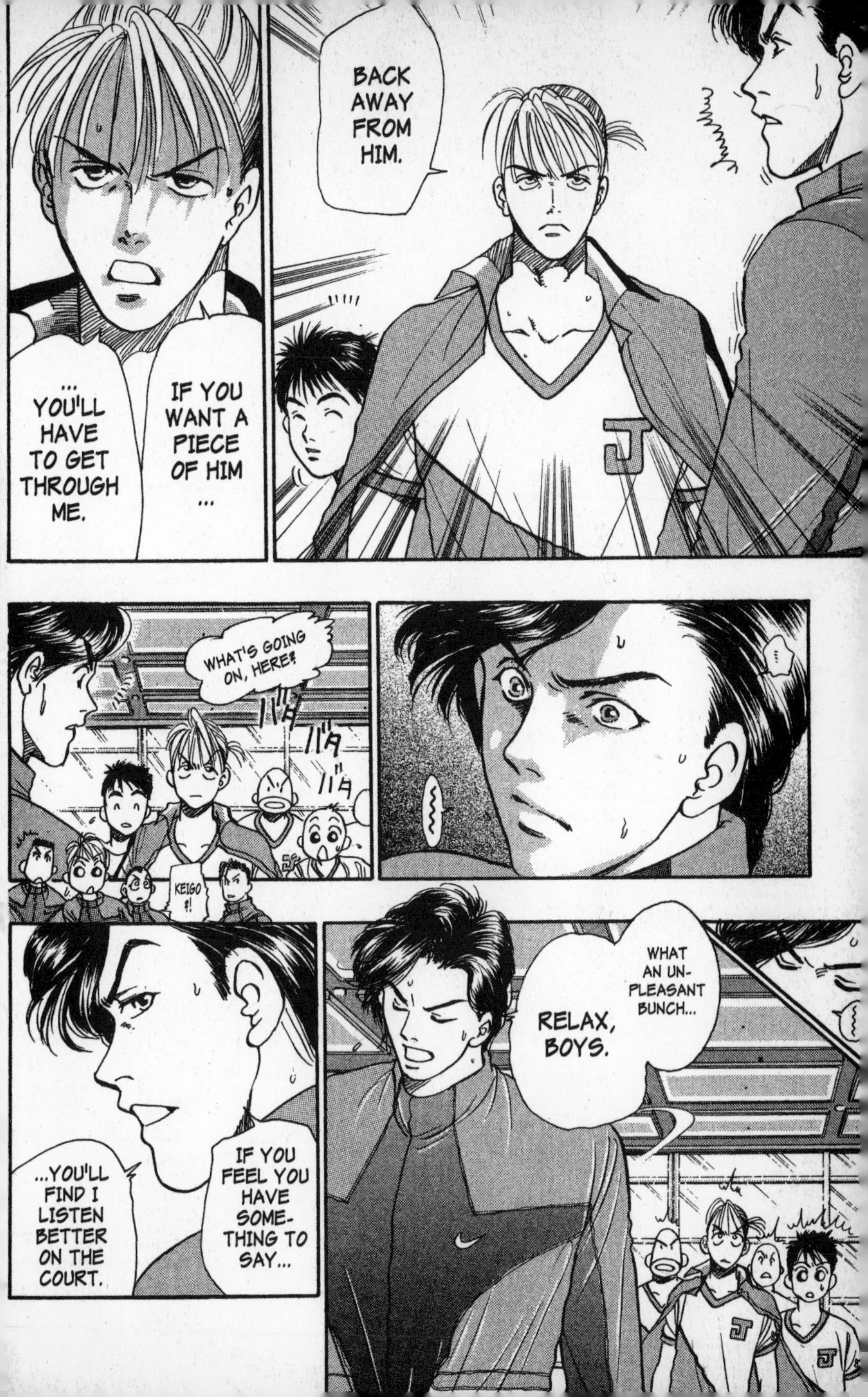
BACK AWAY FROM HIM.
IF YOU WANT A PIECE OF HIM ...
... YOU'LL HAVE TO GET THROUGH ME.
WHAT'S GOING ON, HERE?!
バタ バタ バタ
KEIGO ?!
WHAT AN UN-PLEASANT BUNCH...
RELAX, BOYS.
IF YOU FEEL YOU HAVE SOME-THING TO SAY...
...YOU'LL FIND I LISTEN BETTER ON THE COURT.

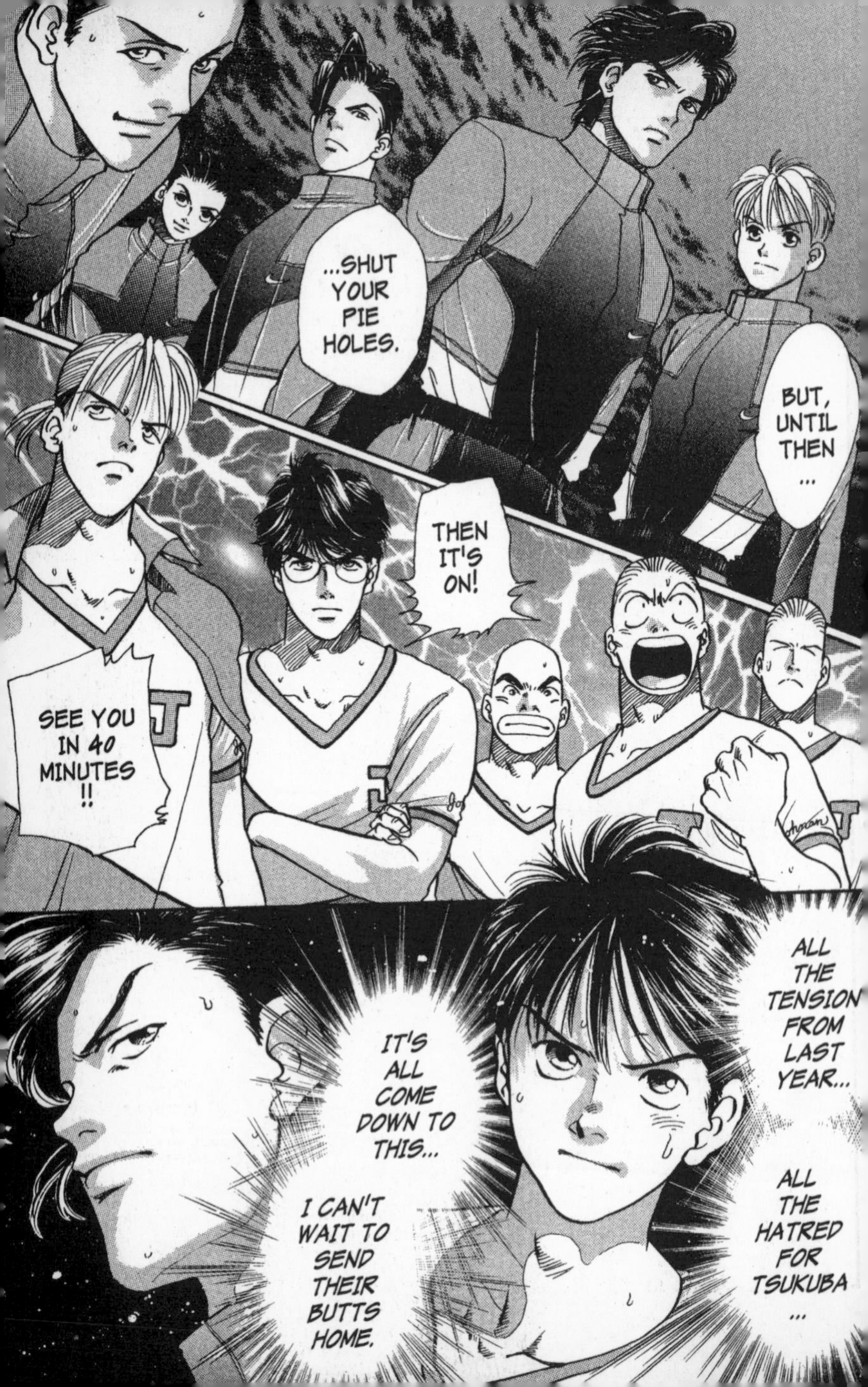
...SHUT YOUR PIE HOLES.
BUT, UNTIL THEN ...
THEN IT'S ON!
SEE YOU IN 40 MINUTES !!
ALL THE TENSION FROM LAST YEAR...
ALL THE HATRED FOR TSUKUBA ...
IT'S ALL COME DOWN TO THIS...
I CAN'T WAIT TO SEND THEIR BUTTS HOME.

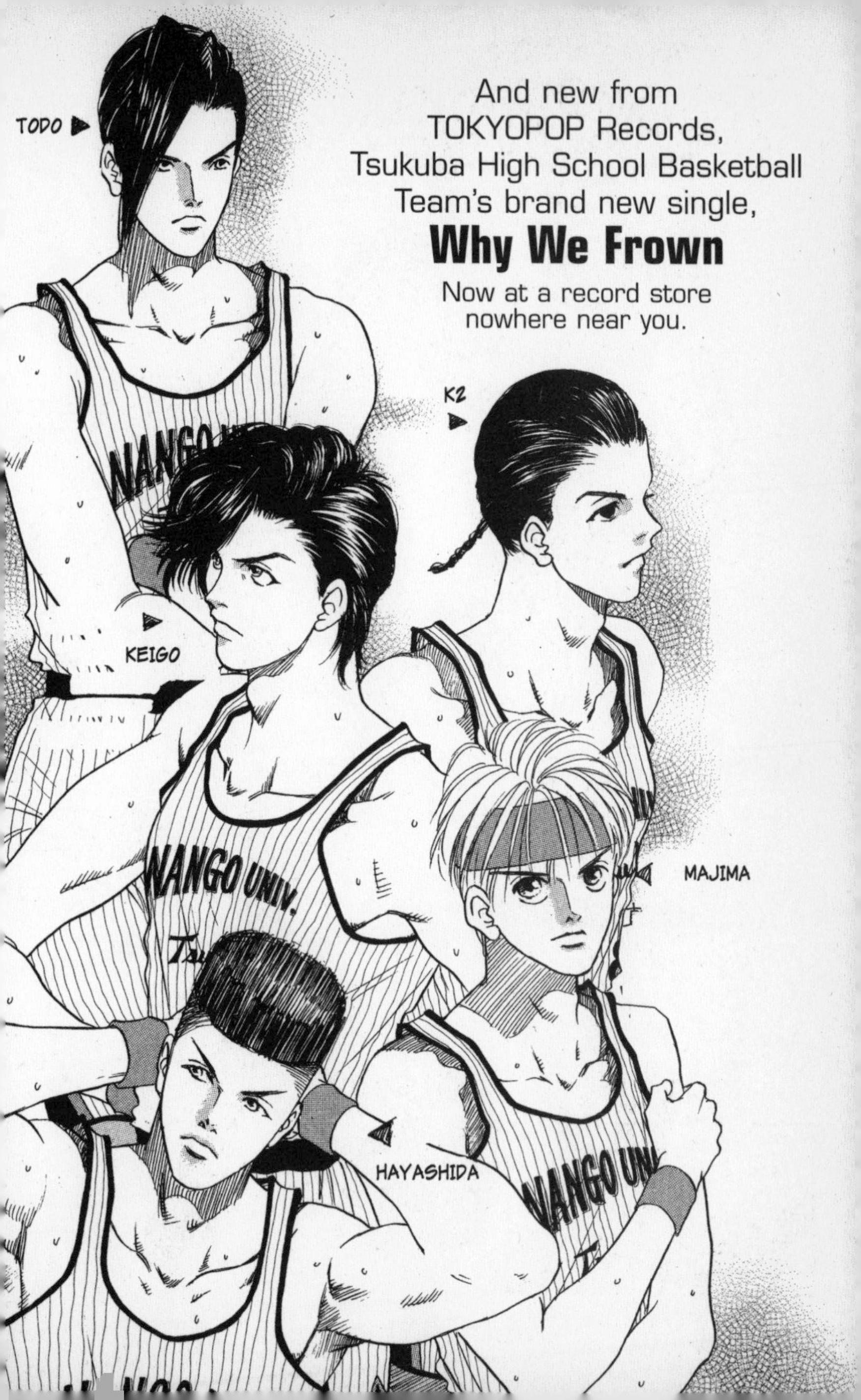

And new from
TOKYOPOP Records,
Tsukuba High School Basketball
Team's brand new single,
Why We Frown
Now at a record store
nowhere near you.
TODO
K2
KEIGO
NANGO UNIV.
MAJIMA
HAYASHIDA

You're reading...

REBOUND

Episode 31: One Heart

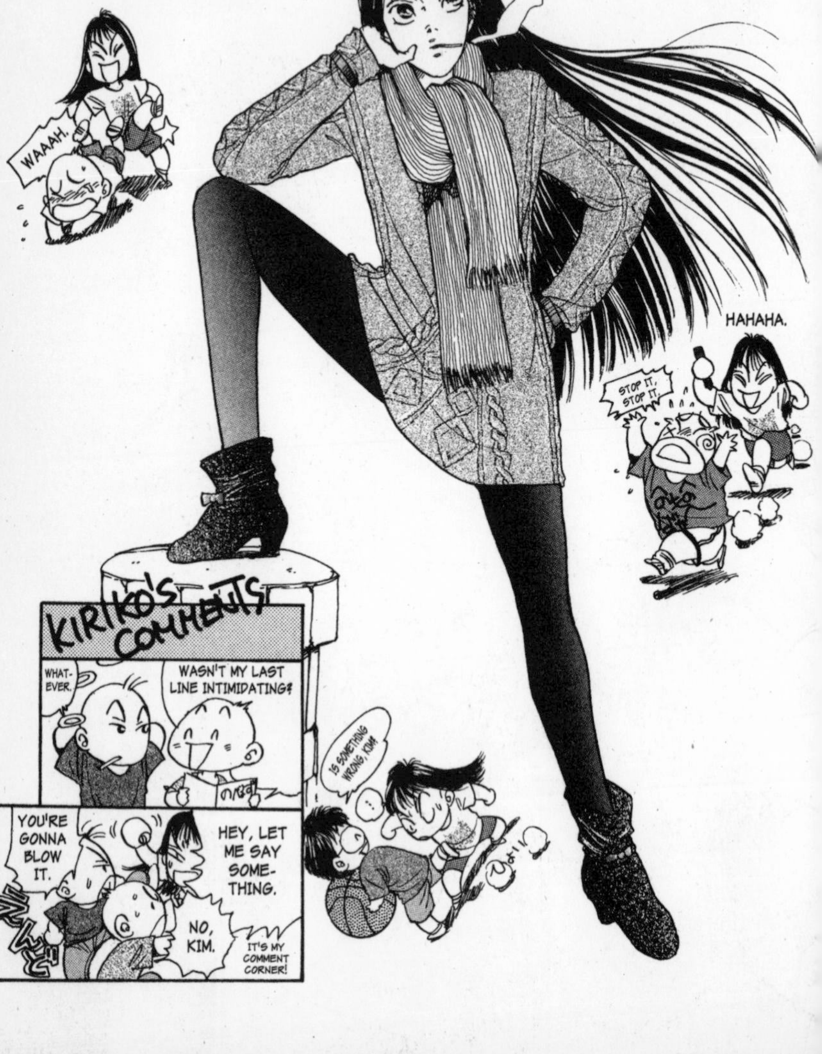
HAHAHA.
STOP IT, STOP IT.
WAAAH.
KIRIKO'S COMMENTS
WASN'T MY LAST LINE INTIMIDATING?
WHAT-EVER.
HEY, LET ME SAY SOME-THING.
YOU'RE GONNA BLOW IT.
IT'S MY COMMENT CORNER!
NO, KIM.
IS SOMETHING WRONG, KIM?
...

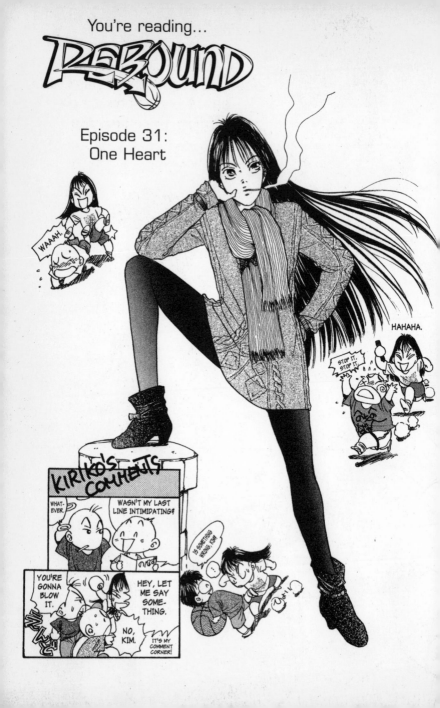

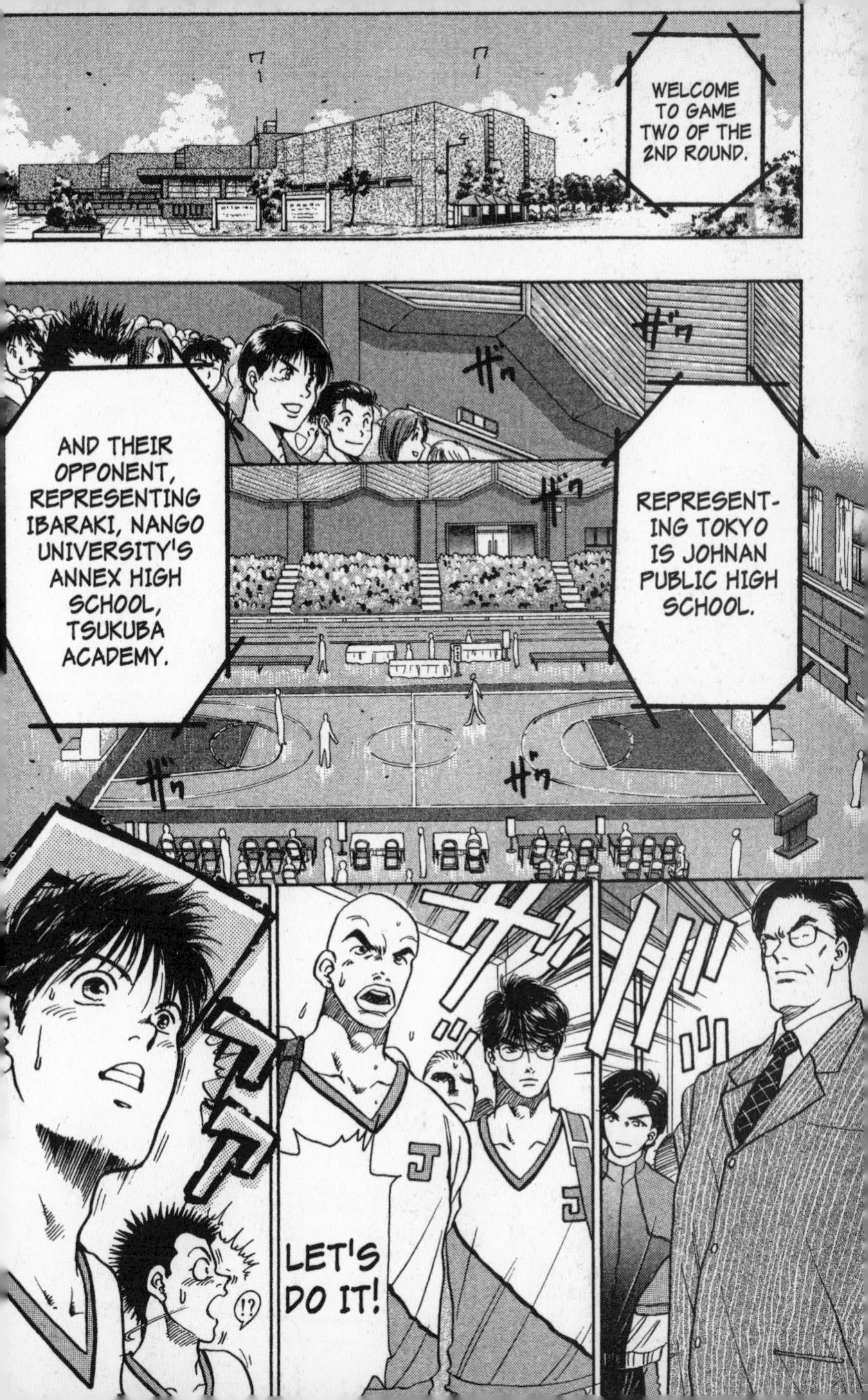
WELCOME TO GAME TWO OF THE 2ND ROUND.
REPRESENTING TOKYO IS JOHNAN PUBLIC HIGH SCHOOL.
AND THEIR OPPONENT, REPRESENTING IBARAKI, NANGO UNIVERSITY'S ANNEX HIGH SCHOOL, TSUKUBA ACADEMY.
LET'S DO IT!
!?

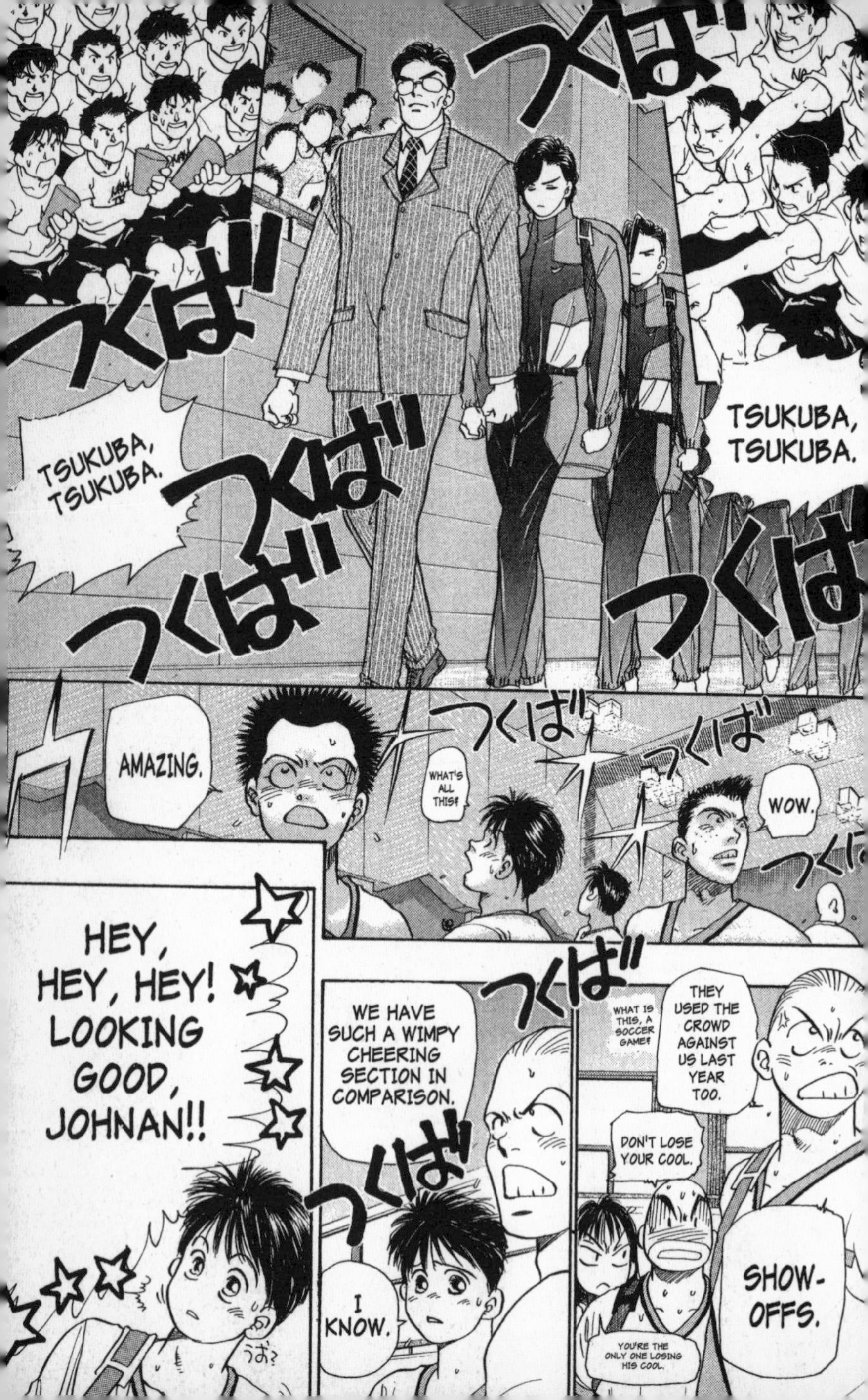
つくば
TSUKUBA, TSUKUBA.
つくば
つくば
TSUKUBA, TSUKUBA.
つくば
WOW.
つくば
つくば
WHAT'S ALL THIS?
AMAZING.
THEY USED THE CROWD AGAINST US LAST YEAR TOO.
WHAT IS THIS, A SOCCER GAME?
DON'T LOSE YOUR COOL.
SHOW-OFFS.
YOU'RE THE ONLY ONE LOSING HIS COOL.
つくば
WE HAVE SUCH A WIMPY CHEERING SECTION IN COMPARISON.
つくば
I KNOW.
HEY, HEY, HEY! LOOKING GOOD, JOHNAN!!
うお?

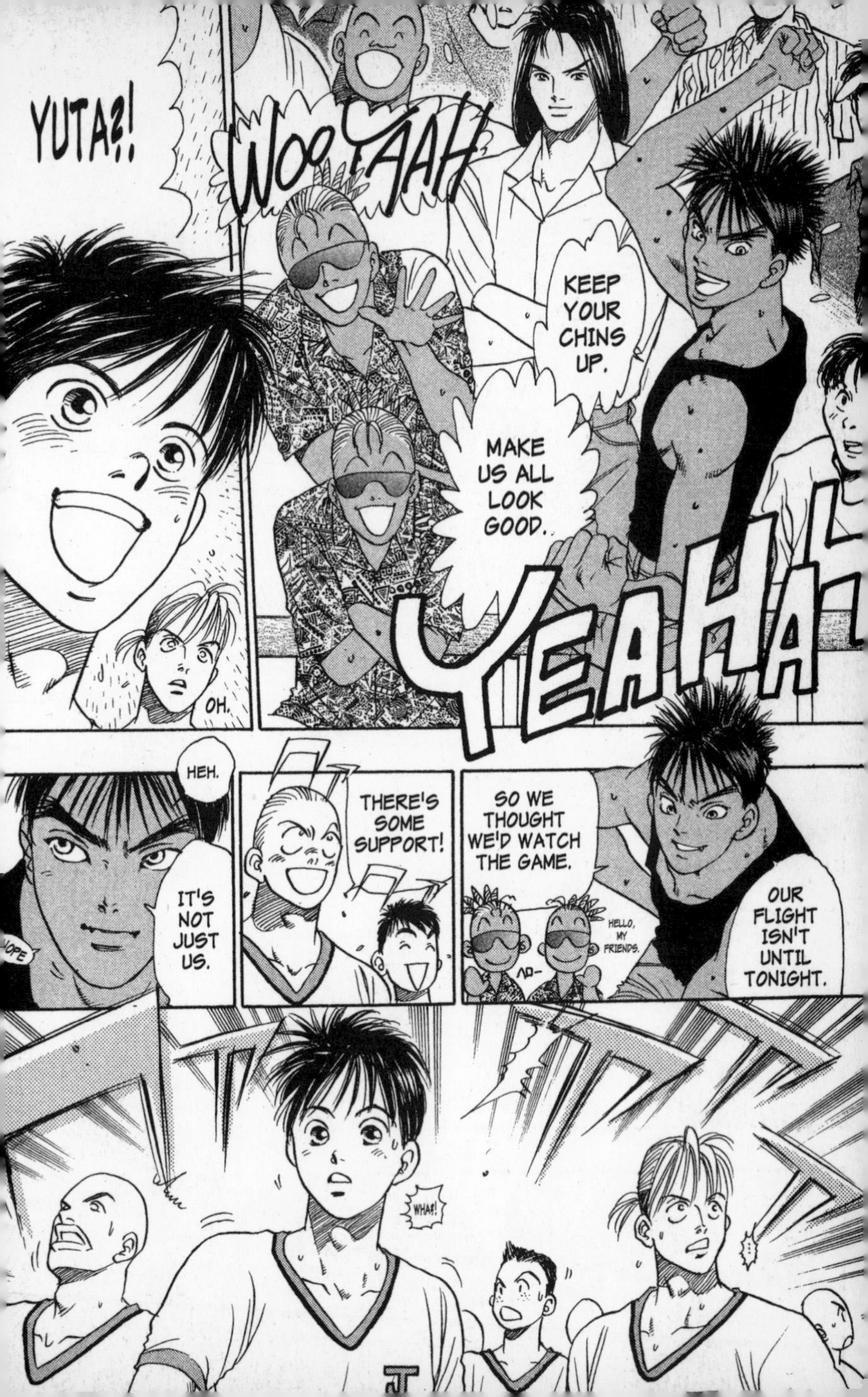
WOO YAAH
KEEP YOUR CHINS UP.
MAKE US ALL LOOK GOOD.
YEAH
YUTA?!
OH.
OUR FLIGHT ISN'T UNTIL TONIGHT.
SO WE THOUGHT WE'D WATCH THE GAME.
HELLO, MY FRIENDS.
THERE'S SOME SUPPORT!
HEH.
IT'S NOT JUST US.
WHA?!

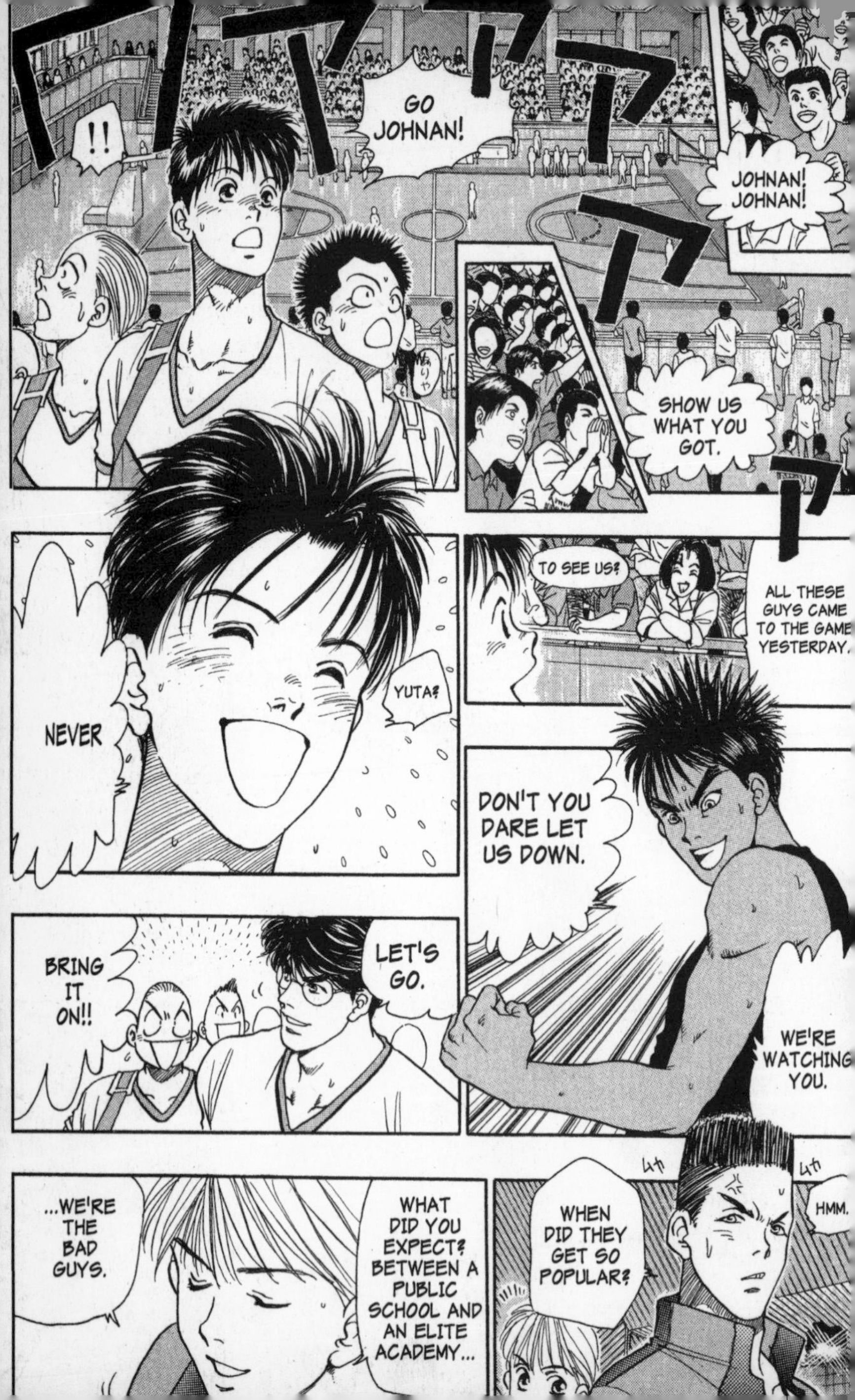
JOHNAN! JOHNAN!
SHOW US WHAT YOU GOT.
GO JOHNAN!
!!
ALL THESE GUYS CAME TO THE GAME YESTERDAY.
TO SEE US?
DON'T YOU DARE LET US DOWN.
WE'RE WATCHING YOU.
YUTA?
NEVER
LET'S GO.
BRING IT ON!!
HMM.
WHEN DID THEY GET SO POPULAR?
WHAT DID YOU EXPECT? BETWEEN A PUBLIC SCHOOL AND AN ELITE ACADEMY...
...WE'RE THE BAD GUYS.

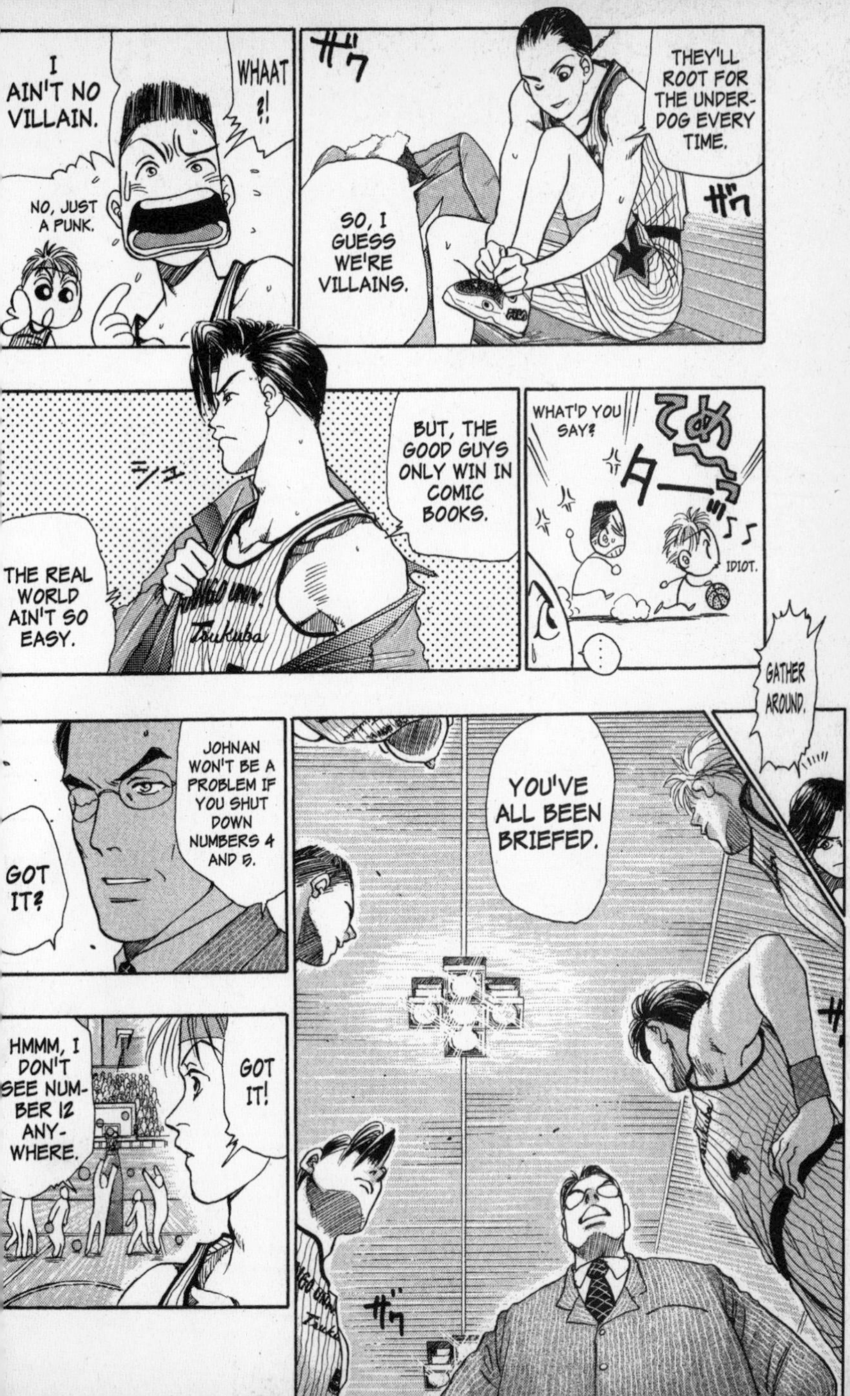
ザワ
THEY'LL ROOT FOR THE UNDER-DOG EVERY TIME.
ザワ
SO, I GUESS WE'RE VILLAINS.
I AIN'T NO VILLAIN.
WHAAT?!
NO, JUST A PUNK.
WHAT'D YOU SAY?
てめ〜〜ター
IDIOT.
...
BUT, THE GOOD GUYS ONLY WIN IN COMIC BOOKS.
THE REAL WORLD AIN'T SO EASY.
GATHER AROUND.
YOU'VE ALL BEEN BRIEFED.
ザワ
JOHNAN WON'T BE A PROBLEM IF YOU SHUT DOWN NUMBERS 4 AND 5.
GOT IT?
GOT IT!
HMMM, I DON'T SEE NUM-BER 12 ANY-WHERE.

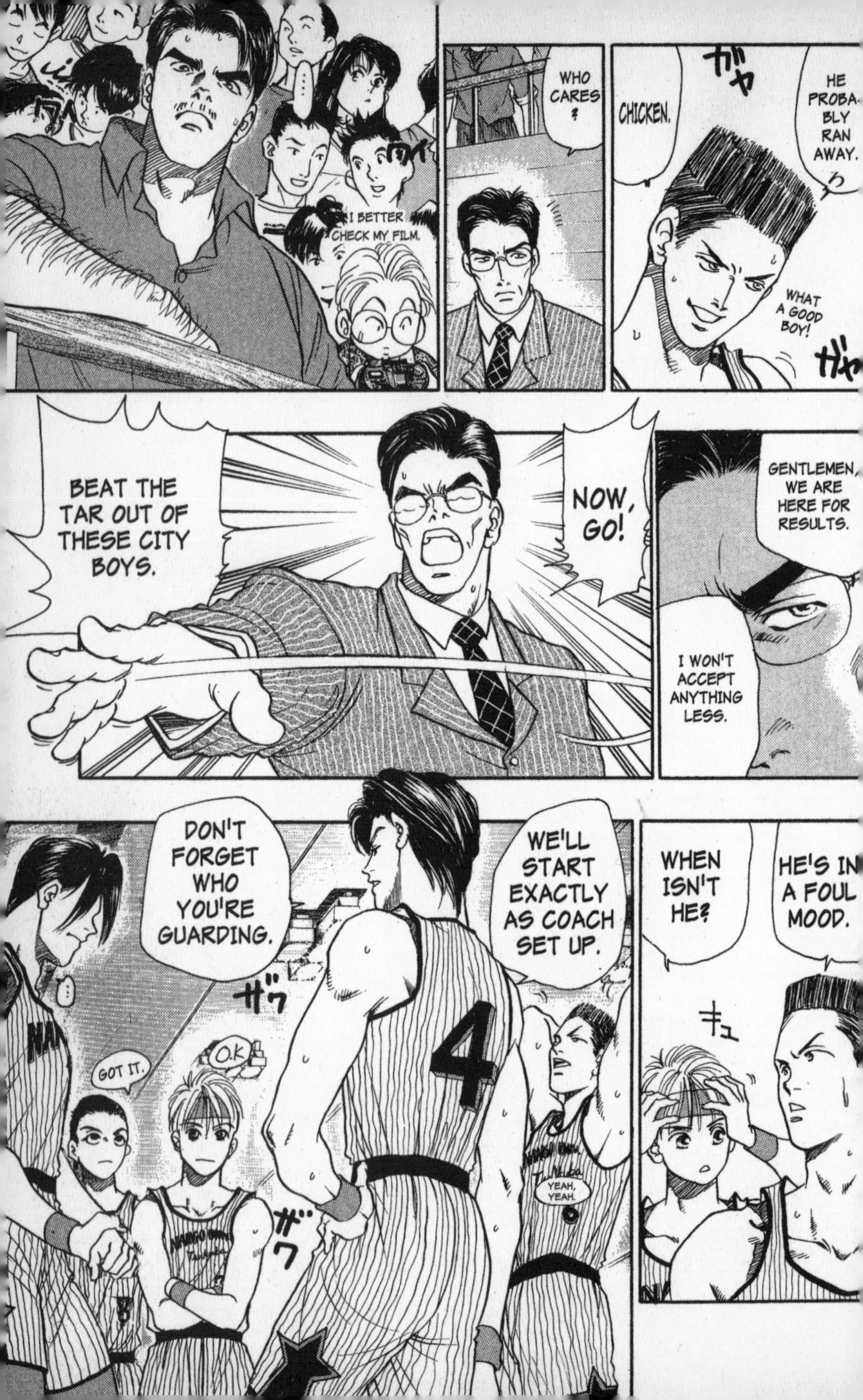

ガヤ
HE PROBABLY RAN AWAY.
CHICKEN.
WHAT A GOOD BOY!
ガヤ
WHO CARES?
...
I BETTER CHECK MY FILM.
GENTLEMEN, WE ARE HERE FOR RESULTS.
I WON'T ACCEPT ANYTHING LESS.
NOW, GO!
BEAT THE TAR OUT OF THESE CITY BOYS.
HE'S IN A FOUL MOOD.
WHEN ISN'T HE?
キュ
WE'LL START EXACTLY AS COACH SET UP.
YEAH, YEAH.
DON'T FORGET WHO YOU'RE GUARDING.
...
O.K
GOT IT.
ザワ
ザワ

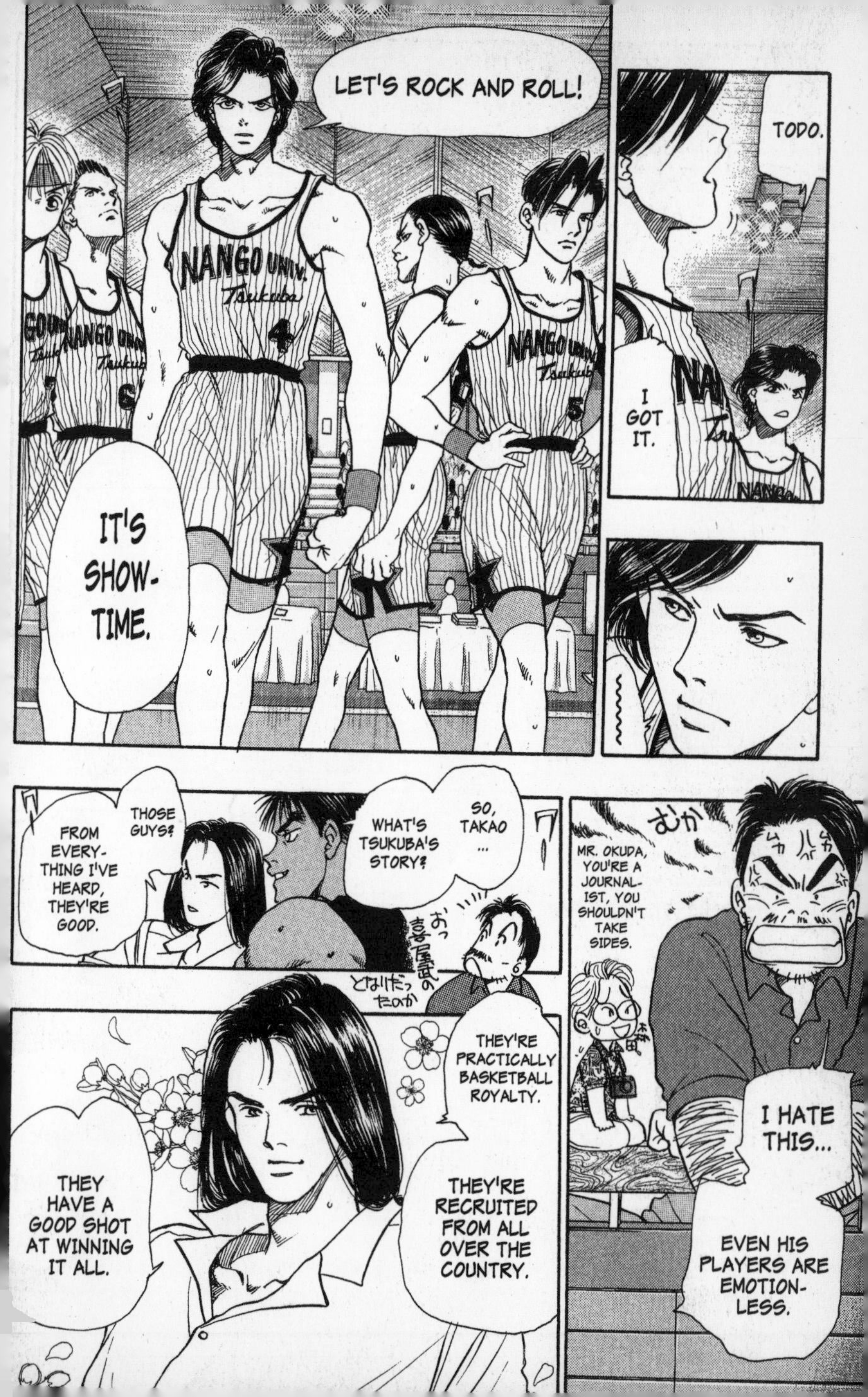
TODO.
I GOT IT.
LET'S ROCK AND ROLL!
IT'S SHOW-TIME.
むか
MR. OKUDA, YOU'RE A JOURNAL-IST, YOU SHOULDN'T TAKE SIDES.
I HATE THIS...
EVEN HIS PLAYERS ARE EMOTION-LESS.
SO, TAKAO ...
WHAT'S TSUKUBA'S STORY?
THOSE GUYS?
FROM EVERY-THING I'VE HEARD, THEY'RE GOOD.
おっ 喜屋武の
となりだったのか
THEY'RE PRACTICALLY BASKETBALL ROYALTY.
THEY'RE RECRUITED FROM ALL OVER THE COUNTRY.
THEY HAVE A GOOD SHOT AT WINNING IT ALL.

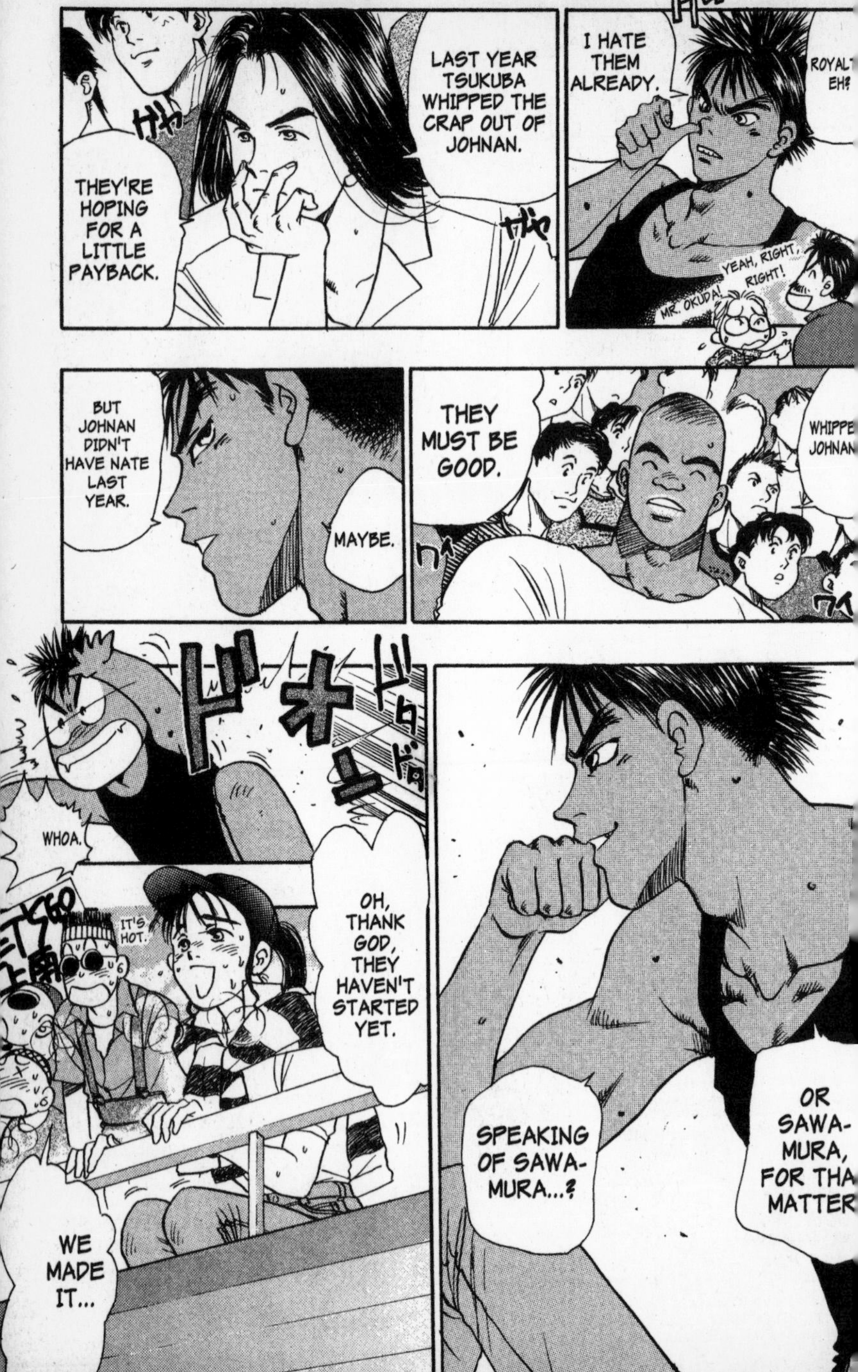

ROYALT EH?
I HATE THEM ALREADY.
YEAH, RIGHT, RIGHT!
MR. OKUDA!
LAST YEAR TSUKUBA WHIPPED THE CRAP OUT OF JOHNAN.
THEY'RE HOPING FOR A LITTLE PAYBACK.
WHIPPE JOHNAN
THEY MUST BE GOOD.
BUT JOHNAN DIDN'T HAVE NATE LAST YEAR.
MAYBE.
OR SAWA-MURA, FOR THA MATTER
SPEAKING OF SAWA-MURA...?
WHOA.
OH, THANK GOD, THEY HAVEN'T STARTED YET.
IT'S HOT.
WE MADE IT...

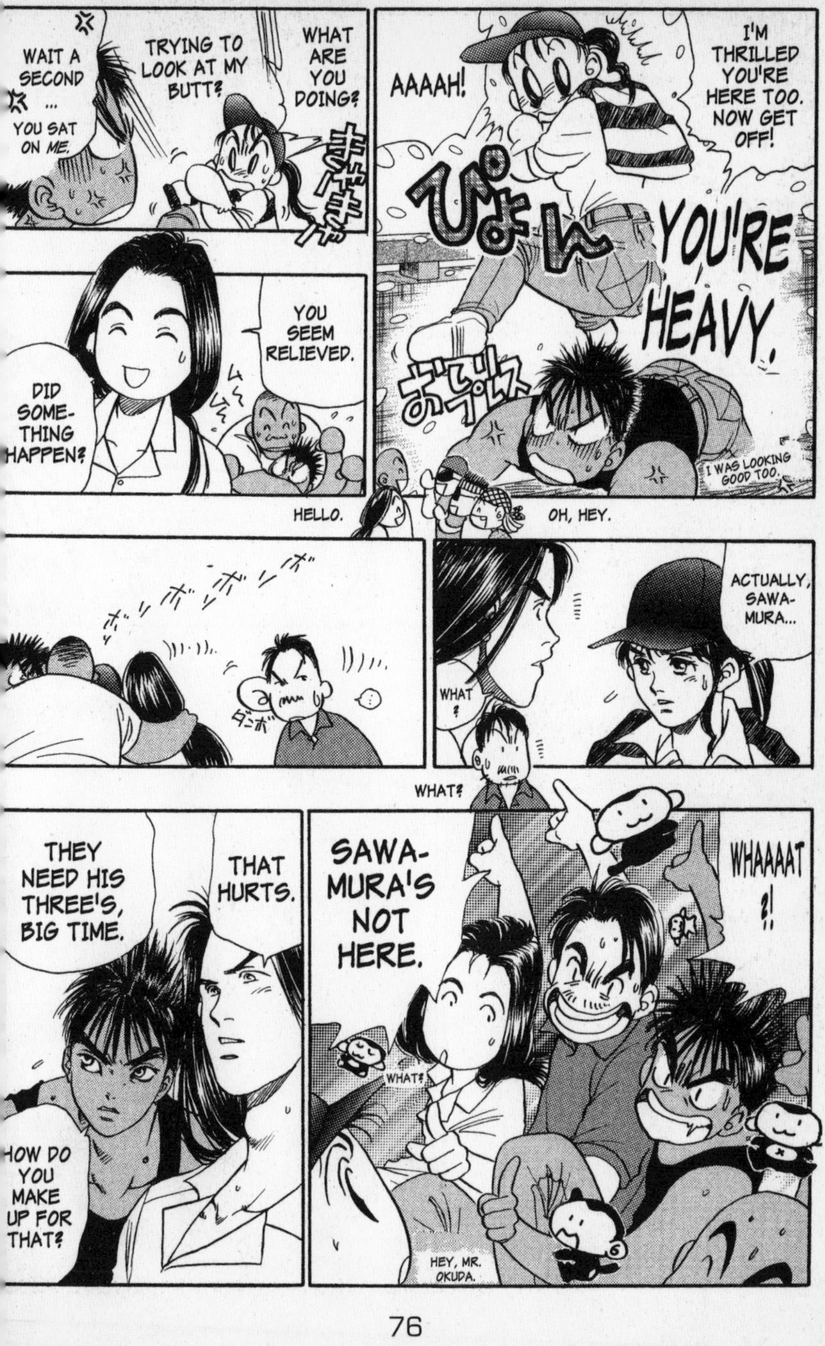
AAAAH!
I'M THRILLED YOU'RE HERE TOO. NOW GET OFF!
ぴょん
YOU'RE HEAVY.
I WAS LOOKING GOOD TOO.
WHAT ARE YOU DOING?
TRYING TO LOOK AT MY BUTT?
WAIT A SECOND ... YOU SAT ON ME.
YOU SEEM RELIEVED.
DID SOMETHING HAPPEN?
OH, HEY.
HELLO.
ACTUALLY, SAWA-MURA...
WHAT?
WHAT?
WHAAAAT?!
SAWA-MURA'S NOT HERE.
WHAT?
HEY, MR. OKUDA.
THAT HURTS.
THEY NEED HIS THREE'S, BIG TIME.
HOW DO YOU MAKE UP FOR THAT?

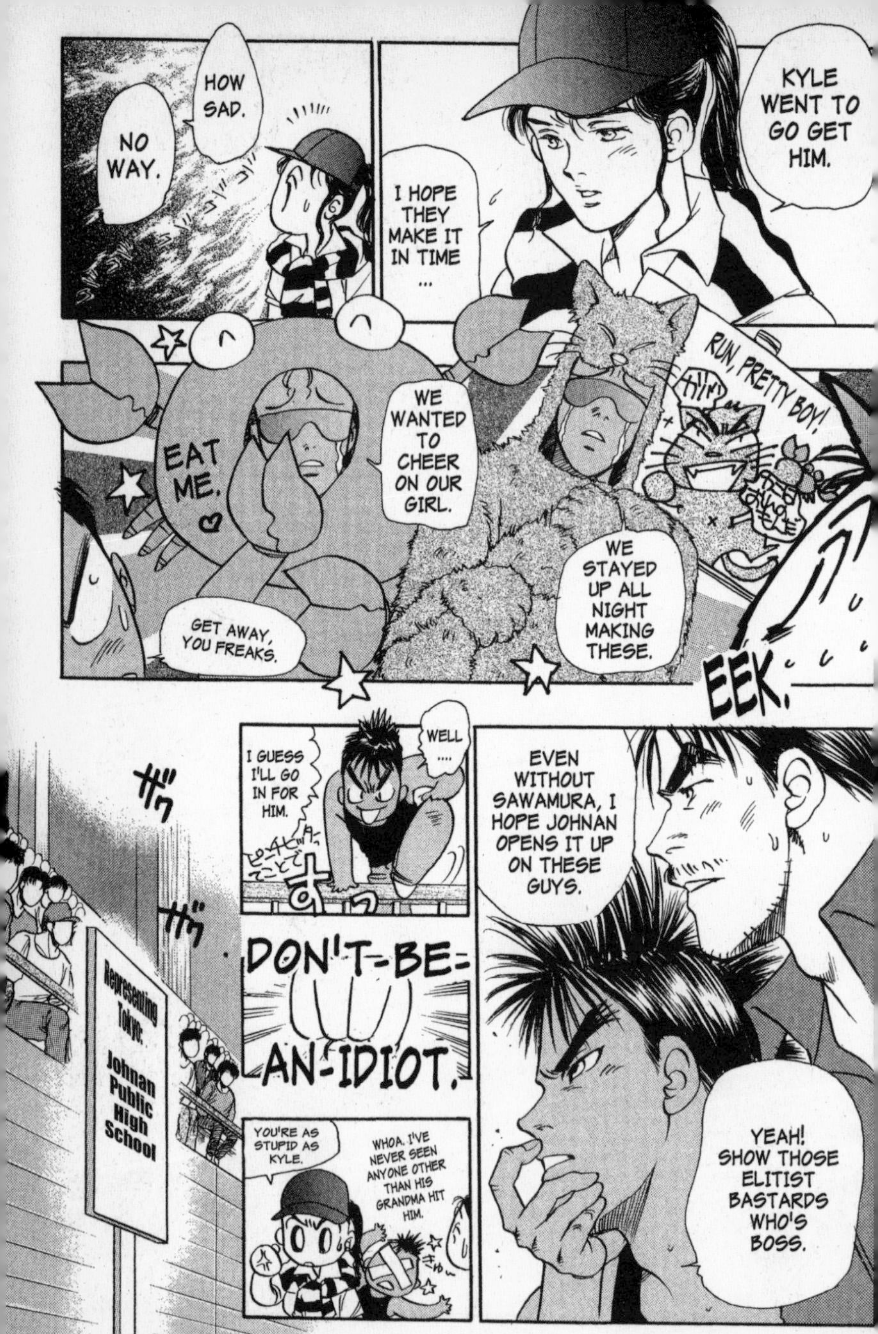
KYLE WENT TO GO GET HIM.
I HOPE THEY MAKE IT IN TIME ...
HOW SAD.
NO WAY.
EEK.
RUN, PRETTY BOY!
WE WANTED TO CHEER ON OUR GIRL.
WE STAYED UP ALL NIGHT MAKING THESE.
EAT ME.
GET AWAY, YOU FREAKS.
EVEN WITHOUT SAWAMURA, I HOPE JOHNAN OPENS IT UP ON THESE GUYS.
YEAH! SHOW THOSE ELITIST BASTARDS WHO'S BOSS.
WELL ....
I GUESS I'LL GO IN FOR HIM.
DON'T-BE-AN-IDIOT.
YOU'RE AS STUPID AS KYLE.
WHOA. I'VE NEVER SEEN ANYONE OTHER THAN HIS GRANDMA HIT HIM.
Representing Tokyo:
Johnan Public High School

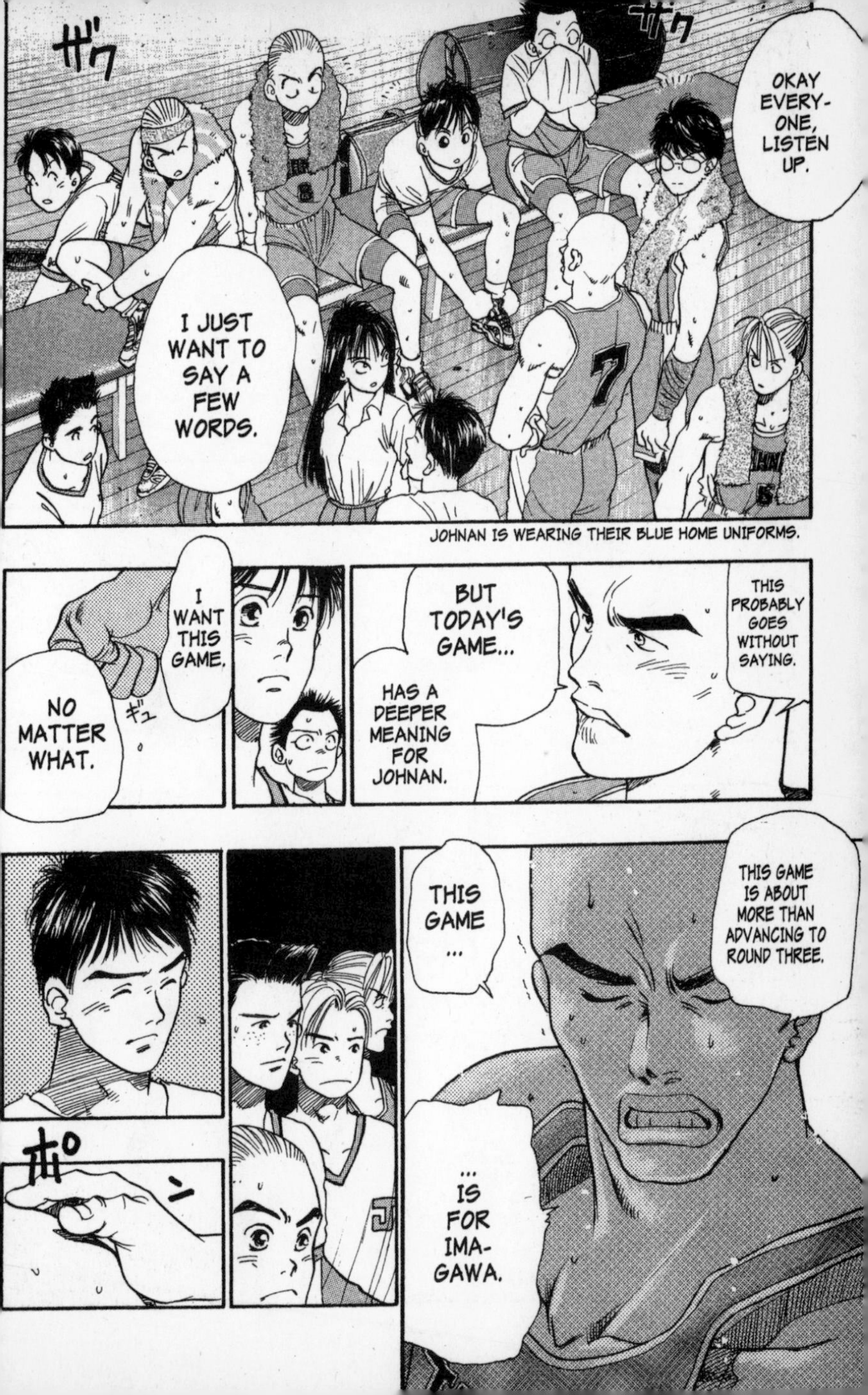
ザク
ザク
OKAY EVERY-ONE, LISTEN UP.
I JUST WANT TO SAY A FEW WORDS.
THIS PROBABLY GOES WITHOUT SAYING.
BUT TODAY'S GAME...
HAS A DEEPER MEANING FOR JOHNAN.
I WANT THIS GAME.
ギュ
NO MATTER WHAT.
THIS GAME IS ABOUT MORE THAN ADVANCING TO ROUND THREE.
THIS GAME ...
... IS FOR IMA-GAWA.
ポン
JOHNAN IS WEARING THEIR BLUE HOME UNIFORMS.

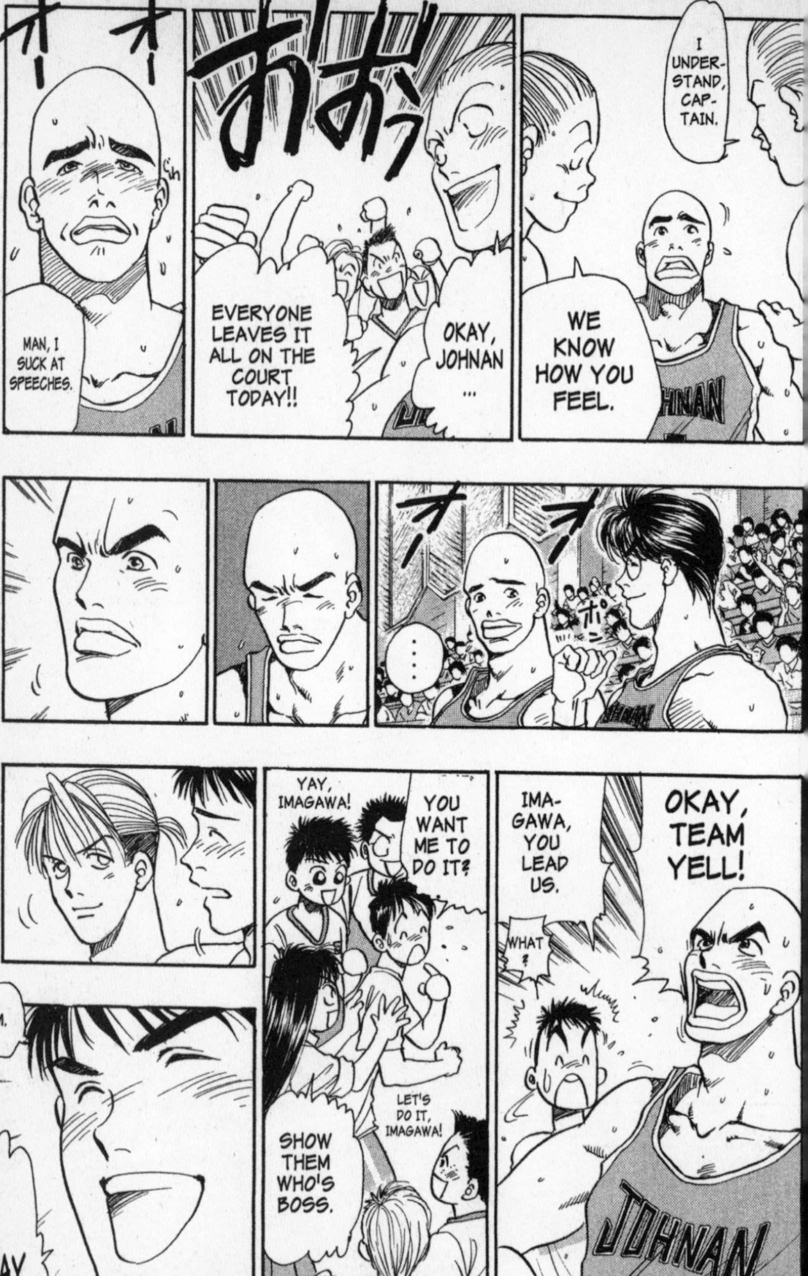
I UNDERSTAND, CAPTAIN.
WE KNOW HOW YOU FEEL.
おおっ
OKAY, JOHNAN ...
EVERYONE LEAVES IT ALL ON THE COURT TODAY!!
オー オー
MAN, I SUCK AT SPEECHES.
....
OKAY, TEAM YELL!
IMAGAWA, YOU LEAD US.
WHAT?
YOU WANT ME TO DO IT?
YAY, IMAGAWA!
LET'S DO IT, IMAGAWA!
SHOW THEM WHO'S BOSS.
HMM.
OKAY.

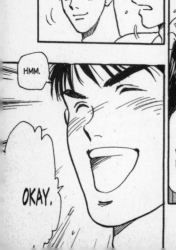

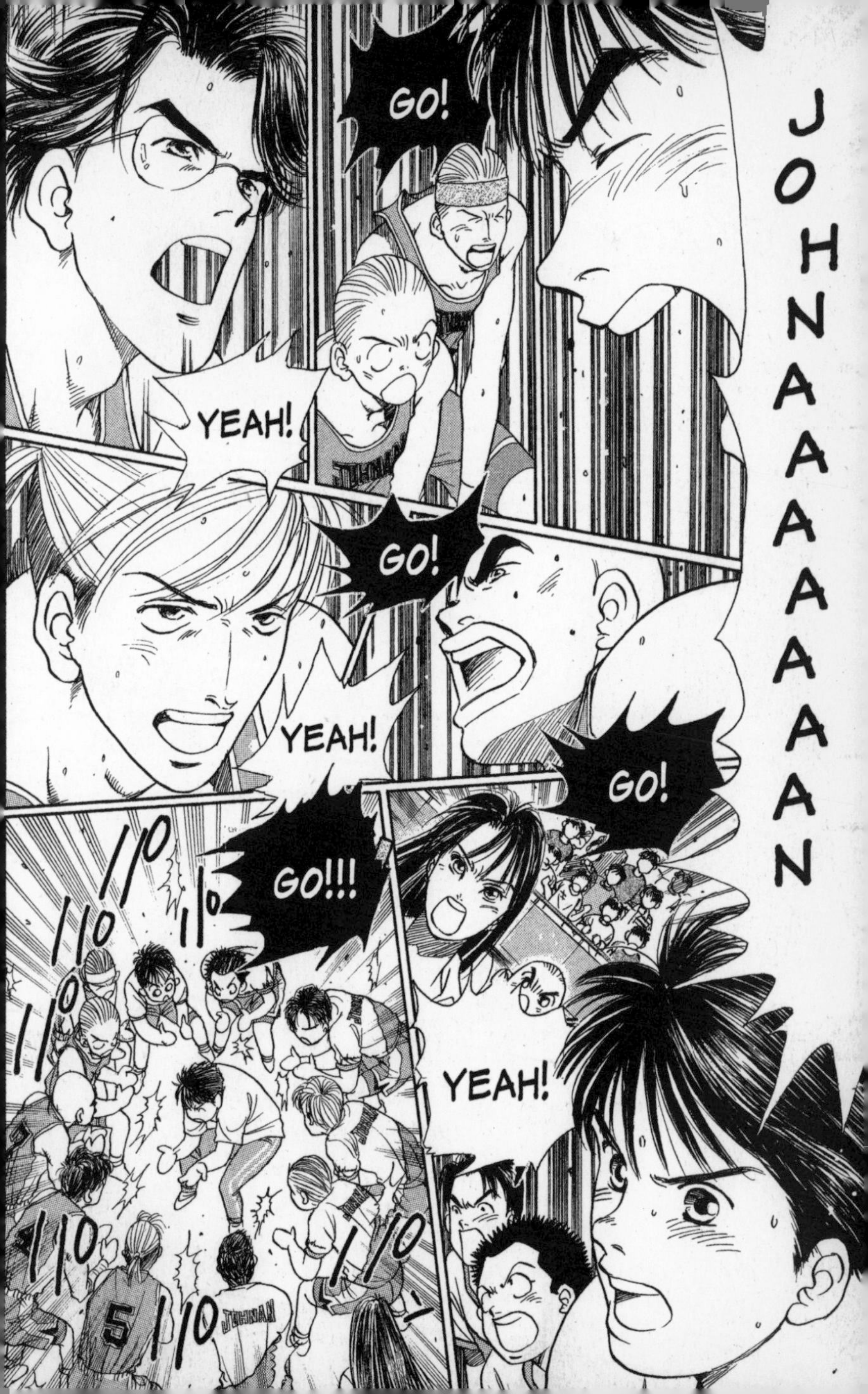
JOHNAAAAAAAN
GO!
YEAH!
GO!
YEAH!
GO!
YEAH!
GO!!!

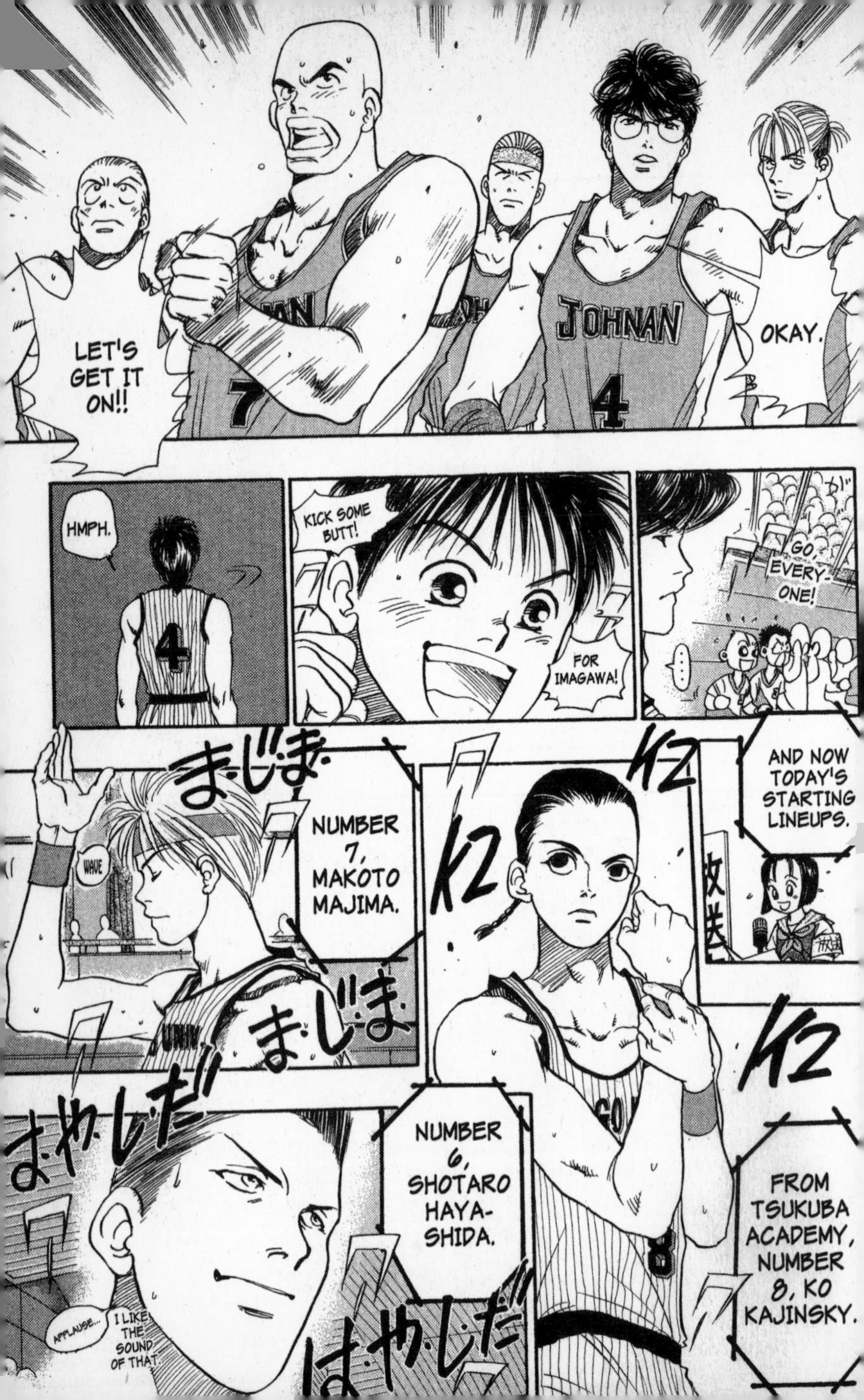
OKAY.
LET'S GET IT ON!!
GO, EVERY-ONE!
...
KICK SOME BUTT!
FOR IMAGAWA!
HMPH.
AND NOW TODAY'S STARTING LINEUPS.
FROM TSUKUBA ACADEMY, NUMBER 8, KO KAJINSKY.
NUMBER 7, MAKOTO MAJIMA.
まじま
まじま
WAVE
NUMBER 6, SHOTARO HAYA-SHIDA.
はやしだ
はやしだ
APPLAUSE...
I LIKE THE SOUND OF THAT.

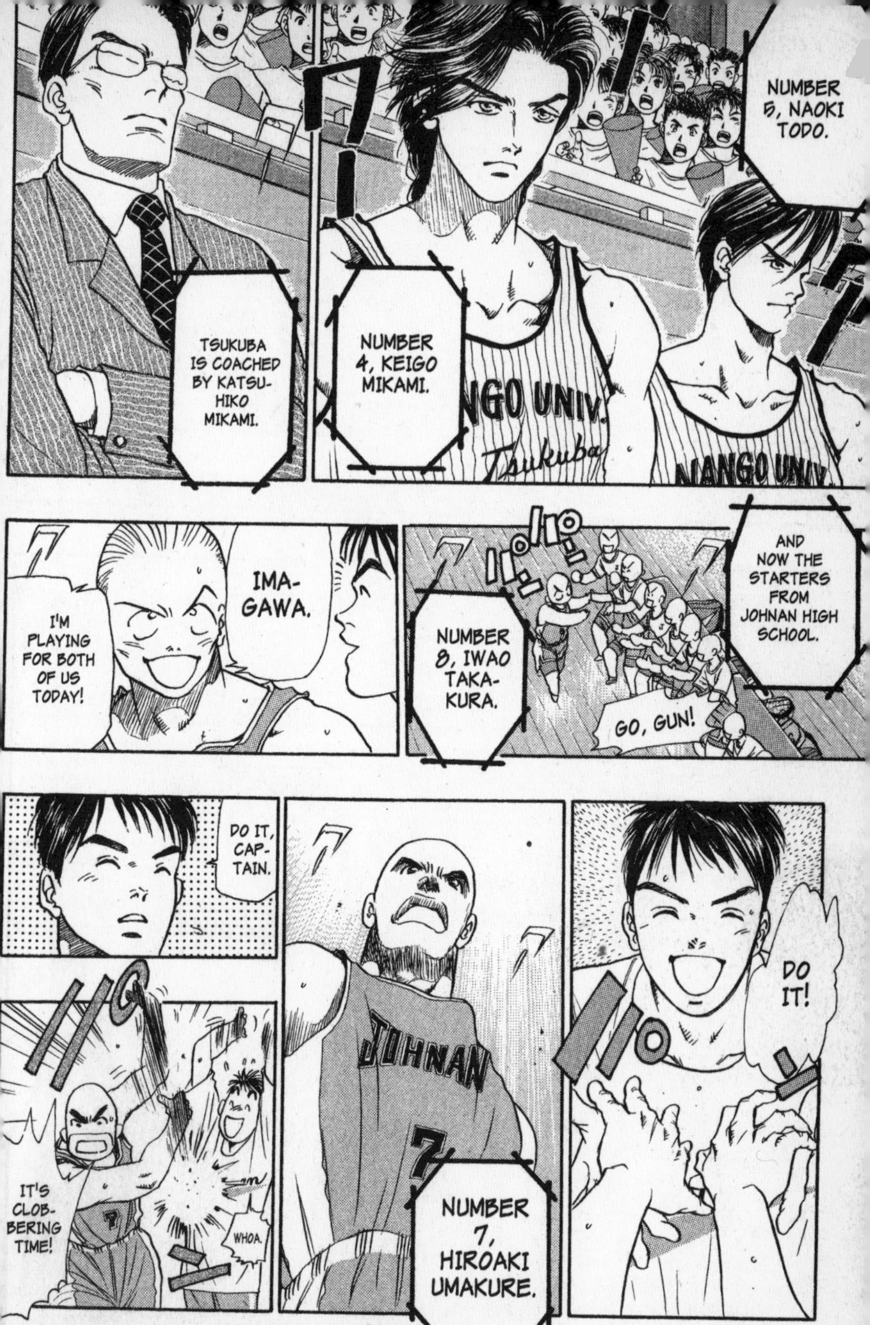
NUMBER 5, NAOKI TODO.
NUMBER 4, KEIGO MIKAMI.
TSUKUBA IS COACHED BY KATSU-HIKO MIKAMI.
AND NOW THE STARTERS FROM JOHNAN HIGH SCHOOL.
NUMBER 8, IWAO TAKA-KURA.
GO, GUN!
IMA-GAWA.
I'M PLAYING FOR BOTH OF US TODAY!
DO IT!
NUMBER 7, HIROAKI UMAKURE.
DO IT, CAP-TAIN.
WHOA.
IT'S CLOB-BERING TIME!

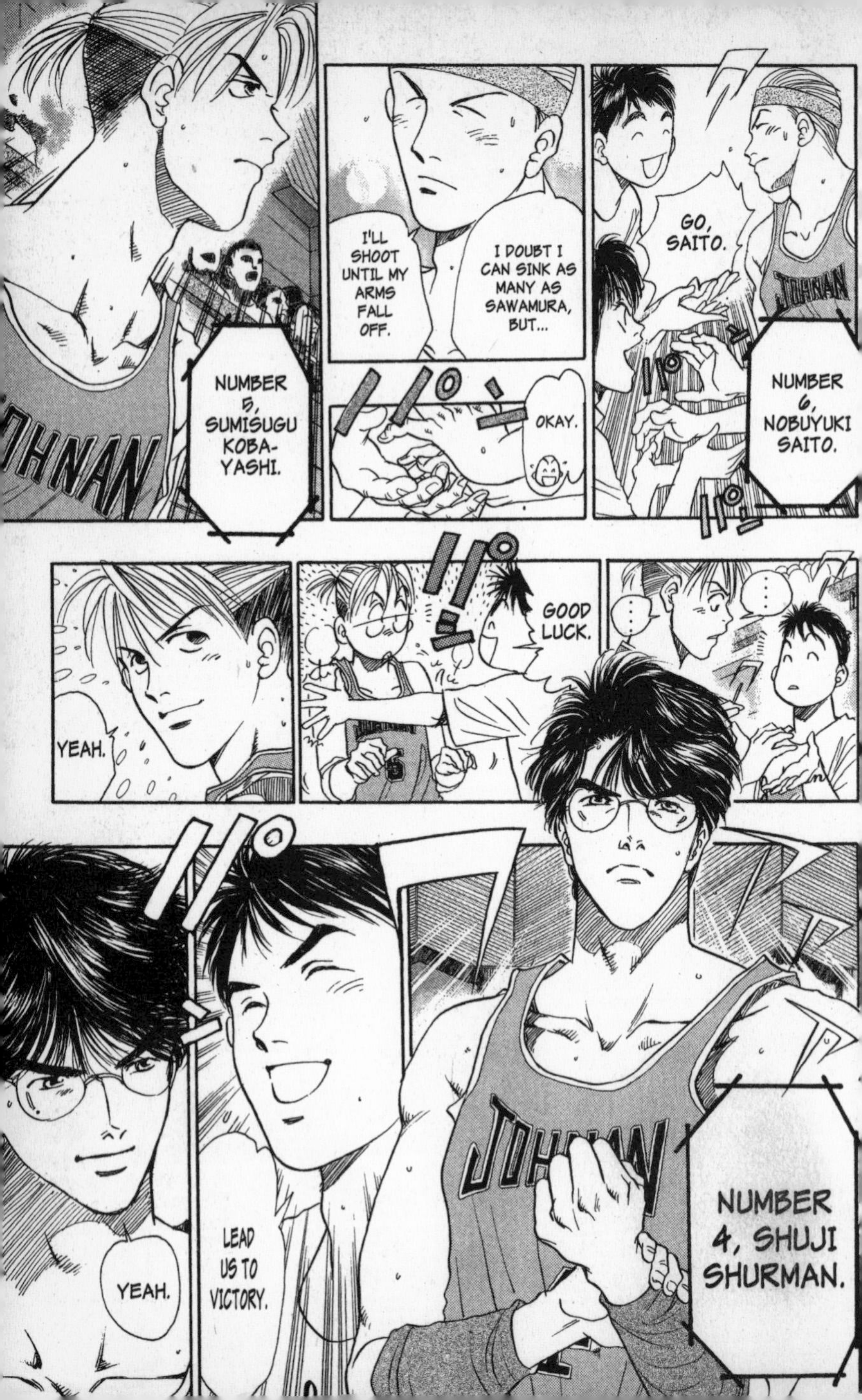
GO, SAITO.
NUMBER 6, NOBUYUKI SAITO.
I DOUBT I CAN SINK AS MANY AS SAWAMURA, BUT...
I'LL SHOOT UNTIL MY ARMS FALL OFF.
OKAY.
NUMBER 5, SUMISUGU KOBA-YASHI.
...
...
GOOD LUCK.
YEAH.
NUMBER 4, SHUJI SHURMAN.
LEAD US TO VICTORY.
YEAH.

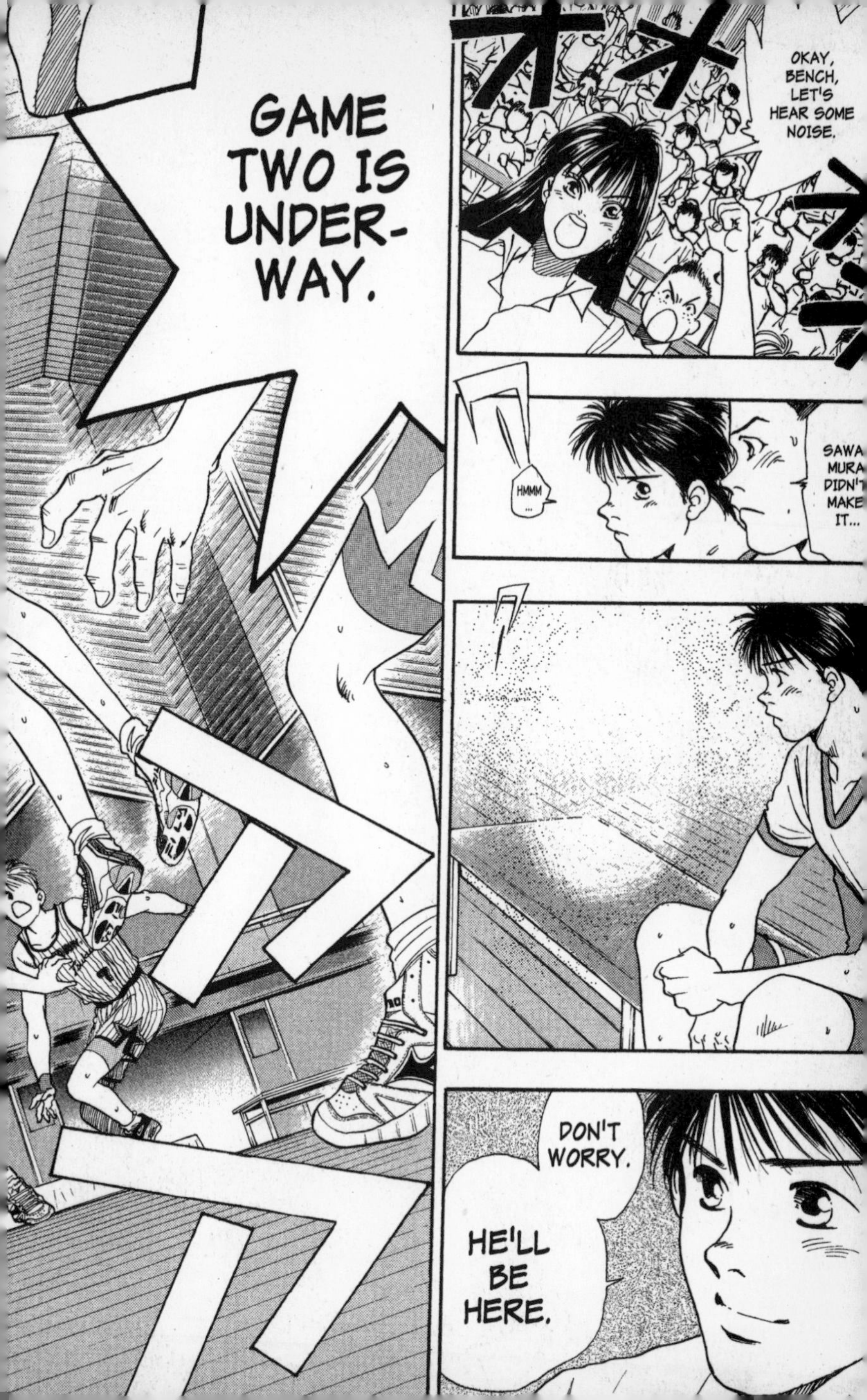
オオ
OKAY, BENCH, LET'S HEAR SOME NOISE.
SAWAMURA DIDN'T MAKE IT...
HMMM...
DON'T WORRY.
HE'LL BE HERE.
GAME TWO IS UNDER-WAY.

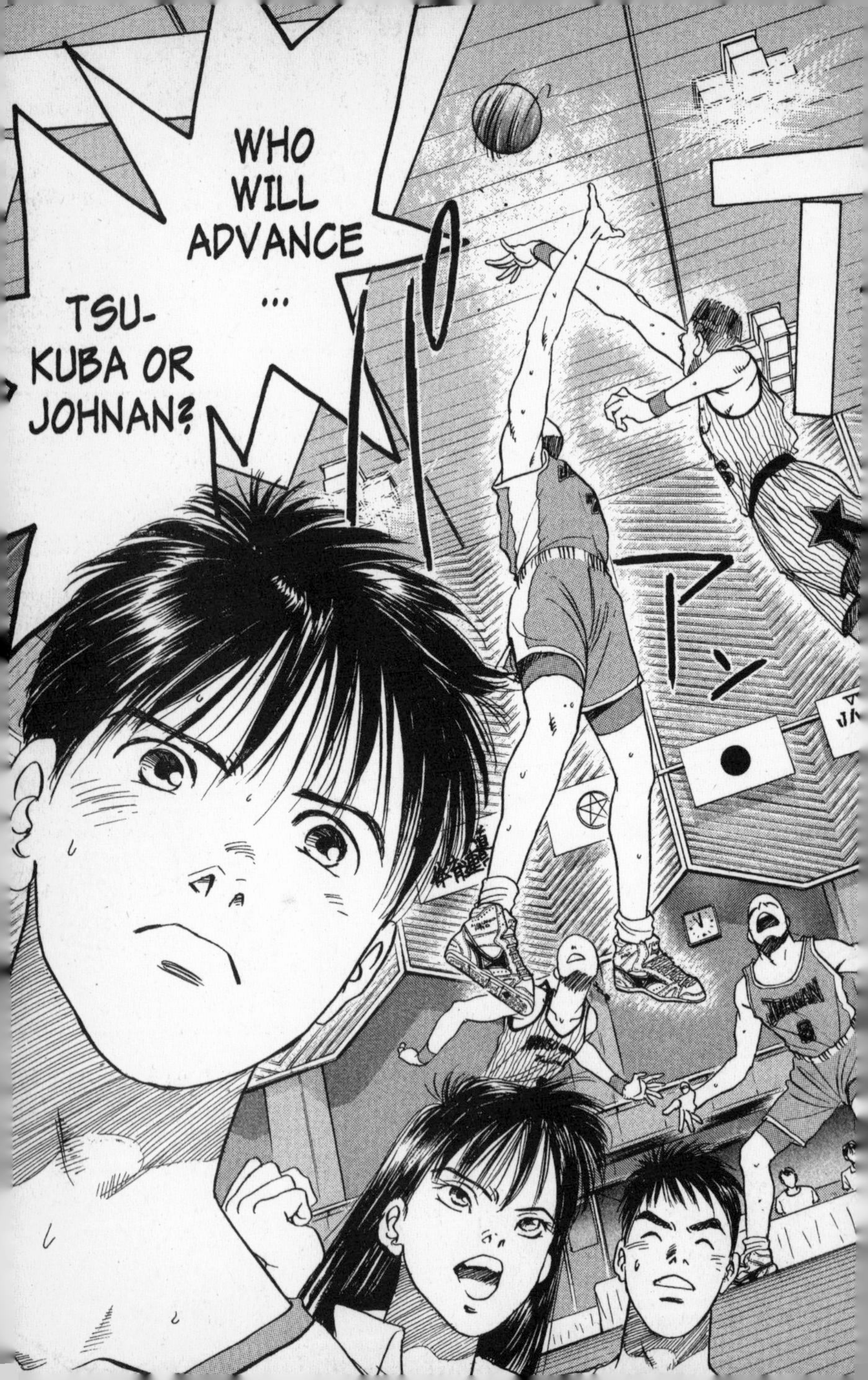
WHO WILL ADVANCE ...
TSU-KUBA OR JOHNAN?

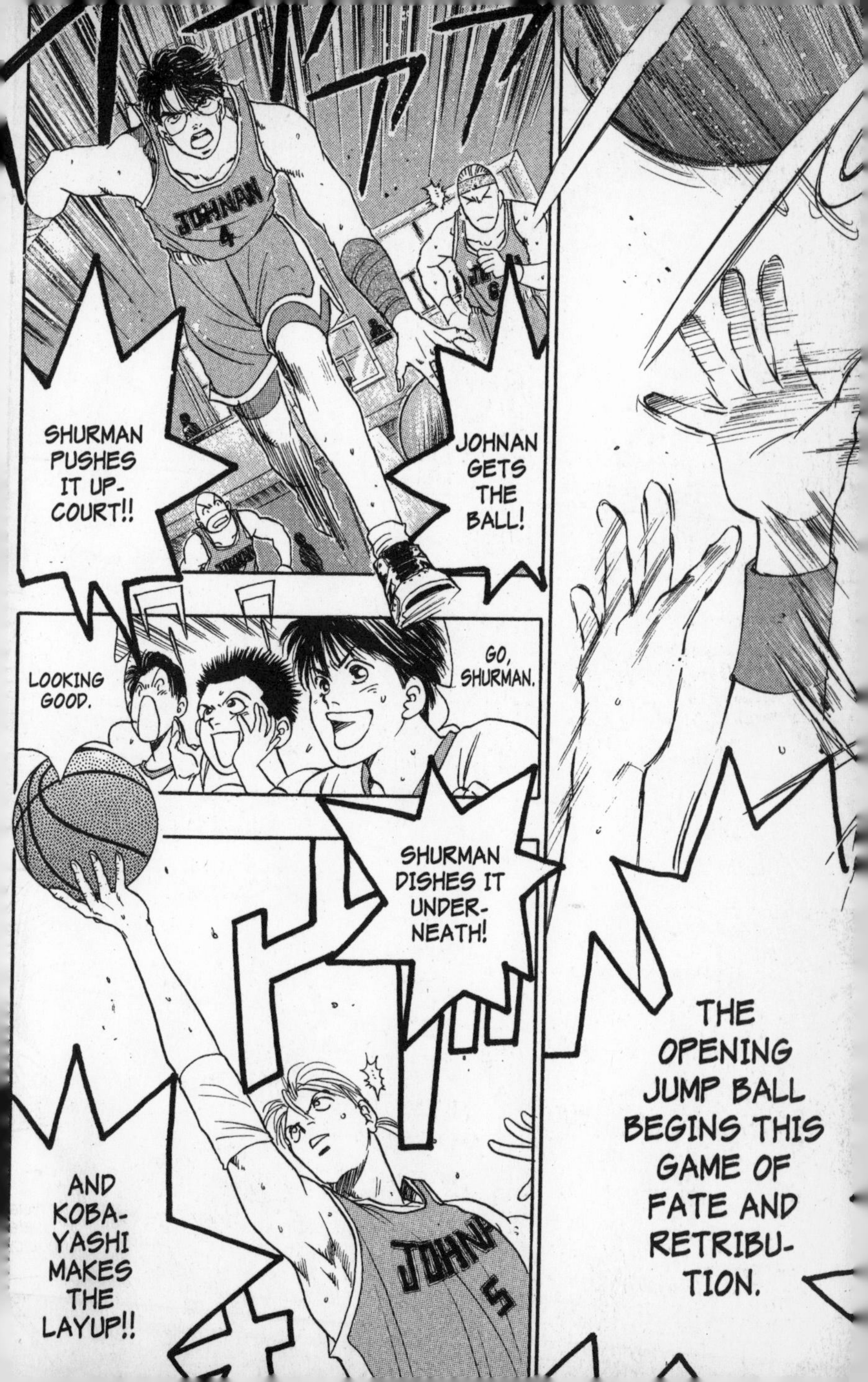
THE OPENING JUMP BALL BEGINS THIS GAME OF FATE AND RETRIBU-TION.
JOHNAN GETS THE BALL!
SHURMAN PUSHES IT UP-COURT!!
GO, SHURMAN.
LOOKING GOOD.
SHURMAN DISHES IT UNDER-NEATH!
AND KOBA-YASHI MAKES THE LAYUP!!

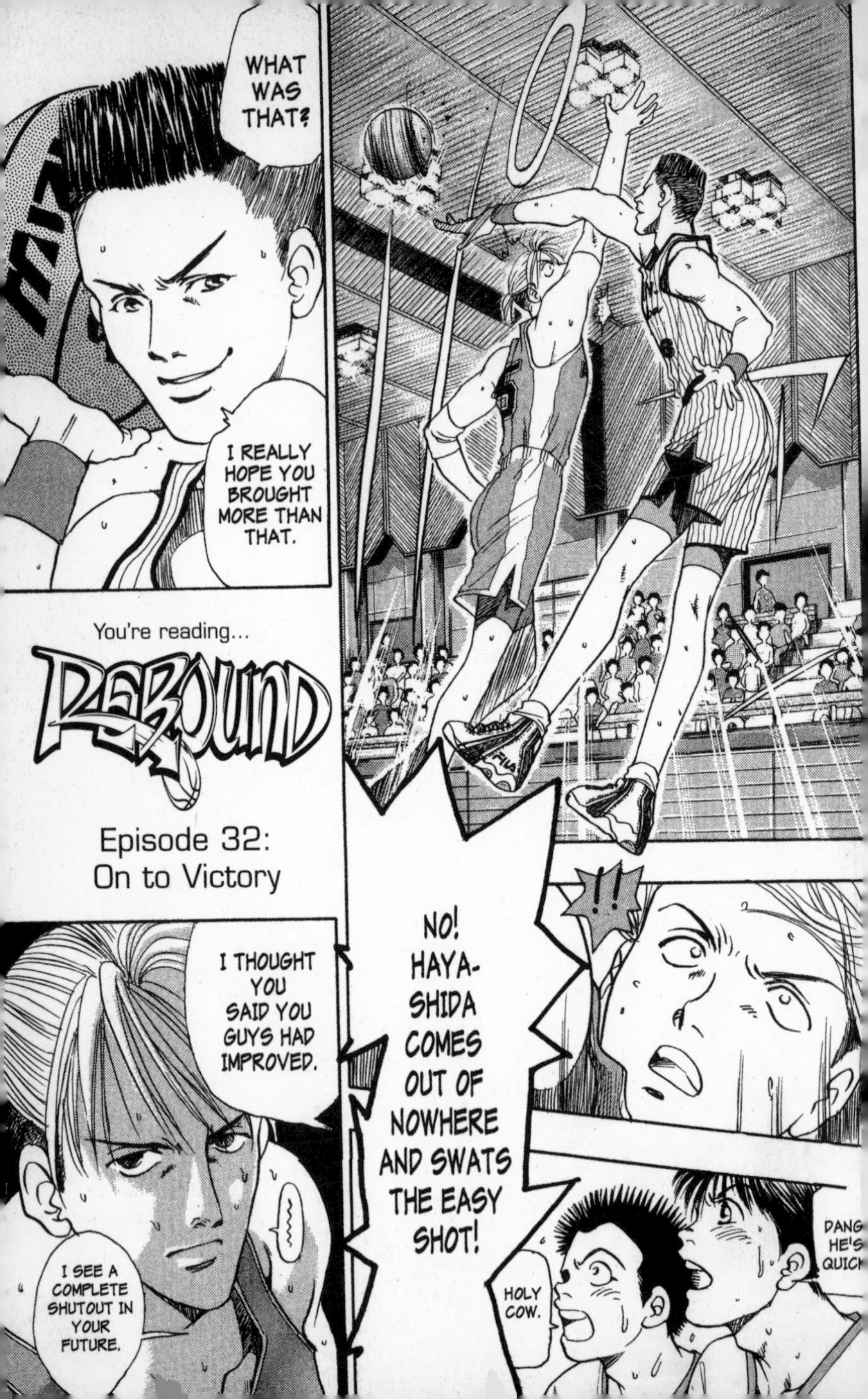
NO! HAYA-SHIDA COMES OUT OF NOWHERE AND SWATS THE EASY SHOT!
!!
DANG HE'S QUICK
HOLY COW.
WHAT WAS THAT?
I REALLY HOPE YOU BROUGHT MORE THAN THAT.
You're reading...
REBOUND
Episode 32: On to Victory
I THOUGHT YOU SAID YOU GUYS HAD IMPROVED.
......
I SEE A COMPLETE SHUTOUT IN YOUR FUTURE.

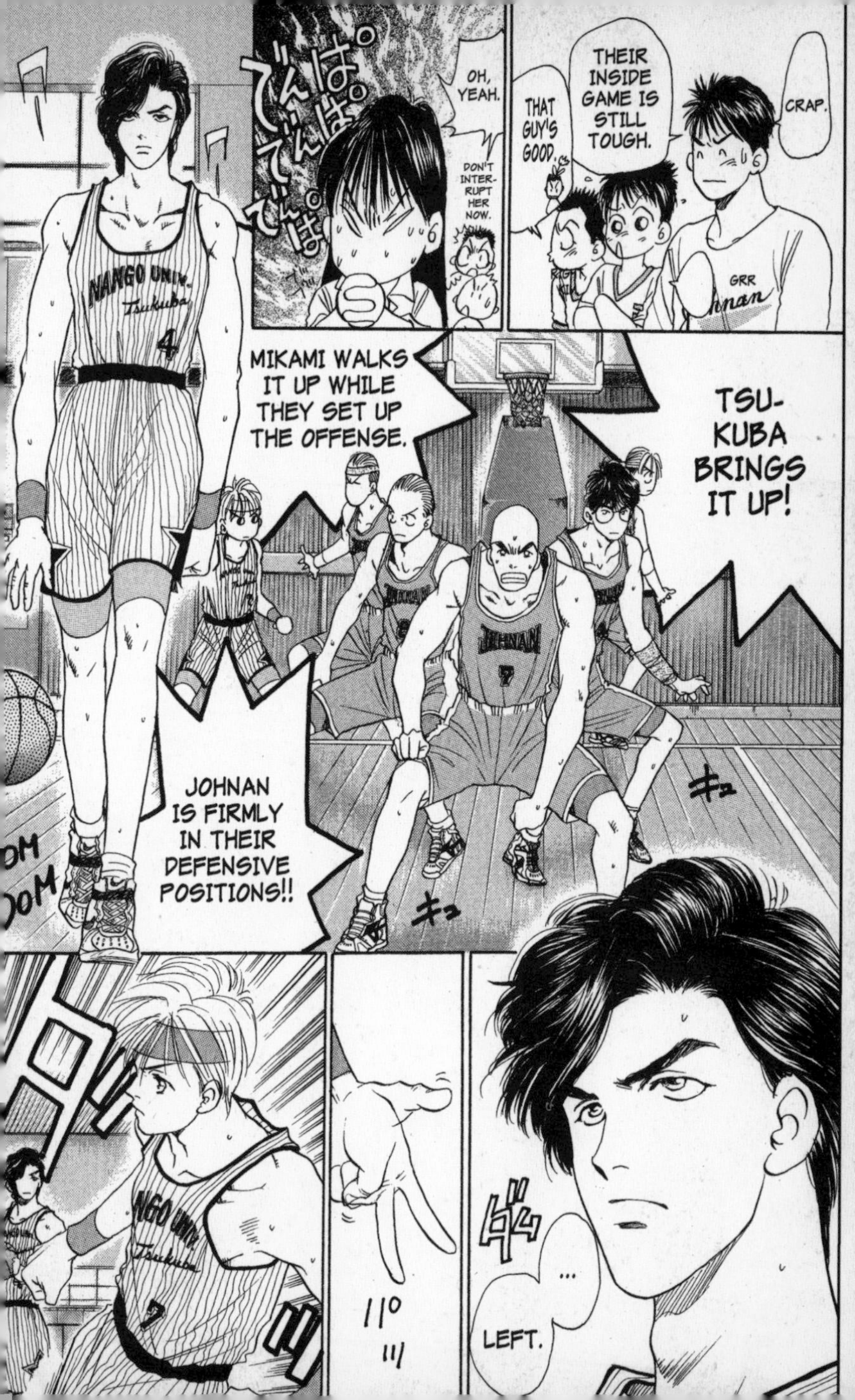
CRAP.
THEIR INSIDE GAME IS STILL TOUGH.
THAT GUY'S GOOD.
GRR
OH, YEAH.
DON'T INTER-RUPT HER NOW.
TSU-KUBA BRINGS IT UP!
MIKAMI WALKS IT UP WHILE THEY SET UP THE OFFENSE.
JOHNAN IS FIRMLY IN THEIR DEFENSIVE POSITIONS!!
...
LEFT.

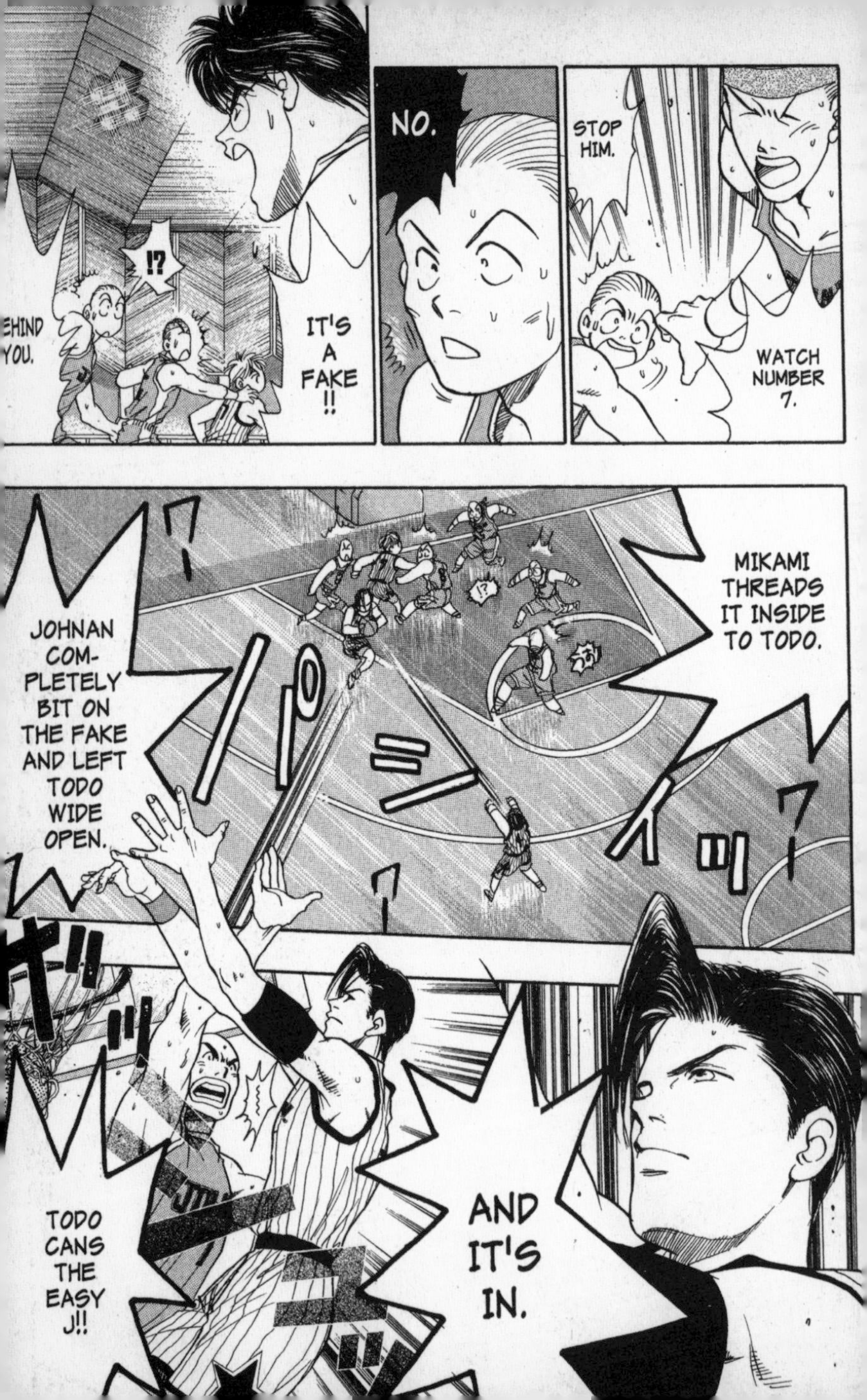

STOP HIM.
WATCH NUMBER 7.
NO.
IT'S A FAKE!!
!?
EHIND YOU.
MIKAMI THREADS IT INSIDE TO TODO.
!?
JOHNAN COM-PLETELY BIT ON THE FAKE AND LEFT TODO WIDE OPEN.
AND IT'S IN.
TODO CANS THE EASY J!!

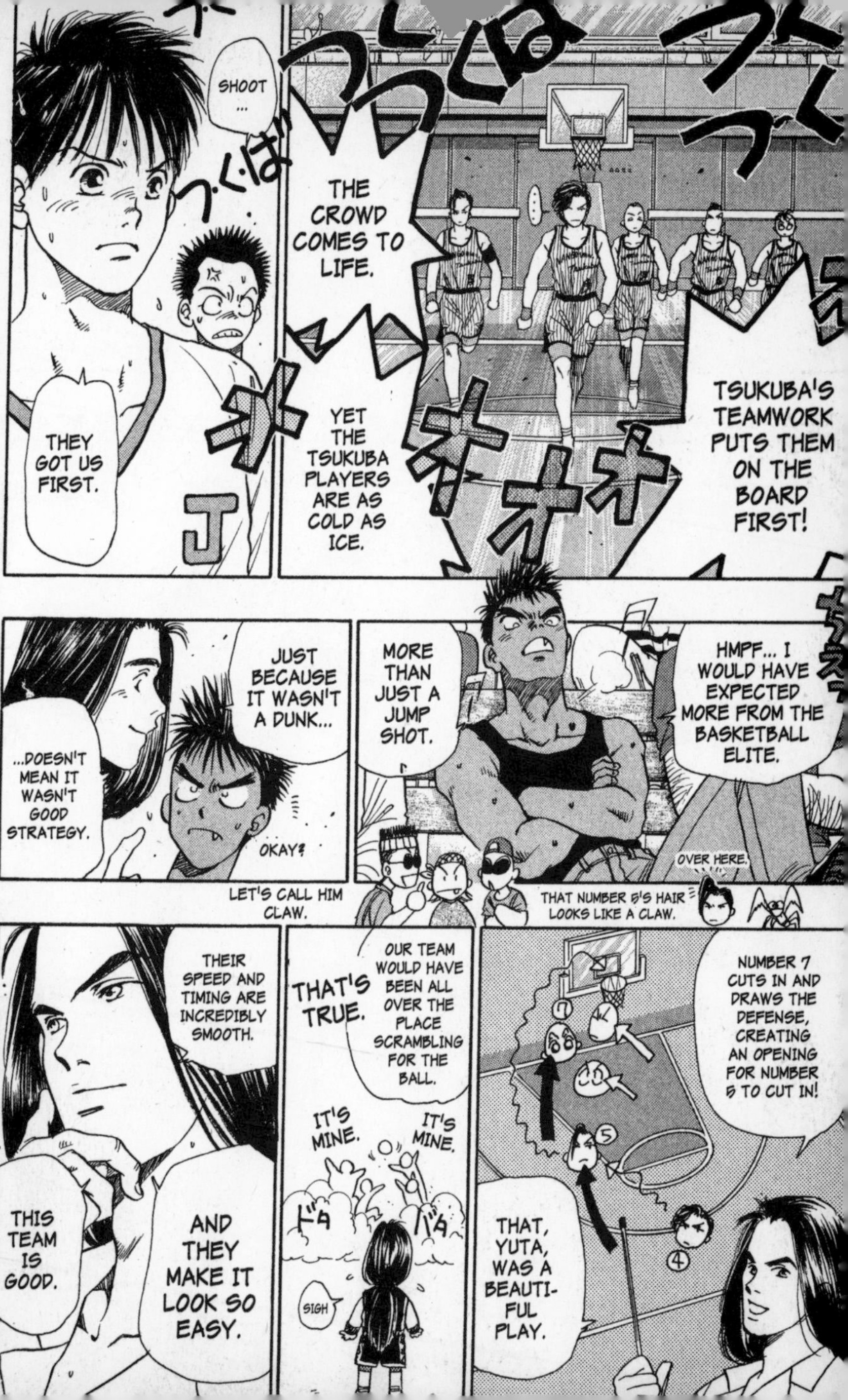
つく
つくば
TSUKUBA'S TEAMWORK PUTS THEM ON THE BOARD FIRST!
THE CROWD COMES TO LIFE.
YET THE TSUKUBA PLAYERS ARE AS COLD AS ICE.
オオオ
SHOOT ...
つ・く・ば
THEY GOT US FIRST.
HMPF... I WOULD HAVE EXPECTED MORE FROM THE BASKETBALL ELITE.
MORE THAN JUST A JUMP SHOT.
OVER HERE.
JUST BECAUSE IT WASN'T A DUNK...
...DOESN'T MEAN IT WASN'T GOOD STRATEGY.
OKAY?
THAT NUMBER 5'S HAIR LOOKS LIKE A CLAW.
LET'S CALL HIM CLAW.
NUMBER 7 CUTS IN AND DRAWS THE DEFENSE, CREATING AN OPENING FOR NUMBER 5 TO CUT IN!
THAT, YUTA, WAS A BEAUTIFUL PLAY.
OUR TEAM WOULD HAVE BEEN ALL OVER THE PLACE SCRAMBLING FOR THE BALL.
THAT'S TRUE.
IT'S MINE.
IT'S MINE.
バタ
ドタ
SIGH
THEIR SPEED AND TIMING ARE INCREDIBLY SMOOTH.
AND THEY MAKE IT LOOK SO EASY.
THIS TEAM IS GOOD.

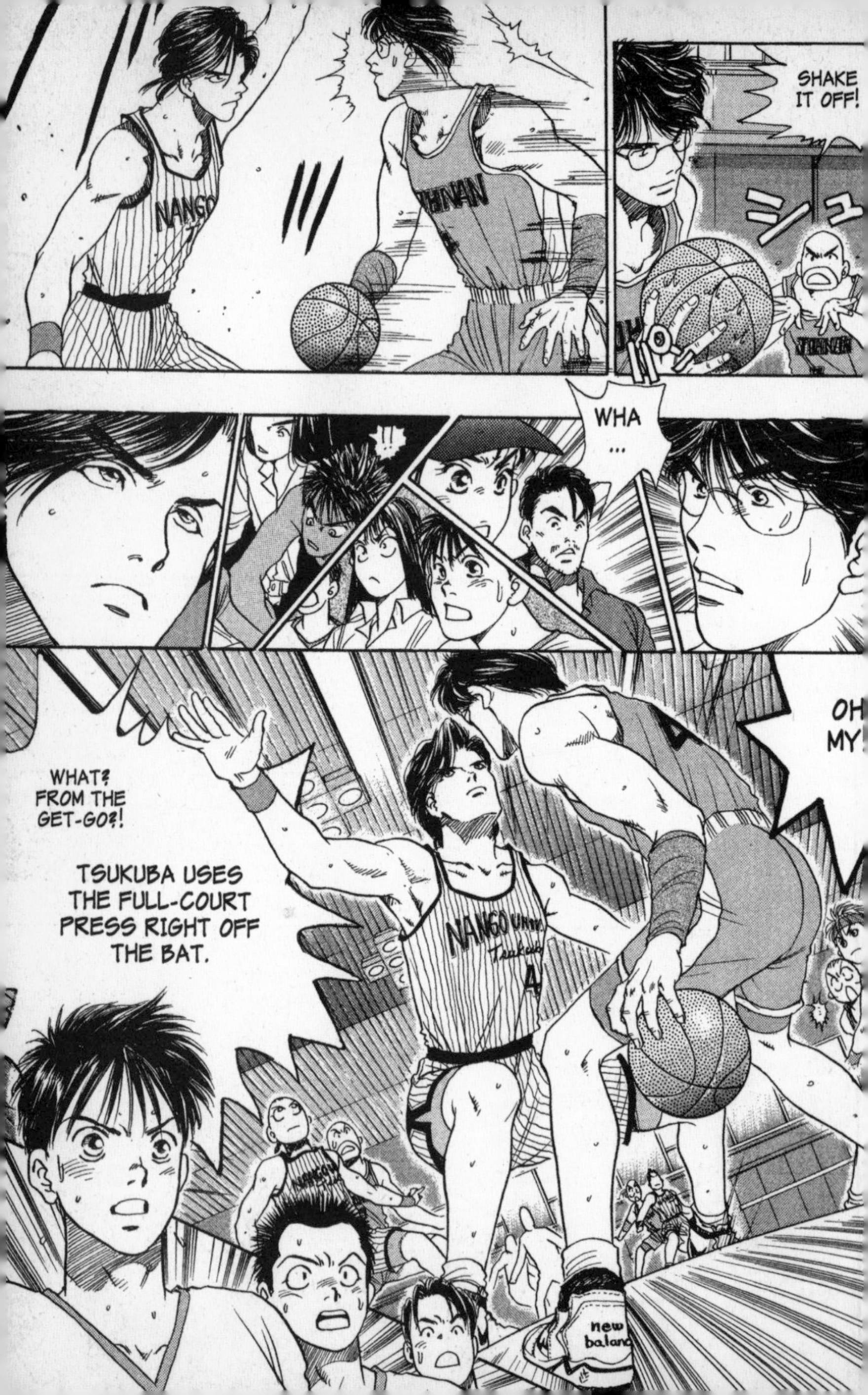
SHAKE IT OFF!
シュ
WHA ...
OH MY!
WHAT? FROM THE GET-GO?!
TSUKUBA USES THE FULL-COURT PRESS RIGHT OFF THE BAT.

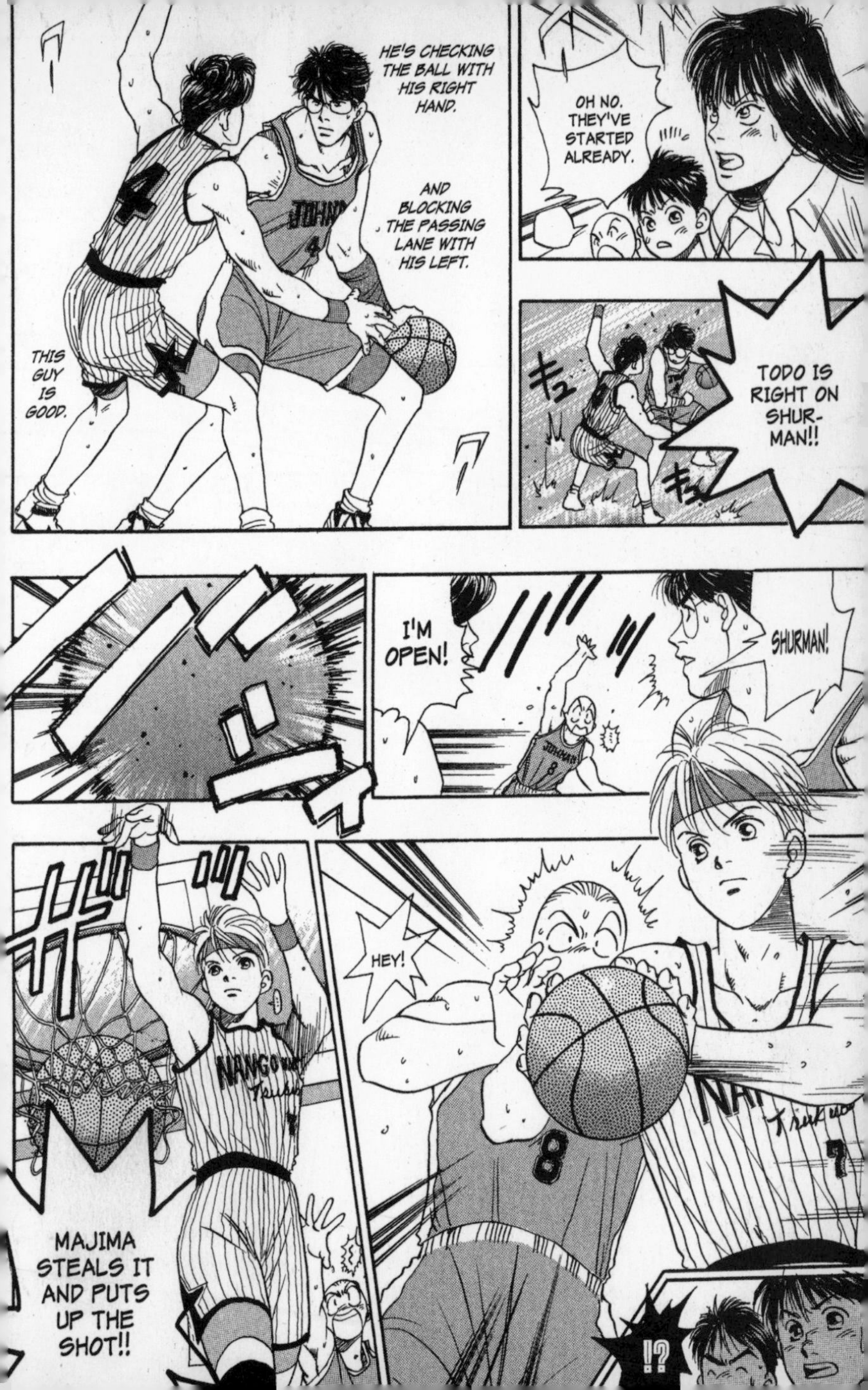
OH NO. THEY'VE STARTED ALREADY.
TODO IS RIGHT ON SHUR-MAN!!
HE'S CHECKING THE BALL WITH HIS RIGHT HAND.
AND BLOCKING THE PASSING LANE WITH HIS LEFT.
THIS GUY IS GOOD.
SHURMAN!
I'M OPEN!
HEY!
!?
MAJIMA STEALS IT AND PUTS UP THE SHOT!!

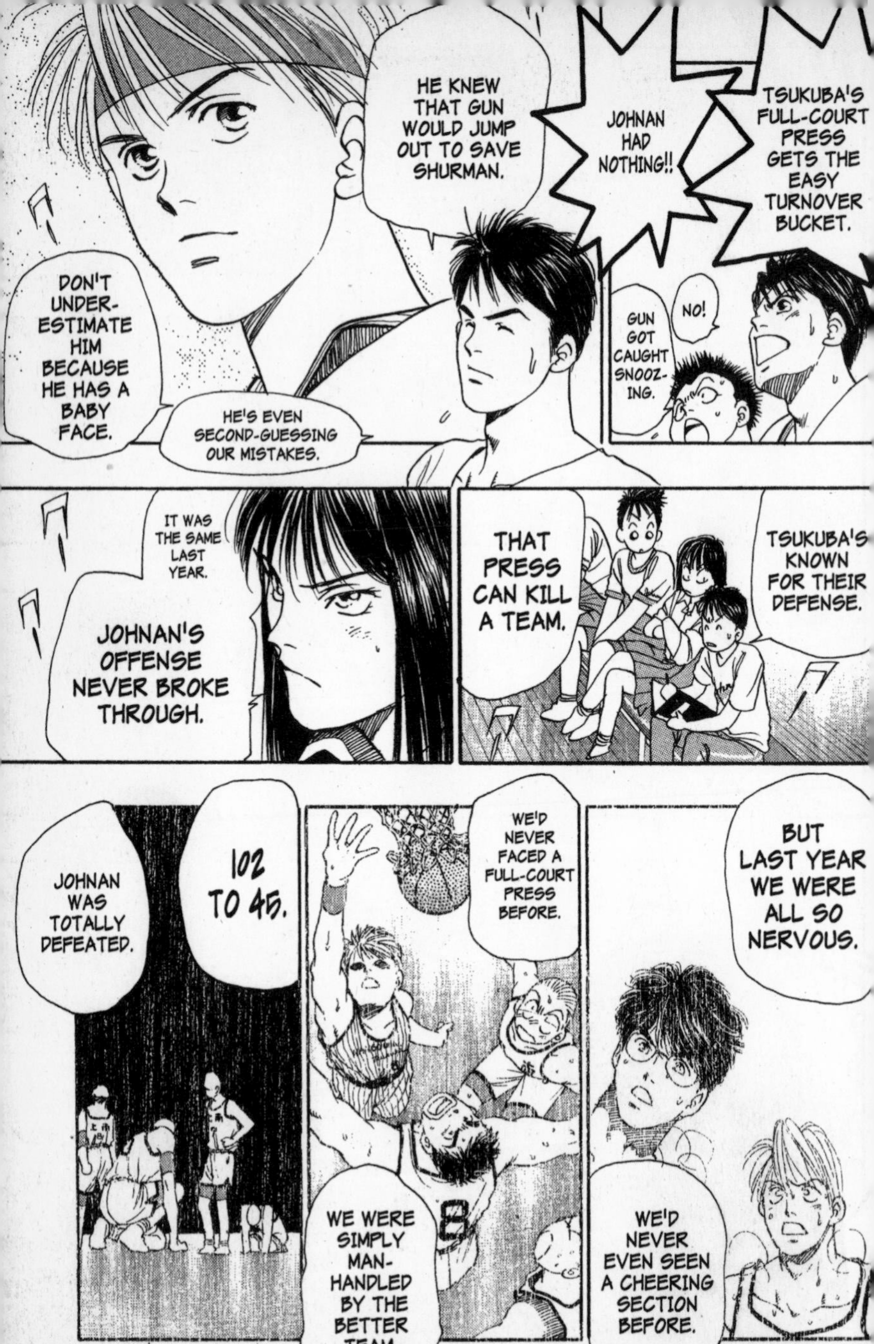
TSUKUBA'S FULL-COURT PRESS GETS THE EASY TURNOVER BUCKET.
JOHNAN HAD NOTHING!!
NO!
GUN GOT CAUGHT SNOOZING.
HE KNEW THAT GUN WOULD JUMP OUT TO SAVE SHURMAN.
DON'T UNDERESTIMATE HIM BECAUSE HE HAS A BABY FACE.
HE'S EVEN SECOND-GUESSING OUR MISTAKES.
TSUKUBA'S KNOWN FOR THEIR DEFENSE.
THAT PRESS CAN KILL A TEAM.
IT WAS THE SAME LAST YEAR.
JOHNAN'S OFFENSE NEVER BROKE THROUGH.
BUT LAST YEAR WE WERE ALL SO NERVOUS.
WE'D NEVER EVEN SEEN A CHEERING SECTION BEFORE.
WE'D NEVER FACED A FULL-COURT PRESS BEFORE.
WE WERE SIMPLY MANHANDLED BY THE BETTER TEAM.
102 TO 45.
JOHNAN WAS TOTALLY DEFEATED.

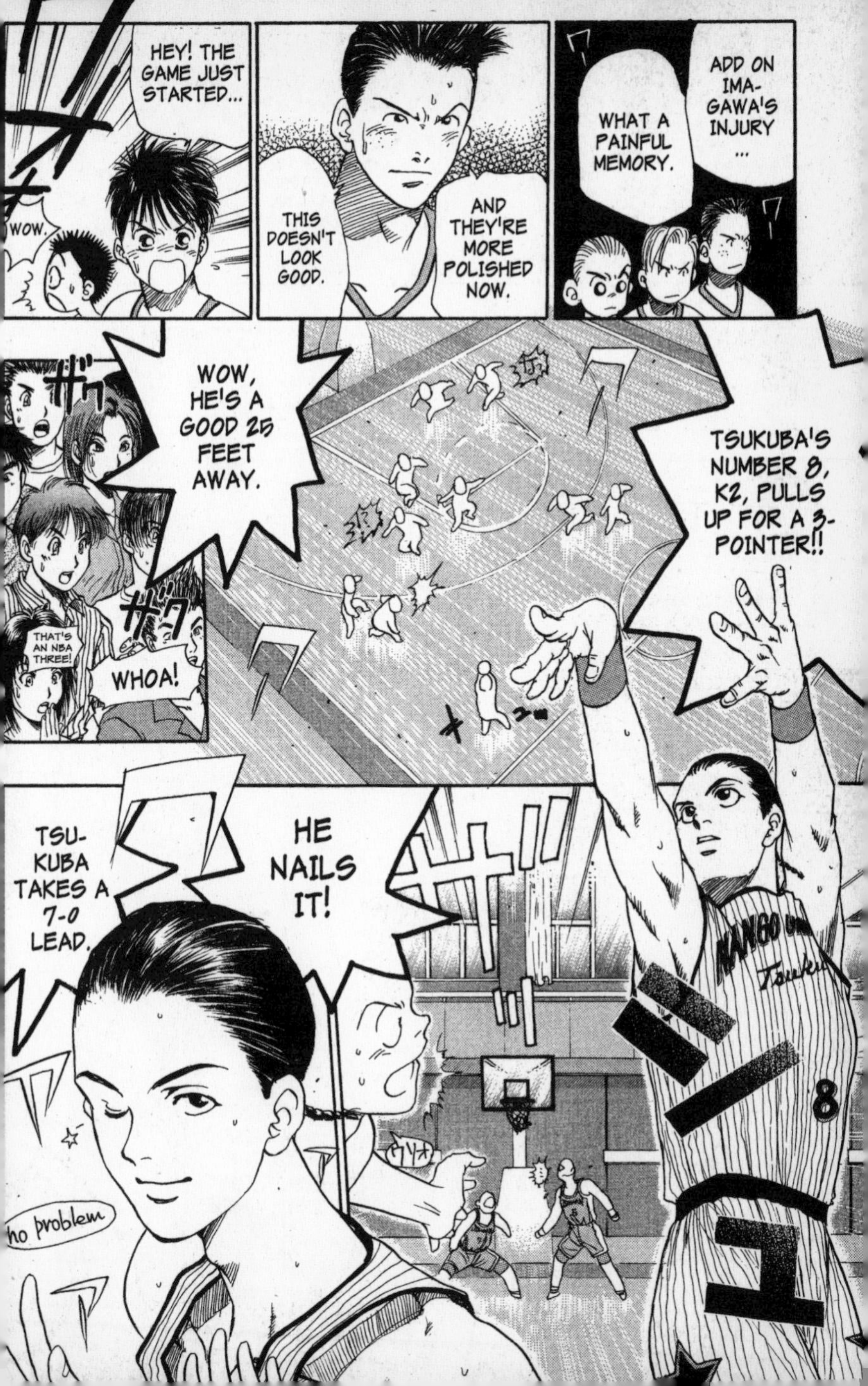
ADD ON IMA-GAWA'S INJURY ...
WHAT A PAINFUL MEMORY.
AND THEY'RE MORE POLISHED NOW.
THIS DOESN'T LOOK GOOD.
HEY! THE GAME JUST STARTED...
WOW.
TSUKUBA'S NUMBER 8, K2, PULLS UP FOR A 3-POINTER!!
WOW, HE'S A GOOD 25 FEET AWAY.
THAT'S AN NBA THREE!
WHOA!
HE NAILS IT!
TSU-KUBA TAKES A 7-0 LEAD.
no problem

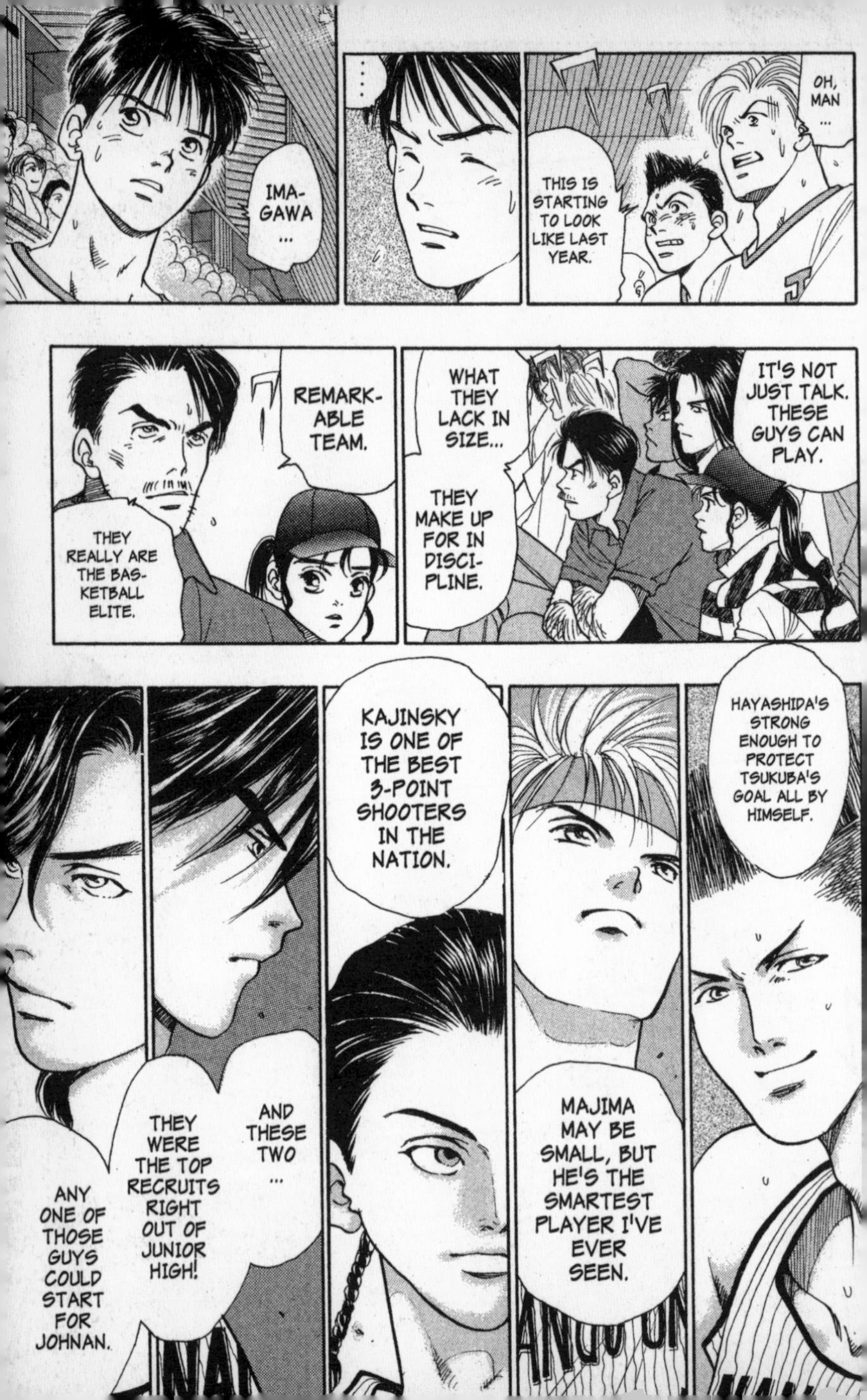

OH, MAN ...
THIS IS STARTING TO LOOK LIKE LAST YEAR.
....
IMA-GAWA ...
IT'S NOT JUST TALK. THESE GUYS CAN PLAY.
WHAT THEY LACK IN SIZE...
THEY MAKE UP FOR IN DISCI-PLINE.
REMARK-ABLE TEAM.
THEY REALLY ARE THE BAS-KETBALL ELITE.
HAYASHIDA'S STRONG ENOUGH TO PROTECT TSUKUBA'S GOAL ALL BY HIMSELF.
MAJIMA MAY BE SMALL, BUT HE'S THE SMARTEST PLAYER I'VE EVER SEEN.
KAJINSKY IS ONE OF THE BEST 3-POINT SHOOTERS IN THE NATION.
AND THESE TWO ...
THEY WERE THE TOP RECRUITS RIGHT OUT OF JUNIOR HIGH!
ANY ONE OF THOSE GUYS COULD START FOR JOHNAN.

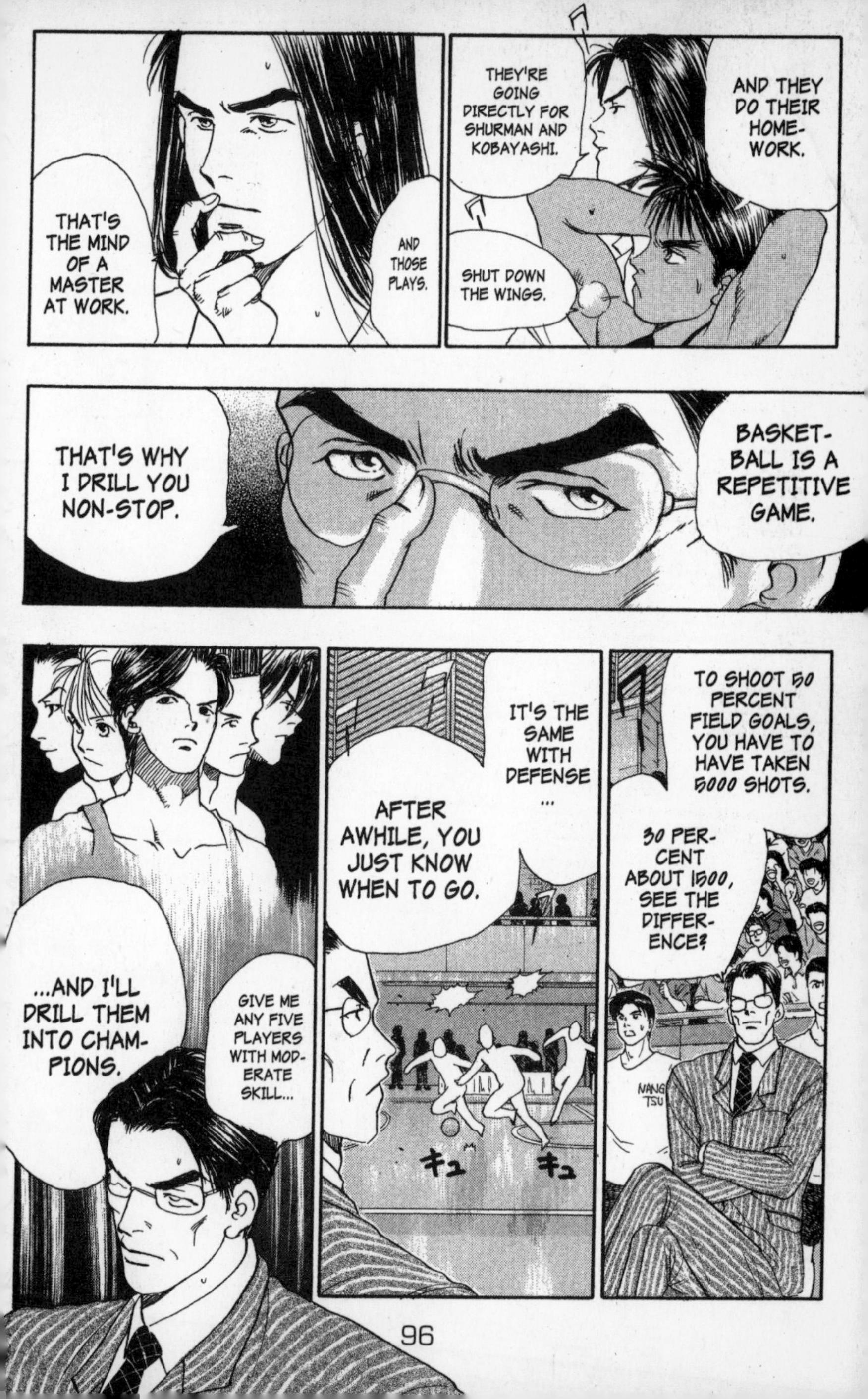
AND THEY DO THEIR HOME-WORK.
THEY'RE GOING DIRECTLY FOR SHURMAN AND KOBAYASHI.
SHUT DOWN THE WINGS.
AND THOSE PLAYS.
THAT'S THE MIND OF A MASTER AT WORK.
BASKET-BALL IS A REPETITIVE GAME.
THAT'S WHY I DRILL YOU NON-STOP.
TO SHOOT 50 PERCENT FIELD GOALS, YOU HAVE TO HAVE TAKEN 5000 SHOTS.
30 PER-CENT ABOUT 1500, SEE THE DIFFER-ENCE?
NANG TSU
IT'S THE SAME WITH DEFENSE ...
AFTER AWHILE, YOU JUST KNOW WHEN TO GO.
キュ
キュ
GIVE ME ANY FIVE PLAYERS WITH MOD-ERATE SKILL...
...AND I'LL DRILL THEM INTO CHAM-PIONS.

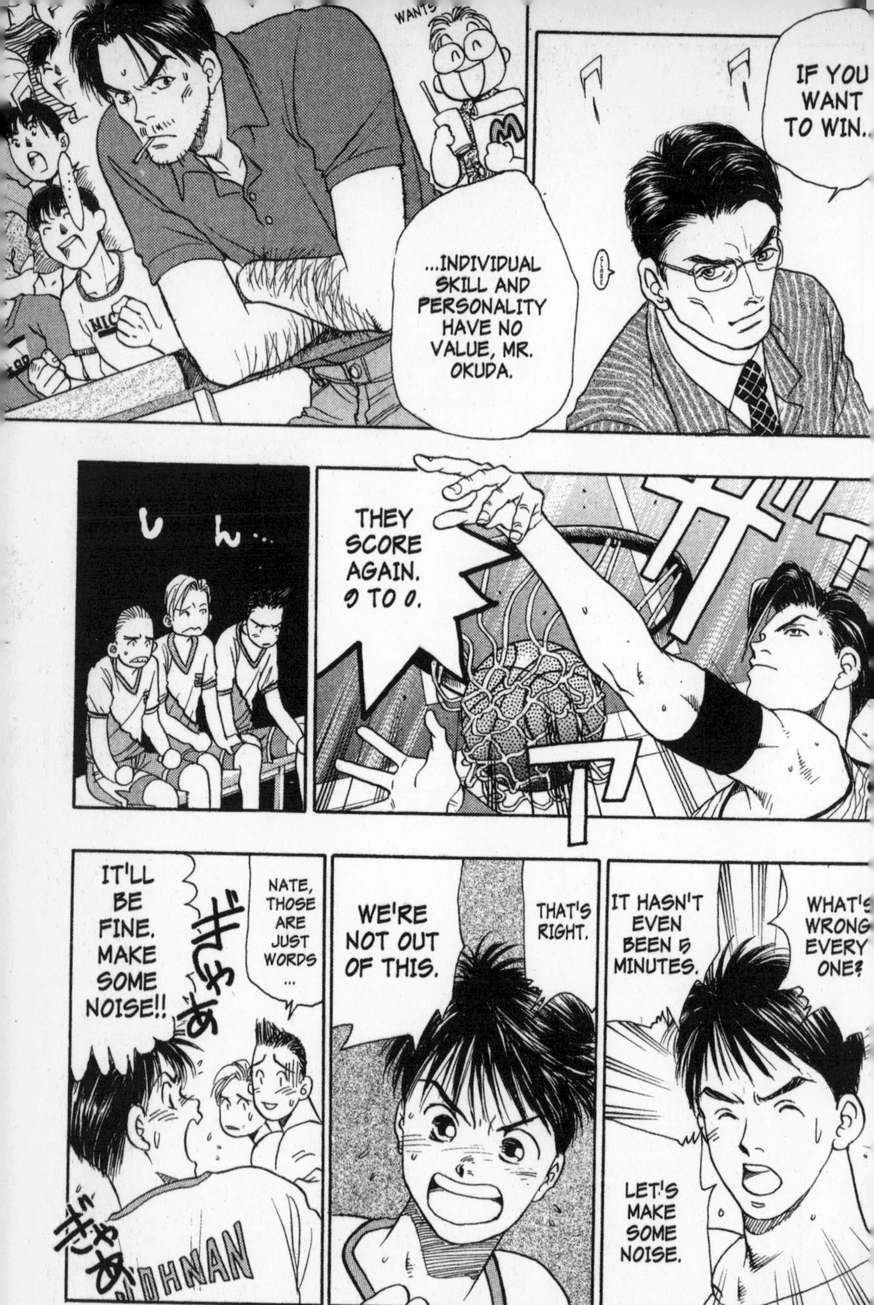
IF YOU WANT TO WIN...
...INDIVIDUAL SKILL AND PERSONALITY HAVE NO VALUE, MR. OKUDA.
WANTS
THEY SCORE AGAIN. 9 TO 0.
しん…
WHAT'S WRONG EVERYONE?
IT HASN'T EVEN BEEN 5 MINUTES.
LET'S MAKE SOME NOISE.
THAT'S RIGHT.
WE'RE NOT OUT OF THIS.
NATE, THOSE ARE JUST WORDS ...
IT'LL BE FINE. MAKE SOME NOISE!!
ぎゃあ
ぎゃあ

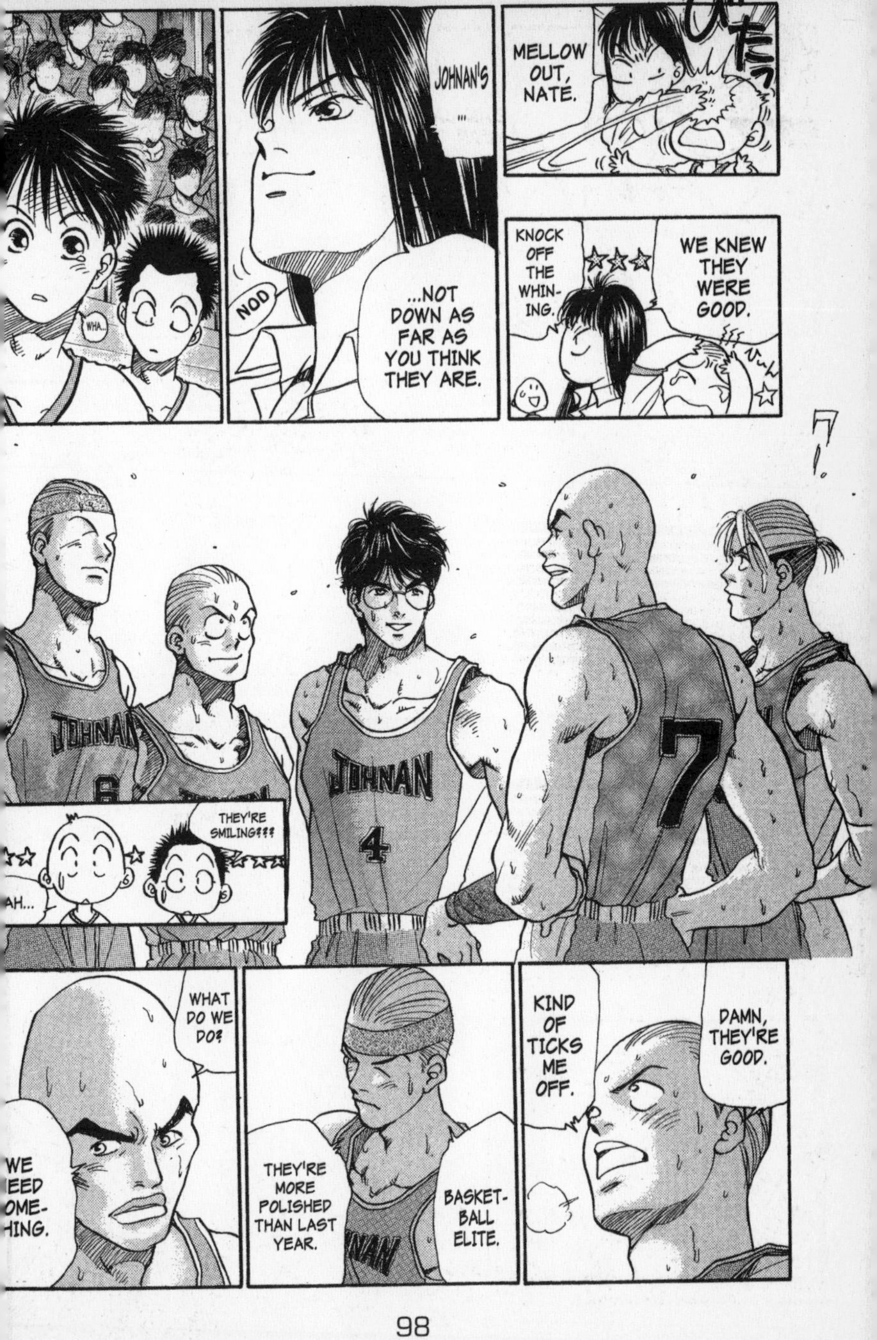
MELLOW OUT, NATE.
WE KNEW THEY WERE GOOD.
KNOCK OFF THE WHIN-ING.
JOHNAN'S ...
NOD
...NOT DOWN AS FAR AS YOU THINK THEY ARE.
WHA...
THEY'RE SMILING???
AH...
DAMN, THEY'RE GOOD.
KIND OF TICKS ME OFF.
BASKET-BALL ELITE.
THEY'RE MORE POLISHED THAN LAST YEAR.
JOHNAN
WHAT DO WE DO?
WE EED OME-HING.

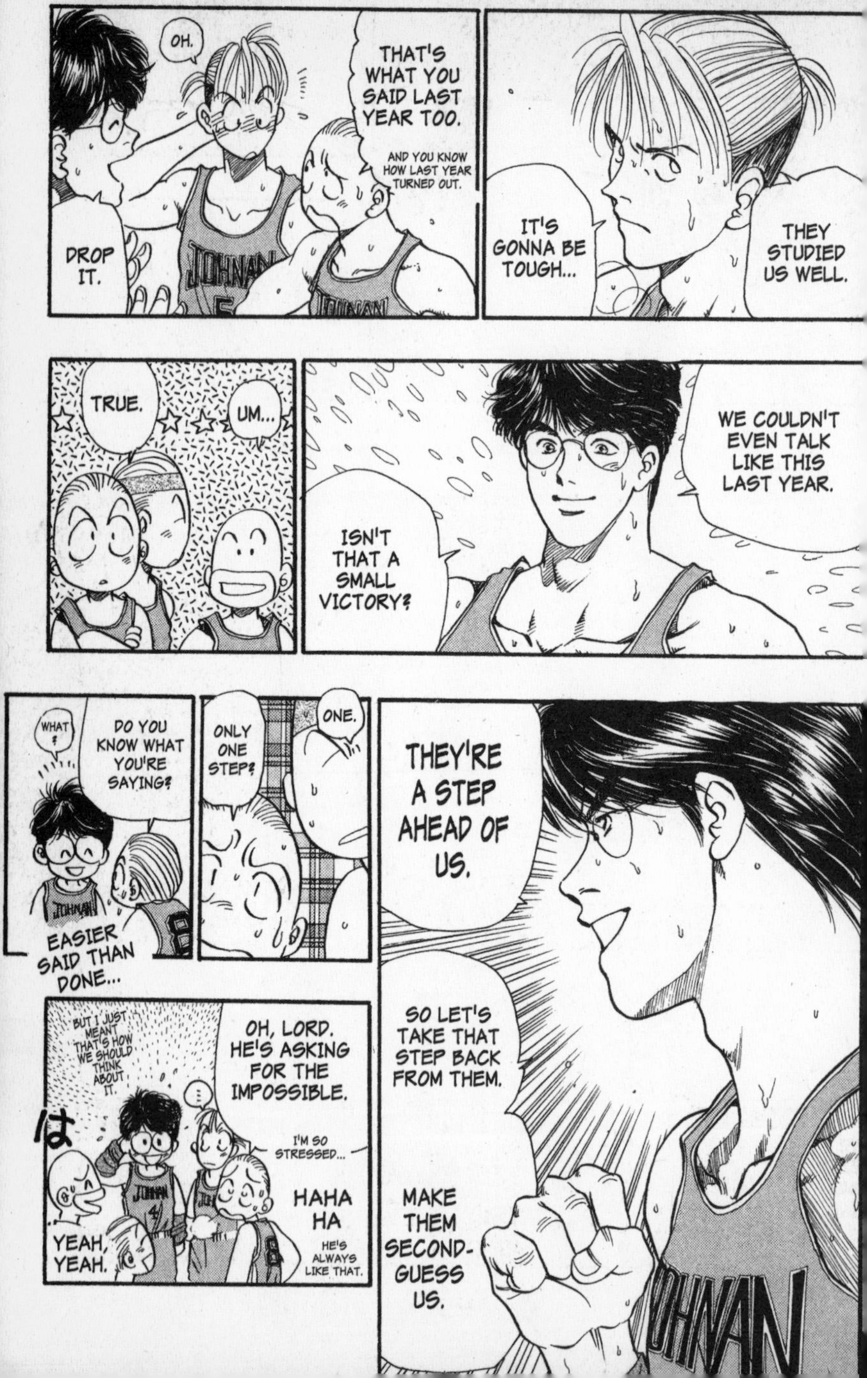

THEY STUDIED US WELL.
IT'S GONNA BE TOUGH...
THAT'S WHAT YOU SAID LAST YEAR TOO.
AND YOU KNOW HOW LAST YEAR TURNED OUT.
OH.
DROP IT.
WE COULDN'T EVEN TALK LIKE THIS LAST YEAR.
ISN'T THAT A SMALL VICTORY?
UM...
TRUE.
THEY'RE A STEP AHEAD OF US.
SO LET'S TAKE THAT STEP BACK FROM THEM.
MAKE THEM SECOND-GUESS US.
ONE.
ONLY ONE STEP?
DO YOU KNOW WHAT YOU'RE SAYING?
WHAT?
EASIER SAID THAN DONE...
OH, LORD. HE'S ASKING FOR THE IMPOSSIBLE.
BUT I JUST MEANT THAT'S HOW WE SHOULD THINK ABOUT IT.
...
I'M SO STRESSED...
HAHA HA
HE'S ALWAYS LIKE THAT.
YEAH, YEAH.
は

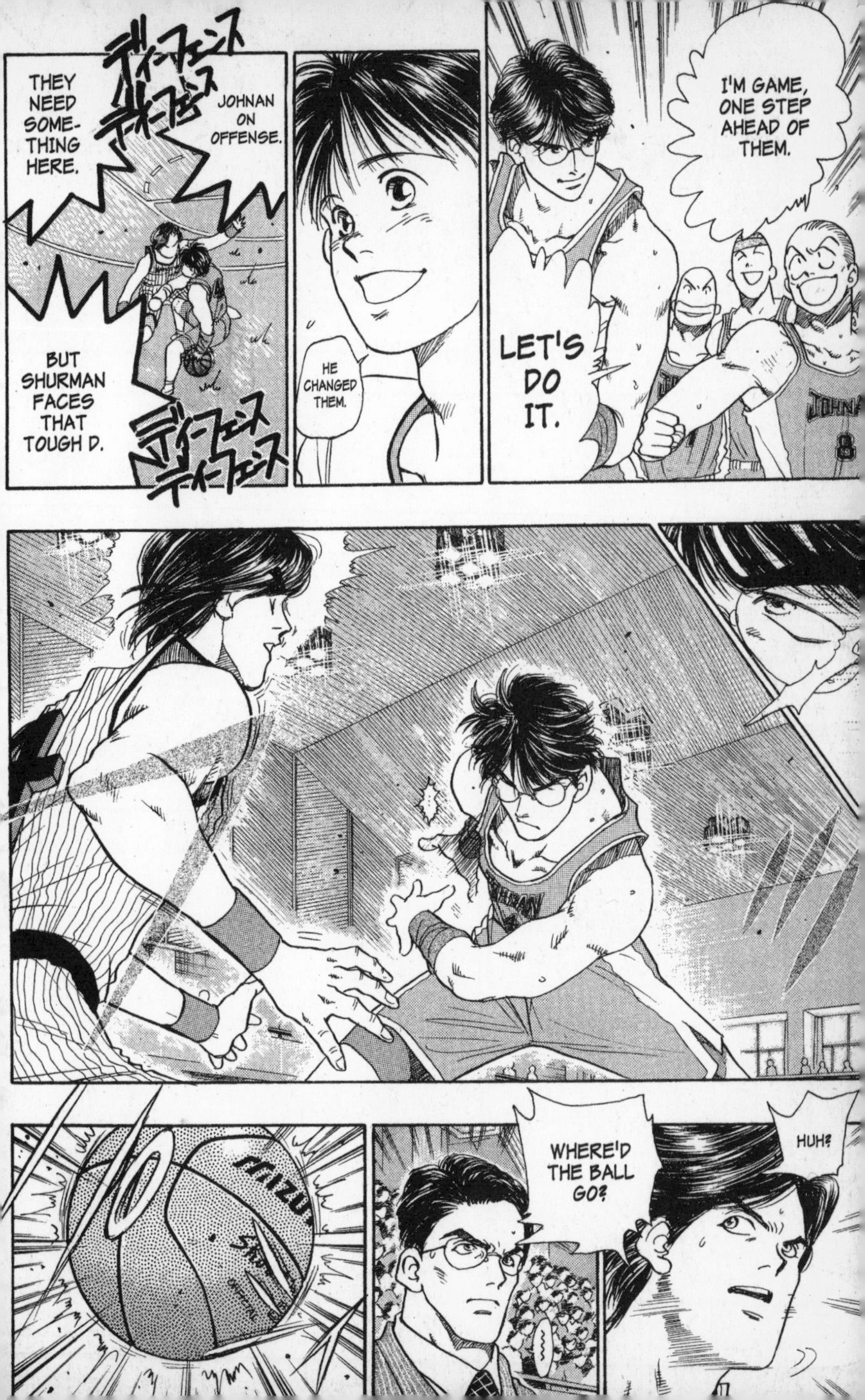
I'M GAME, ONE STEP AHEAD OF THEM.
LET'S DO IT.
HE CHANGED THEM.
JOHNAN ON OFFENSE.
THEY NEED SOMETHING HERE.
BUT SHURMAN FACES THAT TOUGH D.
HUH?
WHERE'D THE BALL GO?

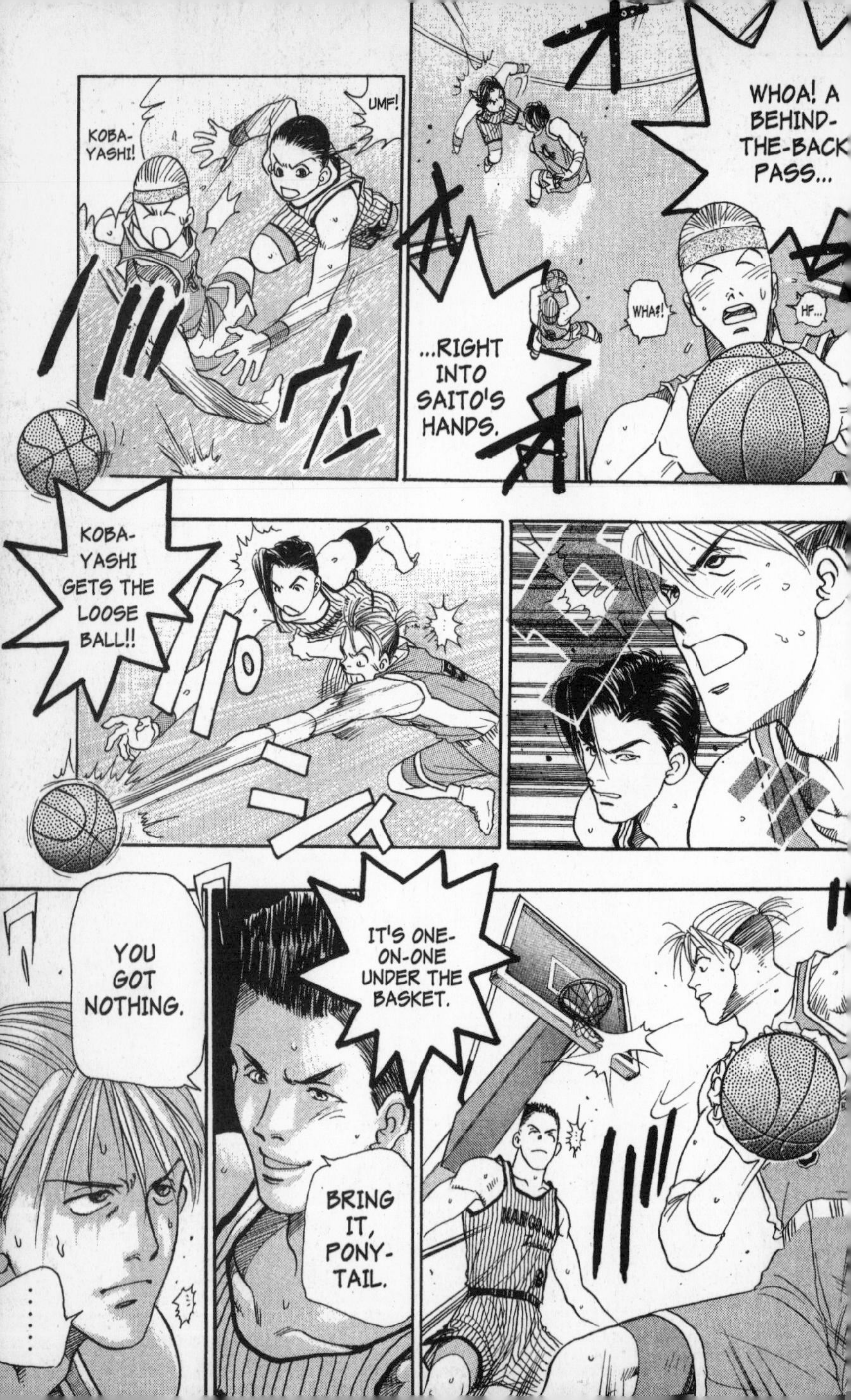
WHOA! A BEHIND-THE-BACK PASS...
WHA?!
HF...
...RIGHT INTO SAITO'S HANDS.
UMF!
KOBA-YASHI!
KOBA-YASHI GETS THE LOOSE BALL!!
IT'S ONE-ON-ONE UNDER THE BASKET.
BRING IT, PONY-TAIL.
YOU GOT NOTHING.
......

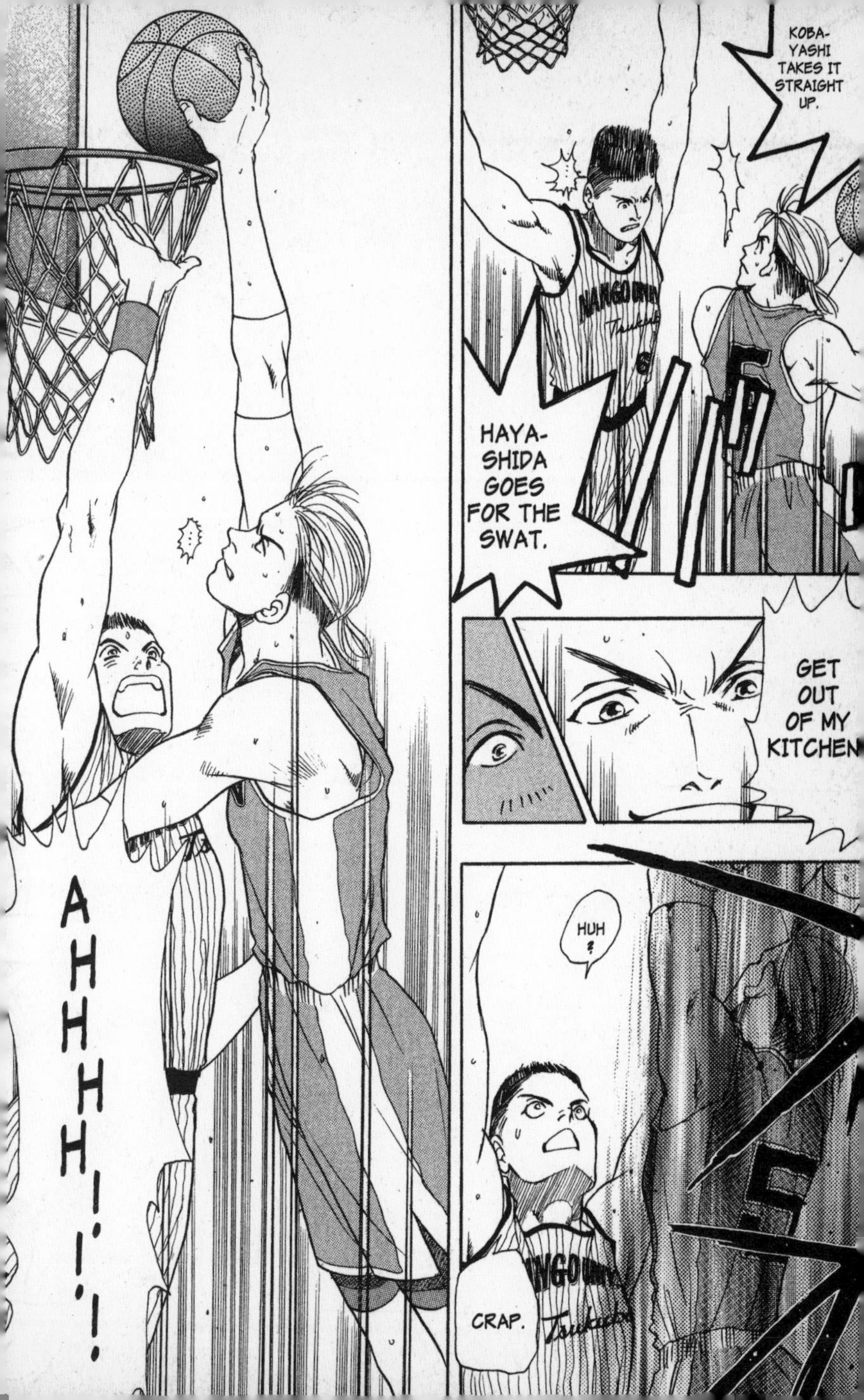
KOBA-YASHI TAKES IT STRAIGHT UP.
HAYA-SHIDA GOES FOR THE SWAT.
GET OUT OF MY KITCHEN
HUH?
CRAP.
AHHHH!!!

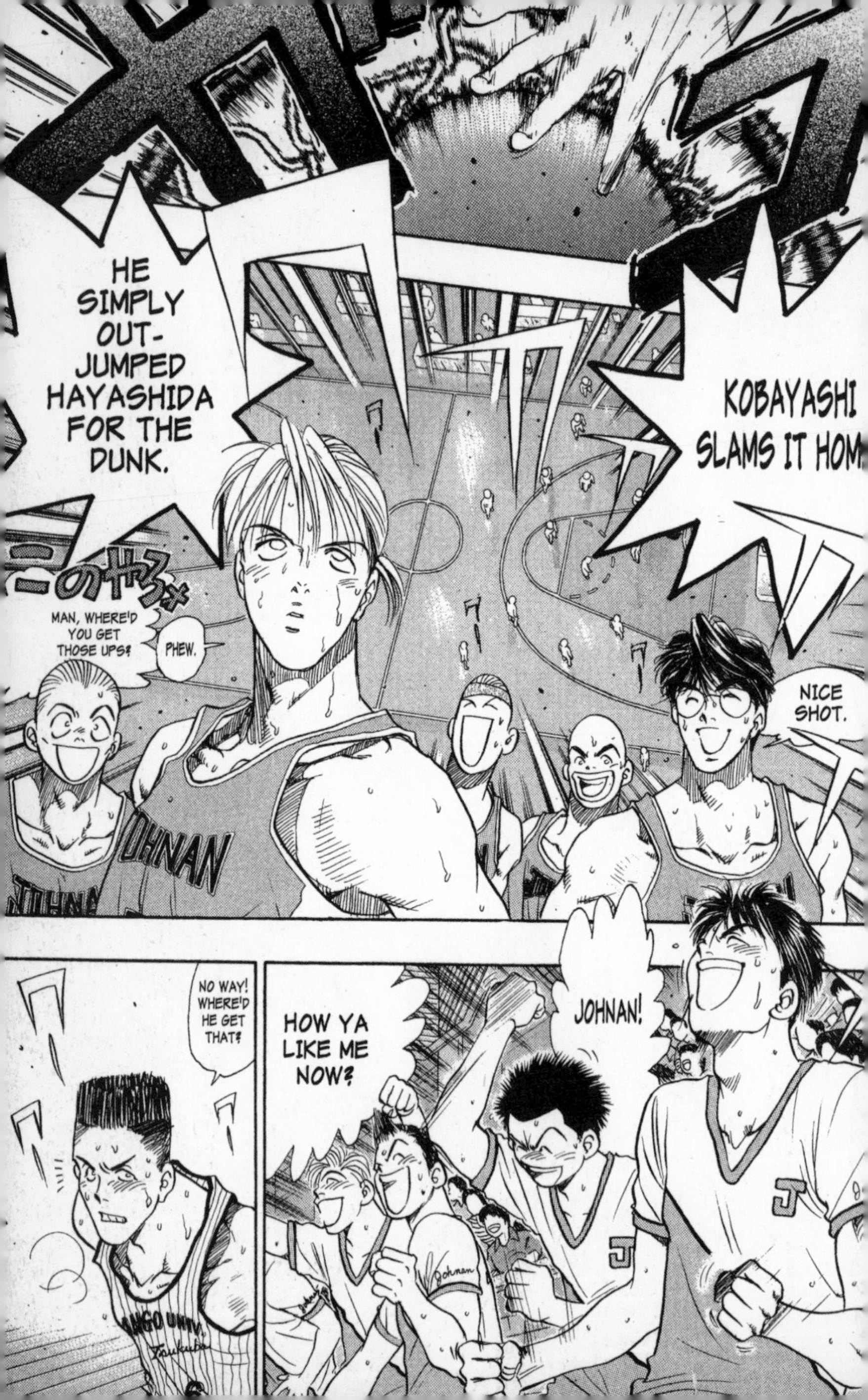
KOBAYASHI SLAMS IT HOM
HE SIMPLY OUT-JUMPED HAYASHIDA FOR THE DUNK.
NICE SHOT.
PHEW.
このやろォ
MAN, WHERE'D YOU GET THOSE UPS?
JOHNAN!
HOW YA LIKE ME NOW?
NO WAY! WHERE'D HE GET THAT?

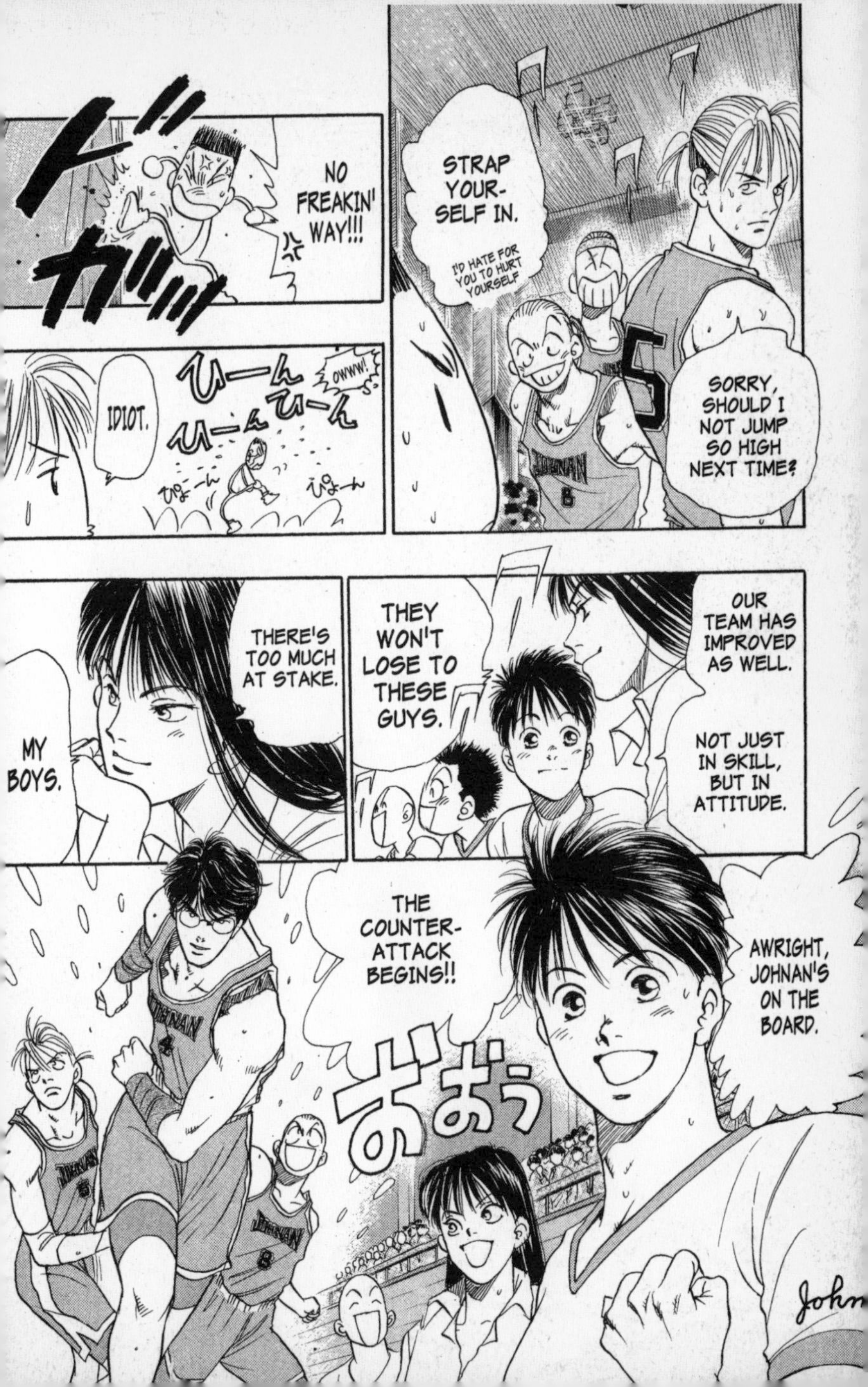
STRAP YOUR-SELF IN.
I'D HATE FOR YOU TO HURT YOURSELF
SORRY, SHOULD I NOT JUMP SO HIGH NEXT TIME?
NO FREAKIN' WAY!!!
IDIOT.
ひーん ひーん ひーん
OWWW!
ぴょーん ぴょーん
OUR TEAM HAS IMPROVED AS WELL.
THEY WON'T LOSE TO THESE GUYS.
NOT JUST IN SKILL, BUT IN ATTITUDE.
THERE'S TOO MUCH AT STAKE.
MY BOYS.
AWRIGHT, JOHNAN'S ON THE BOARD.
THE COUNTER-ATTACK BEGINS!!
おおう

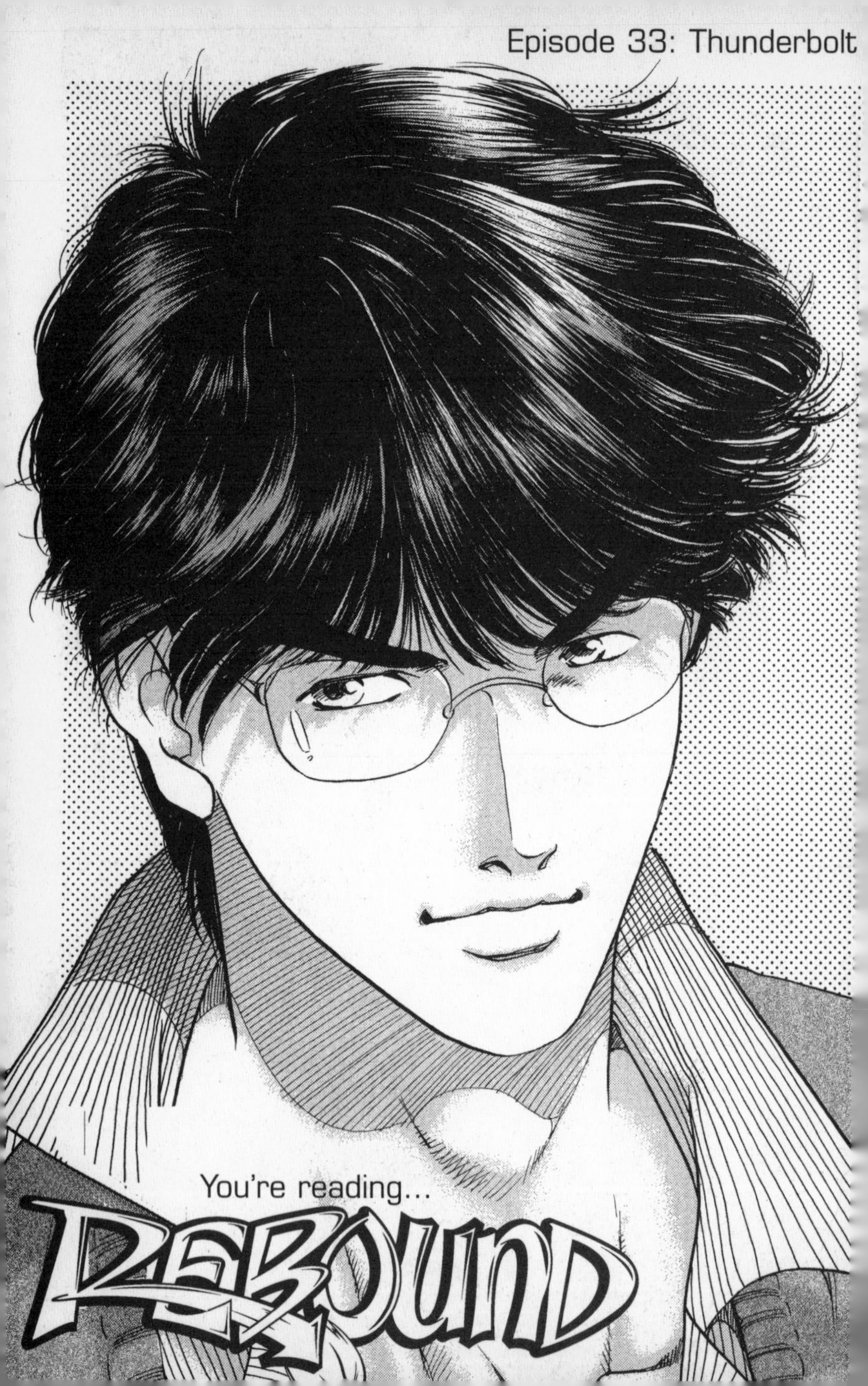
Episode 33: Thunderbolt
You're reading...
REBOUND

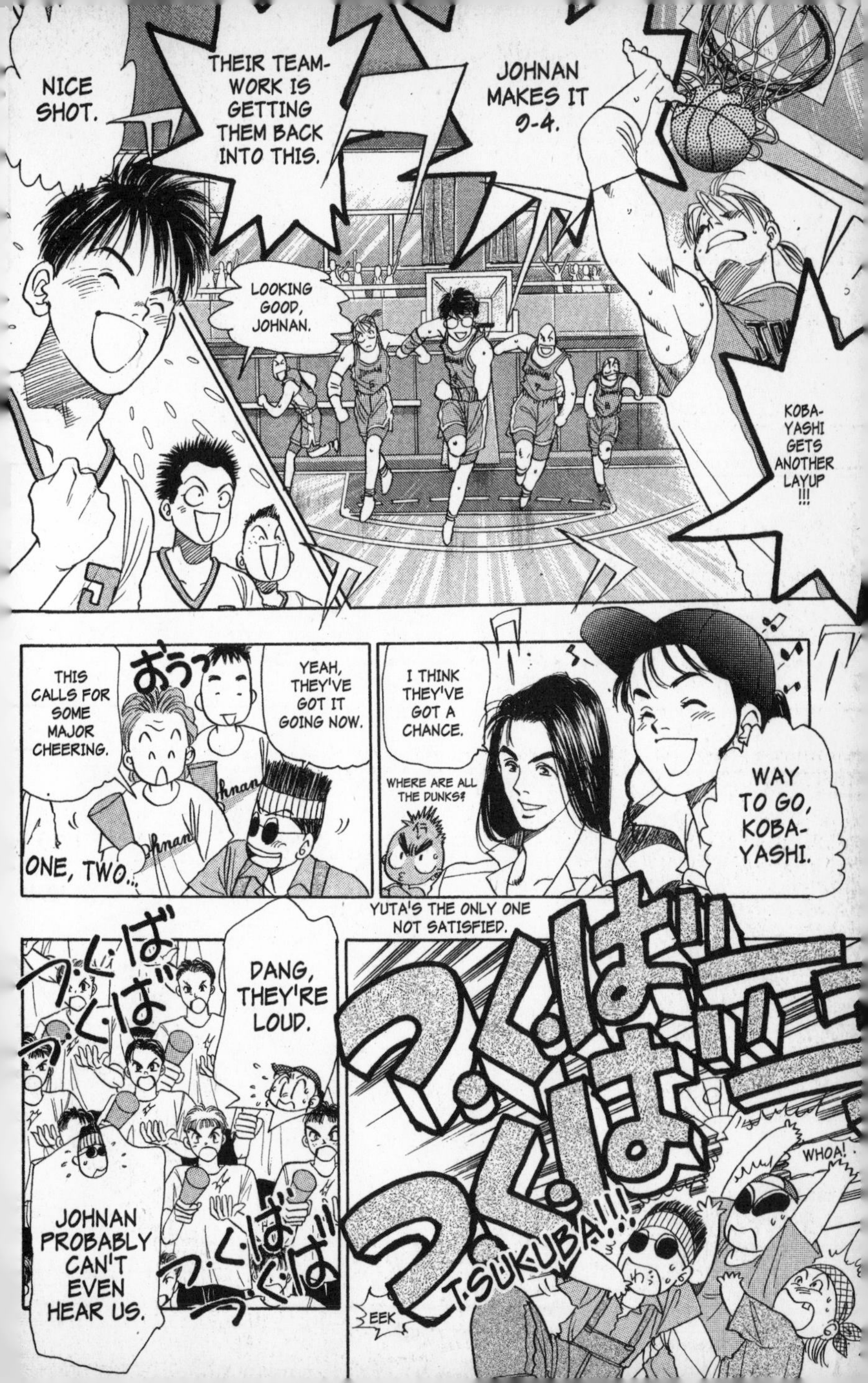
JOHNAN MAKES IT 9-4.
KOBA-YASHI GETS ANOTHER LAYUP!!!
THEIR TEAM-WORK IS GETTING THEM BACK INTO THIS.
NICE SHOT.
LOOKING GOOD, JOHNAN.
WAY TO GO, KOBA-YASHI.
I THINK THEY'VE GOT A CHANCE.
WHERE ARE ALL THE DUNKS?
YUTA'S THE ONLY ONE NOT SATISFIED.
YEAH, THEY'VE GOT IT GOING NOW.
おうっ
THIS CALLS FOR SOME MAJOR CHEERING.
ONE, TWO...
つ・く・ば つ・く・ば
TSUKUBA!!!
WHOA!
EEK
つくば つくば
DANG, THEY'RE LOUD.
JOHNAN PROBABLY CAN'T EVEN HEAR US.
つくば つくば

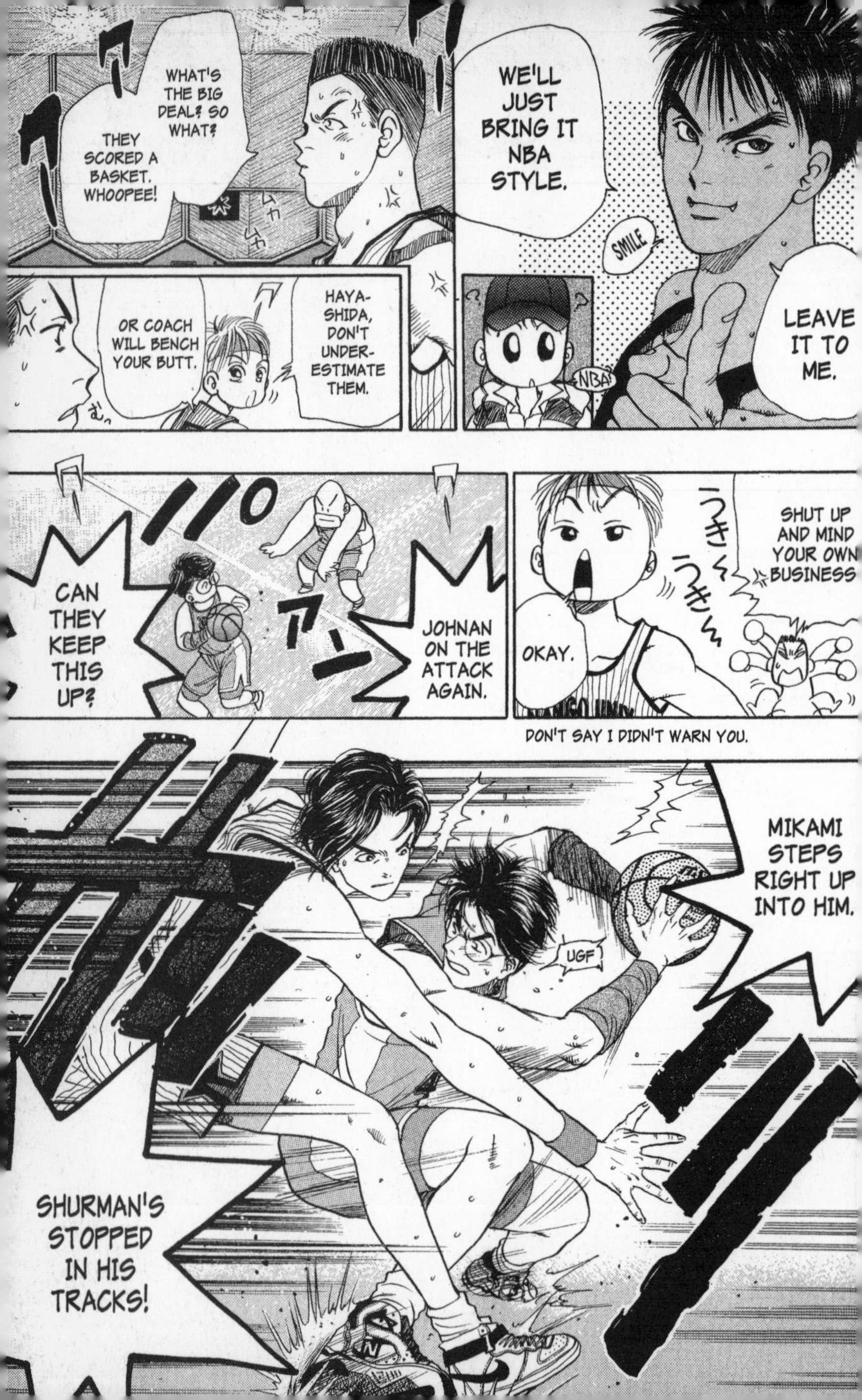
WE'LL JUST BRING IT NBA STYLE.
SMILE
LEAVE IT TO ME.
NBA!
WHAT'S THE BIG DEAL? SO WHAT?
THEY SCORED A BASKET. WHOOPEE!
HAYA-SHIDA, DON'T UNDER-ESTIMATE THEM.
OR COACH WILL BENCH YOUR BUTT.
SHUT UP AND MIND YOUR OWN BUSINESS
OKAY.
DON'T SAY I DIDN'T WARN YOU.
JOHNAN ON THE ATTACK AGAIN.
CAN THEY KEEP THIS UP?
MIKAMI STEPS RIGHT UP INTO HIM.
UGF
SHURMAN'S STOPPED IN HIS TRACKS!

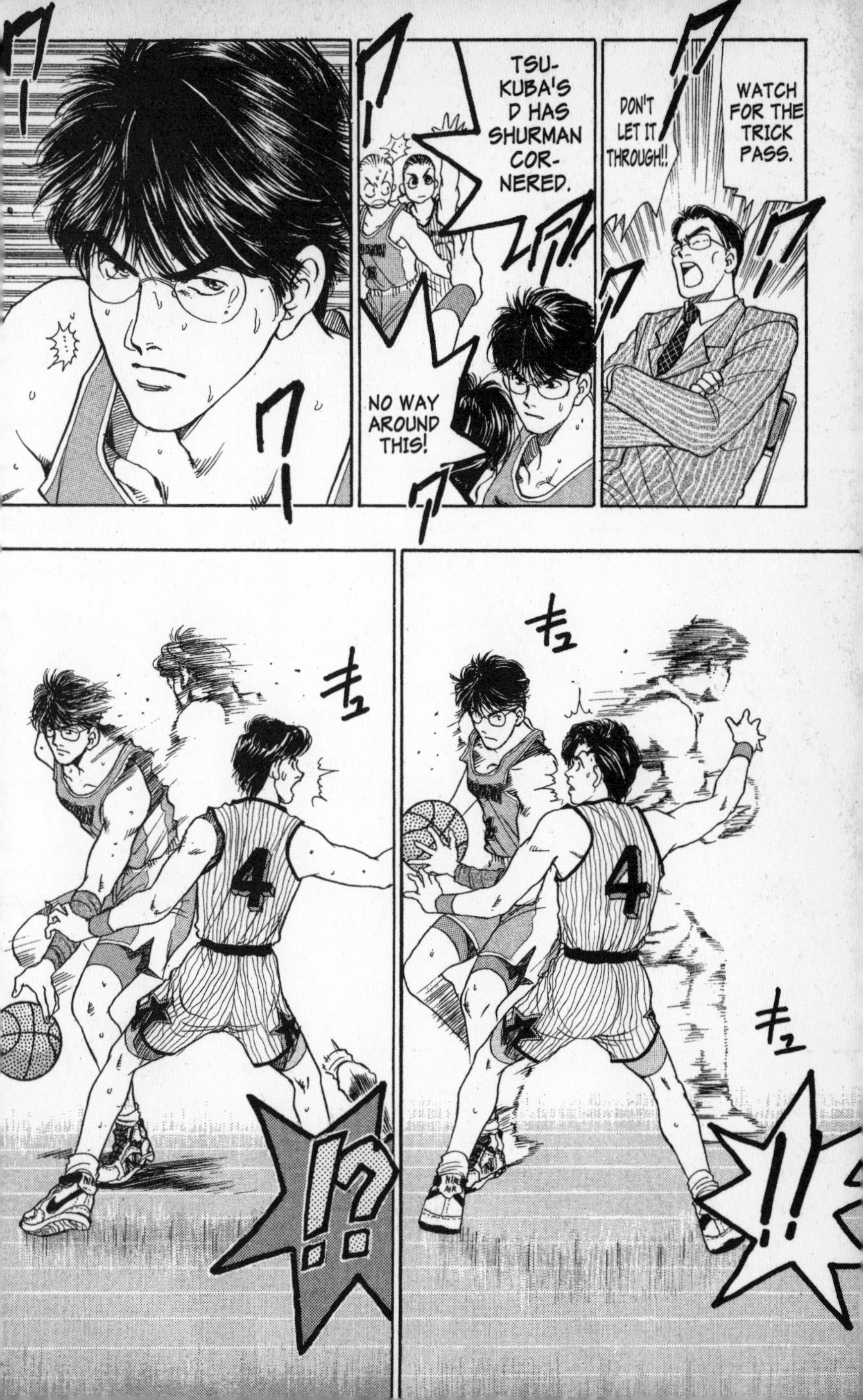
WATCH FOR THE TRICK PASS.
DON'T LET IT THROUGH!!
TSU-KUBA'S D HAS SHURMAN COR-NERED.
NO WAY AROUND THIS!
キュ
キュ
!!
キュ
!?

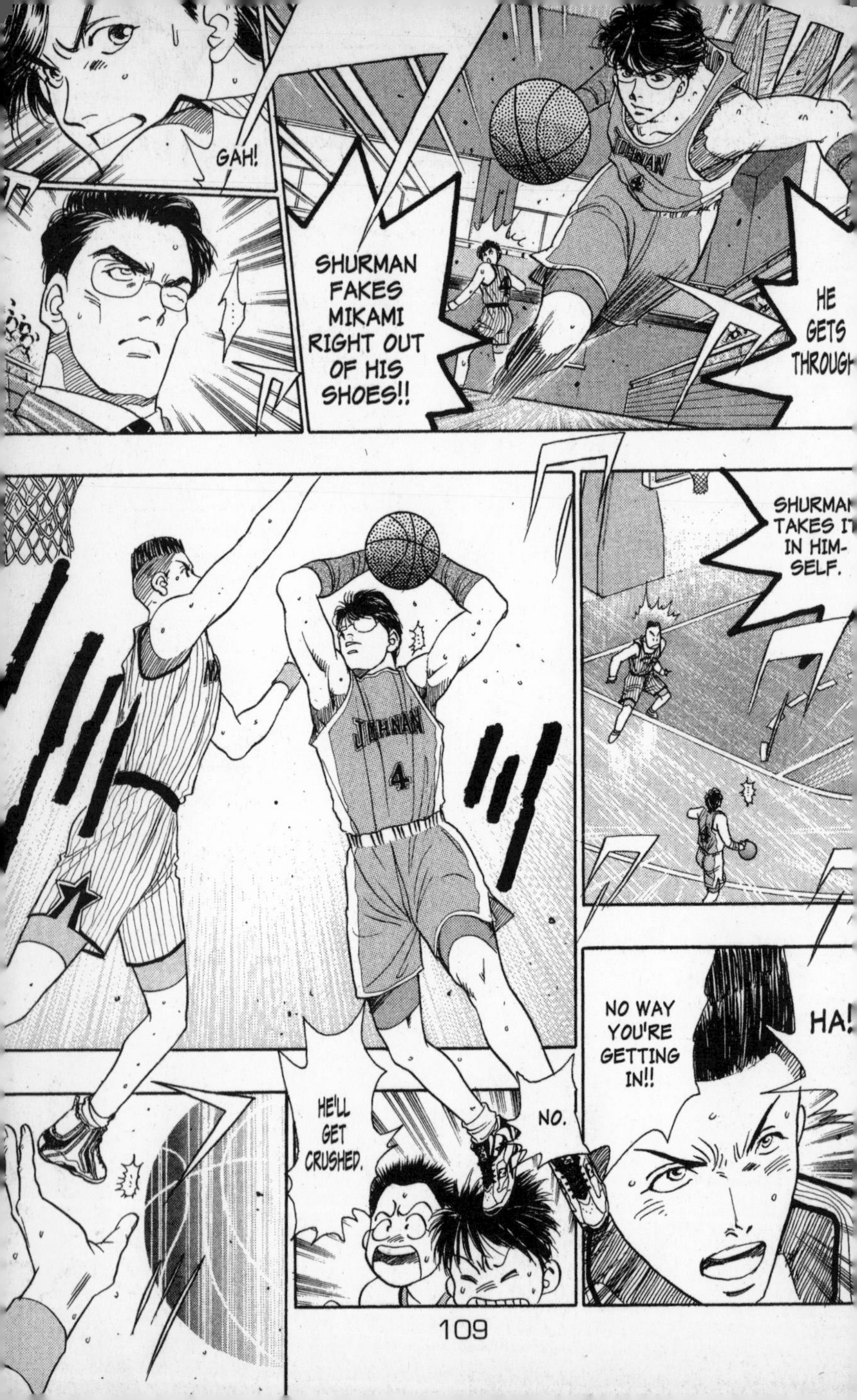

HE GETS THROUGH
SHURMAN FAKES MIKAMI RIGHT OUT OF HIS SHOES!!
GAH!
SHURMAN TAKES IT IN HIM-SELF.
HA!
NO WAY YOU'RE GETTING IN!!
NO.
HE'LL GET CRUSHED.

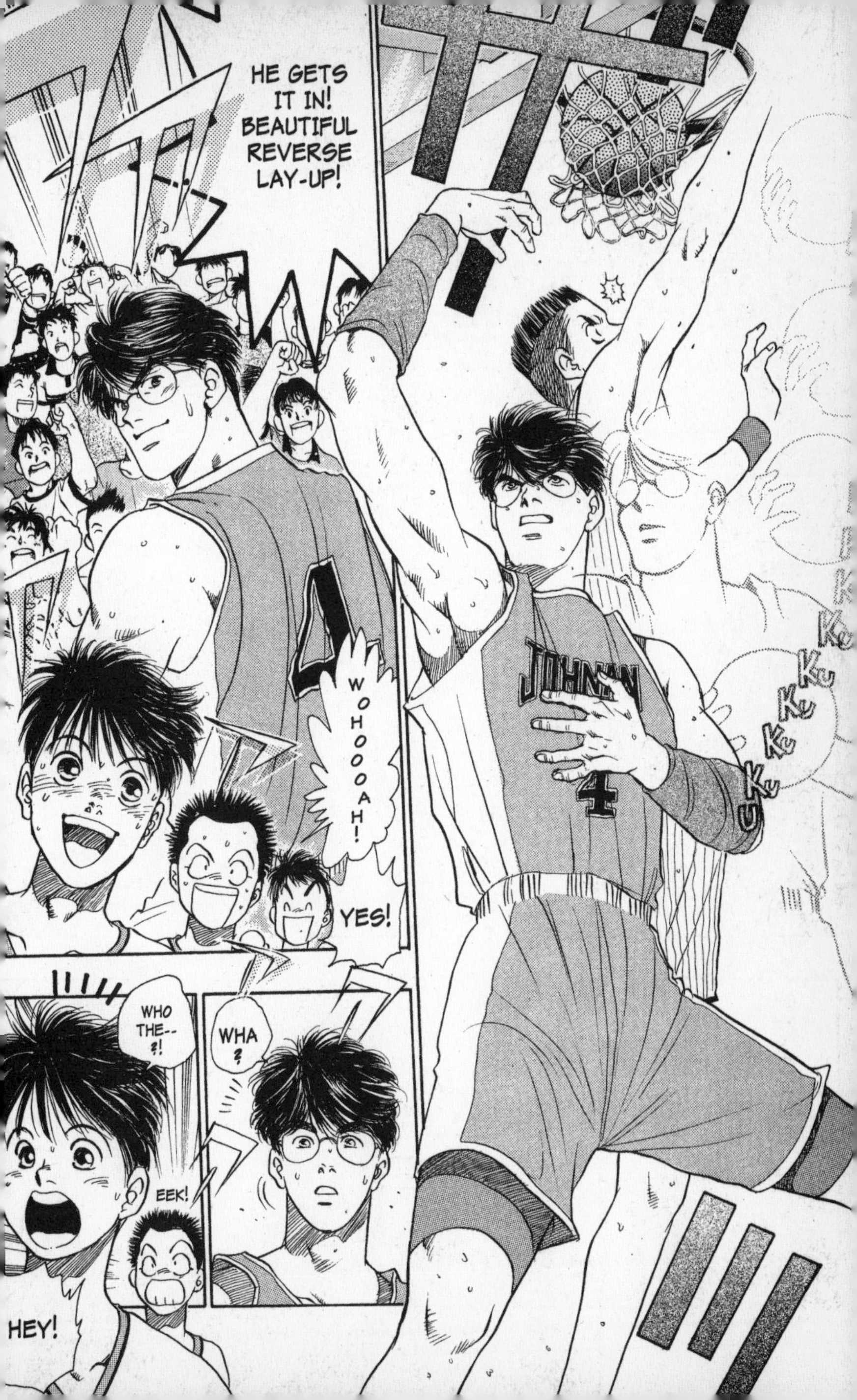
KUKUKUKUKUKU
HE GETS IT IN! BEAUTIFUL REVERSE LAY-UP!
WOHOOOAH!
YES!
WHA?
WHO THE--?!
EEK!
HEY!

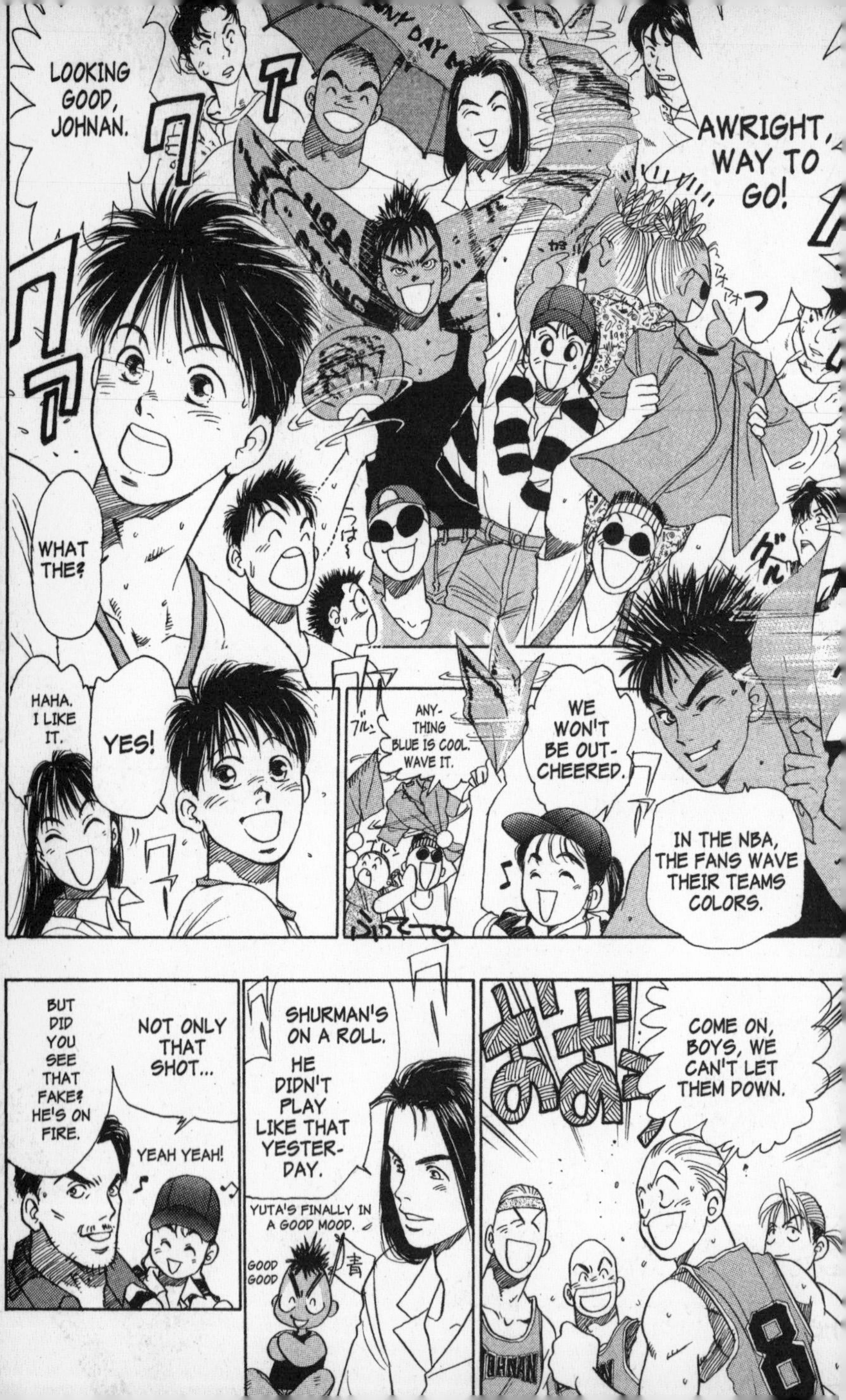
AWRIGHT, WAY TO GO!
LOOKING GOOD, JOHNAN.
WHAT THE?
IN THE NBA, THE FANS WAVE THEIR TEAMS COLORS.
WE WON'T BE OUT-CHEERED.
ANY-THING BLUE IS COOL. WAVE IT.
YES!
HAHA. I LIKE IT.
COME ON, BOYS, WE CAN'T LET THEM DOWN.
SHURMAN'S ON A ROLL.
HE DIDN'T PLAY LIKE THAT YESTER-DAY.
YUTA'S FINALLY IN A GOOD MOOD.
GOOD GOOD
NOT ONLY THAT SHOT...
BUT DID YOU SEE THAT FAKE? HE'S ON FIRE.
YEAH YEAH!

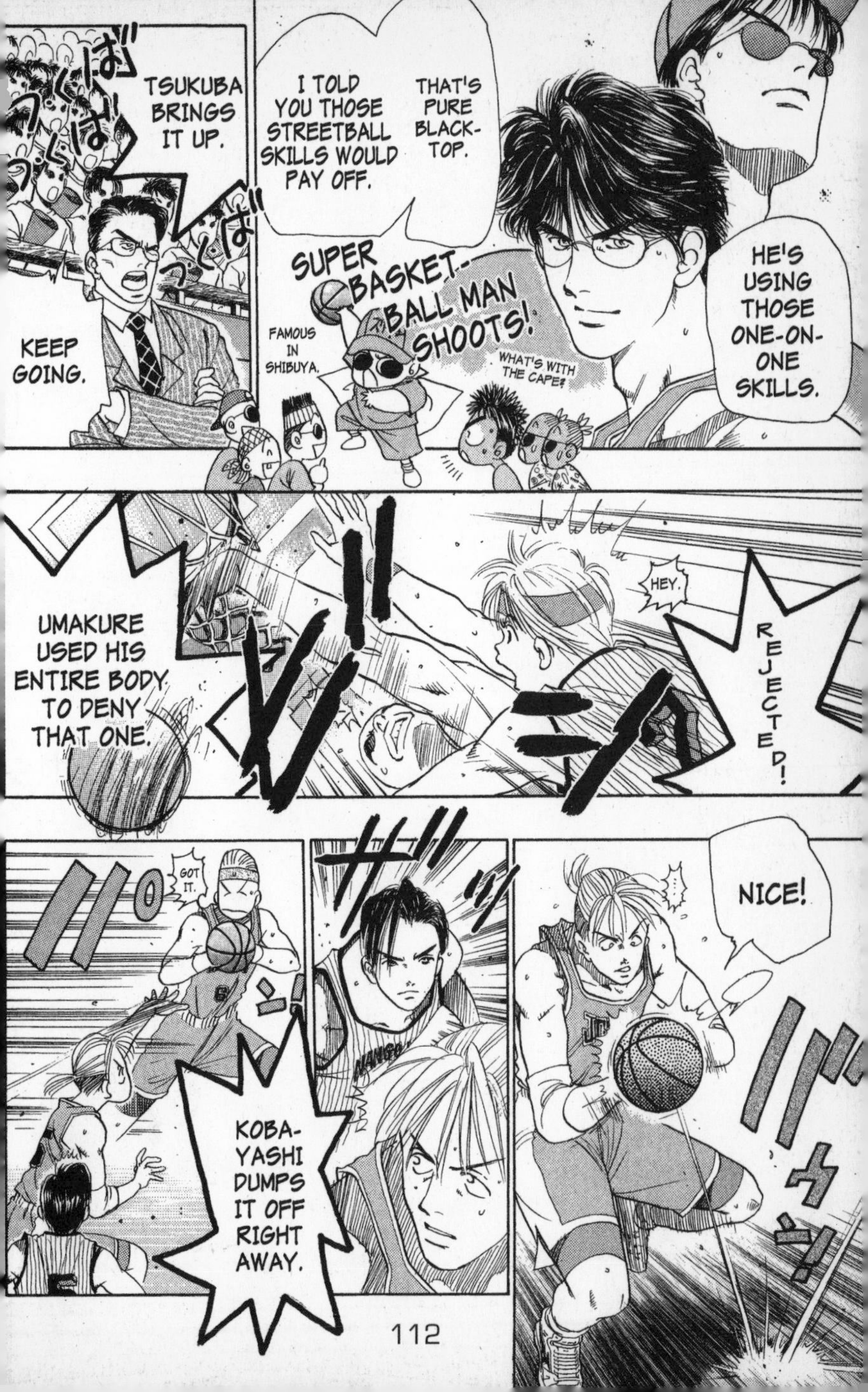
HE'S USING THOSE ONE-ON-ONE SKILLS.
THAT'S PURE BLACK-TOP.
I TOLD YOU THOSE STREETBALL SKILLS WOULD PAY OFF.
SUPER BASKET-BALL MAN SHOOTS!
FAMOUS IN SHIBUYA.
WHAT'S WITH THE CAPE?
TSUKUBA BRINGS IT UP.
KEEP GOING.
HEY.
REJECTED!
UMAKURE USED HIS ENTIRE BODY TO DENY THAT ONE.
NICE!
KOBA-YASHI DUMPS IT OFF RIGHT AWAY.
GOT IT.

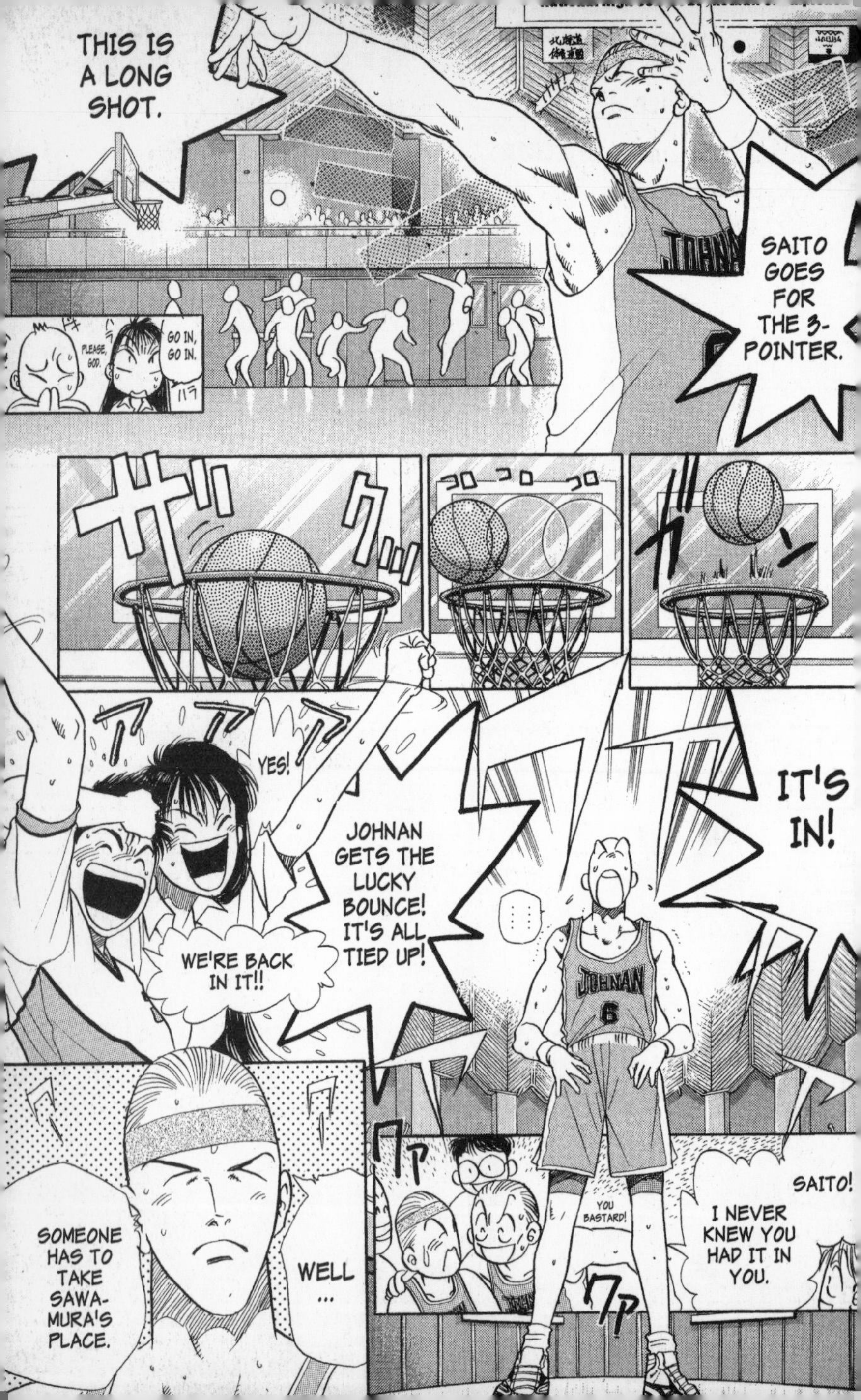

SAITO GOES FOR THE 3-POINTER.
THIS IS A LONG SHOT.
GO IN, GO IN.
PLEASE, GOD.
コロ コロ コロ
IT'S IN!
JOHNAN GETS THE LUCKY BOUNCE! IT'S ALL TIED UP!
......
YES!
WE'RE BACK IN IT!!
SAITO!
I NEVER KNEW YOU HAD IT IN YOU.
YOU BASTARD!
WELL ...
SOMEONE HAS TO TAKE SAWAMURA'S PLACE.

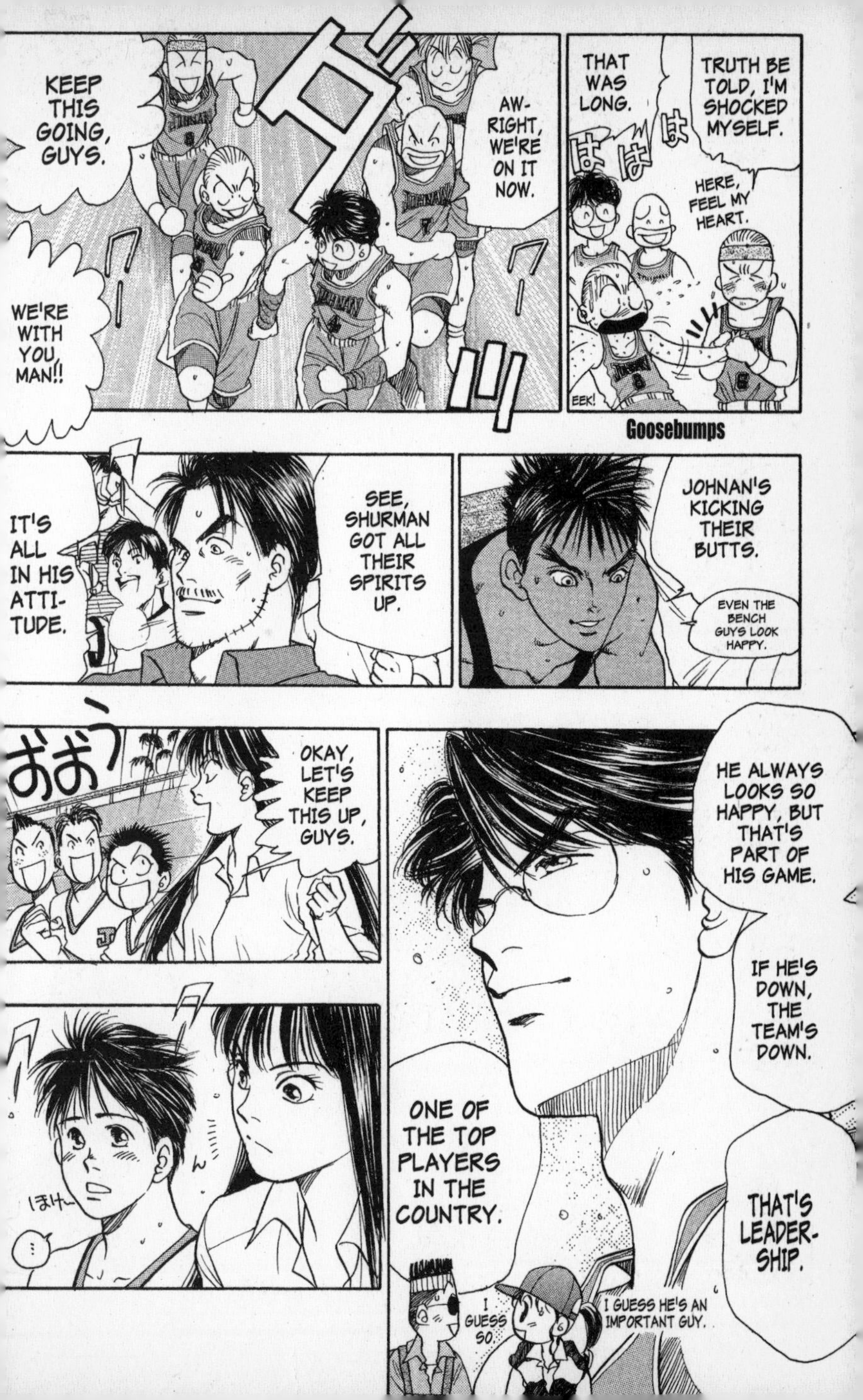
TRUTH BE TOLD, I'M SHOCKED MYSELF.
THAT WAS LONG.
はは
HERE, FEEL MY HEART.
EEK!
Goosebumps
AW-RIGHT, WE'RE ON IT NOW.
ダッ
KEEP THIS GOING, GUYS.
WE'RE WITH YOU, MAN!!
JOHNAN'S KICKING THEIR BUTTS.
EVEN THE BENCH GUYS LOOK HAPPY.
SEE, SHURMAN GOT ALL THEIR SPIRITS UP.
IT'S ALL IN HIS ATTITUDE.
HE ALWAYS LOOKS SO HAPPY, BUT THAT'S PART OF HIS GAME.
IF HE'S DOWN, THE TEAM'S DOWN.
THAT'S LEADER-SHIP.
ONE OF THE TOP PLAYERS IN THE COUNTRY.
I GUESS HE'S AN IMPORTANT GUY.
I GUESS SO.
OKAY, LET'S KEEP THIS UP, GUYS.
おおう
ん
ほけ~
...

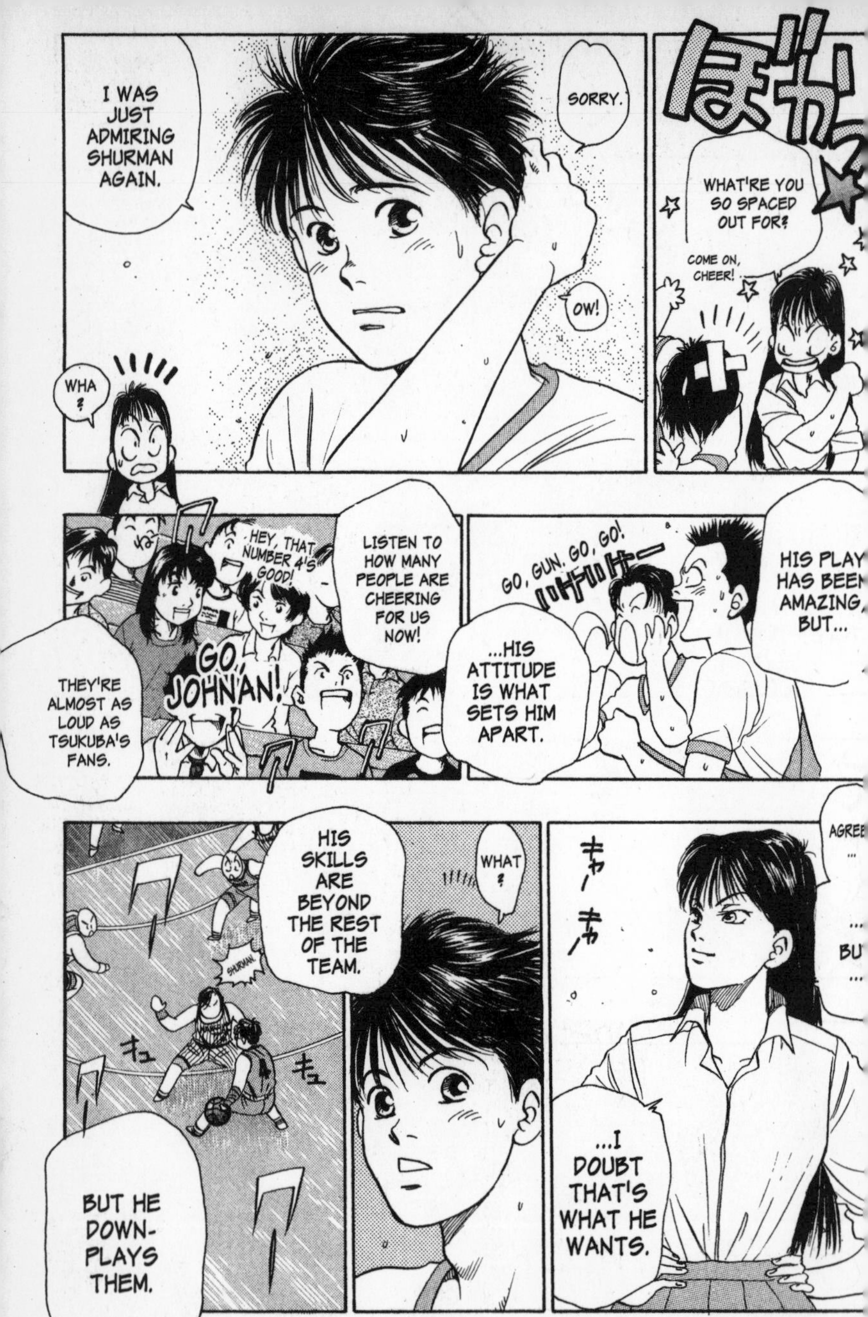
WHAT'RE YOU SO SPACED OUT FOR?
COME ON, CHEER!
SORRY.
I WAS JUST ADMIRING SHURMAN AGAIN.
OW!
WHA?
HIS PLAY HAS BEEN AMAZING, BUT...
GO, GUN. GO, GO!
...HIS ATTITUDE IS WHAT SETS HIM APART.
LISTEN TO HOW MANY PEOPLE ARE CHEERING FOR US NOW!
HEY, THAT NUMBER 4'S GOOD!
GO, JOHNAN!
THEY'RE ALMOST AS LOUD AS TSUKUBA'S FANS.
...I DOUBT THAT'S WHAT HE WANTS.
WHAT?
HIS SKILLS ARE BEYOND THE REST OF THE TEAM.
SHURMAN
BUT HE DOWN-PLAYS THEM.

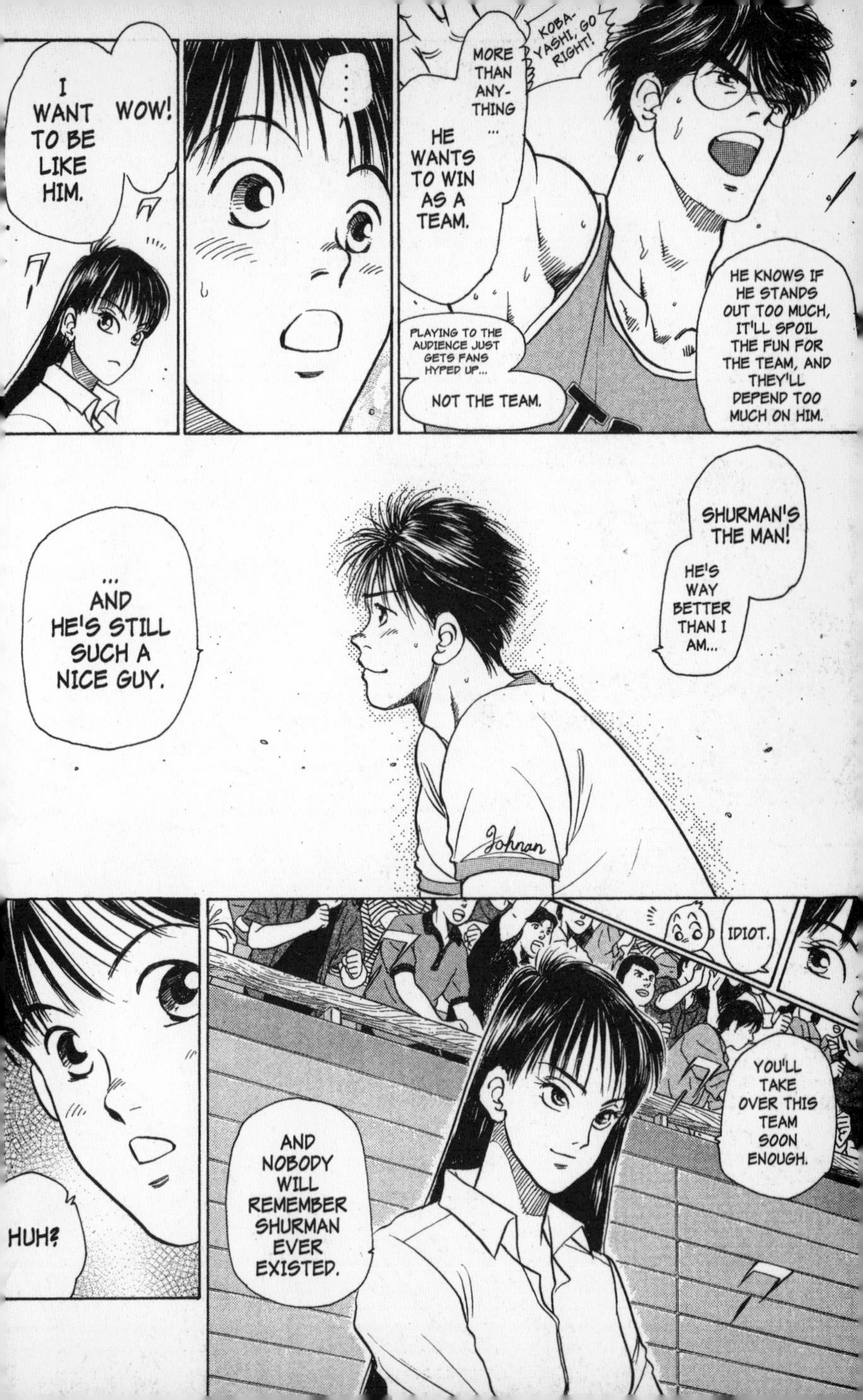
KOBA-YASHI, GO RIGHT!
MORE THAN ANYTHING...
HE WANTS TO WIN AS A TEAM.
HE KNOWS IF HE STANDS OUT TOO MUCH, IT'LL SPOIL THE FUN FOR THE TEAM, AND THEY'LL DEPEND TOO MUCH ON HIM.
PLAYING TO THE AUDIENCE JUST GETS FANS HYPED UP...
NOT THE TEAM.
......
WOW!
I WANT TO BE LIKE HIM.
SHURMAN'S THE MAN!
HE'S WAY BETTER THAN I AM...
...AND HE'S STILL SUCH A NICE GUY.
Johnan
IDIOT.
YOU'LL TAKE OVER THIS TEAM SOON ENOUGH.
AND NOBODY WILL REMEMBER SHURMAN EVER EXISTED.
HUH?

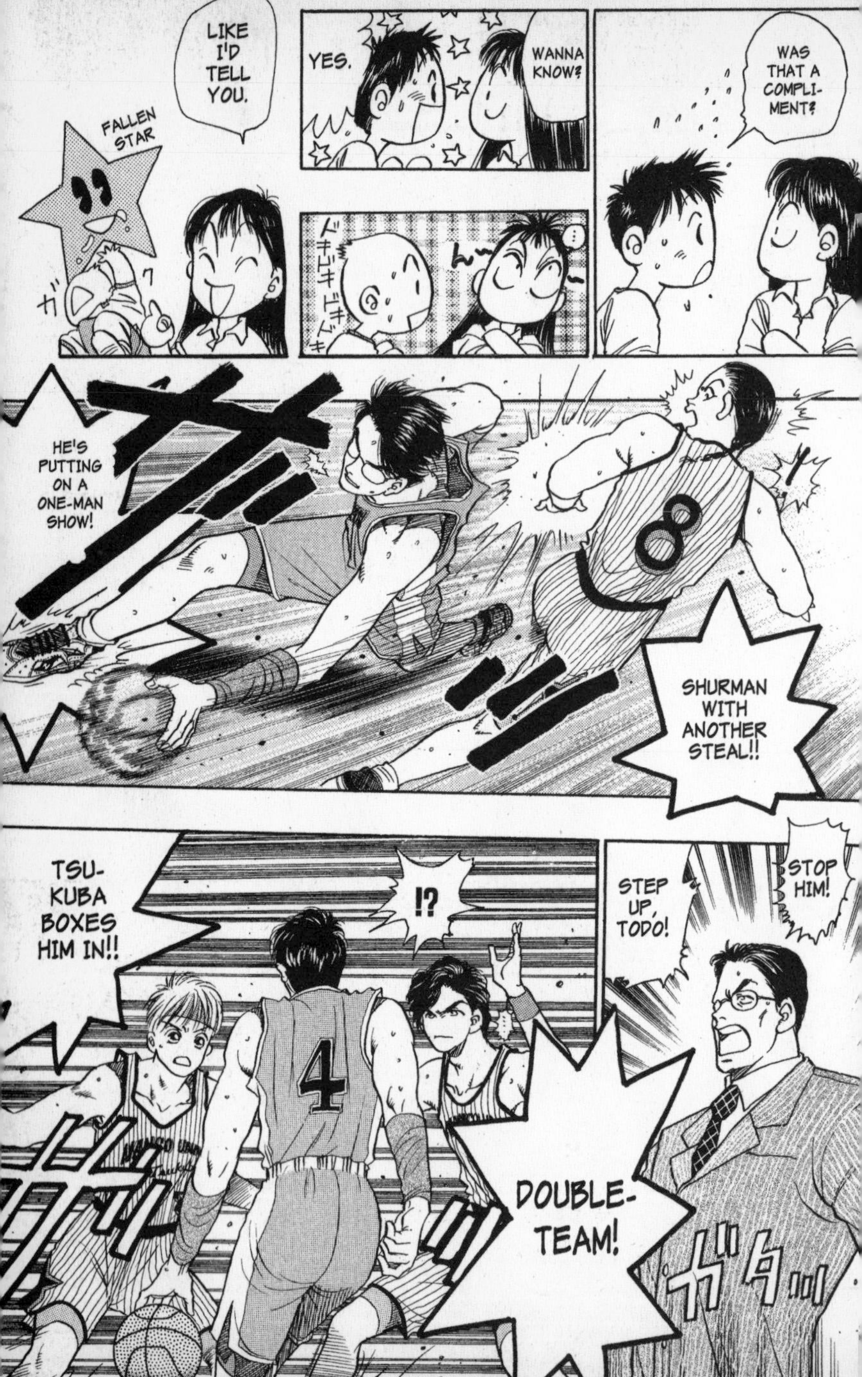
WAS THAT A COMPLIMENT?
WANNA KNOW?
YES.
LIKE I'D TELL YOU.
FALLEN STAR
SHURMAN WITH ANOTHER STEAL!!
HE'S PUTTING ON A ONE-MAN SHOW!
STOP HIM!
STEP UP, TODO!
DOUBLE-TEAM!
!?
TSU-KUBA BOXES HIM IN!!

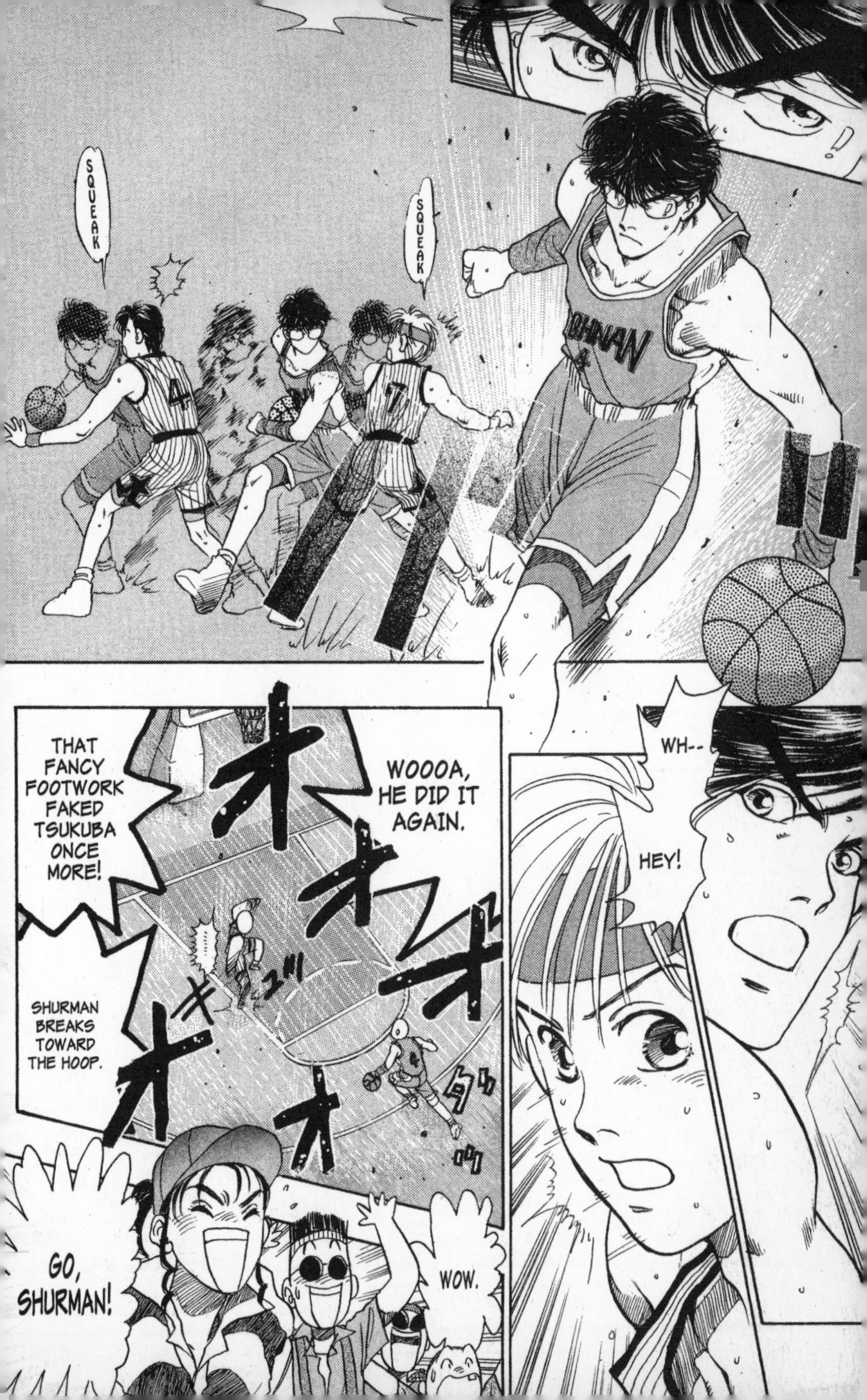
SQUEAK
SQUEAK
WH--
HEY!
WOOOA, HE DID IT AGAIN.
THAT FANCY FOOTWORK FAKED TSUKUBA ONCE MORE!
SHURMAN BREAKS TOWARD THE HOOP.
WOW.
GO, SHURMAN!

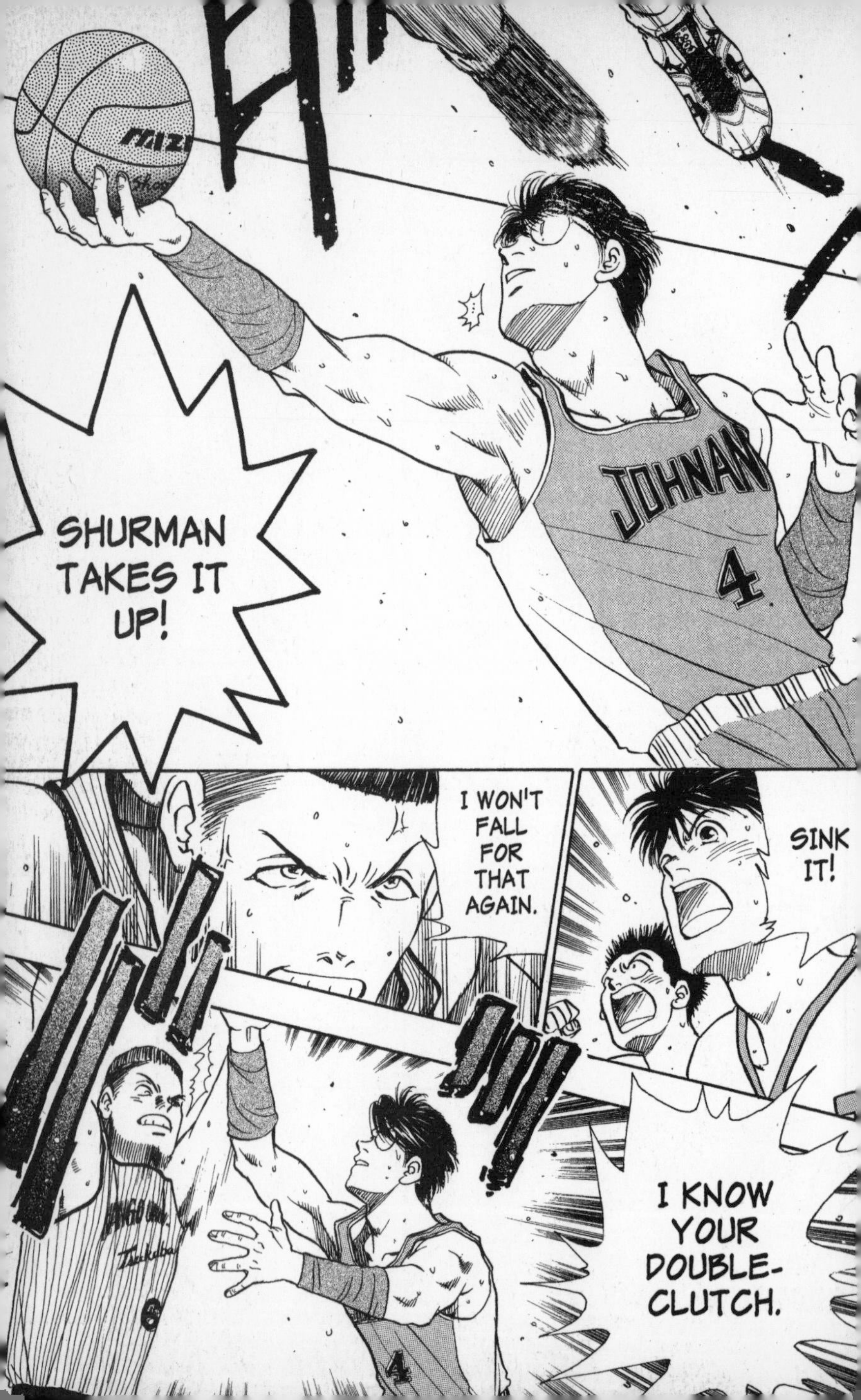
SHURMAN TAKES IT UP!
SINK IT!
I WON'T FALL FOR THAT AGAIN.
I KNOW YOUR DOUBLE-CLUTCH.
JOHNAN

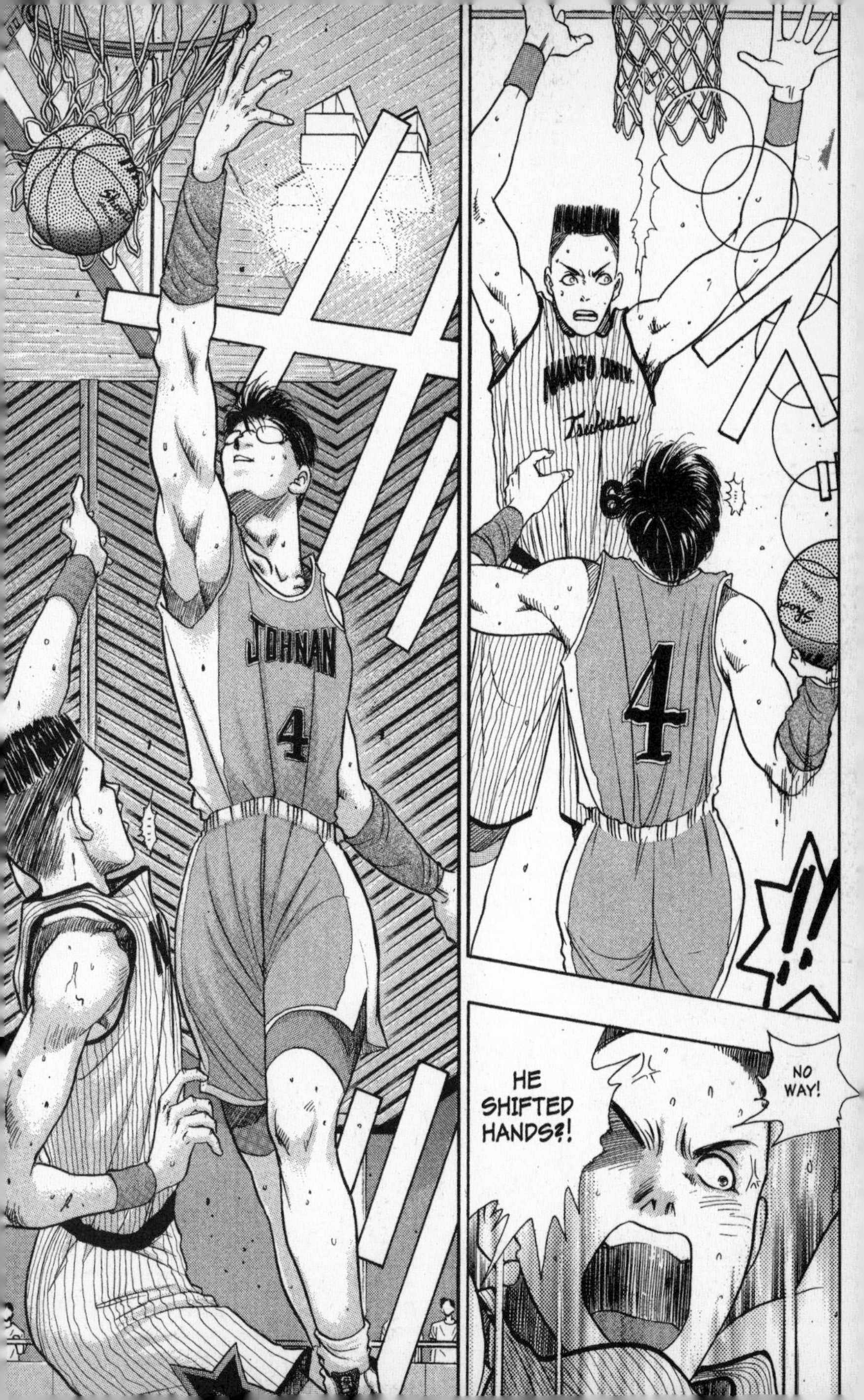
!!
NO WAY!
HE SHIFTED HANDS?!

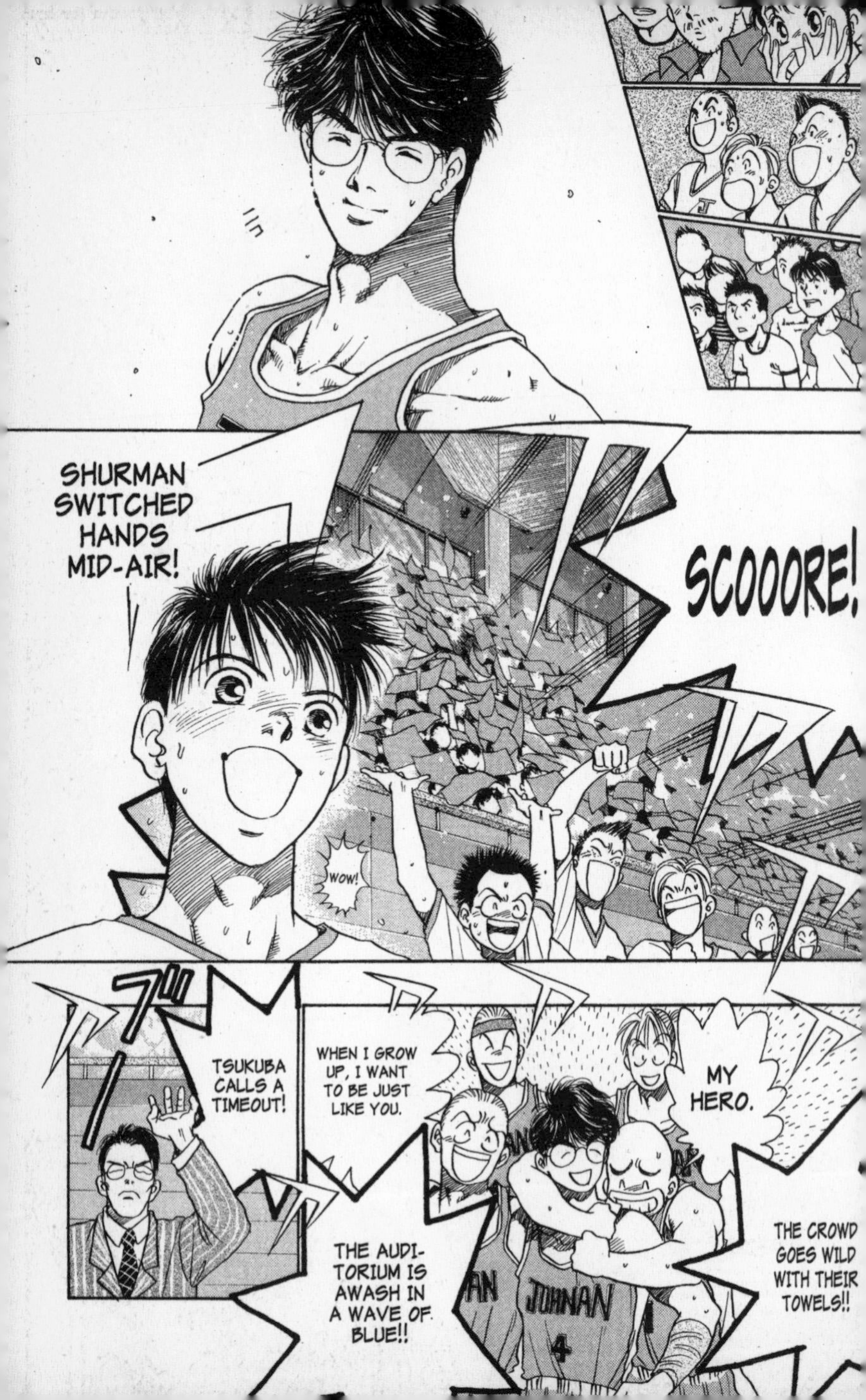
SCOOORE!
SHURMAN SWITCHED HANDS MID-AIR!
WOW!
MY HERO.
WHEN I GROW UP, I WANT TO BE JUST LIKE YOU.
THE CROWD GOES WILD WITH THEIR TOWELS!!
JOHNAN
THE AUDITORIUM IS AWASH IN A WAVE OF BLUE!!
TSUKUBA CALLS A TIMEOUT!
ブッ

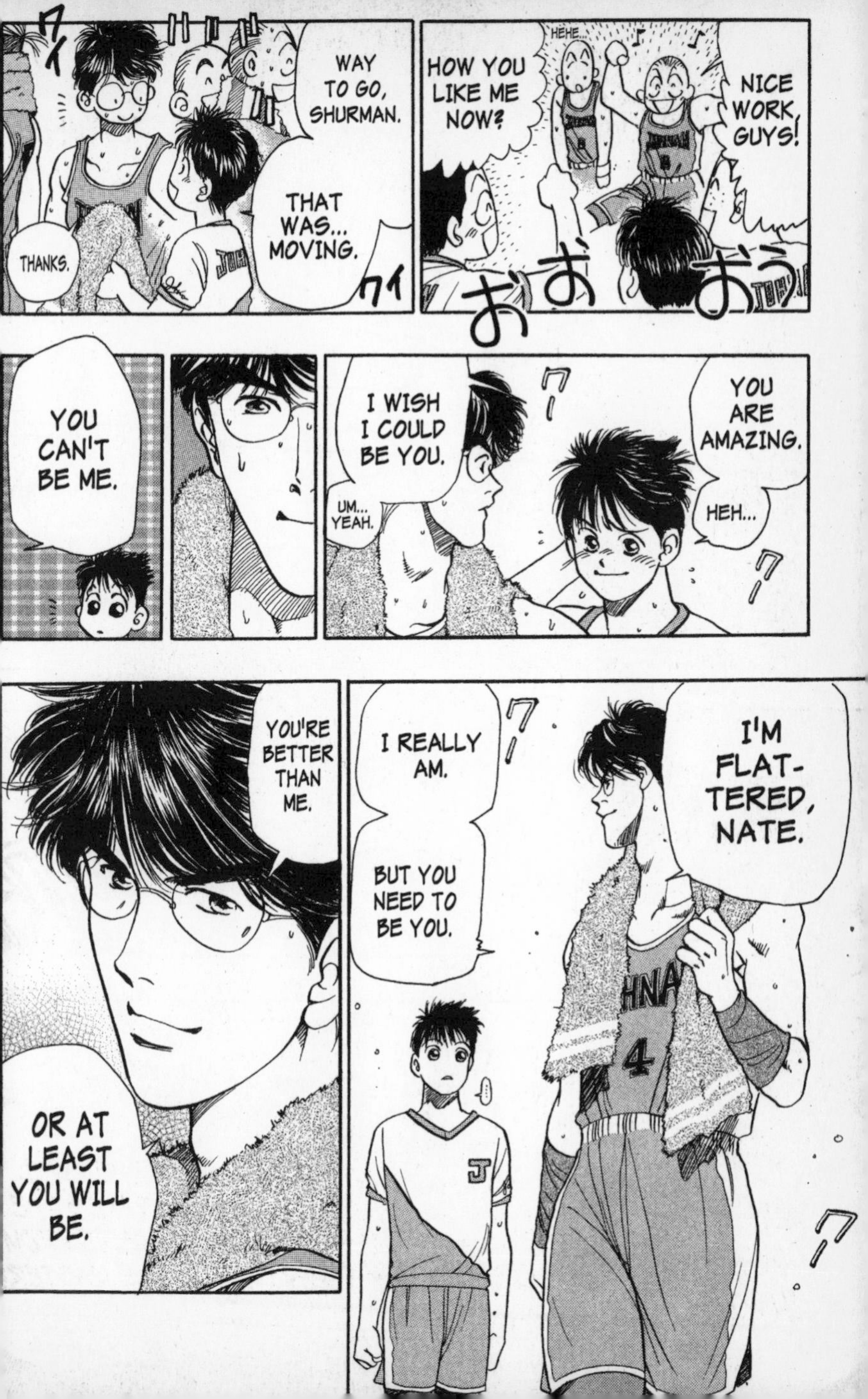
NICE WORK, GUYS!
HEHE...
HOW YOU LIKE ME NOW?
おおおう
WAY TO GO, SHURMAN.
ワイ
THAT WAS... MOVING.
THANKS.
ワイ
YOU ARE AMAZING.
HEH...
I WISH I COULD BE YOU.
UM... YEAH.
YOU CAN'T BE ME.
I'M FLATTERED, NATE.
I REALLY AM.
BUT YOU NEED TO BE YOU.
YOU'RE BETTER THAN ME.
OR AT LEAST YOU WILL BE.

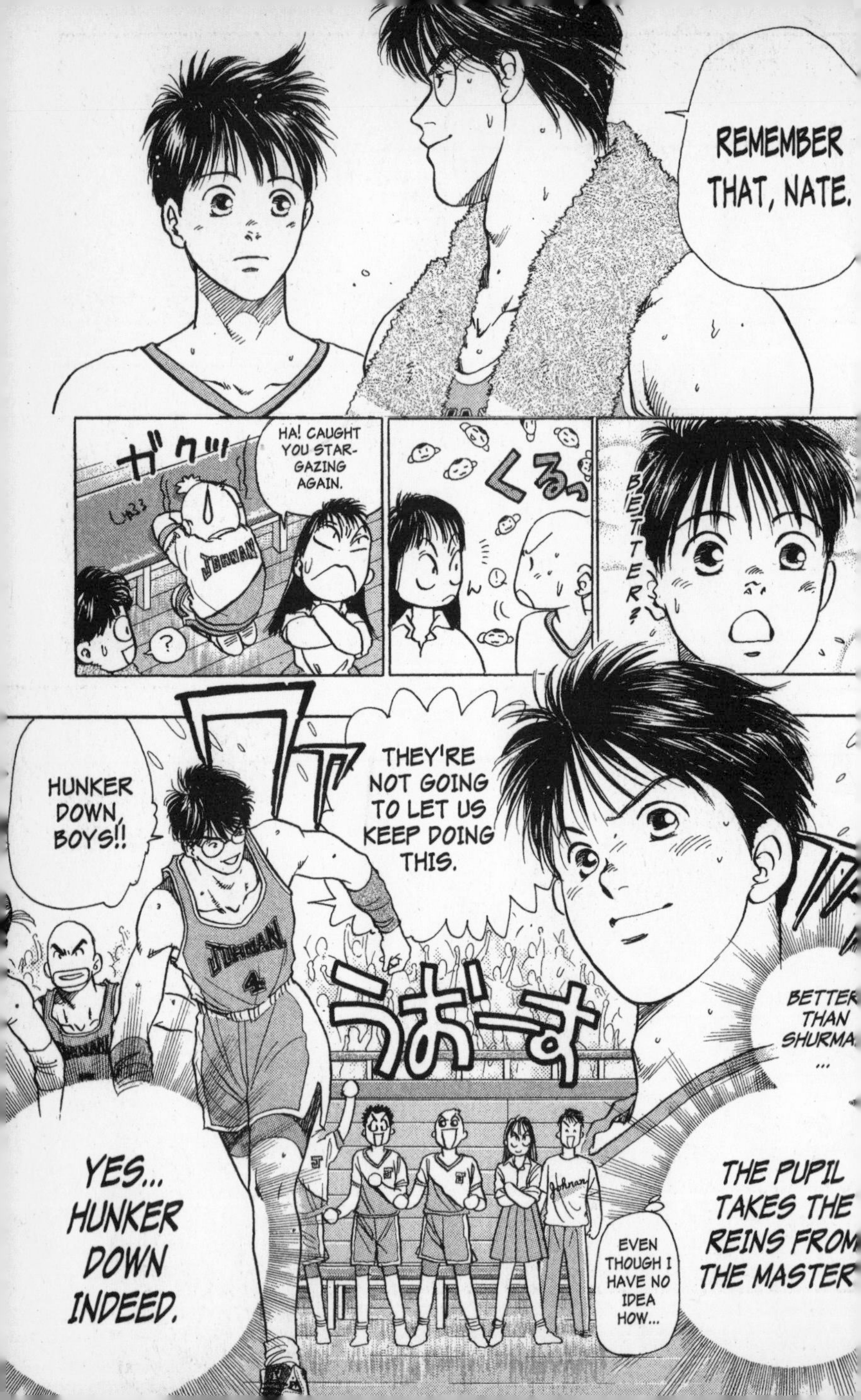
REMEMBER THAT, NATE.
BETTER?
くるっ
HA! CAUGHT YOU STAR-GAZING AGAIN.
ガクッ
?
BETTER THAN SHURMA...
THEY'RE NOT GOING TO LET US KEEP DOING THIS.
HUNKER DOWN, BOYS!!
うおーす
THE PUPIL TAKES THE REINS FROM THE MASTER
EVEN THOUGH I HAVE NO IDEA HOW...
YES... HUNKER DOWN INDEED.

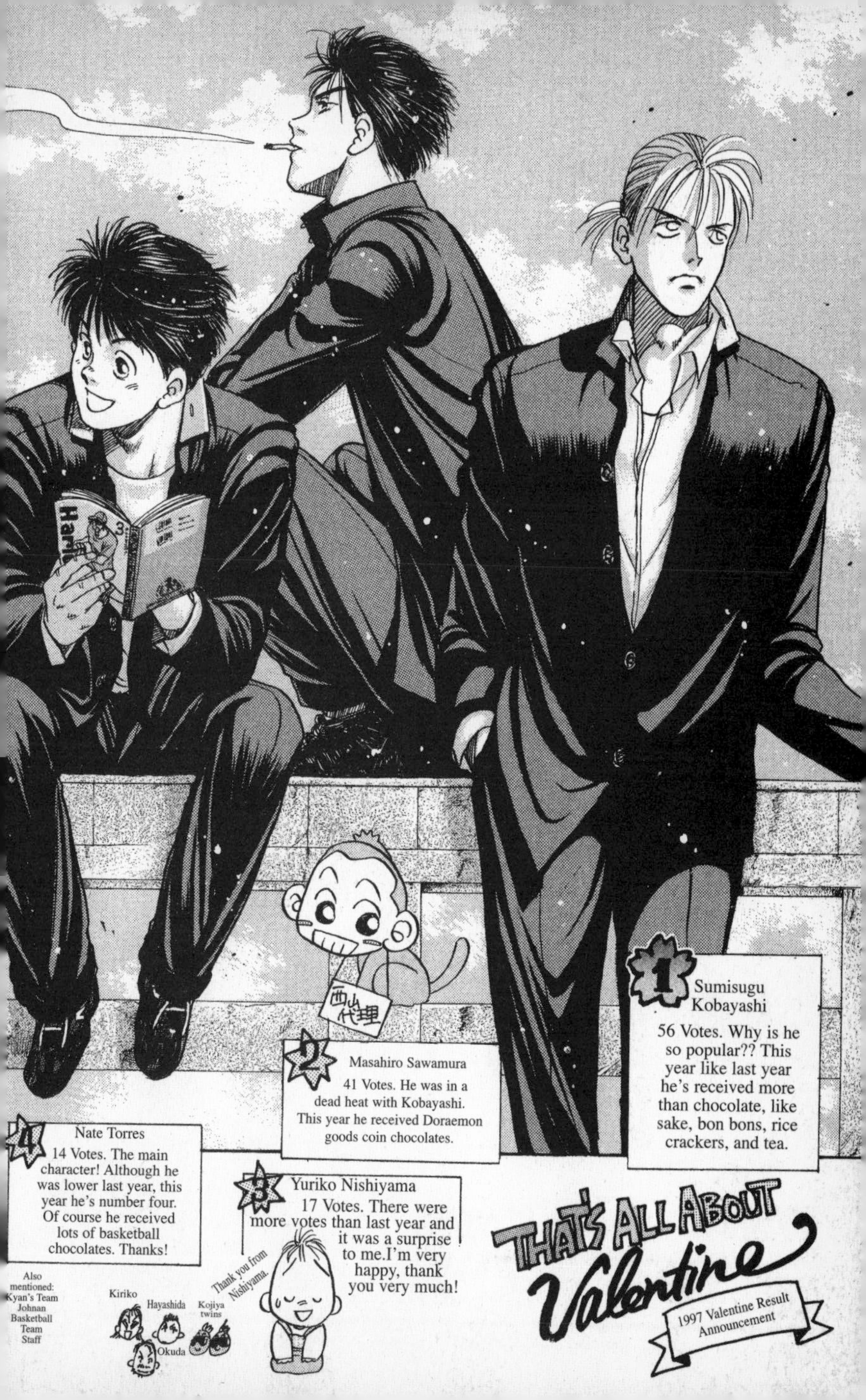
THAT'S ALL ABOUT Valentine
1997 Valentine Result Announcement
1 Sumisugu Kobayashi
56 Votes. Why is he so popular?? This year like last year he's received more than chocolate, like sake, bon bons, rice crackers, and tea.
2 Masahiro Sawamura
41 Votes. He was in a dead heat with Kobayashi. This year he received Doraemon goods coin chocolates.
西山代理
3 Yuriko Nishiyama
17 Votes. There were more votes than last year and it was a surprise to me. I'm very happy, thank you very much!
Thank you from Nishiyama.
4 Nate Torres
14 Votes. The main character! Although he was lower last year, this year he's number four. Of course he received lots of basketball chocolates. Thanks!
Also mentioned: Kyan's Team Johnan Basketball Team Staff
Kiriko
Hayashida
Kojiya twins
Okuda

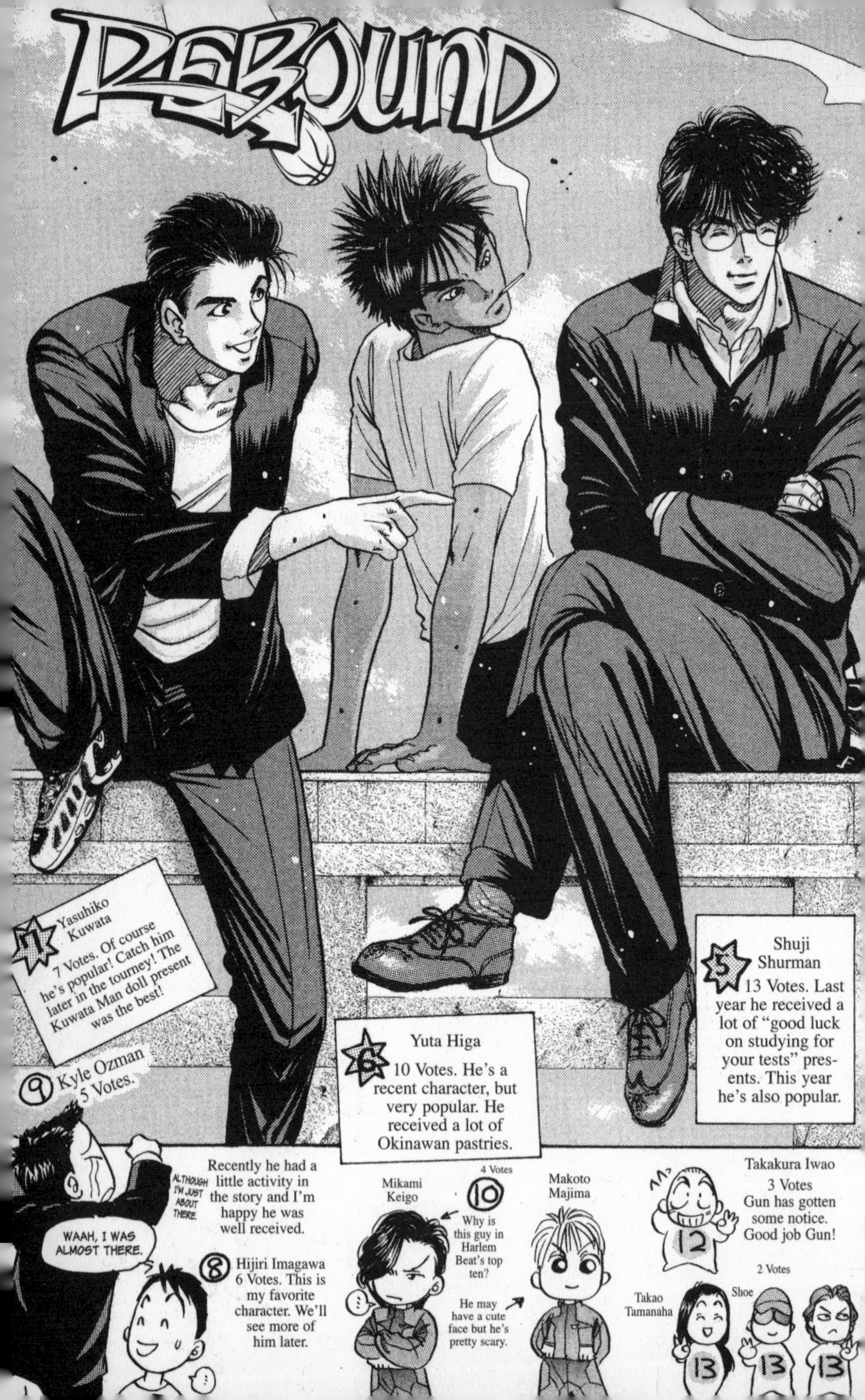

REBOUND
Shuji Shurman
5
13 Votes. Last year he received a lot of "good luck on studying for your tests" presents. This year he's also popular.
Yuta Higa
6
10 Votes. He's a recent character, but very popular. He received a lot of Okinawan pastries.
1
Yasuhiko Kuwata
7 Votes. Of course he's popular! Catch him later in the tourney! The Kuwata Man doll present was the best!
9 Kyle Ozman 5 Votes.
Takakura Iwao
3 Votes
Gun has gotten some notice. Good job Gun!
12
2 Votes
Shoe
Takao Tamanaha
13
13
13
Makoto Majima
He may have a cute face but he's pretty scary.
4 Votes
10
Mikami Keigo
Why is this guy in Harlem Beat's top ten?
Recently he had a little activity in the story and I'm happy he was well received.
ALTHOUGH I'M JUST ABOUT THERE.
WAAH, I WAS ALMOST THERE.
8 Hijiri Imagawa 6 Votes. This is my favorite character. We'll see more of him later.

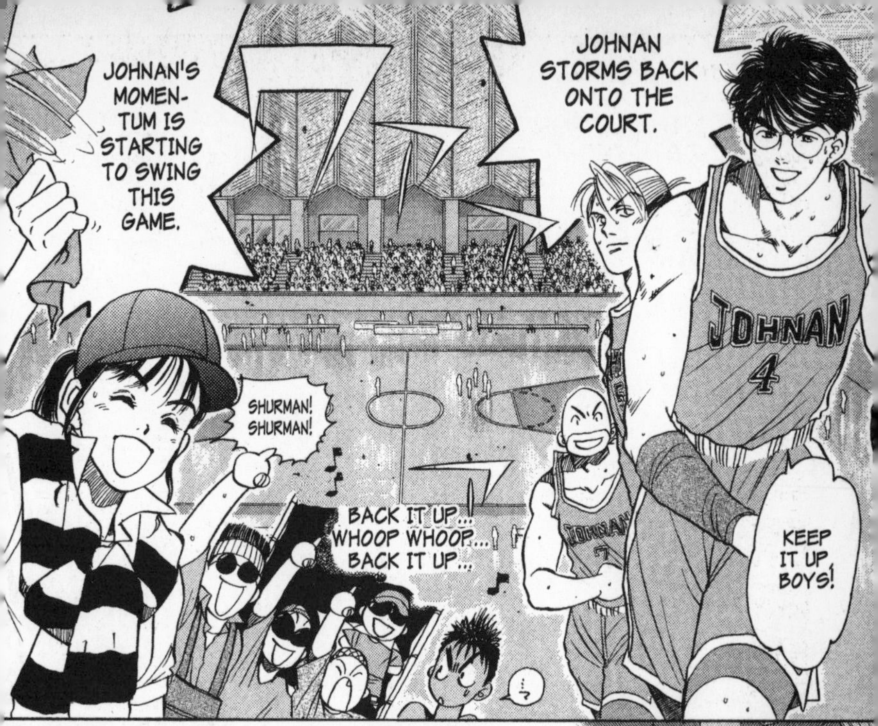
JOHNAN STORMS BACK ONTO THE COURT.
JOHNAN'S MOMEN-TUM IS STARTING TO SWING THIS GAME.
KEEP IT UP BOYS!
SHURMAN! SHURMAN!
BACK IT UP... WHOOP WHOOP... BACK IT UP...
...?

Episode 34: The Truth Is Out There

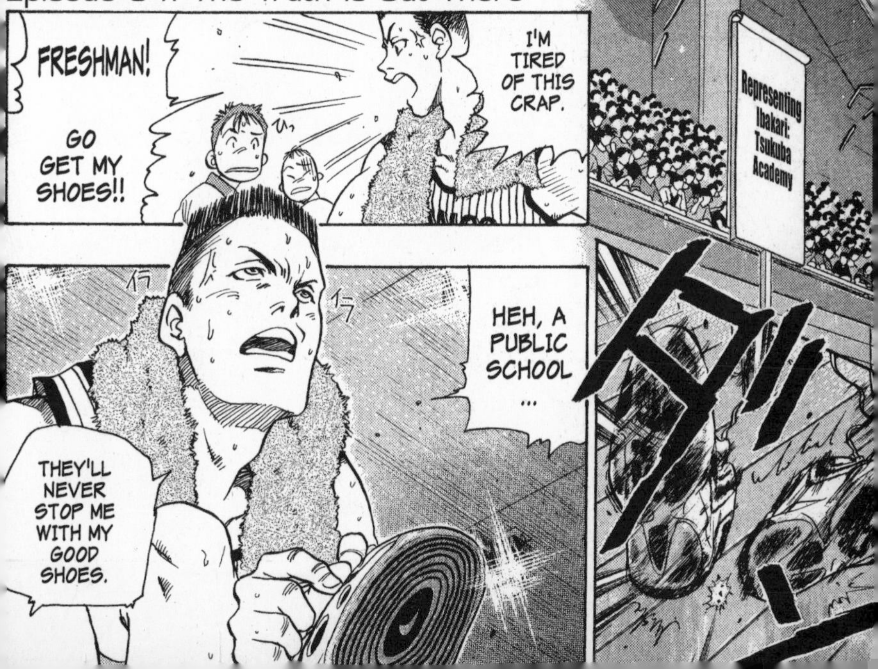
Representing Ibakari: Tsukuba Academy
I'M TIRED OF THIS CRAP.
FRESHMAN!
GO GET MY SHOES!!
HEH, A PUBLIC SCHOOL ...
THEY'LL NEVER STOP ME WITH MY GOOD SHOES.

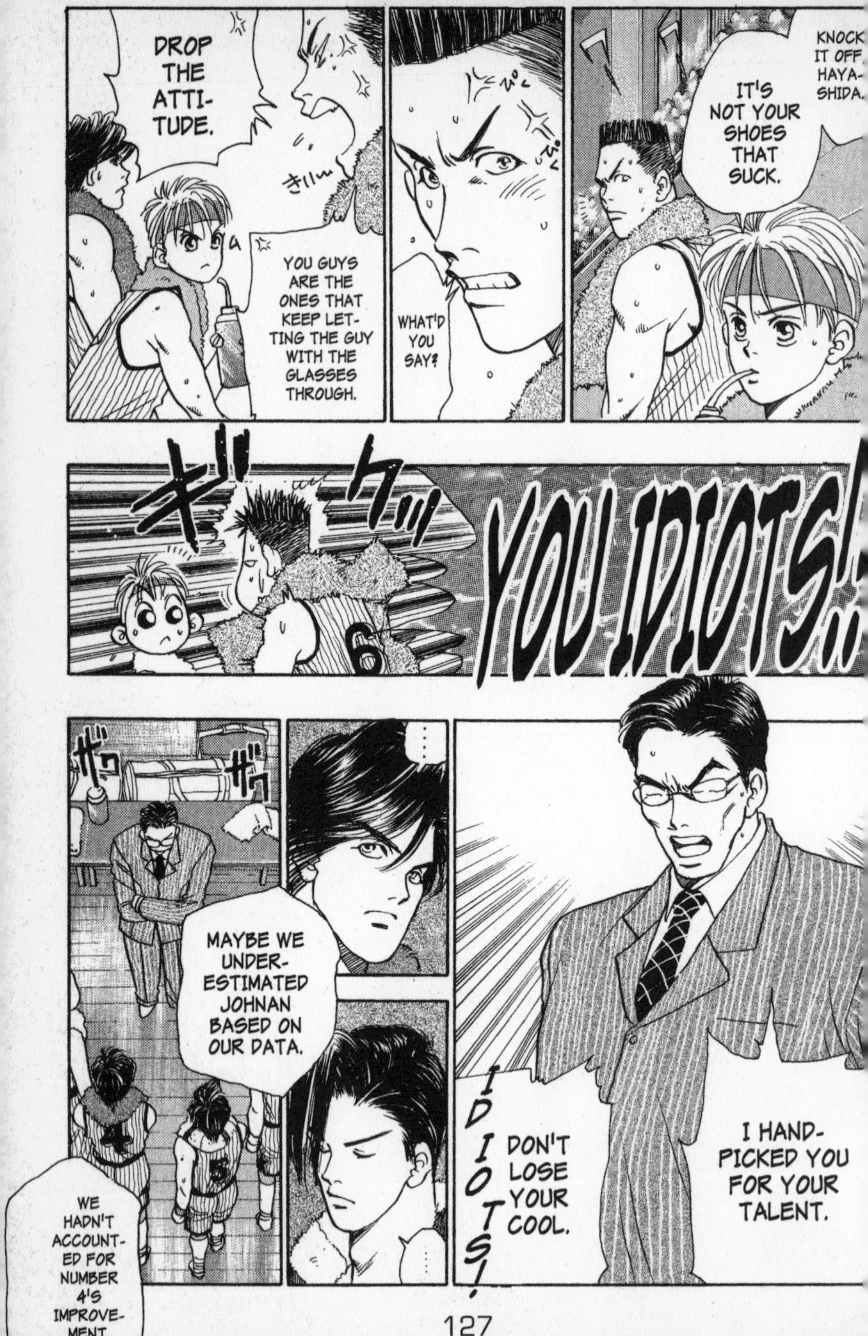
KNOCK IT OFF, HAYASHIDA.
IT'S NOT YOUR SHOES THAT SUCK.
WHAT'D YOU SAY?
YOU GUYS ARE THE ONES THAT KEEP LETTING THE GUY WITH THE GLASSES THROUGH.
DROP THE ATTITUDE.
YOU IDIOTS!!
ギクッ
I HAND-PICKED YOU FOR YOUR TALENT.
DON'T LOSE YOUR COOL.
IDIOTS!
...
MAYBE WE UNDERESTIMATED JOHNAN BASED ON OUR DATA.
...
ザワ ザワ
WE HADN'T ACCOUNTED FOR NUMBER 4'S IMPROVEMENT.

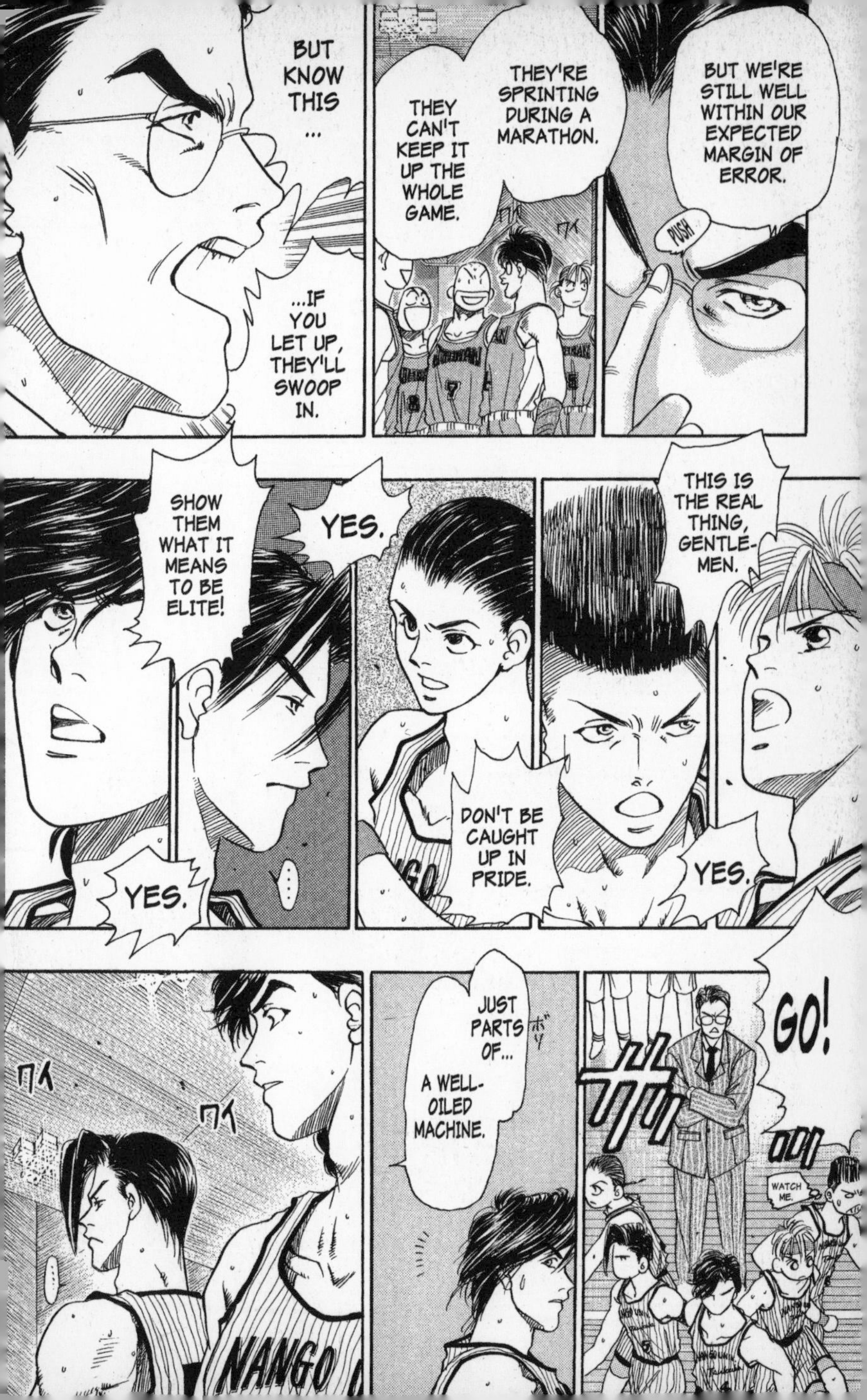
PUSH
BUT WE'RE STILL WELL WITHIN OUR EXPECTED MARGIN OF ERROR.
THEY'RE SPRINTING DURING A MARATHON.
THEY CAN'T KEEP IT UP THE WHOLE GAME.
ワイ
ワイ
BUT KNOW THIS ...
...IF YOU LET UP, THEY'LL SWOOP IN.
THIS IS THE REAL THING, GENTLEMEN.
YES.
DON'T BE CAUGHT UP IN PRIDE.
YES.
SHOW THEM WHAT IT MEANS TO BE ELITE!
YES.
...
YES.
GO!
WATCH ME.
JUST PARTS OF...
ボソ
A WELL-OILED MACHINE.
ワイ
ワイ
...
NANGO

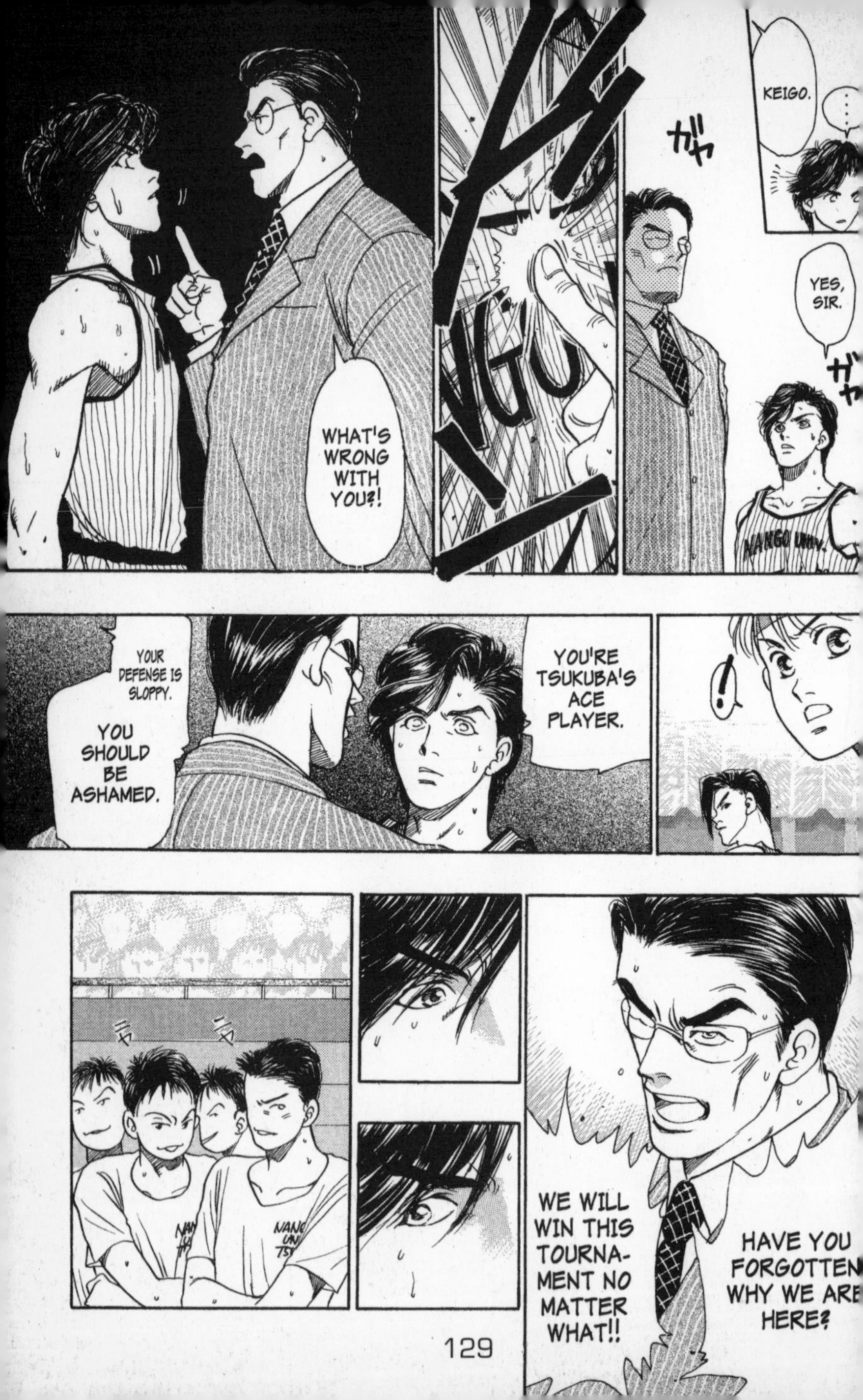
KEIGO.
……
ガヤ
YES, SIR.
ガヤ
WHAT'S WRONG WITH YOU?!
!
YOU'RE TSUKUBA'S ACE PLAYER.
YOUR DEFENSE IS SLOPPY.
YOU SHOULD BE ASHAMED.
HAVE YOU FORGOTTEN WHY WE ARE HERE?
WE WILL WIN THIS TOURNA-MENT NO MATTER WHAT!!
ニヤ
ニヤ

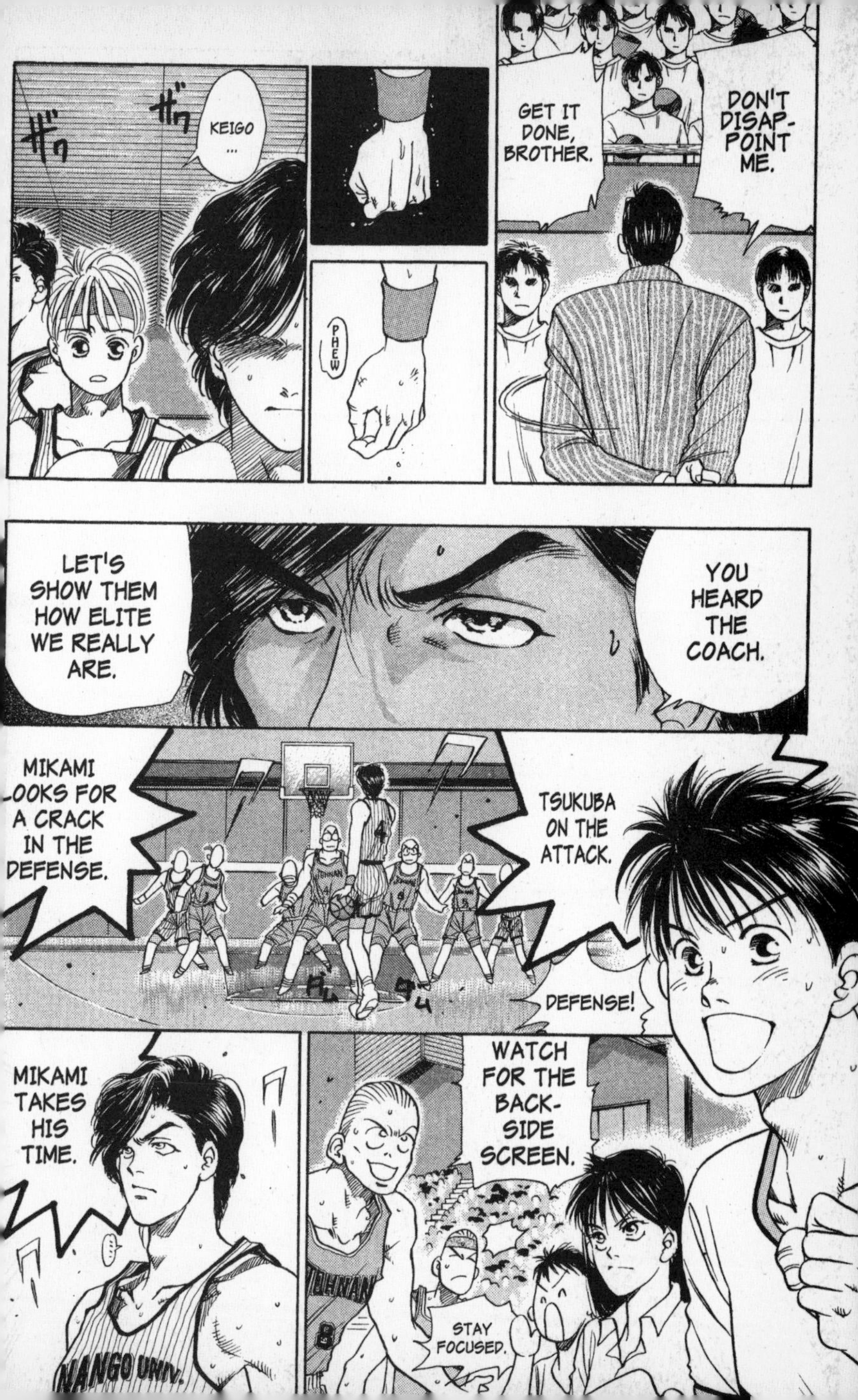
DON'T DISAP-POINT ME.
GET IT DONE, BROTHER.
PHEW
ザワ ザワ
KEIGO ...
YOU HEARD THE COACH.
LET'S SHOW THEM HOW ELITE WE REALLY ARE.
TSUKUBA ON THE ATTACK.
DEFENSE!
MIKAMI LOOKS FOR A CRACK IN THE DEFENSE.
WATCH FOR THE BACK-SIDE SCREEN.
STAY FOCUSED.
MIKAMI TAKES HIS TIME.
NANGO UNIV.

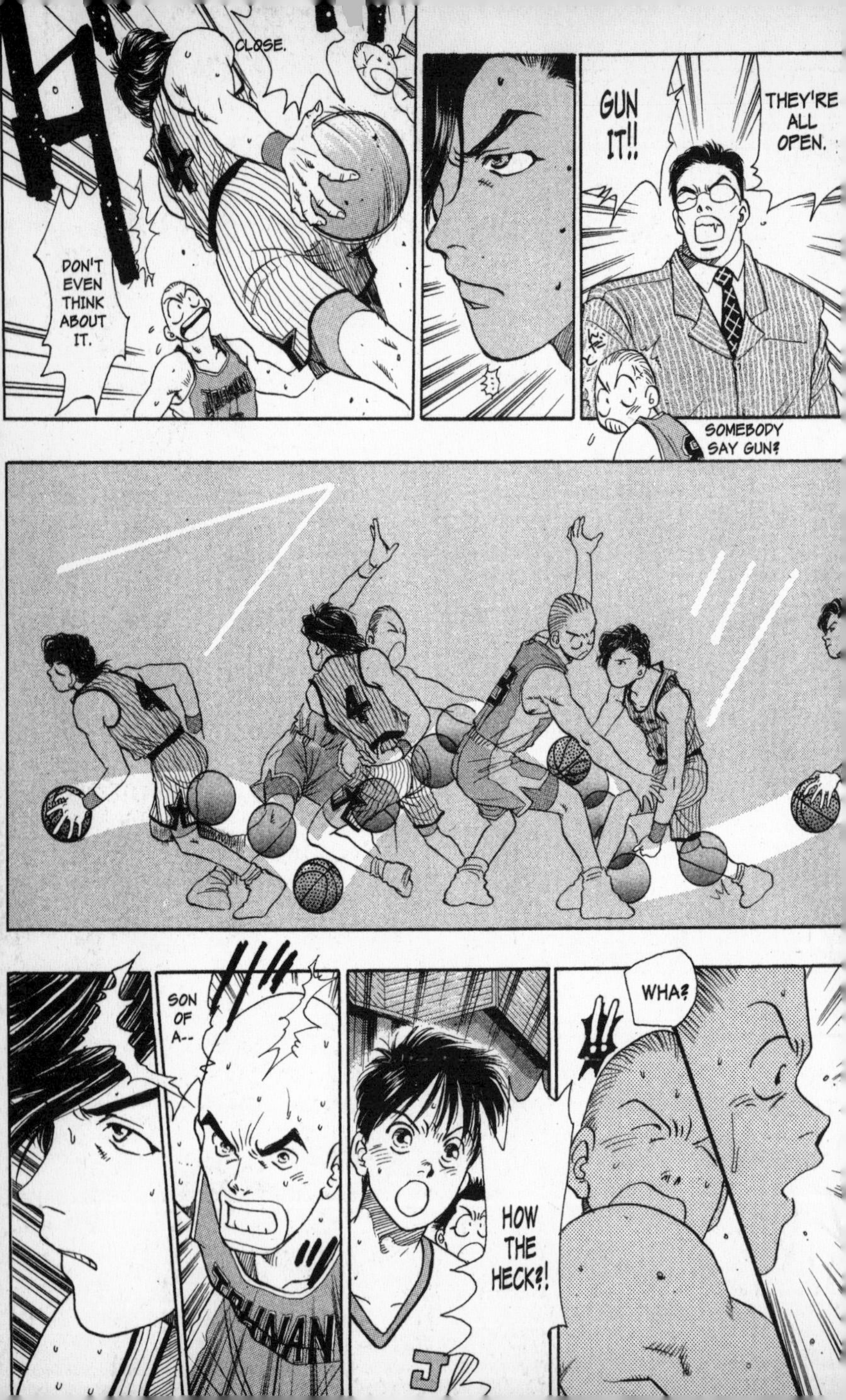
THEY'RE ALL OPEN.
GUN IT!!
SOMEBODY SAY GUN?
CLOSE.
DON'T EVEN THINK ABOUT IT.
WHA?
HOW THE HECK?!
SON OF A--

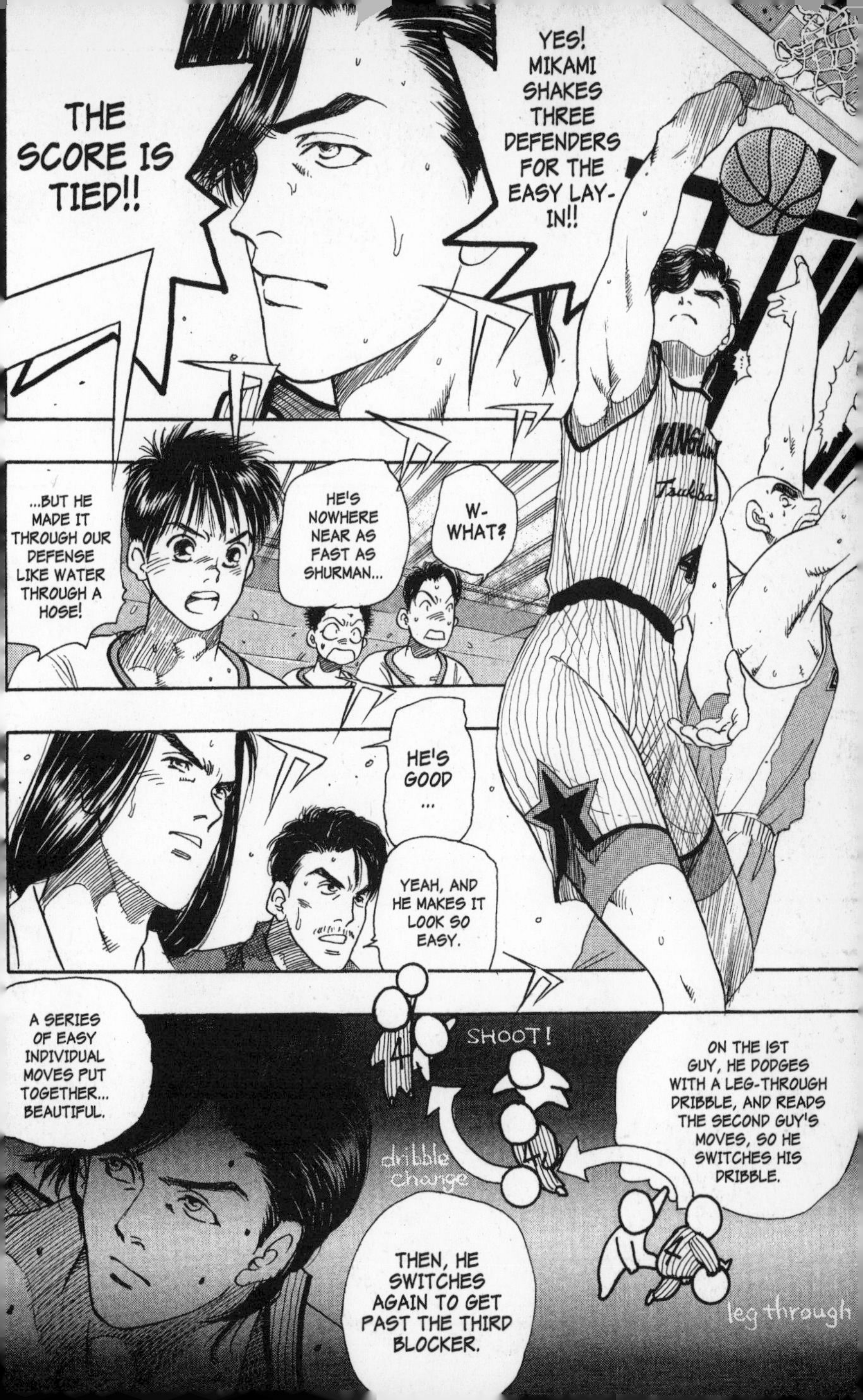
YES! MIKAMI SHAKES THREE DEFENDERS FOR THE EASY LAY-IN!!
THE SCORE IS TIED!!
W-WHAT?
HE'S NOWHERE NEAR AS FAST AS SHURMAN...
...BUT HE MADE IT THROUGH OUR DEFENSE LIKE WATER THROUGH A HOSE!
HE'S GOOD ...
YEAH, AND HE MAKES IT LOOK SO EASY.
ON THE 1ST GUY, HE DODGES WITH A LEG-THROUGH DRIBBLE, AND READS THE SECOND GUY'S MOVES, SO HE SWITCHES HIS DRIBBLE.
SHOOT!
A SERIES OF EASY INDIVIDUAL MOVES PUT TOGETHER... BEAUTIFUL.
dribble change
THEN, HE SWITCHES AGAIN TO GET PAST THE THIRD BLOCKER.
leg through

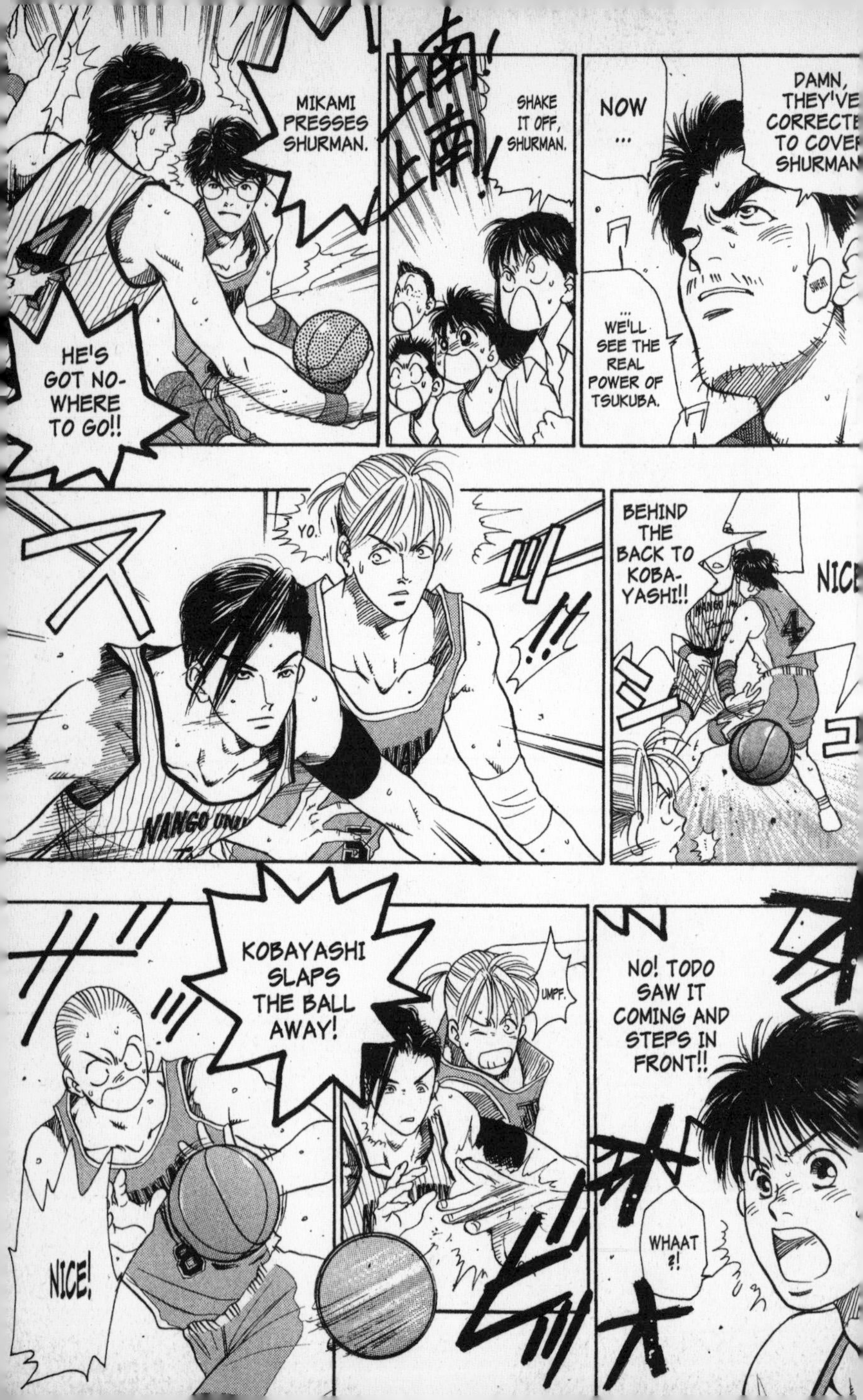
DAMN, THEY'VE CORRECTE TO COVER SHURMAN
SWEAT
NOW ...
... WE'LL SEE THE REAL POWER OF TSUKUBA.
SHAKE IT OFF, SHURMAN.
MIKAMI PRESSES SHURMAN.
HE'S GOT NO-WHERE TO GO!!
BEHIND THE BACK TO KOBA-YASHI!!
NICE
YO.
NO! TODO SAW IT COMING AND STEPS IN FRONT!!
WHAAT ?!
KOBAYASHI SLAPS THE BALL AWAY!
UMPF.
NICE!

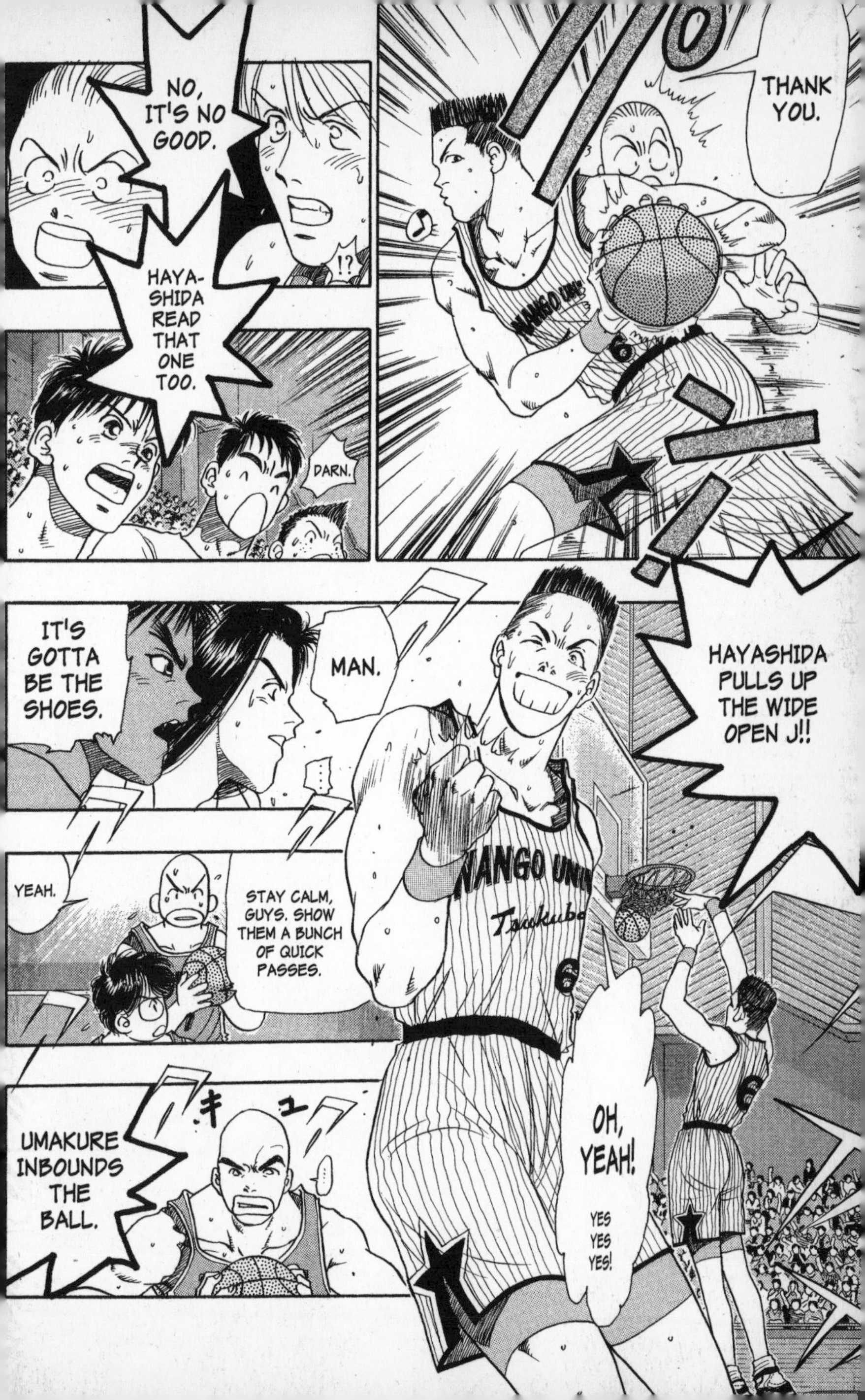
THANK YOU.
NO, IT'S NO GOOD.
!?
HAYA-SHIDA READ THAT ONE TOO.
DARN.
HAYASHIDA PULLS UP THE WIDE OPEN J!!
OH, YEAH!
YES YES YES!
MAN.
IT'S GOTTA BE THE SHOES.
...
STAY CALM, GUYS. SHOW THEM A BUNCH OF QUICK PASSES.
YEAH.
キュ
UMAKURE INBOUNDS THE BALL.
...

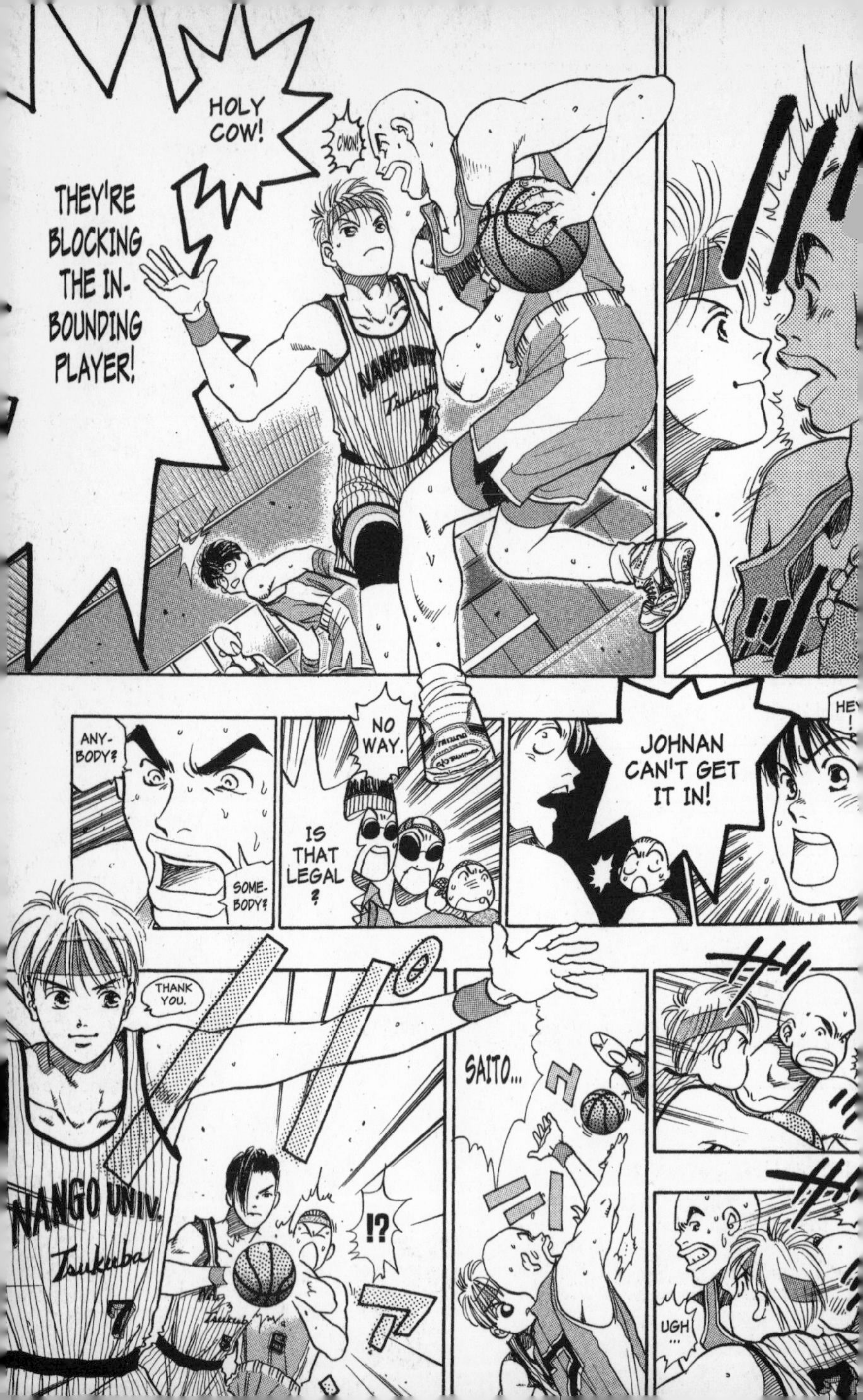
C'MON!
HOLY COW!
THEY'RE BLOCKING THE IN-BOUNDING PLAYER!
HEY!
JOHNAN CAN'T GET IT IN!
NO WAY.
IS THAT LEGAL?
ANYBODY?
SOMEBODY?
UGH...
SAITO...
!?
THANK YOU.

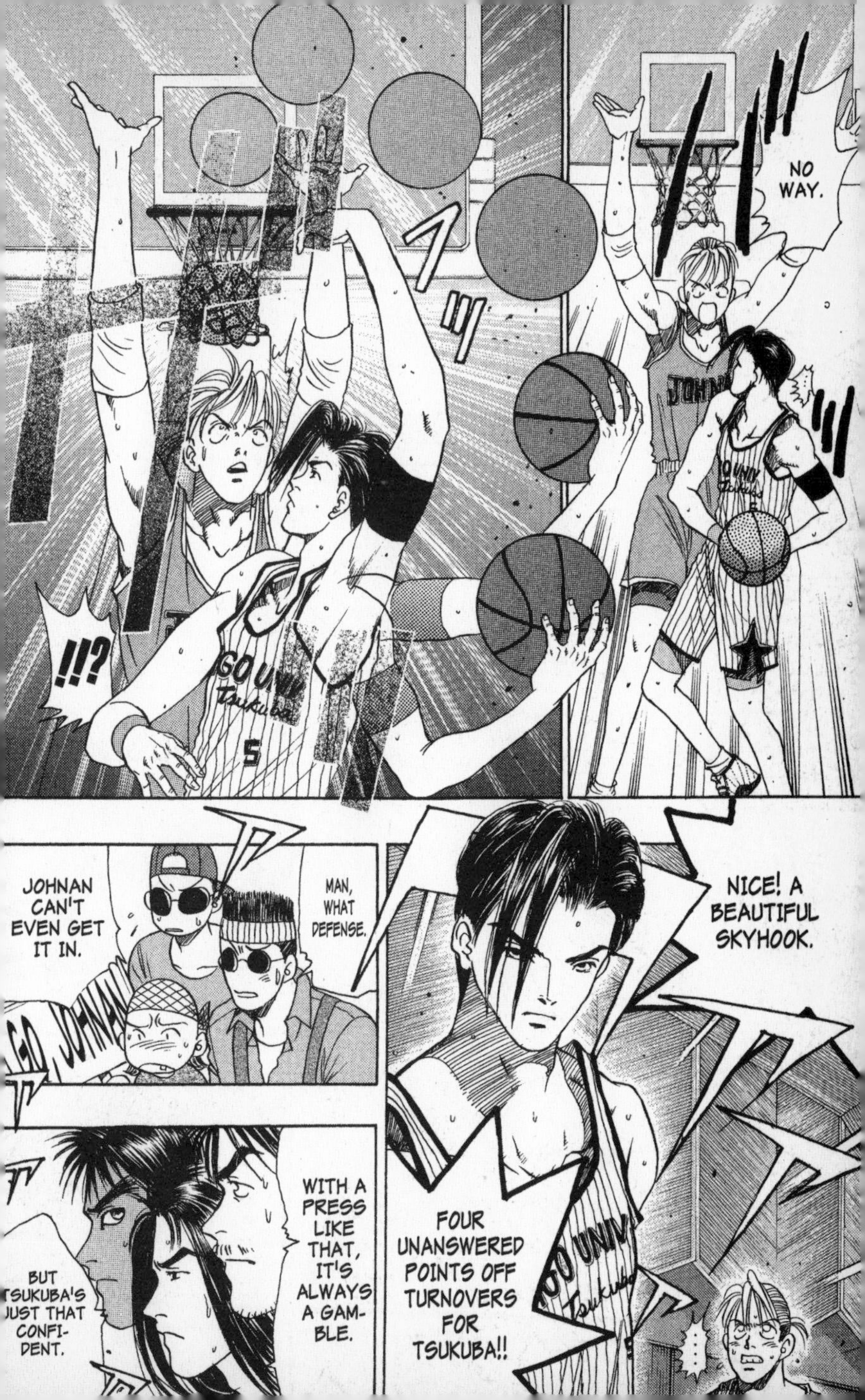
NO WAY.
!!?
NICE! A BEAUTIFUL SKYHOOK.
FOUR UNANSWERED POINTS OFF TURNOVERS FOR TSUKUBA!!
MAN, WHAT DEFENSE.
JOHNAN CAN'T EVEN GET IT IN.
WITH A PRESS LIKE THAT, IT'S ALWAYS A GAMBLE.
BUT TSUKUBA'S JUST THAT CONFIDENT.

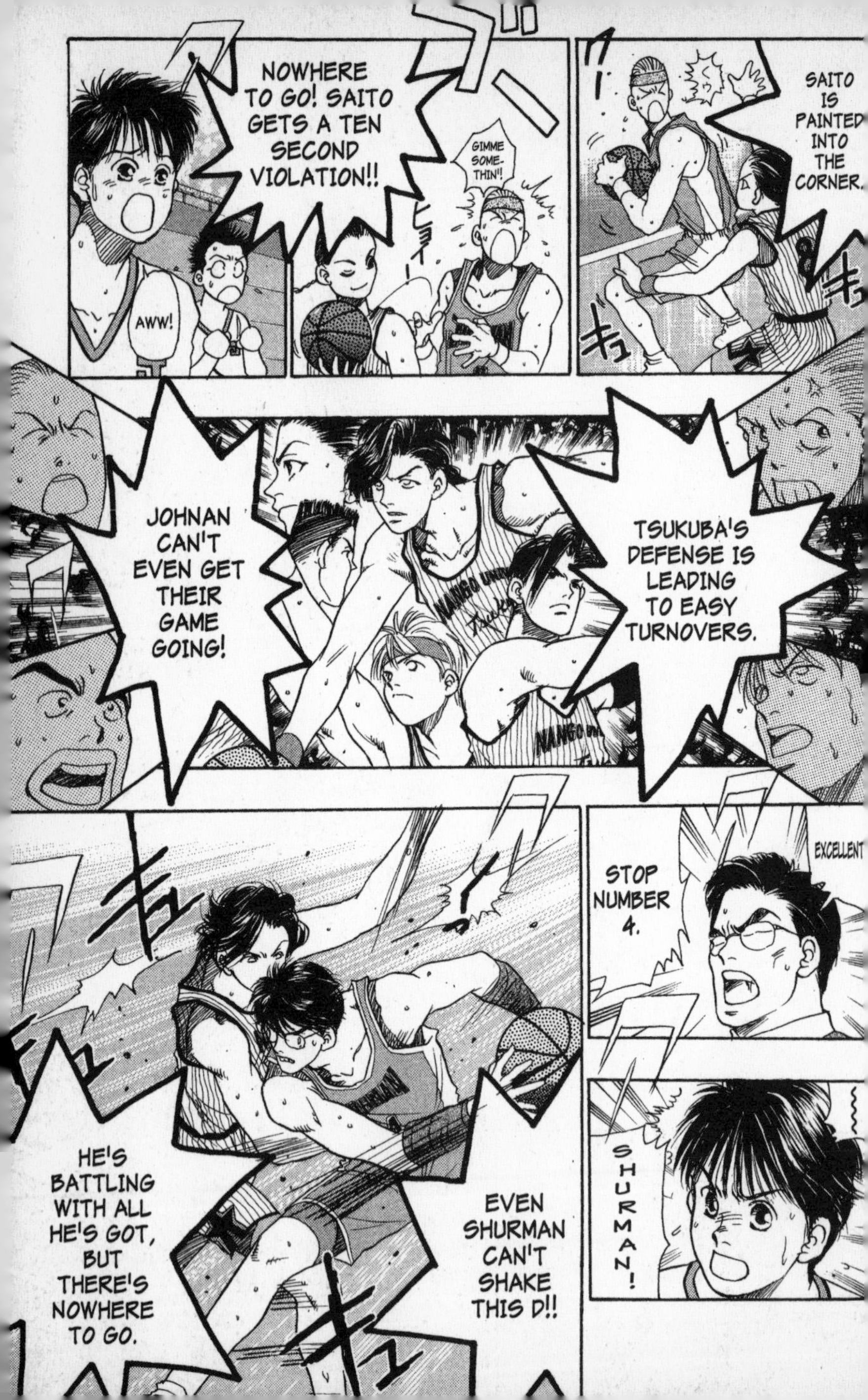
SAITO IS PAINTED INTO THE CORNER.
NOWHERE TO GO! SAITO GETS A TEN SECOND VIOLATION!!
GIMME SOME-THIN'!!
AWW!
TSUKUBA'S DEFENSE IS LEADING TO EASY TURNOVERS.
JOHNAN CAN'T EVEN GET THEIR GAME GOING!
EXCELLENT
STOP NUMBER 4.
SHURMAN!
EVEN SHURMAN CAN'T SHAKE THIS D!!
HE'S BATTLING WITH ALL HE'S GOT, BUT THERE'S NOWHERE TO GO.

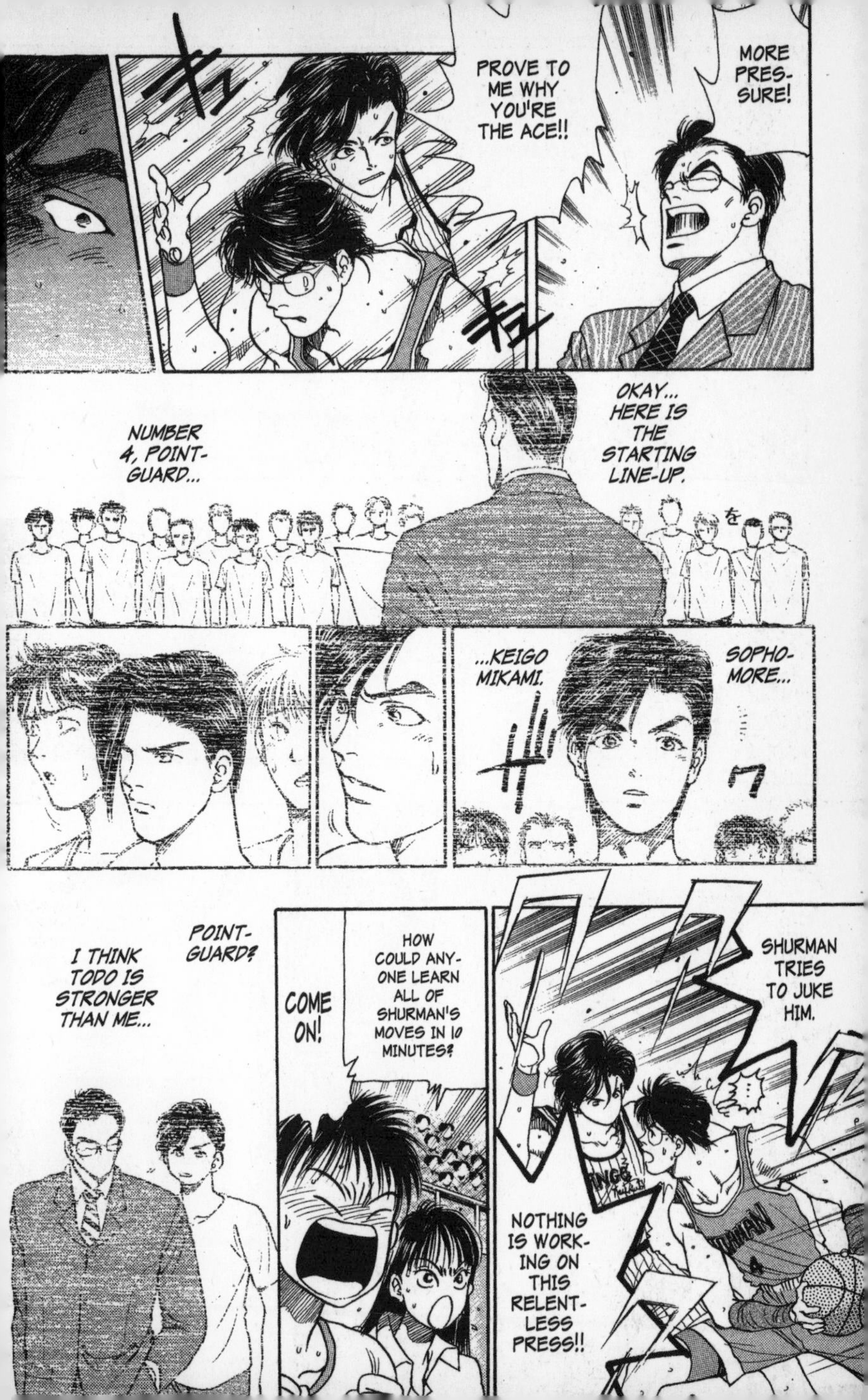
MORE PRES-SURE!
PROVE TO ME WHY YOU'RE THE ACE!!
キュ
キュ
OKAY... HERE IS THE STARTING LINE-UP.
NUMBER 4, POINT-GUARD...
SOPHO-MORE...
...KEIGO MIKAMI.
SHURMAN TRIES TO JUKE HIM.
NOTHING IS WORK-ING ON THIS RELENT-LESS PRESS!!
HOW COULD ANY-ONE LEARN ALL OF SHURMAN'S MOVES IN 10 MINUTES?
COME ON!
POINT-GUARD?
I THINK TODO IS STRONGER THAN ME...

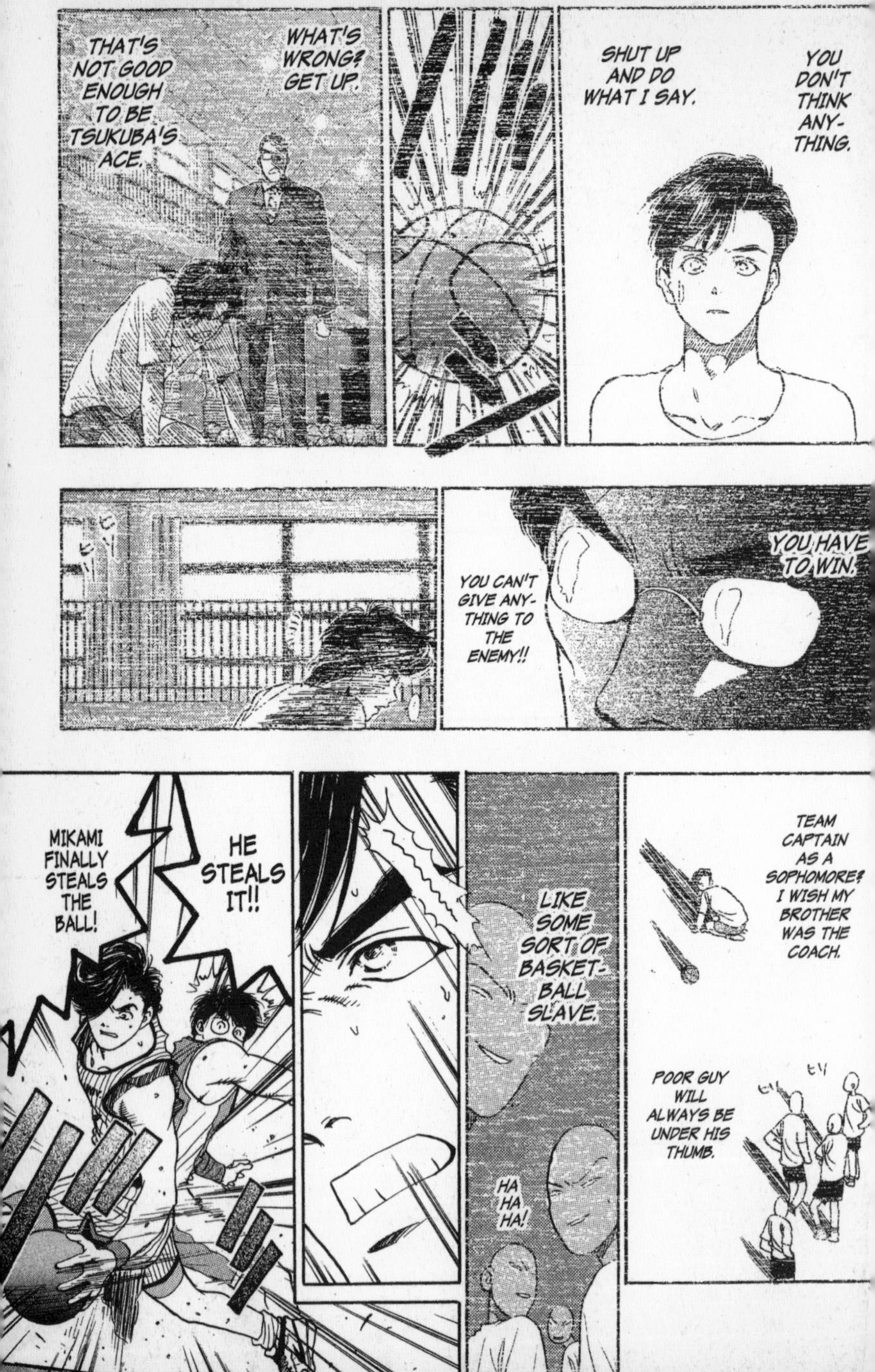
YOU DON'T THINK ANY-THING.
SHUT UP AND DO WHAT I SAY.
WHAT'S WRONG? GET UP.
THAT'S NOT GOOD ENOUGH TO BE TSUKUBA'S ACE.
YOU HAVE TO WIN.
YOU CAN'T GIVE ANY-THING TO THE ENEMY!!
TEAM CAPTAIN AS A SOPHOMORE? I WISH MY BROTHER WAS THE COACH.
POOR GUY WILL ALWAYS BE UNDER HIS THUMB.
LIKE SOME SORT OF BASKET-BALL SLAVE.
HA HA HA!
HE STEALS IT!!
MIKAMI FINALLY STEALS THE BALL!

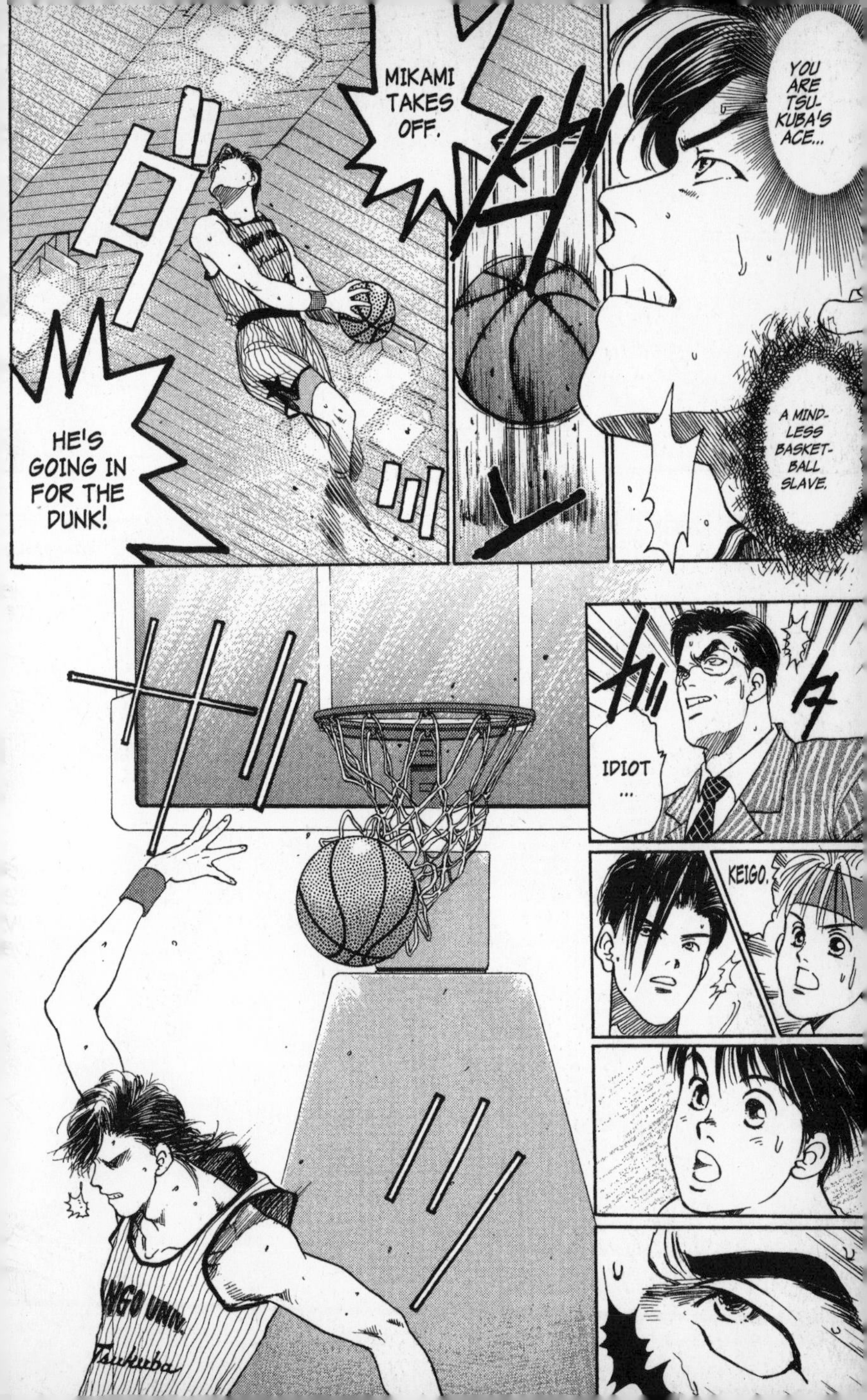
YOU ARE TSU-KUBA'S ACE...
A MIND-LESS BASKET-BALL SLAVE.
MIKAMI TAKES OFF.
HE'S GOING IN FOR THE DUNK!
IDIOT ...
KEIGO.
Tsukuba

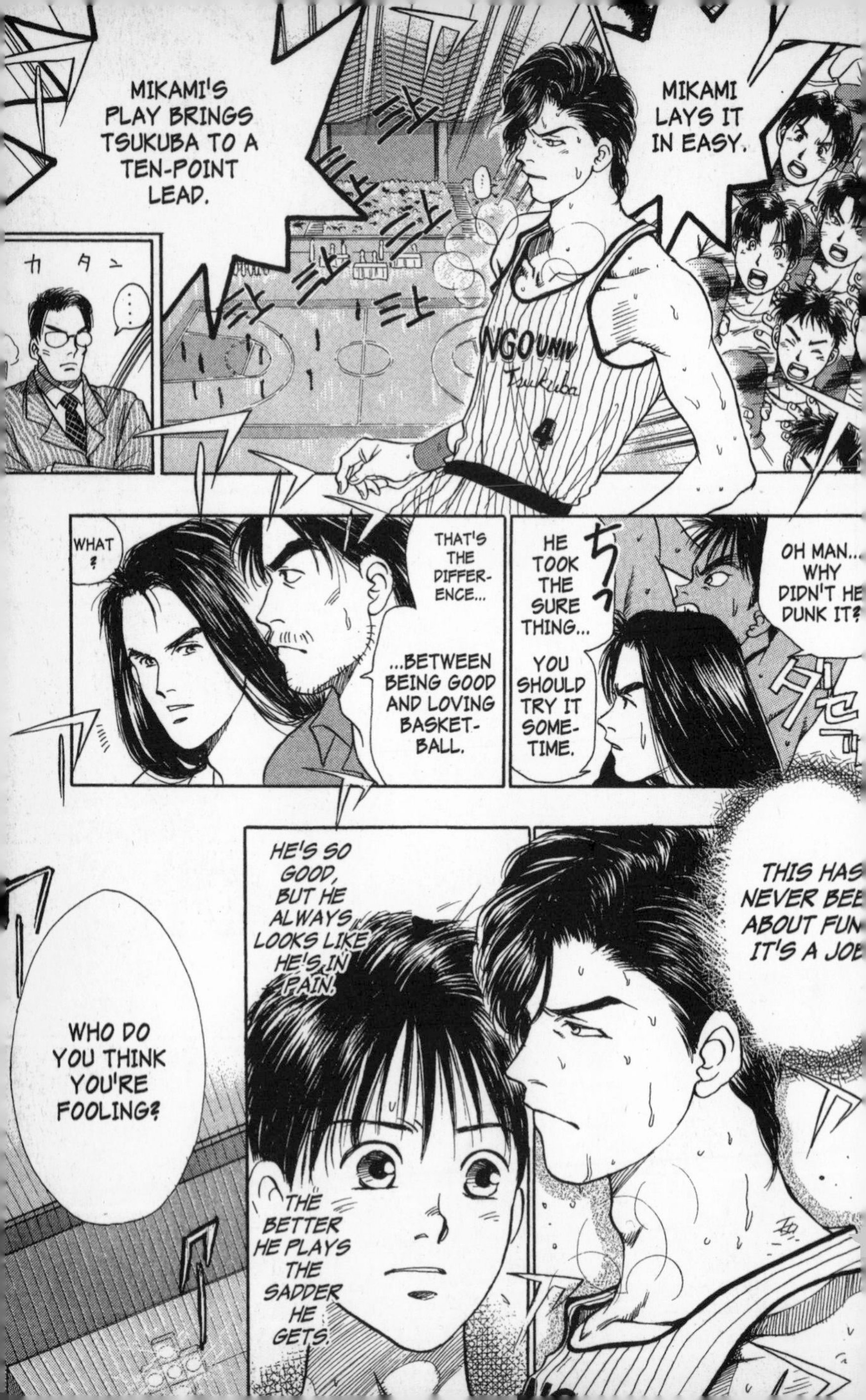
MIKAMI LAYS IT IN EASY.
MIKAMI'S PLAY BRINGS TSUKUBA TO A TEN-POINT LEAD.
カタン
...
OH MAN... WHY DIDN'T HE DUNK IT?
HE TOOK THE SURE THING...
YOU SHOULD TRY IT SOMETIME.
WHAT?
THAT'S THE DIFFERENCE...
...BETWEEN BEING GOOD AND LOVING BASKETBALL.
THIS HAS NEVER BEE ABOUT FUN IT'S A JOB
HE'S SO GOOD, BUT HE ALWAYS LOOKS LIKE HE'S IN PAIN.
THE BETTER HE PLAYS THE SADDER HE GETS.
WHO DO YOU THINK YOU'RE FOOLING?

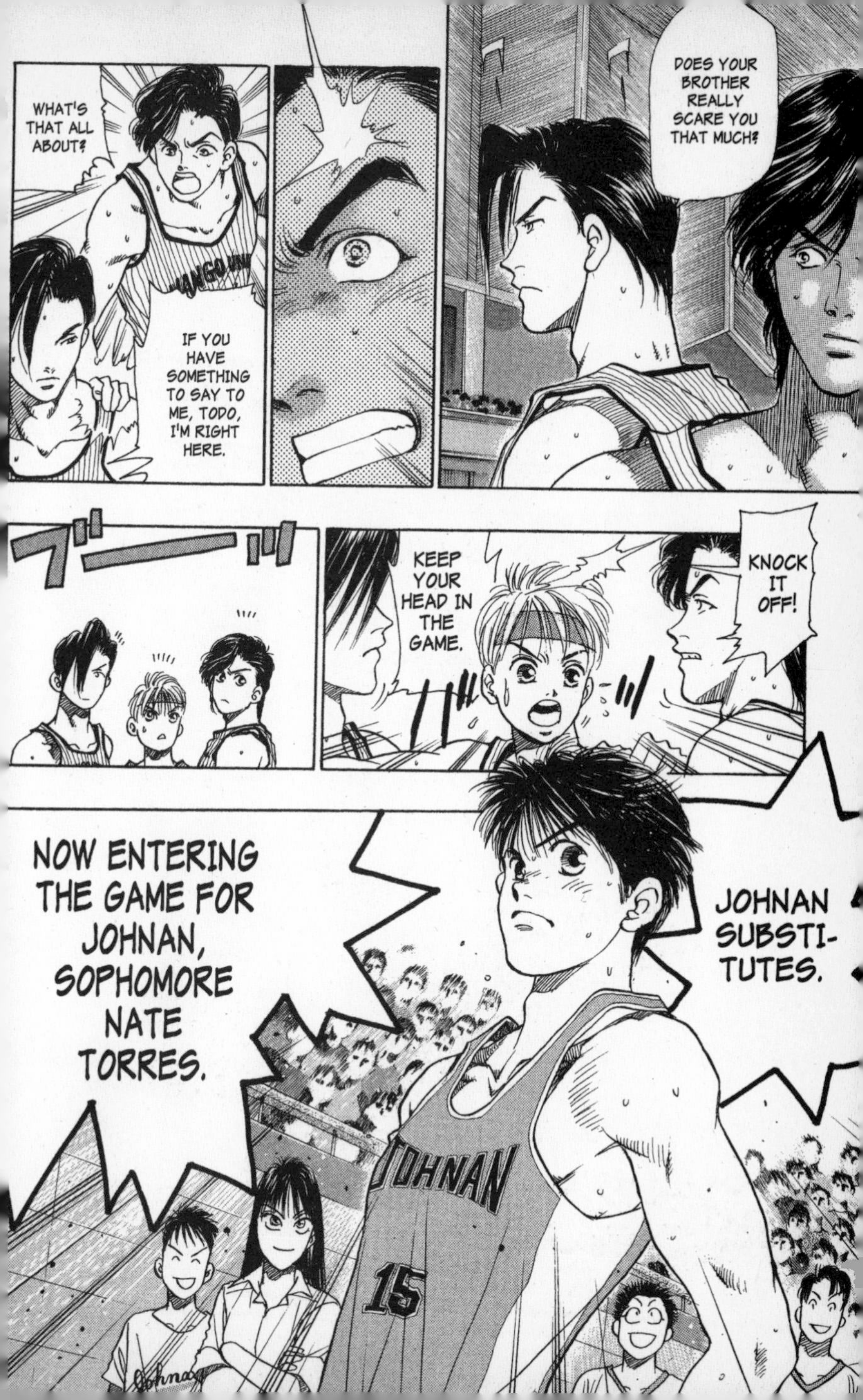
DOES YOUR BROTHER REALLY SCARE YOU THAT MUCH?
WHAT'S THAT ALL ABOUT?
IF YOU HAVE SOMETHING TO SAY TO ME, TODO, I'M RIGHT HERE.
KNOCK IT OFF!
KEEP YOUR HEAD IN THE GAME.
ブーーッ
JOHNAN SUBSTITUTES.
NOW ENTERING THE GAME FOR JOHNAN, SOPHOMORE NATE TORRES.

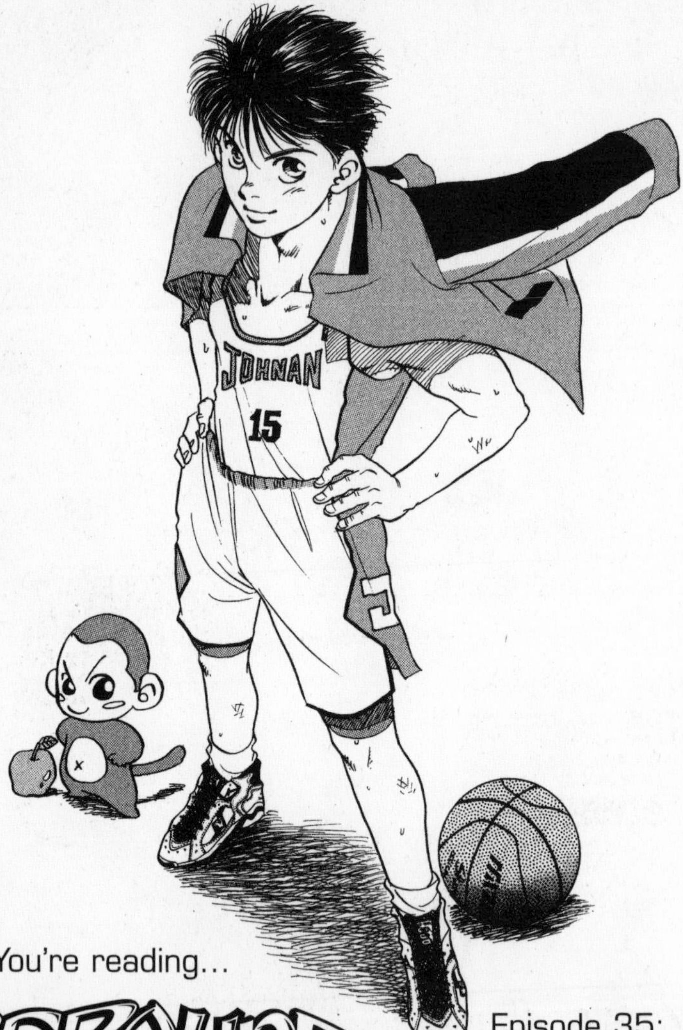
JOHNAN
15

You're reading...

REBOUND

Episode 35:
Miracle J

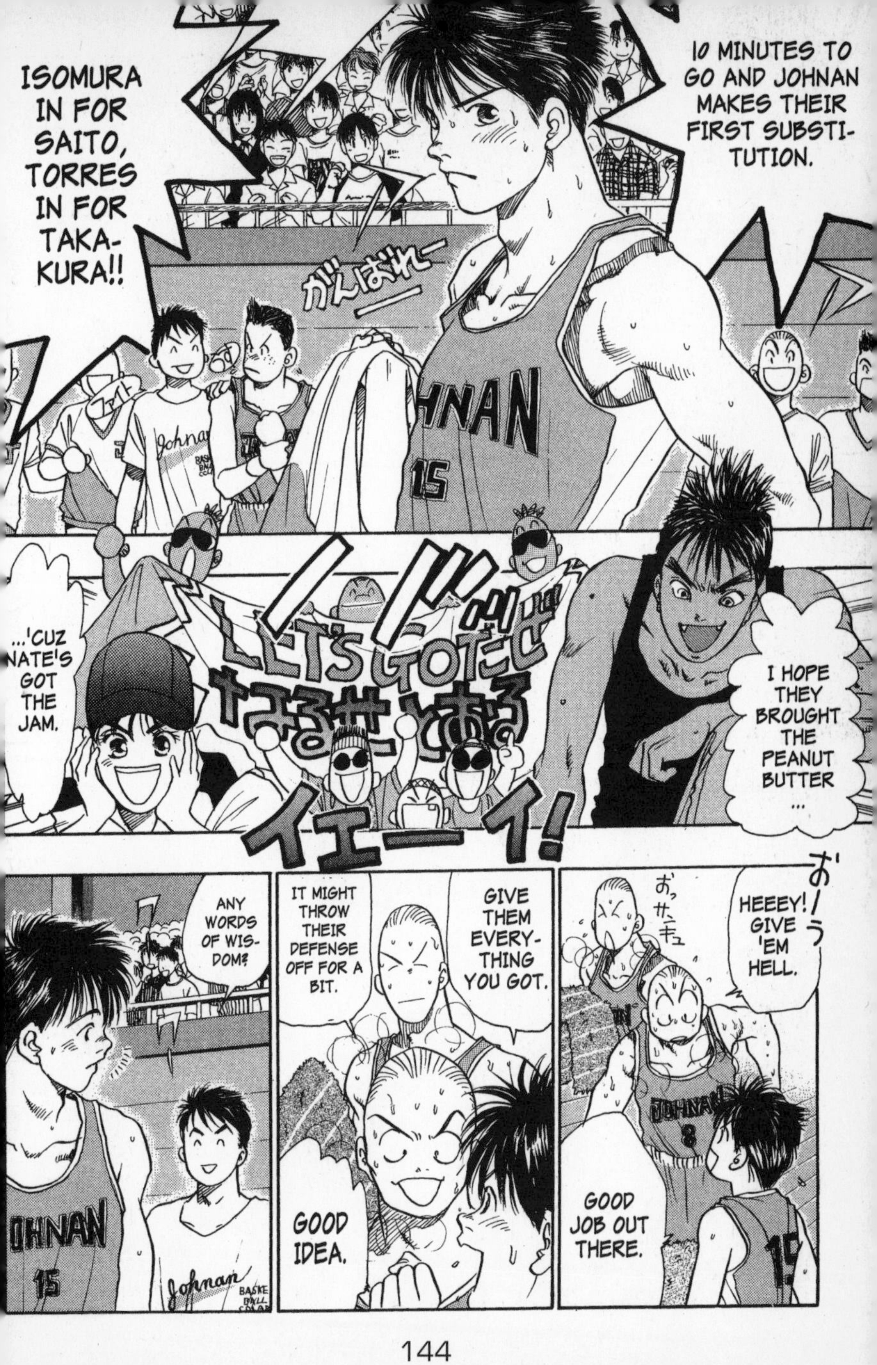
10 MINUTES TO GO AND JOHNAN MAKES THEIR FIRST SUBSTI-TUTION.
ISOMURA IN FOR SAITO, TORRES IN FOR TAKA-KURA!!
がんばれー
I HOPE THEY BROUGHT THE PEANUT BUTTER ...
LET'S GOだぜ
イエーイ!
...'CUZ NATE'S GOT THE JAM.
おーう
HEEEY! GIVE 'EM HELL.
GOOD JOB OUT THERE.
GIVE THEM EVERY-THING YOU GOT.
IT MIGHT THROW THEIR DEFENSE OFF FOR A BIT.
GOOD IDEA.
ANY WORDS OF WIS-DOM?

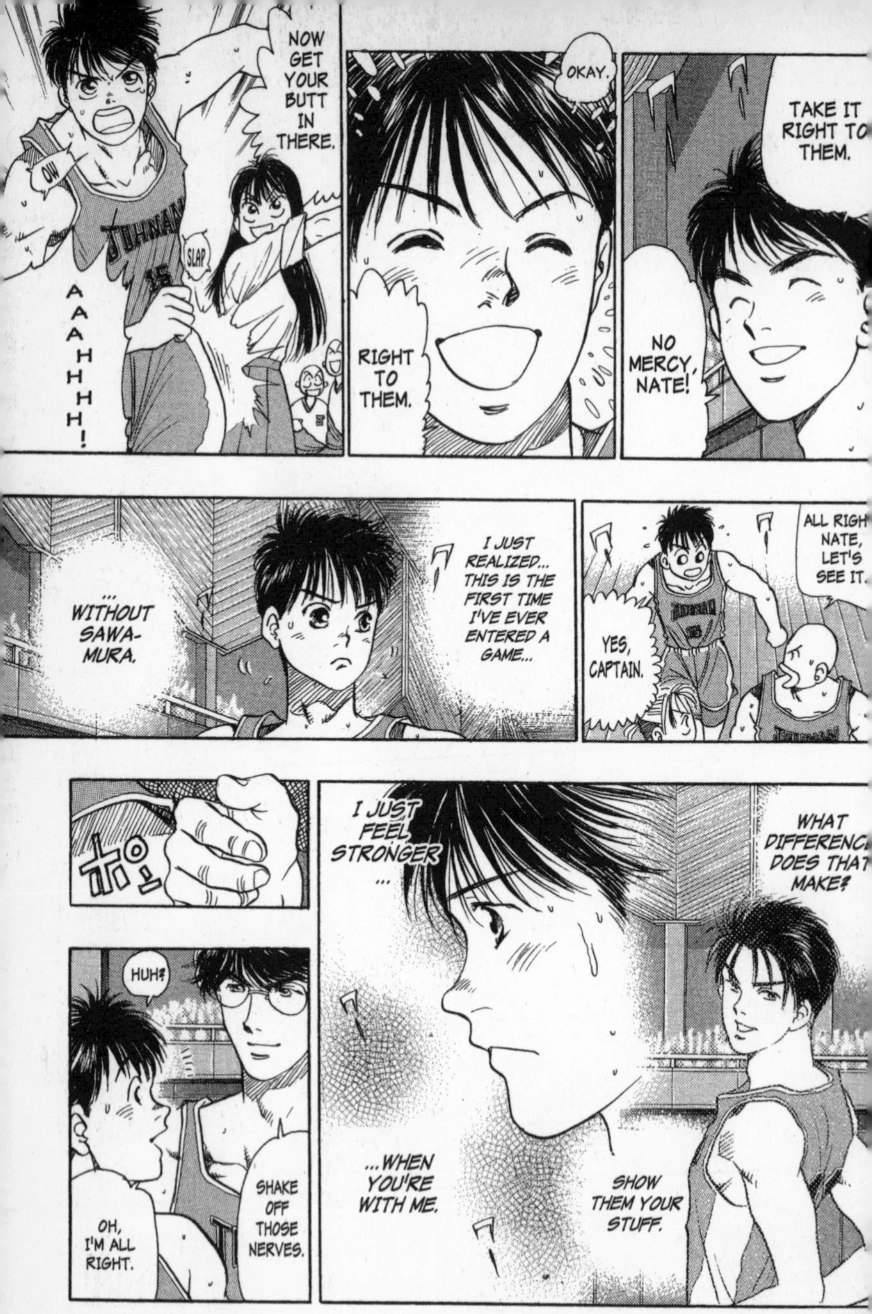
TAKE IT RIGHT TO THEM.
NO MERCY, NATE!
OKAY.
RIGHT TO THEM.
NOW GET YOUR BUTT IN THERE.
OW
SLAP
AAAHHHH!
ALL RIGH NATE, LET'S SEE IT.
YES, CAPTAIN.
I JUST REALIZED... THIS IS THE FIRST TIME I'VE EVER ENTERED A GAME...
...WITHOUT SAWAMURA.
WHAT DIFFERENC DOES THAT MAKE?
I JUST FEEL STRONGER...
...WHEN YOU'RE WITH ME.
SHOW THEM YOUR STUFF.
HUH?
SHAKE OFF THOSE NERVES.
OH, I'M ALL RIGHT.

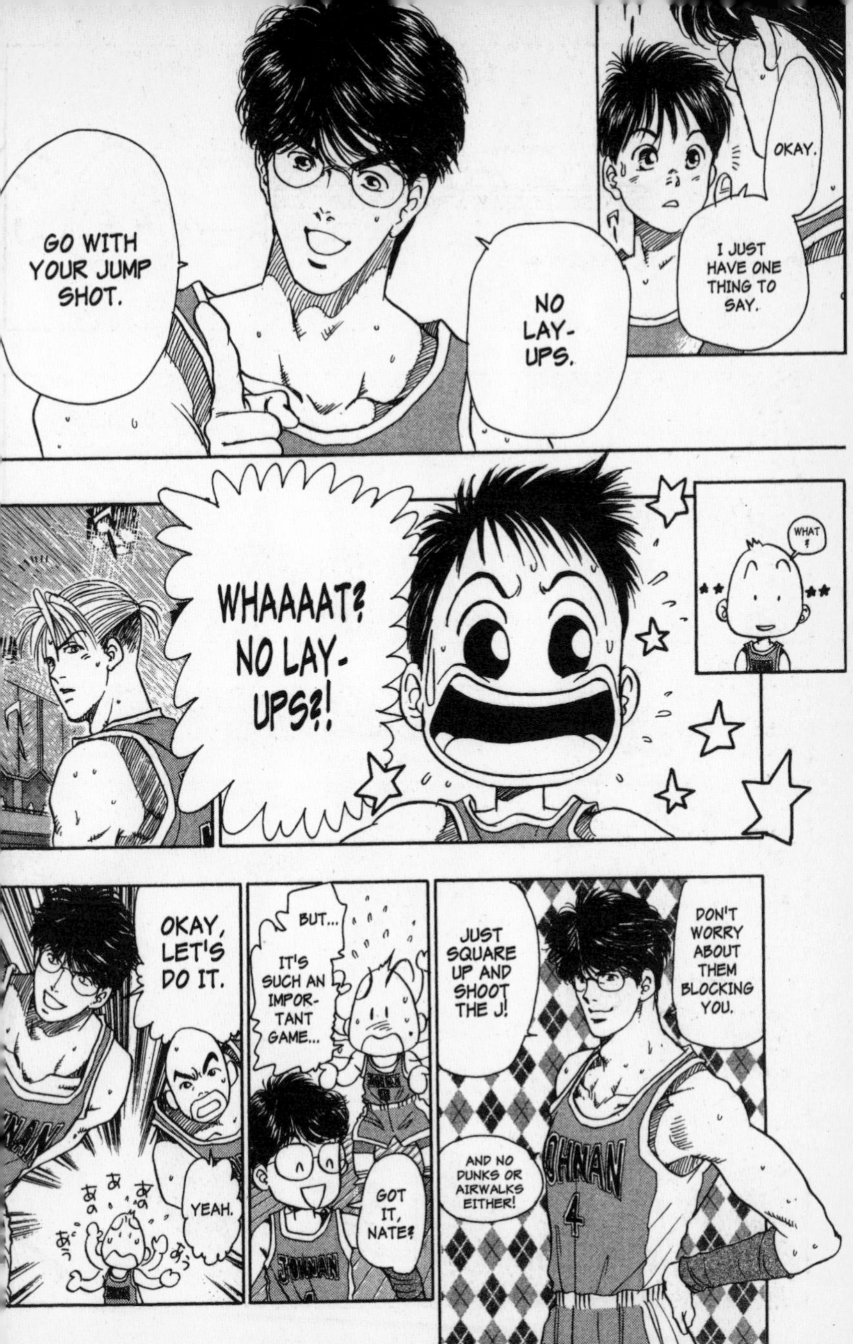
OKAY.
I JUST HAVE ONE THING TO SAY.
NO LAY-UPS.
GO WITH YOUR JUMP SHOT.
WHAT?
WHAAAAT? NO LAY-UPS?!
DON'T WORRY ABOUT THEM BLOCKING YOU.
JUST SQUARE UP AND SHOOT THE J!
AND NO DUNKS OR AIRWALKS EITHER!
BUT...
IT'S SUCH AN IMPOR-TANT GAME...
GOT IT, NATE?
OKAY, LET'S DO IT.
YEAH.

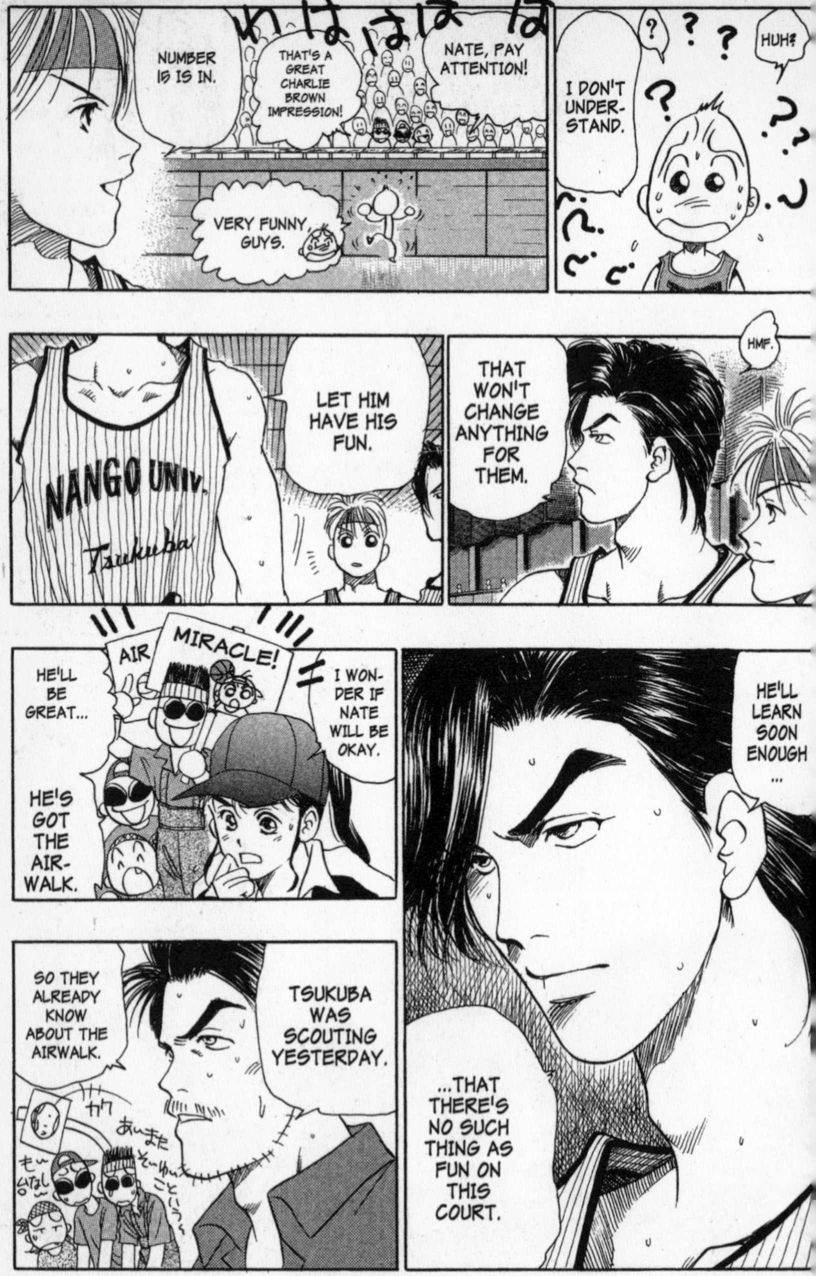

HUH?
I DON'T UNDER-STAND.
わはははは
NATE, PAY ATTENTION!
THAT'S A GREAT CHARLIE BROWN IMPRESSION!
NUMBER 15 IS IN.
VERY FUNNY, GUYS.
HMF.
THAT WON'T CHANGE ANYTHING FOR THEM.
LET HIM HAVE HIS FUN.
NANGO UNIV.
Tsukuba
HE'LL LEARN SOON ENOUGH...
...THAT THERE'S NO SUCH THING AS FUN ON THIS COURT.
I WON-DER IF NATE WILL BE OKAY.
AIR MIRACLE!
HE'LL BE GREAT...
HE'S GOT THE AIR-WALK.
TSUKUBA WAS SCOUTING YESTERDAY.
SO THEY ALREADY KNOW ABOUT THE AIRWALK.
カク

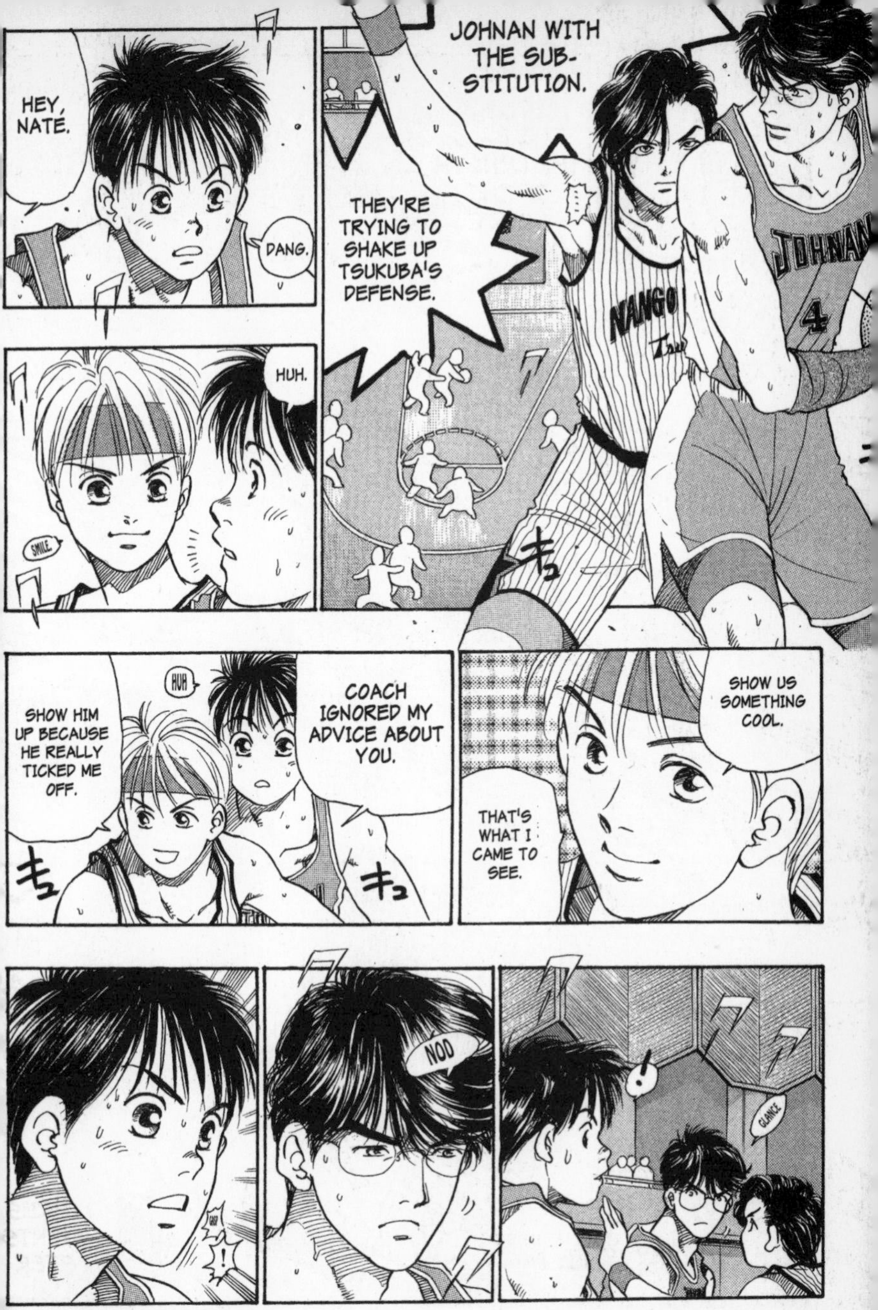
JOHNAN WITH THE SUB-STITUTION.
THEY'RE TRYING TO SHAKE UP TSUKUBA'S DEFENSE.
HEY, NATE.
DANG.
HUH.
SMILE.
SHOW US SOMETHING COOL.
THAT'S WHAT I CAME TO SEE.
COACH IGNORED MY ADVICE ABOUT YOU.
HUH
SHOW HIM UP BECAUSE HE REALLY TICKED ME OFF.
GLANCE
NOD
GASP
!

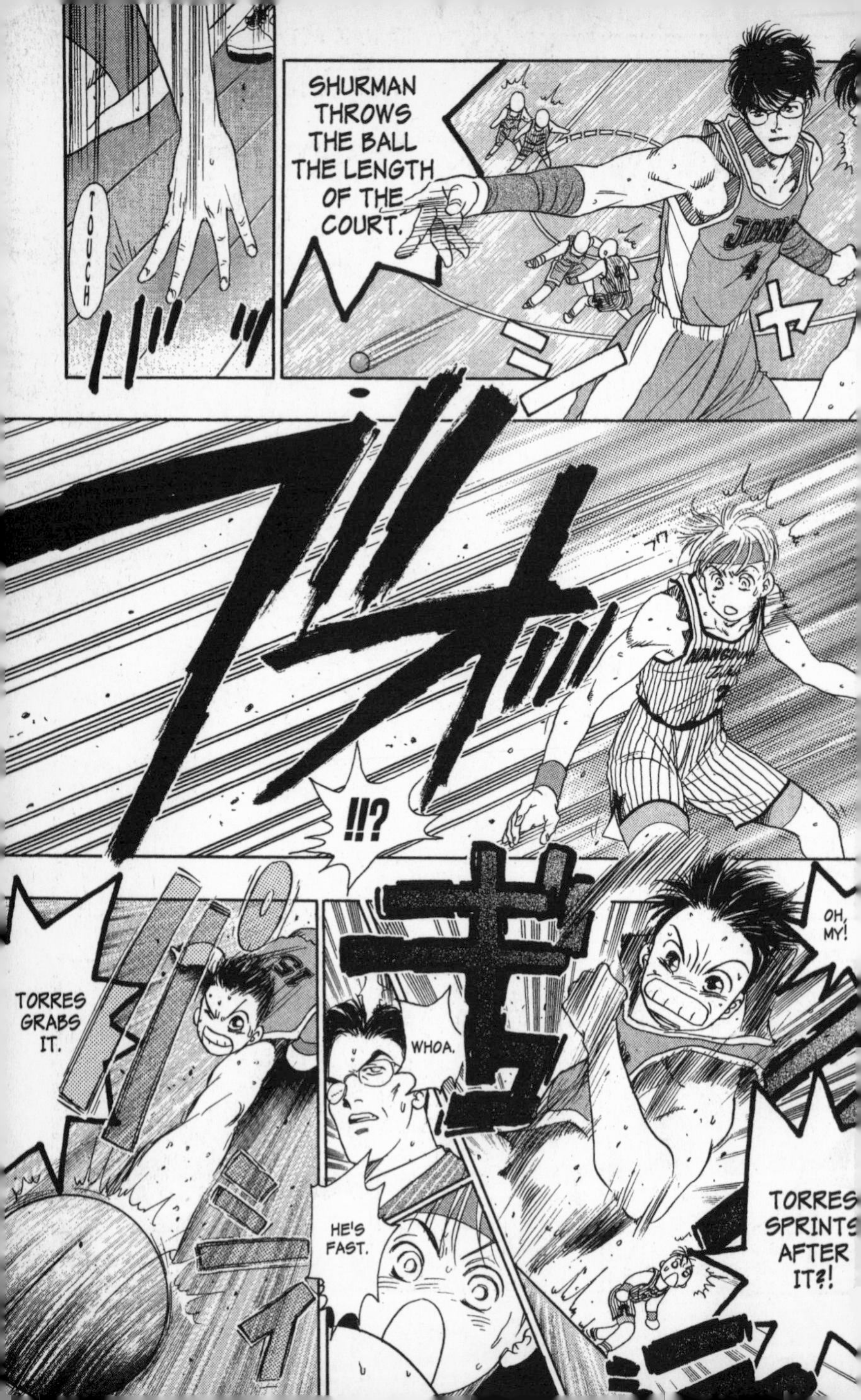
SHURMAN THROWS THE BALL THE LENGTH OF THE COURT.
TOUCH
!!?
OH, MY!
WHOA.
TORRES SPRINTS AFTER IT?!
HE'S FAST.
TORRES GRABS IT.

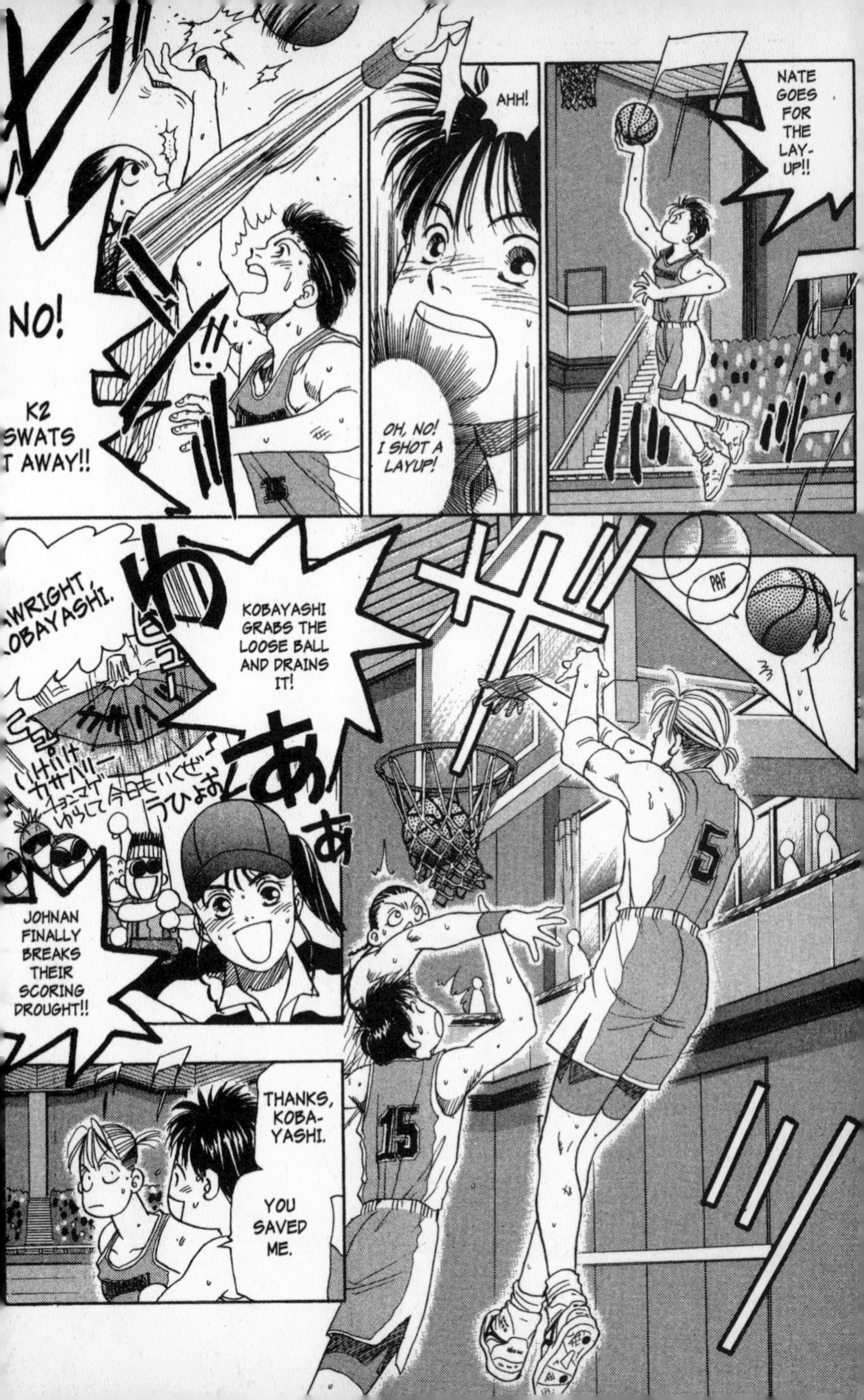
NATE GOES FOR THE LAY-UP!!
AHH!
OH, NO! I SHOT A LAYUP!
NO!
K2 SWATS
T AWAY!!
PAF
KOBAYASHI GRABS THE LOOSE BALL AND DRAINS IT!
AWRIGHT, OBAYASHI.
わ
あぁ
JOHNAN FINALLY BREAKS THEIR SCORING DROUGHT!!
THANKS, KOBA-YASHI.
YOU SAVED ME.

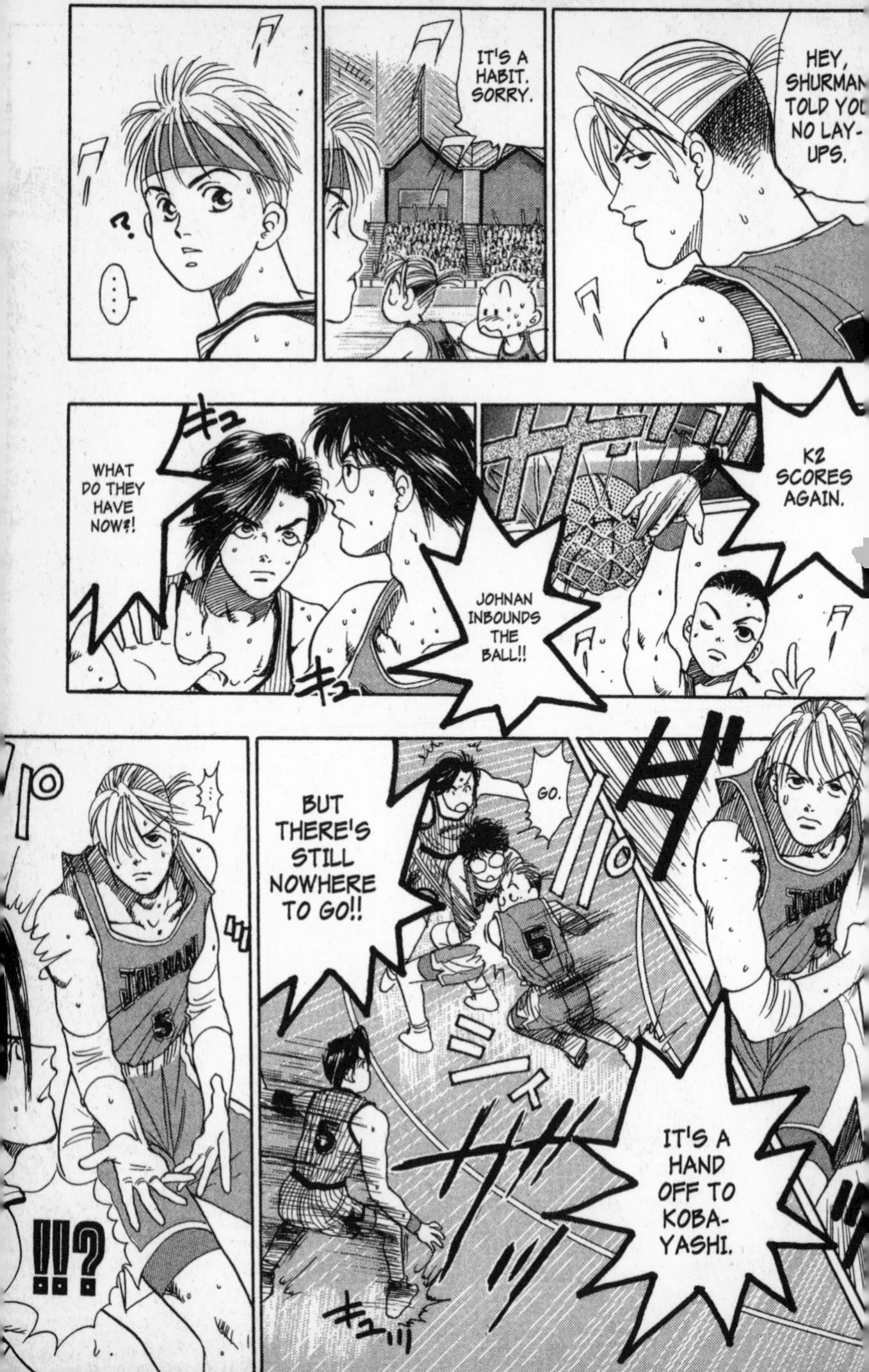
HEY, SHURMAN TOLD YOU NO LAY-UPS.
IT'S A HABIT. SORRY.
K2 SCORES AGAIN.
JOHNAN INBOUNDS THE BALL!!
WHAT DO THEY HAVE NOW?!
GO.
BUT THERE'S STILL NOWHERE TO GO!!
IT'S A HAND OFF TO KOBA-YASHI.
!!?

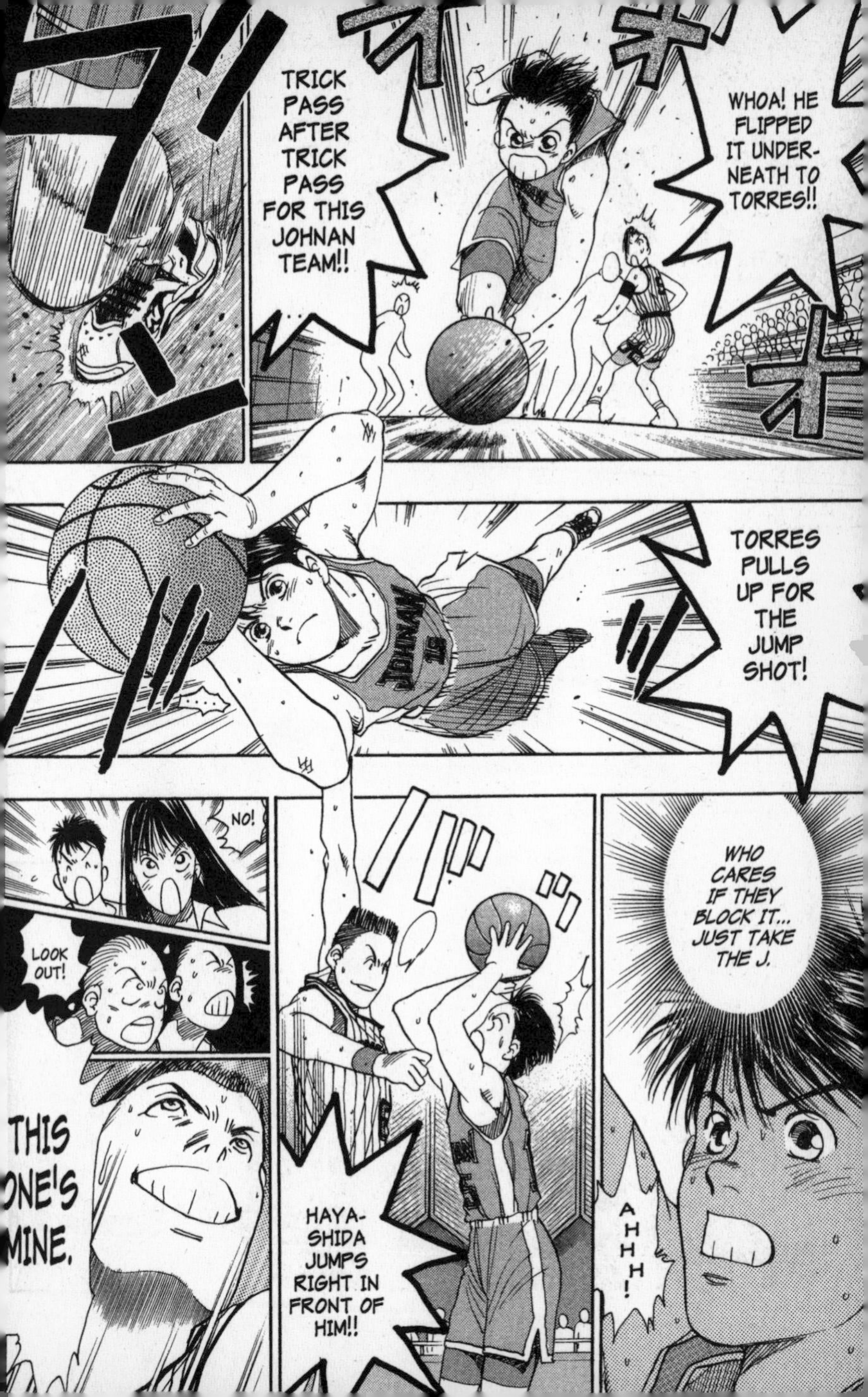
WHOA! HE FLIPPED IT UNDER-NEATH TO TORRES!!
TRICK PASS AFTER TRICK PASS FOR THIS JOHNAN TEAM!!
TORRES PULLS UP FOR THE JUMP SHOT!
JOHNAN
WHO CARES IF THEY BLOCK IT... JUST TAKE THE J.
AHHH!
HAYA-SHIDA JUMPS RIGHT IN FRONT OF HIM!!
NO!
LOOK OUT!
THIS ONE'S MINE.

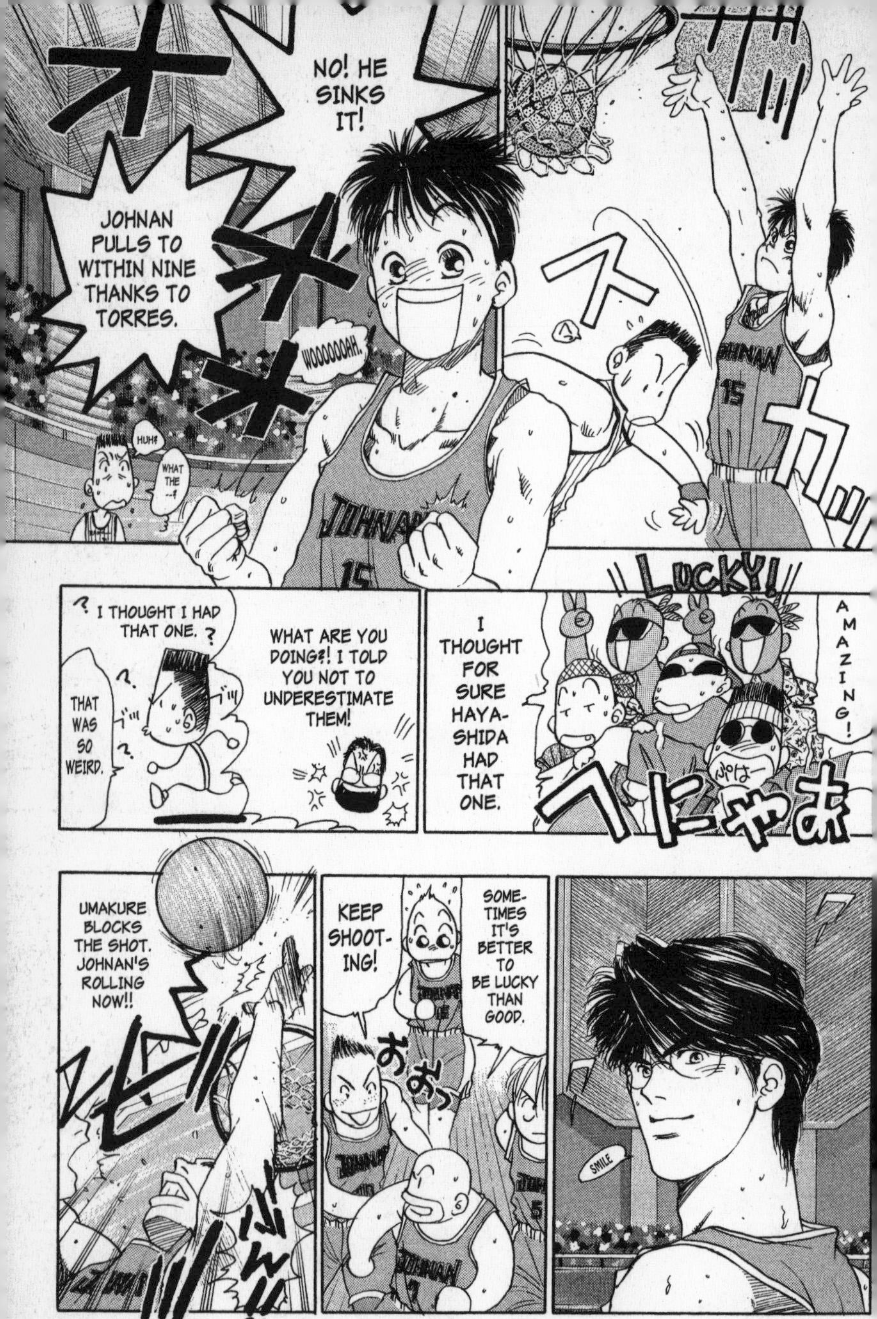
NO! HE SINKS IT!
ス
カッ
JOHNAN PULLS TO WITHIN NINE THANKS TO TORRES.
WOOOOOOAH.
HUH?
WHAT THE --?
LUCKY!
AMAZING!
I THOUGHT FOR SURE HAYA-SHIDA HAD THAT ONE.
ぷはー
へにゃあ
WHAT ARE YOU DOING?! I TOLD YOU NOT TO UNDERESTIMATE THEM!
I THOUGHT I HAD THAT ONE.
THAT WAS SO WEIRD.
SMILE
SOME-TIMES IT'S BETTER TO BE LUCKY THAN GOOD.
KEEP SHOOT-ING!
おおっ
UMAKURE BLOCKS THE SHOT. JOHNAN'S ROLLING NOW!!

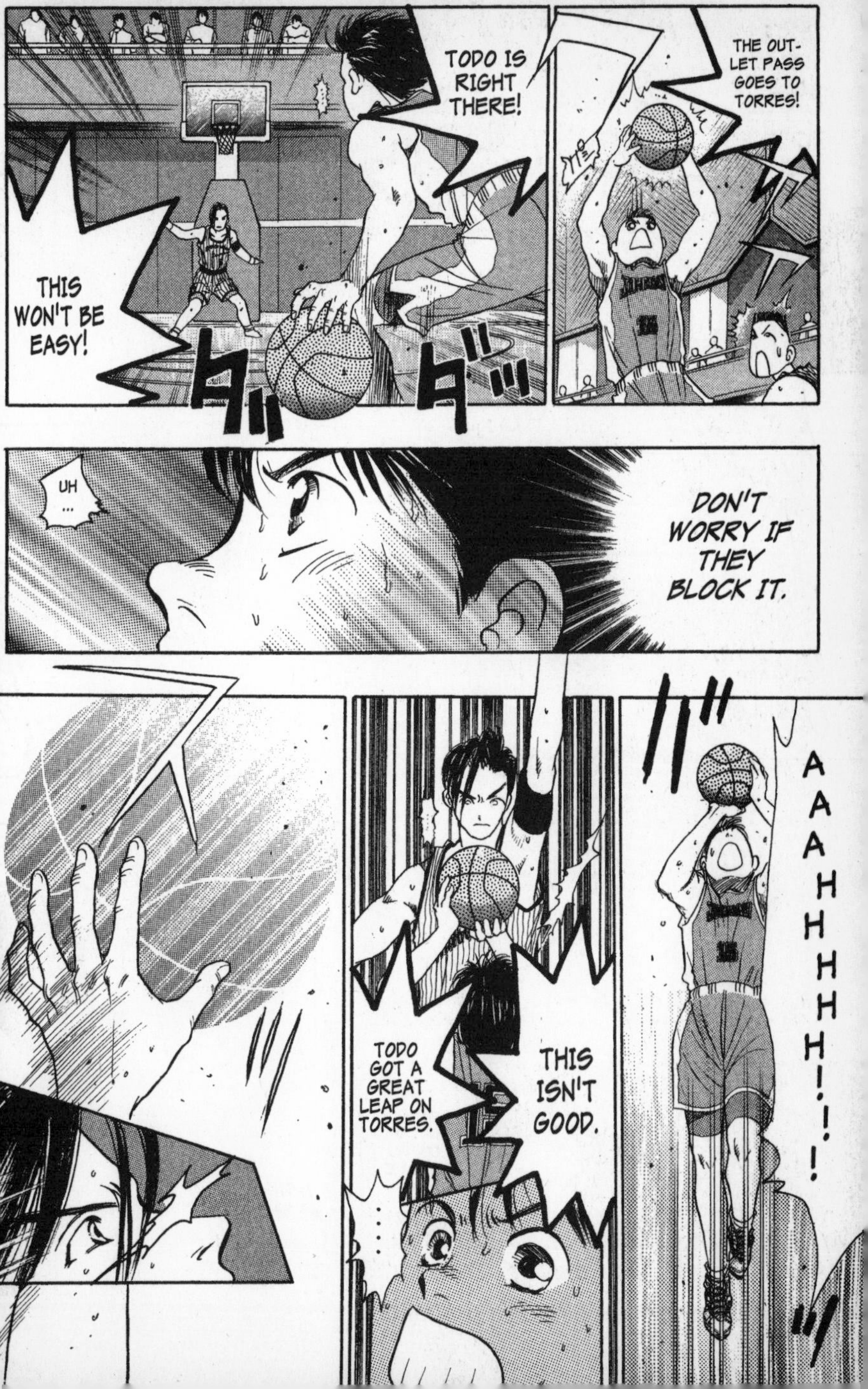
THE OUT-LET PASS GOES TO TORRES!
TODO IS RIGHT THERE!
THIS WON'T BE EASY!
タッ
ダッ
DON'T WORRY IF THEY BLOCK IT.
UH ...
AAAHHHHH!!!
THIS ISN'T GOOD.
TODO GOT A GREAT LEAP ON TORRES.

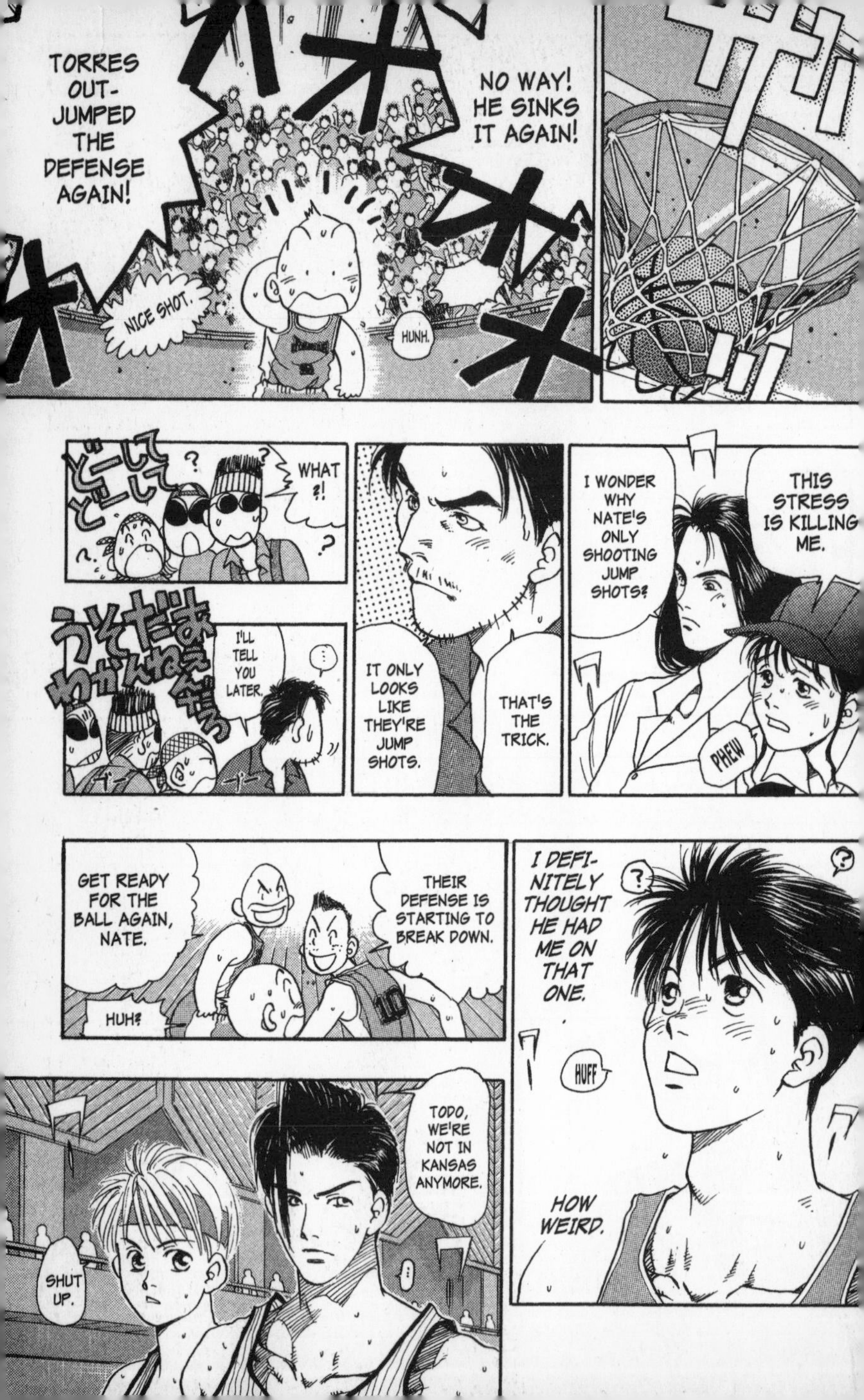
NO WAY! HE SINKS IT AGAIN!
TORRES OUT-JUMPED THE DEFENSE AGAIN!
HUNH.
NICE SHOT.
THIS STRESS IS KILLING ME.
I WONDER WHY NATE'S ONLY SHOOTING JUMP SHOTS?
PHEW
THAT'S THE TRICK.
IT ONLY LOOKS LIKE THEY'RE JUMP SHOTS.
WHAT?!
どーして どーして
...
I'LL TELL YOU LATER.
うそだぁ
I DEFINITELY THOUGHT HE HAD ME ON THAT ONE.
HUFF
HOW WEIRD.
THEIR DEFENSE IS STARTING TO BREAK DOWN.
GET READY FOR THE BALL AGAIN, NATE.
HUH?
TODO, WE'RE NOT IN KANSAS ANYMORE.
...
SHUT UP.

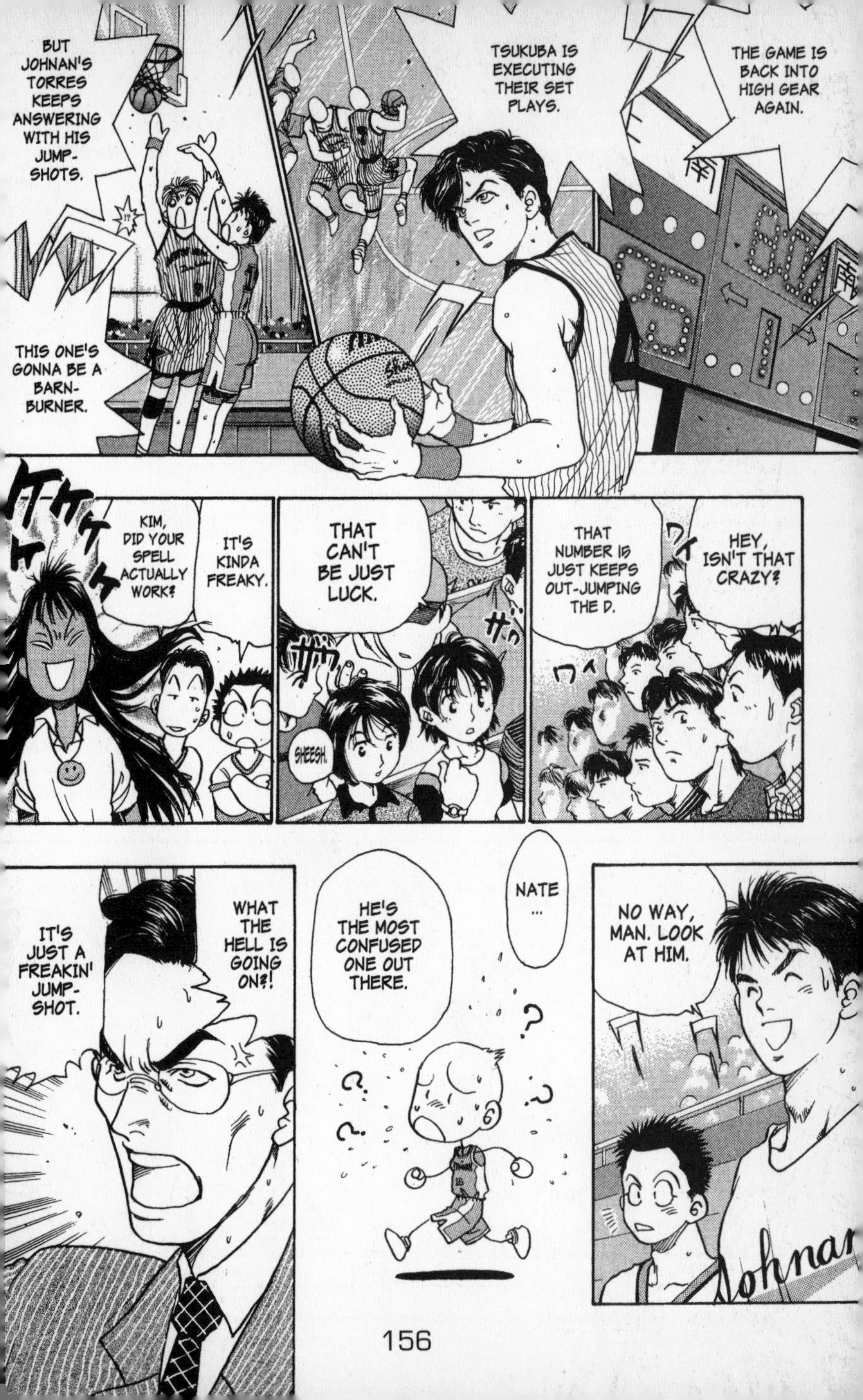
THE GAME IS BACK INTO HIGH GEAR AGAIN.
TSUKUBA IS EXECUTING THEIR SET PLAYS.
BUT JOHNAN'S TORRES KEEPS ANSWERING WITH HIS JUMP-SHOTS.
!?
THIS ONE'S GONNA BE A BARN-BURNER.
HEY, ISN'T THAT CRAZY?
THAT NUMBER IS JUST KEEPS OUT-JUMPING THE D.
THAT CAN'T BE JUST LUCK.
SHEESH.
IT'S KINDA FREAKY.
KIM, DID YOUR SPELL ACTUALLY WORK?
NO WAY, MAN. LOOK AT HIM.
NATE ...
HE'S THE MOST CONFUSED ONE OUT THERE.
WHAT THE HELL IS GOING ON?!
IT'S JUST A FREAKIN' JUMP-SHOT.

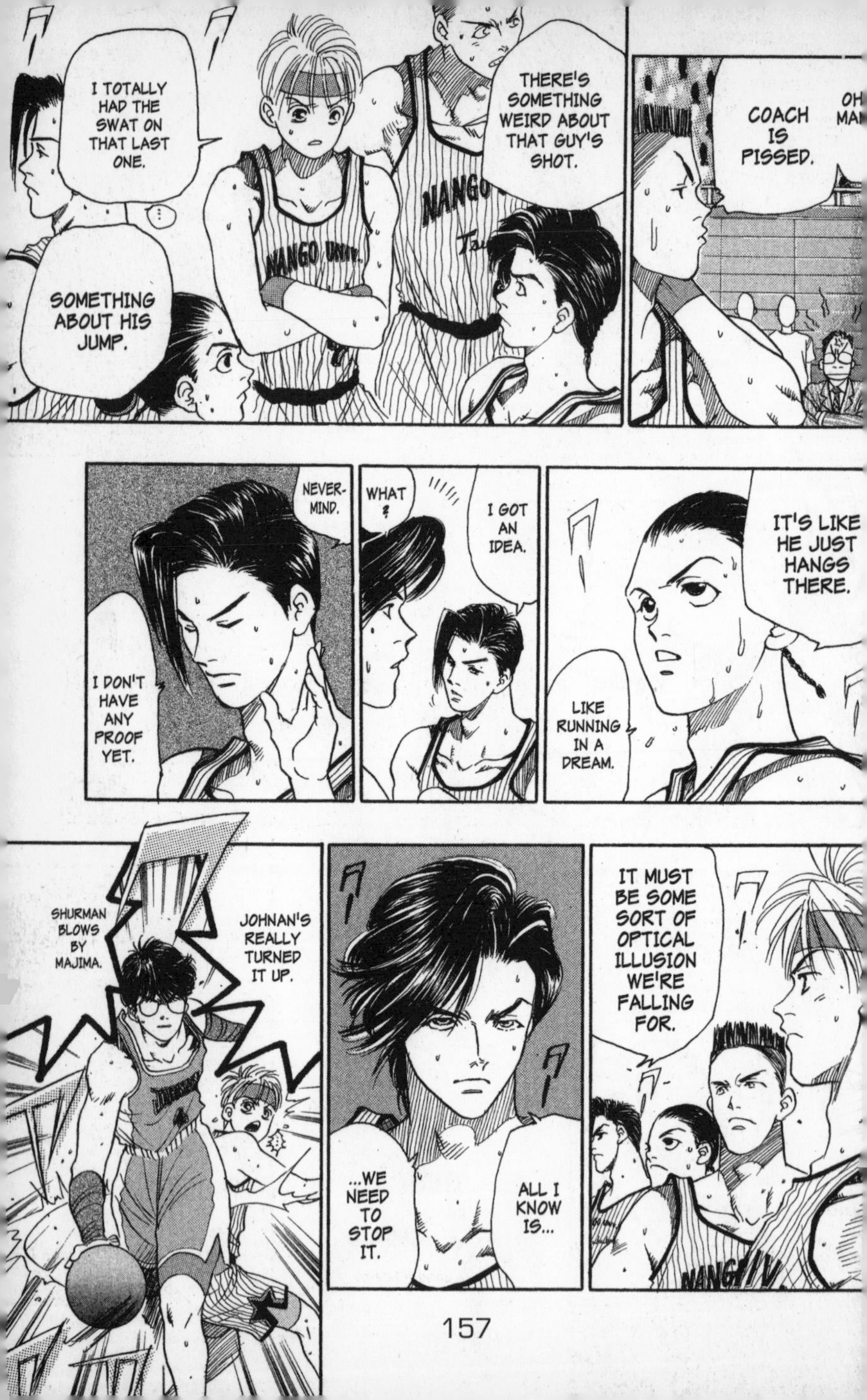

OH
COACH IS PISSED.
THERE'S SOMETHING WEIRD ABOUT THAT GUY'S SHOT.
I TOTALLY HAD THE SWAT ON THAT LAST ONE.
...
SOMETHING ABOUT HIS JUMP.
IT'S LIKE HE JUST HANGS THERE.
LIKE RUNNING IN A DREAM.
I GOT AN IDEA.
WHAT?
NEVER-MIND.
I DON'T HAVE ANY PROOF YET.
IT MUST BE SOME SORT OF OPTICAL ILLUSION WE'RE FALLING FOR.
ALL I KNOW IS...
...WE NEED TO STOP IT.
JOHNAN'S REALLY TURNED IT UP.
SHURMAN BLOWS BY MAJIMA.

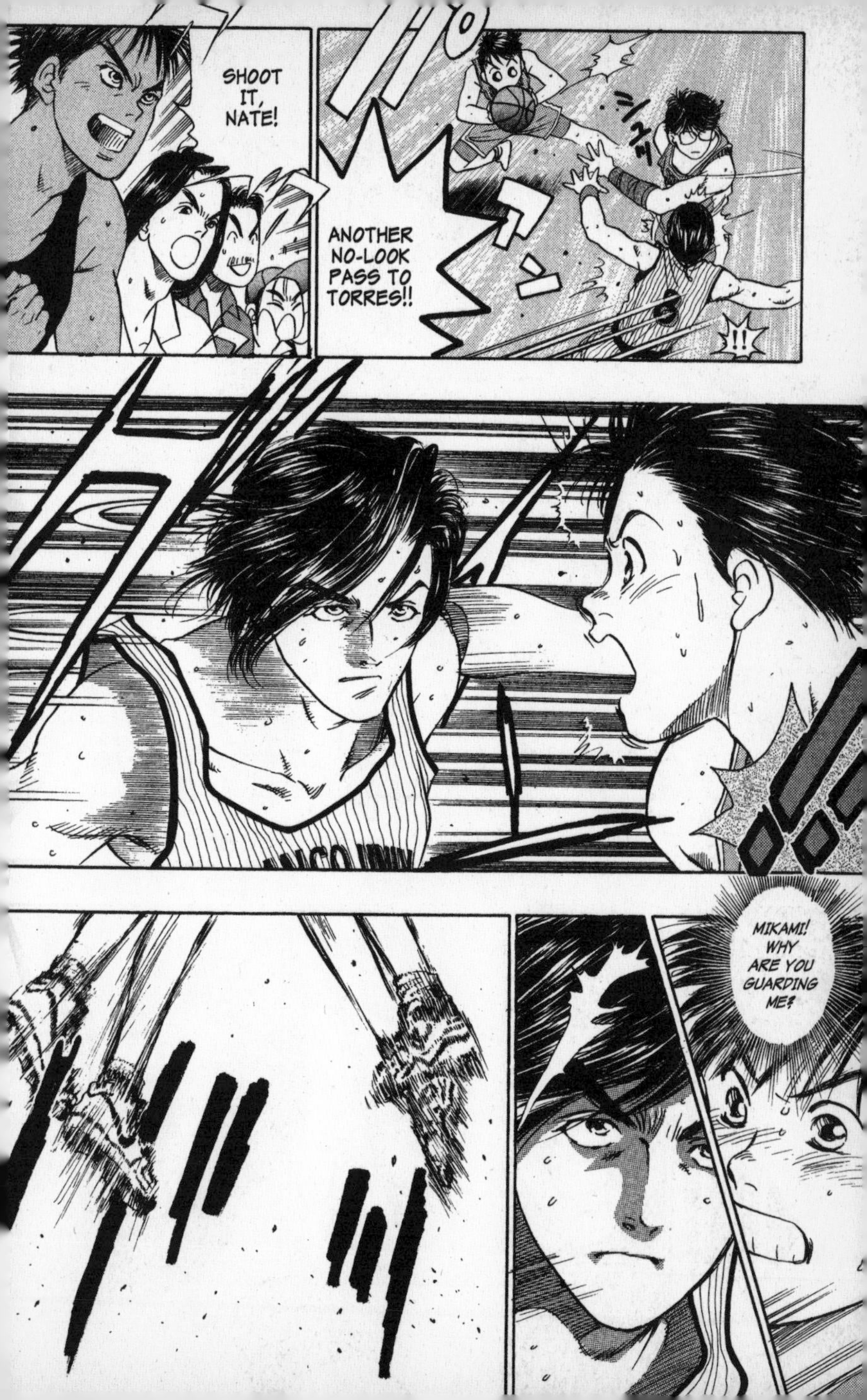
ANOTHER NO-LOOK PASS TO TORRES!!
!!
SHOOT IT, NATE!
MIKAMI! WHY ARE YOU GUARDING ME?

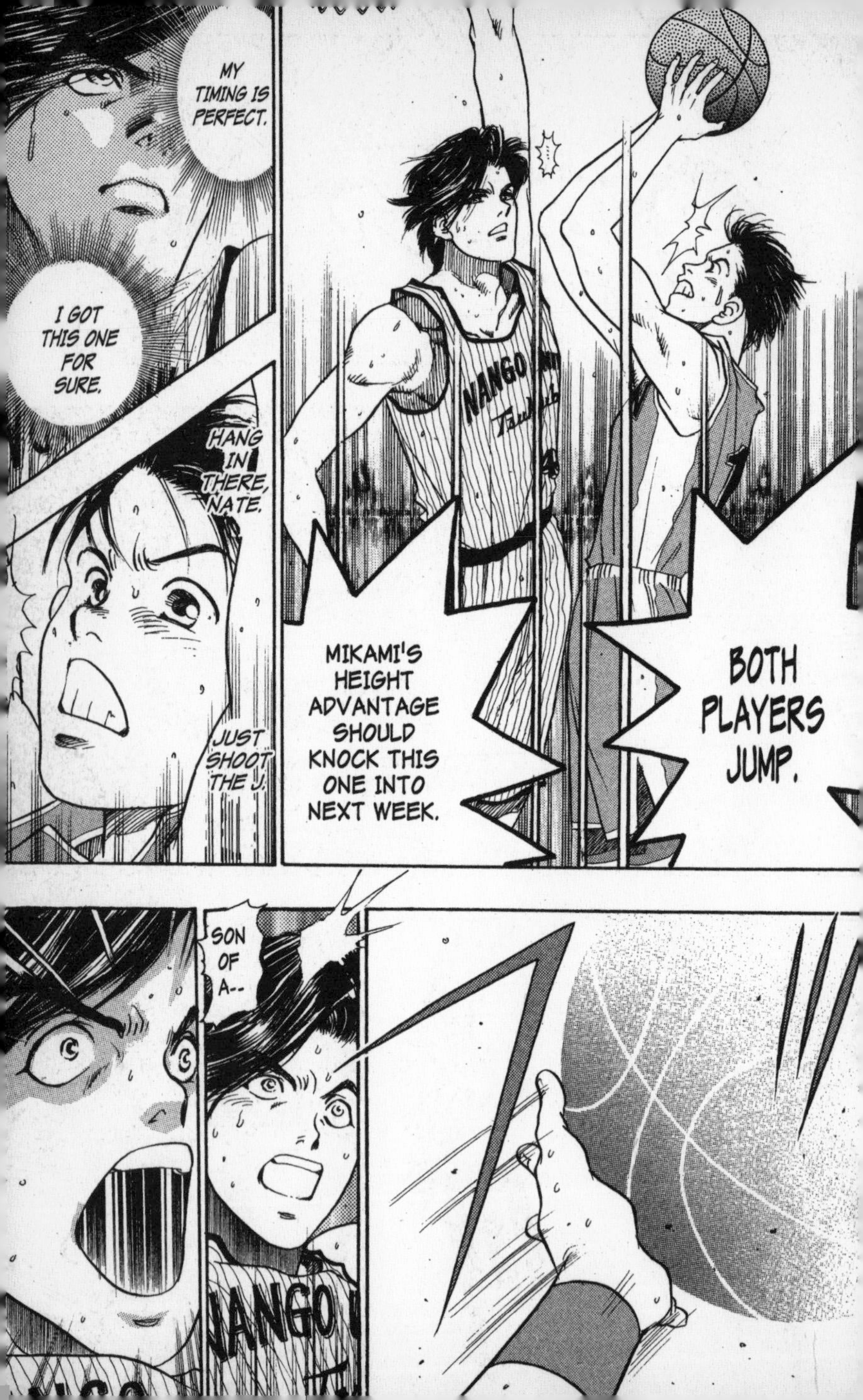
BOTH PLAYERS JUMP.
MIKAMI'S HEIGHT ADVANTAGE SHOULD KNOCK THIS ONE INTO NEXT WEEK.
MY TIMING IS PERFECT.
I GOT THIS ONE FOR SURE.
HANG IN THERE, NATE.
JUST SHOOT THE J.
SON OF A--
NANGO
NANGO

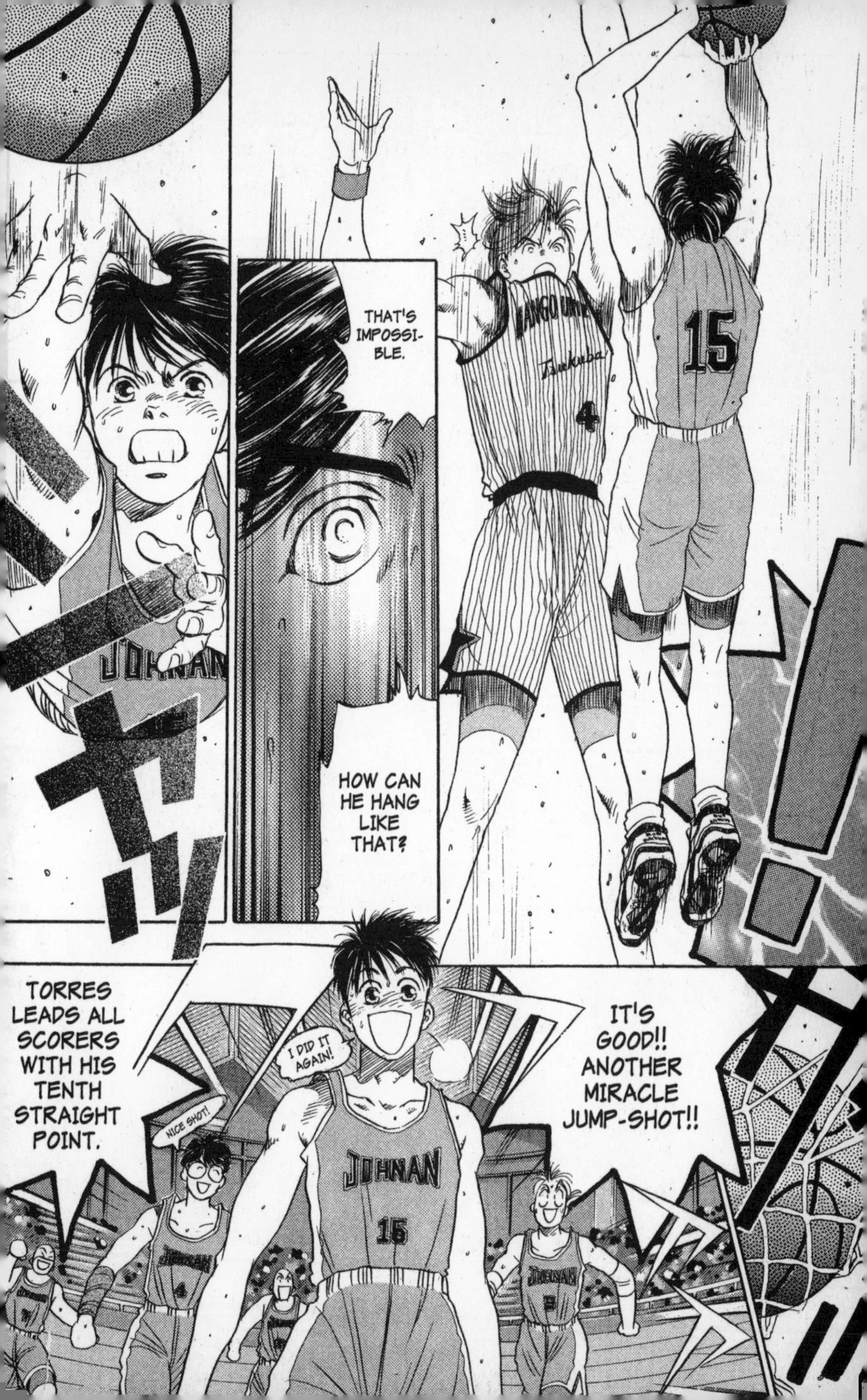
THAT'S IMPOSSI-BLE.
HOW CAN HE HANG LIKE THAT?
IT'S GOOD!! ANOTHER MIRACLE JUMP-SHOT!!
I DID IT AGAIN!
NICE SHOT!
TORRES LEADS ALL SCORERS WITH HIS TENTH STRAIGHT POINT.

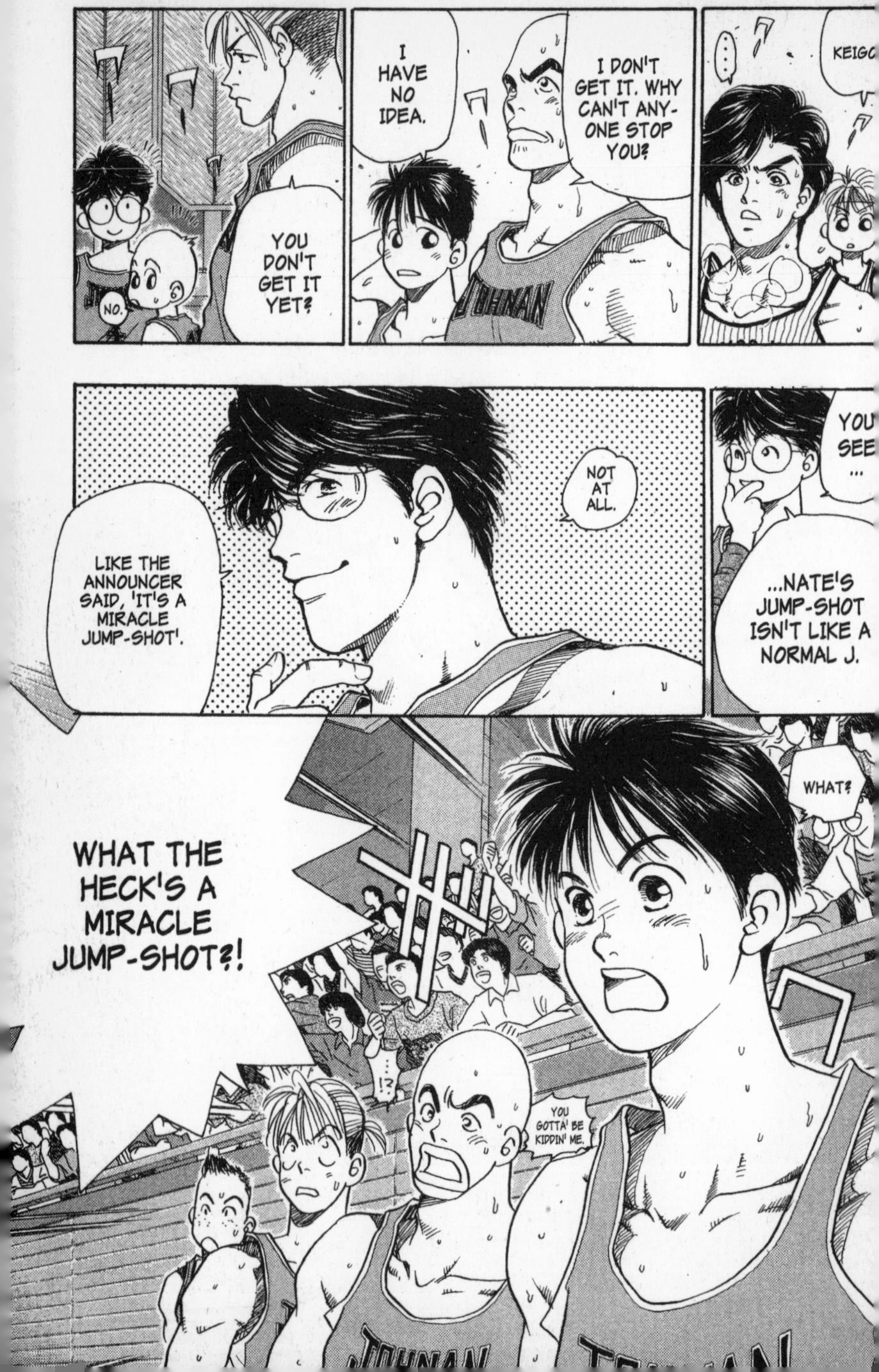
...
KEIG
I DON'T GET IT. WHY CAN'T ANY-ONE STOP YOU?
I HAVE NO IDEA.
YOU DON'T GET IT YET?
NO.
YOU SEE ...
...NATE'S JUMP-SHOT ISN'T LIKE A NORMAL J.
NOT AT ALL.
LIKE THE ANNOUNCER SAID, 'IT'S A MIRACLE JUMP-SHOT'.
WHAT?
WHAT THE HECK'S A MIRACLE JUMP-SHOT?!
...!?
YOU GOTTA' BE KIDDIN' ME.

What indeed is a **MIRACLE JUMP SHOT?** The answers to this and other questions to come in the next thrilling episode of...

And if its answers you seek, try TOKYOPOP's new Magic Basketball.

"Hey, Magic Basketball, will I have loads of fun asking you loads of questions?"

"Signs point to YES!"

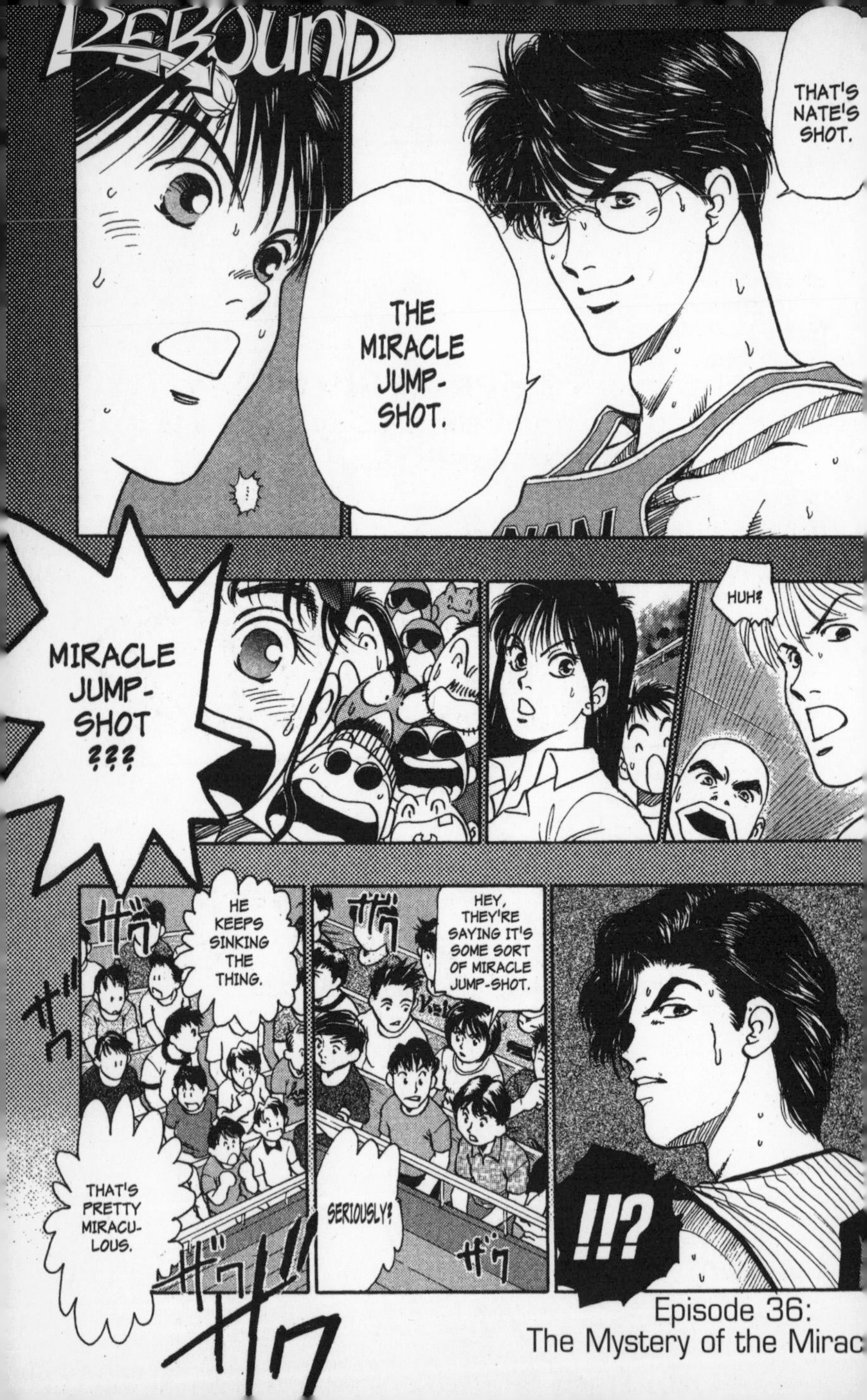
REBOUND
THAT'S NATE'S SHOT.
THE MIRACLE JUMP-SHOT.
...
HUH?
MIRACLE JUMP-SHOT???
!!?
HEY, THEY'RE SAYING IT'S SOME SORT OF MIRACLE JUMP-SHOT.
SERIOUSLY?
HE KEEPS SINKING THE THING.
THAT'S PRETTY MIRACULOUS.

Episode 36:
The Mystery of the Mirac

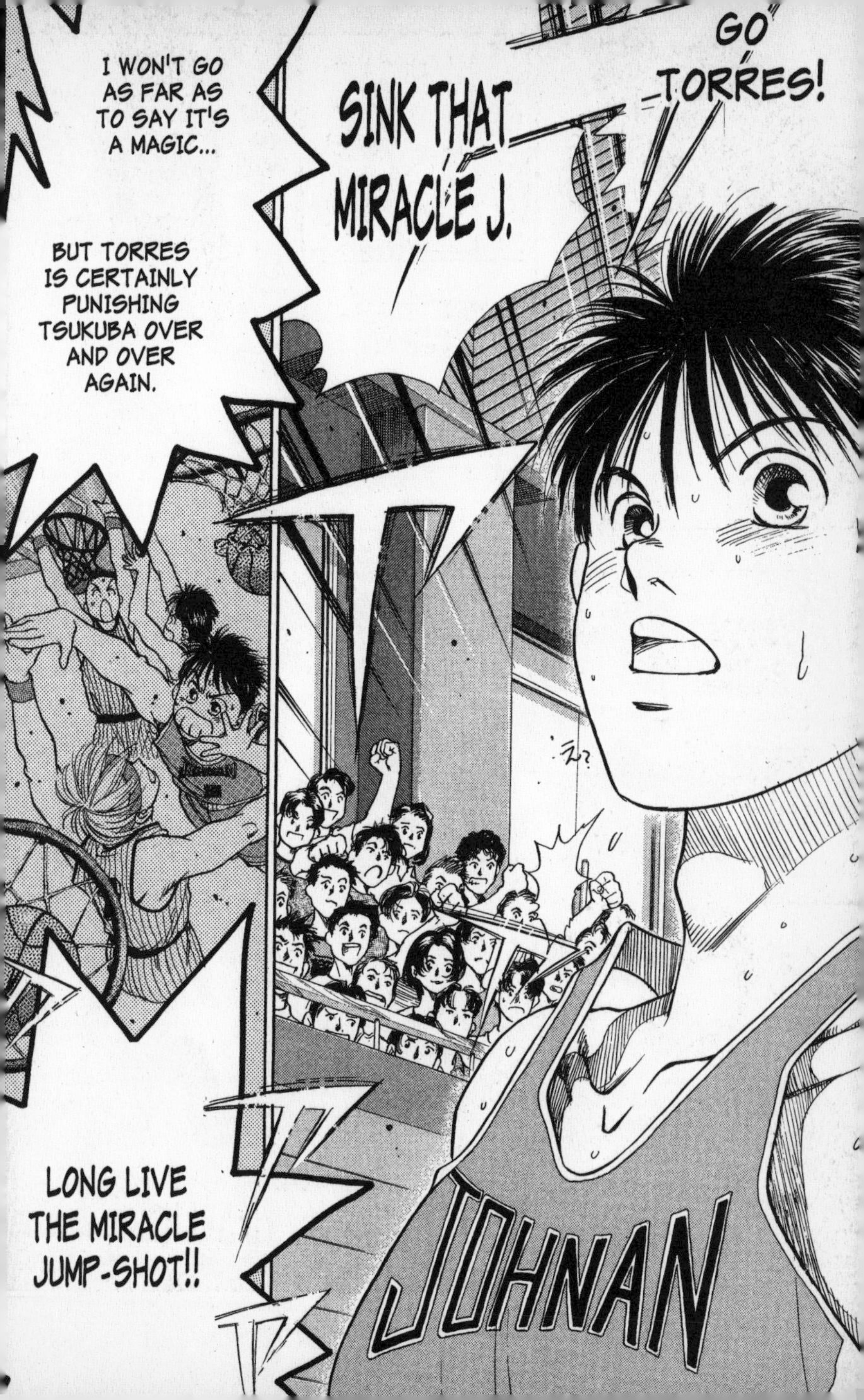
GO TORRES!
SINK THAT MIRACLE J.
I WON'T GO AS FAR AS TO SAY IT'S A MAGIC...
BUT TORRES IS CERTAINLY PUNISHING TSUKUBA OVER AND OVER AGAIN.
LONG LIVE THE MIRACLE JUMP-SHOT!!
JOHNAN

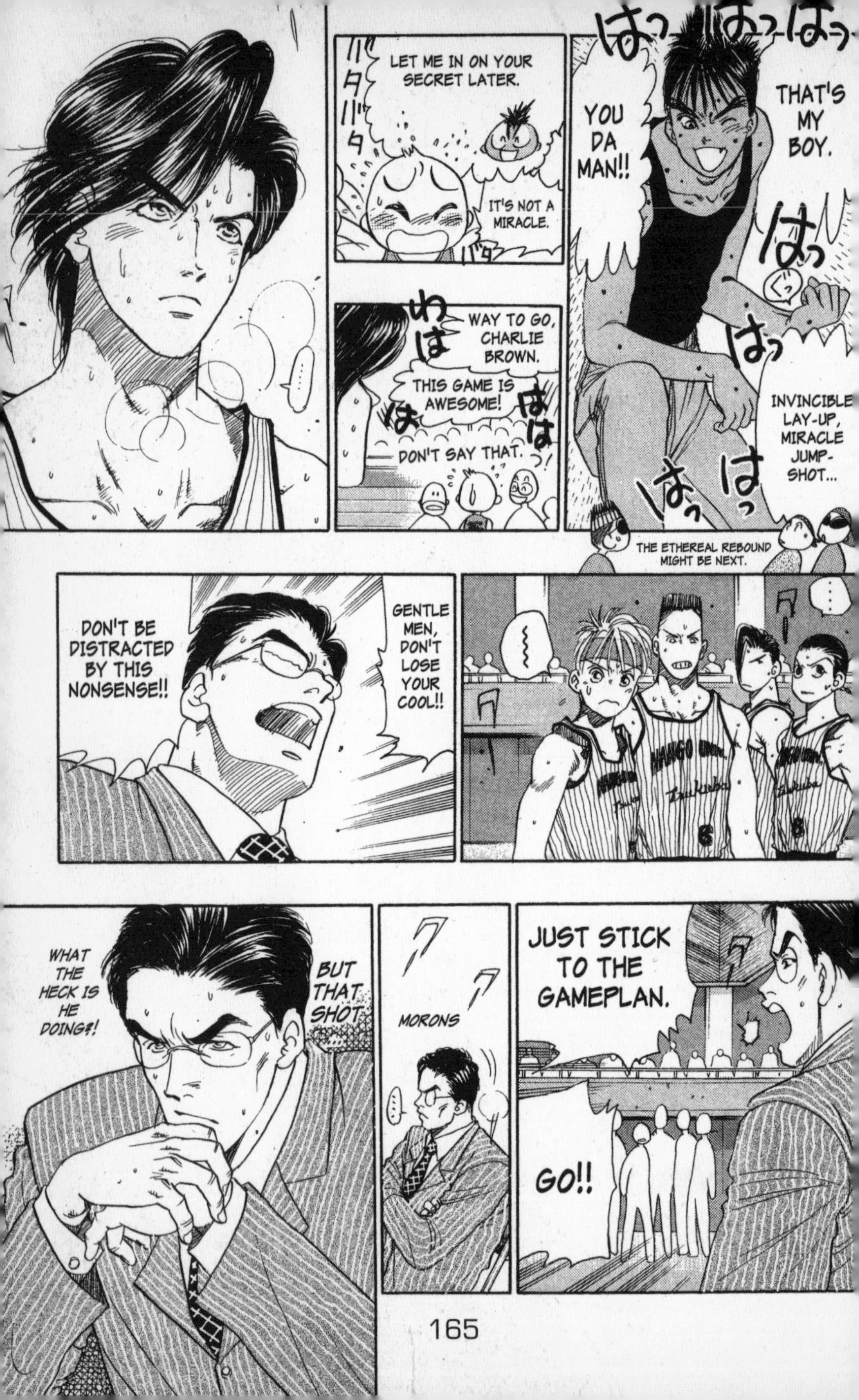
はっ はっ はっ
YOU DA MAN!!
THAT'S MY BOY.
はっ
はっ
INVINCIBLE LAY-UP, MIRACLE JUMP-SHOT...
はっ はっ
THE ETHEREAL REBOUND MIGHT BE NEXT.
LET ME IN ON YOUR SECRET LATER.
IT'S NOT A MIRACLE.
WAY TO GO, CHARLIE BROWN.
THIS GAME IS AWESOME!
DON'T SAY THAT.
GENTLE MEN, DON'T LOSE YOUR COOL!!
DON'T BE DISTRACTED BY THIS NONSENSE!!
JUST STICK TO THE GAMEPLAN.
GO!!
MORONS
BUT THAT SHOT...
WHAT THE HECK IS HE DOING?!

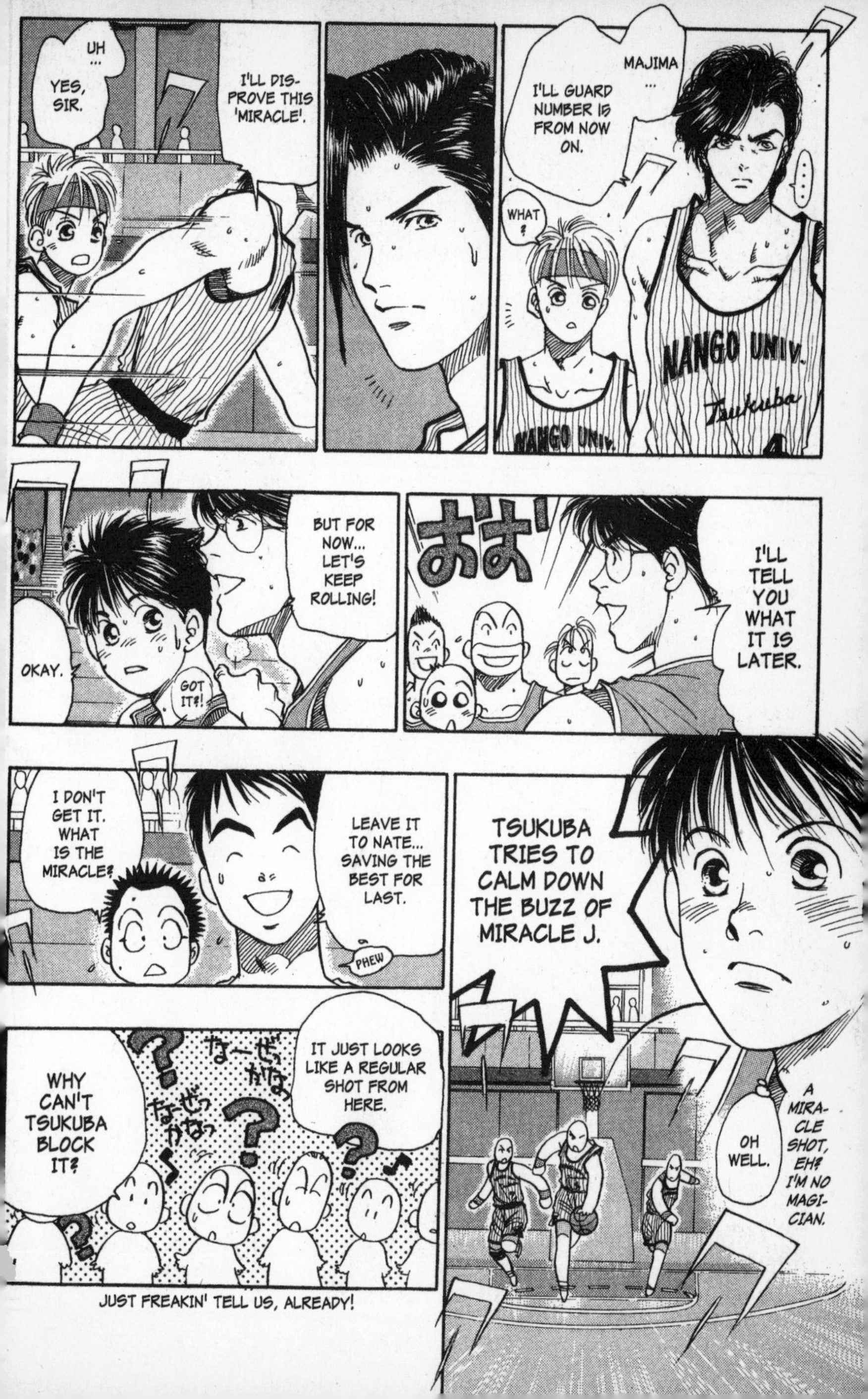
MAJIMA ...
I'LL GUARD NUMBER 15 FROM NOW ON.
...
WHAT?
I'LL DIS-PROVE THIS 'MIRACLE'.
UH ... YES, SIR.
I'LL TELL YOU WHAT IT IS LATER.
おお!
BUT FOR NOW... LET'S KEEP ROLLING!
GOT IT?!
OKAY.
TSUKUBA TRIES TO CALM DOWN THE BUZZ OF MIRACLE J.
A MIRA-CLE SHOT, EH? I'M NO MAGI-CIAN.
OH WELL.
LEAVE IT TO NATE... SAVING THE BEST FOR LAST.
PHEW
I DON'T GET IT. WHAT IS THE MIRACLE?
IT JUST LOOKS LIKE A REGULAR SHOT FROM HERE.
なーぜっかなっ
なぜっかなっ
WHY CAN'T TSUKUBA BLOCK IT?
JUST FREAKIN' TELL US, ALREADY!

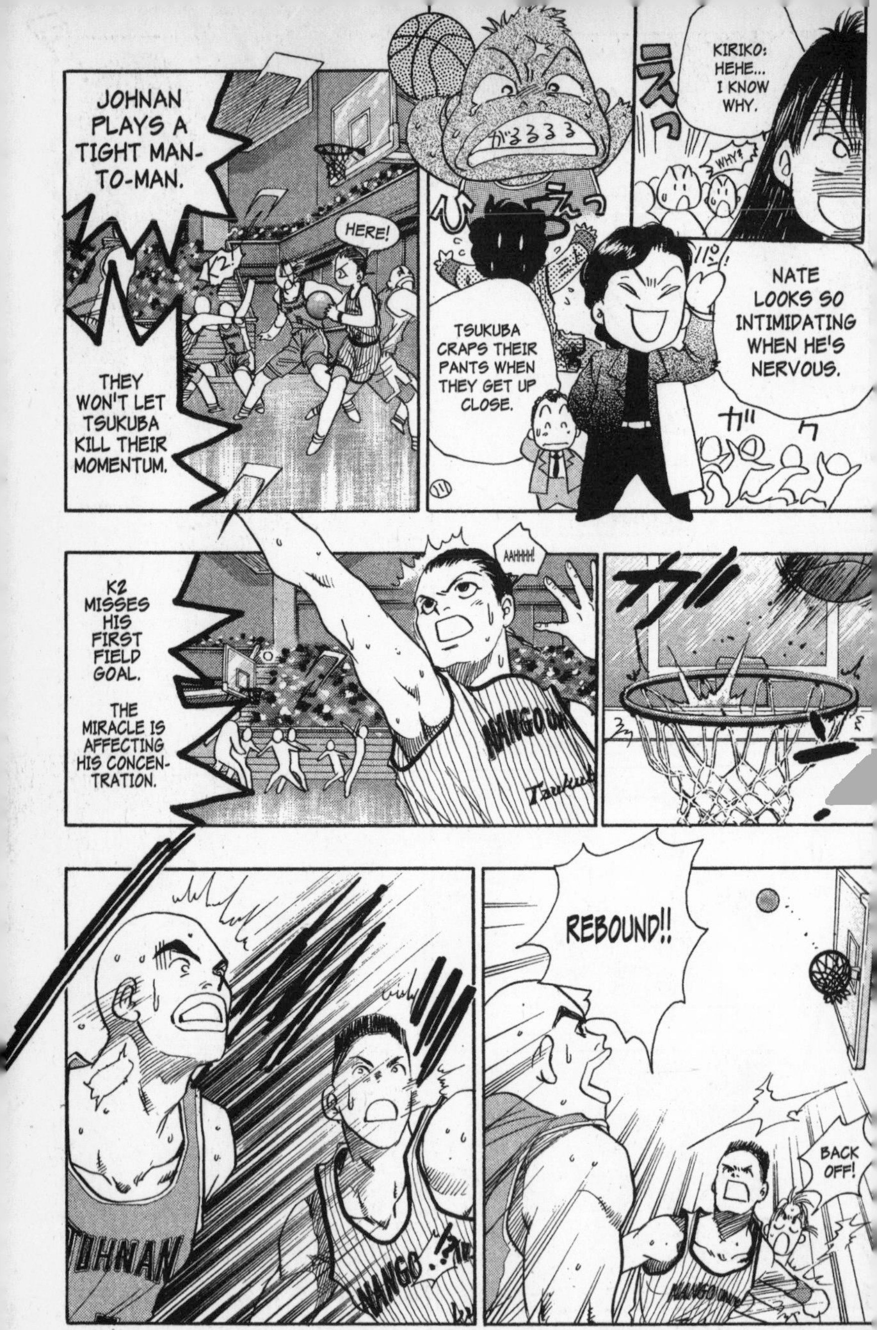
KIRIKO: HEHE... I KNOW WHY.
WHY?
NATE LOOKS SO INTIMIDATING WHEN HE'S NERVOUS.
TSUKUBA CRAPS THEIR PANTS WHEN THEY GET UP CLOSE.
JOHNAN PLAYS A TIGHT MAN-TO-MAN.
HERE!
THEY WON'T LET TSUKUBA KILL THEIR MOMENTUM.
AAHHHH!
K2 MISSES HIS FIRST FIELD GOAL.
THE MIRACLE IS AFFECTING HIS CONCENTRATION.
REBOUND!!
BACK OFF!

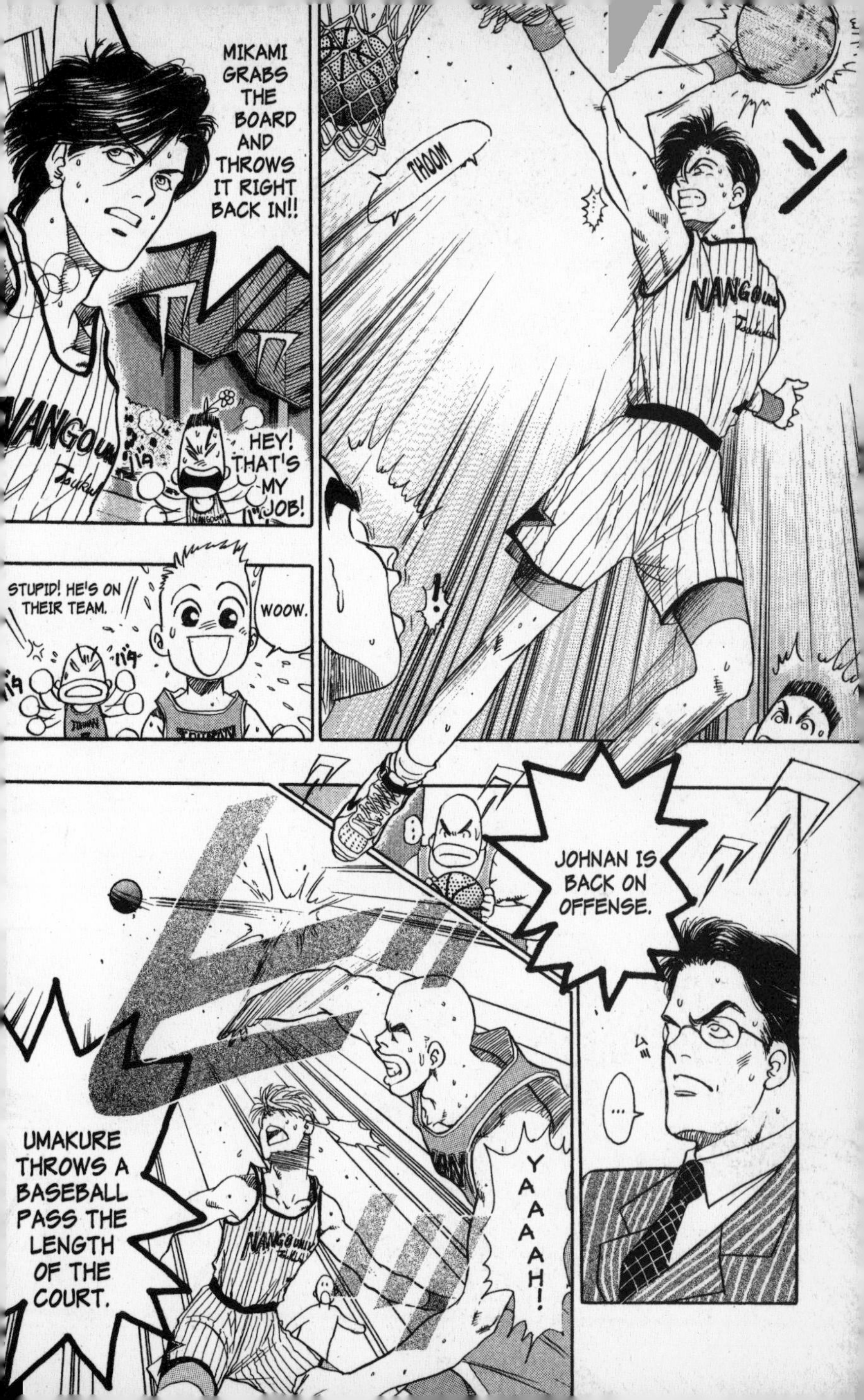
THOOM
MIKAMI GRABS THE BOARD AND THROWS IT RIGHT BACK IN!!
HEY! THAT'S MY JOB!
WOOW.
STUPID! HE'S ON THEIR TEAM.
JOHNAN IS BACK ON OFFENSE.
...
UMAKURE THROWS A BASEBALL PASS THE LENGTH OF THE COURT.
YAAAAH!

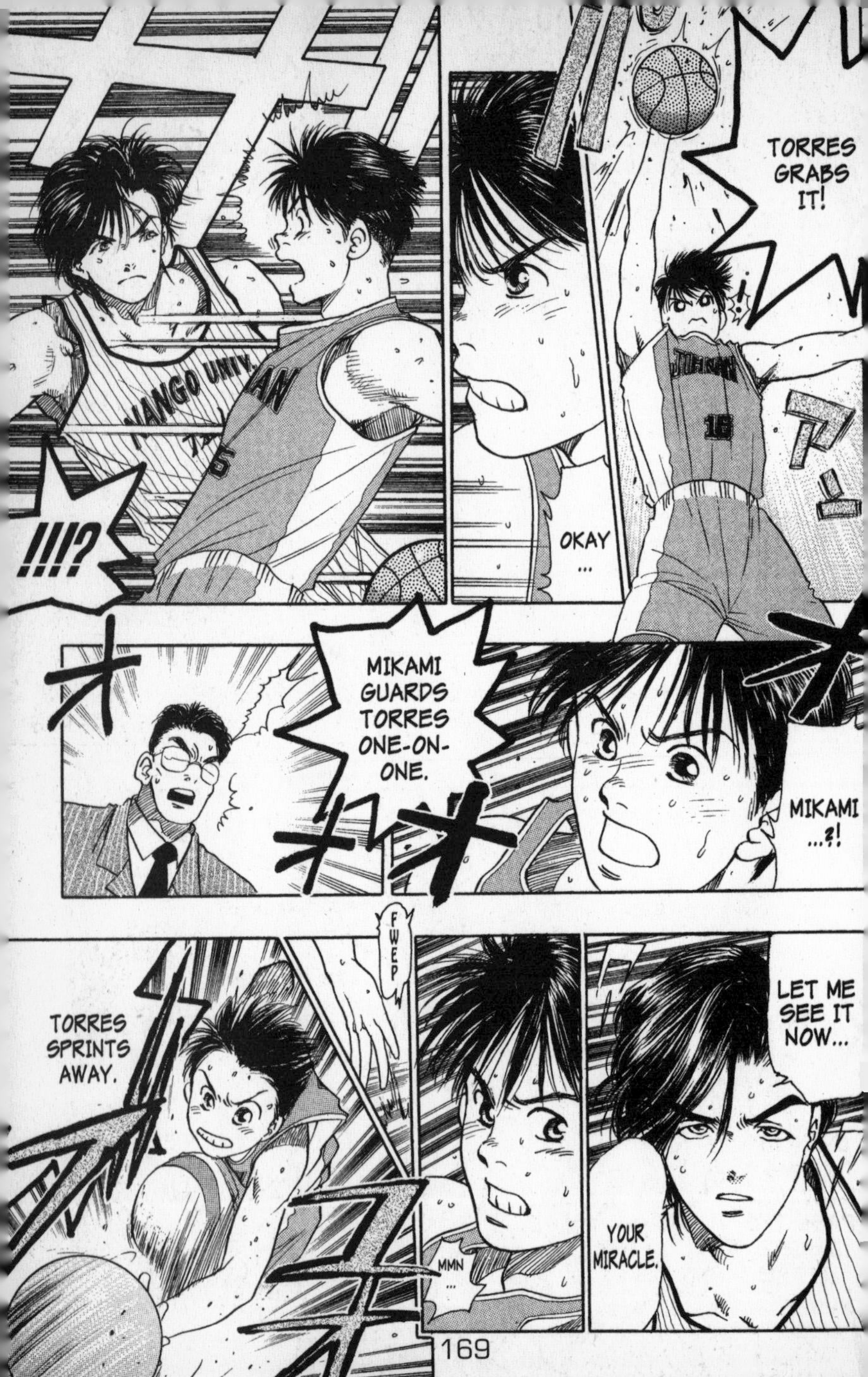
TORRES GRABS IT!
OKAY ...
!!!?
MIKAMI ...?!
MIKAMI GUARDS TORRES ONE-ON-ONE.
LET ME SEE IT NOW...
YOUR MIRACLE.
MMN ...
FWEP
TORRES SPRINTS AWAY.

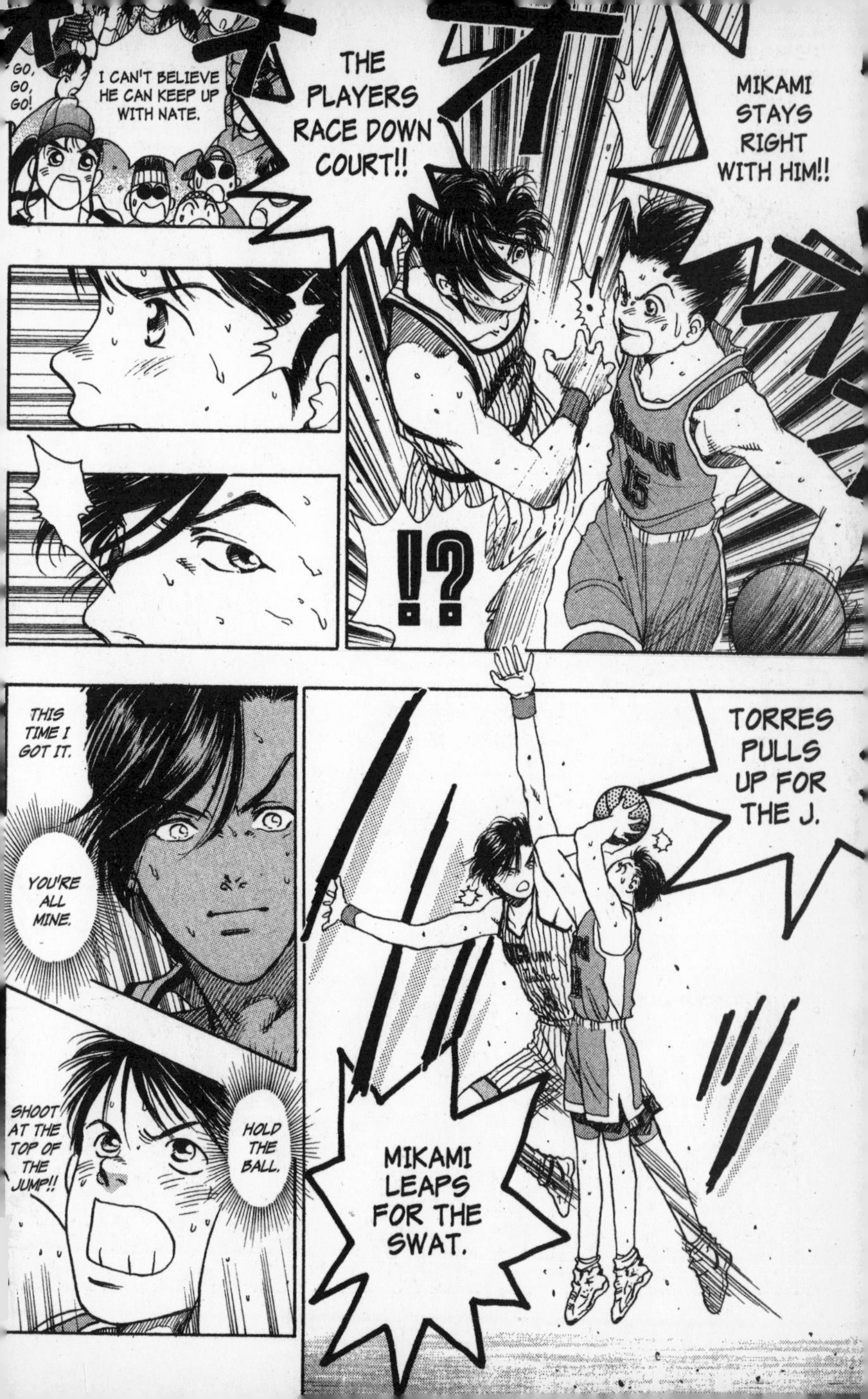
THE PLAYERS RACE DOWN COURT!!
MIKAMI STAYS RIGHT WITH HIM!!
!?
I CAN'T BELIEVE HE CAN KEEP UP WITH NATE.
GO, GO, GO!
TORRES PULLS UP FOR THE J.
MIKAMI LEAPS FOR THE SWAT.
THIS TIME I GOT IT.
YOU'RE ALL MINE.
HOLD THE BALL.
SHOOT AT THE TOP OF THE JUMP!!

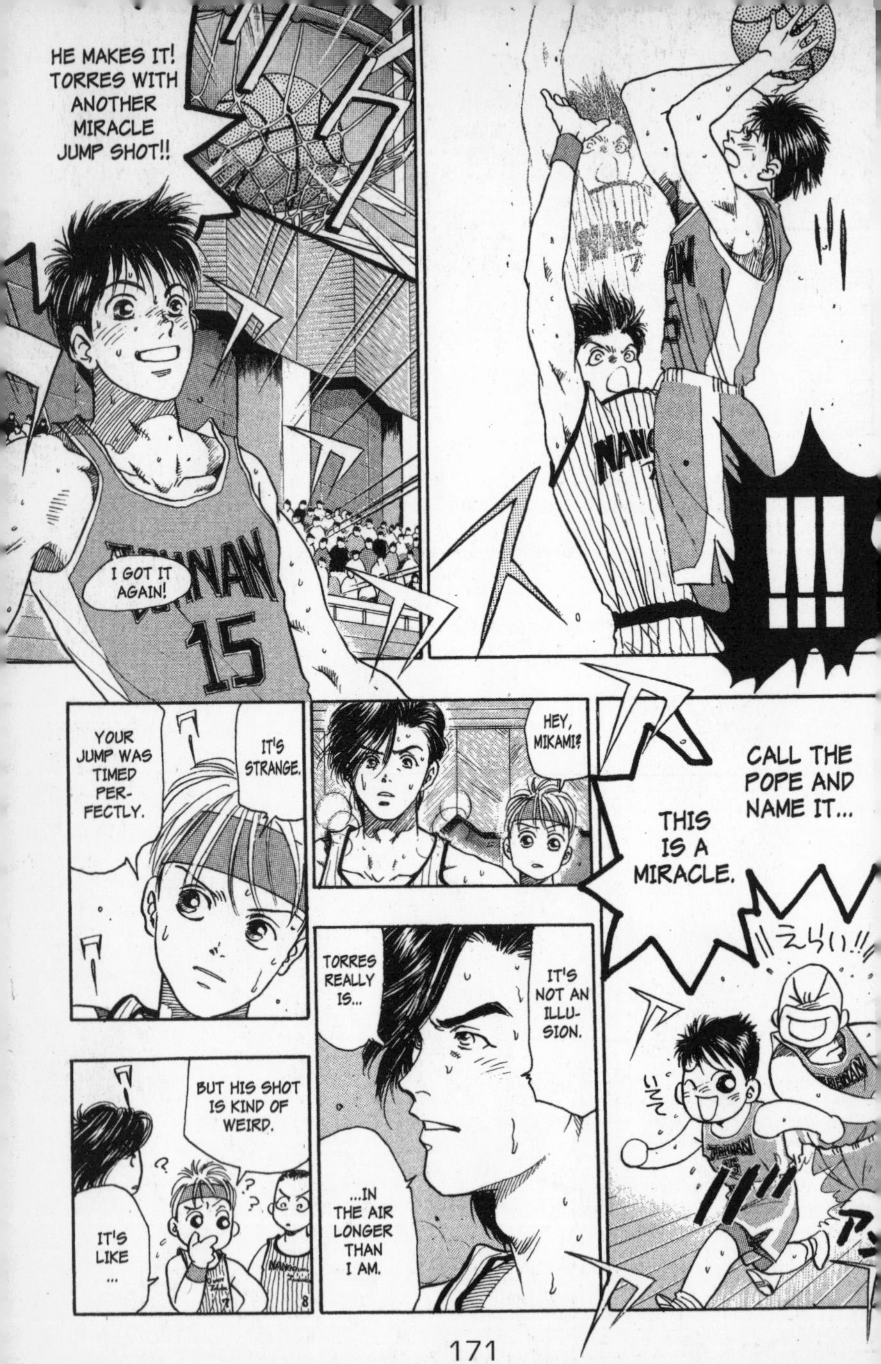
!!!
HE MAKES IT! TORRES WITH ANOTHER MIRACLE JUMP SHOT!!
I GOT IT AGAIN!
CALL THE POPE AND NAME IT...
THIS IS A MIRACLE.
えらい!!
HEY, MIKAMI?
IT'S STRANGE.
YOUR JUMP WAS TIMED PER-FECTLY.
IT'S NOT AN ILLU-SION.
TORRES REALLY IS...
...IN THE AIR LONGER THAN I AM.
BUT HIS SHOT IS KIND OF WEIRD.
IT'S LIKE ...

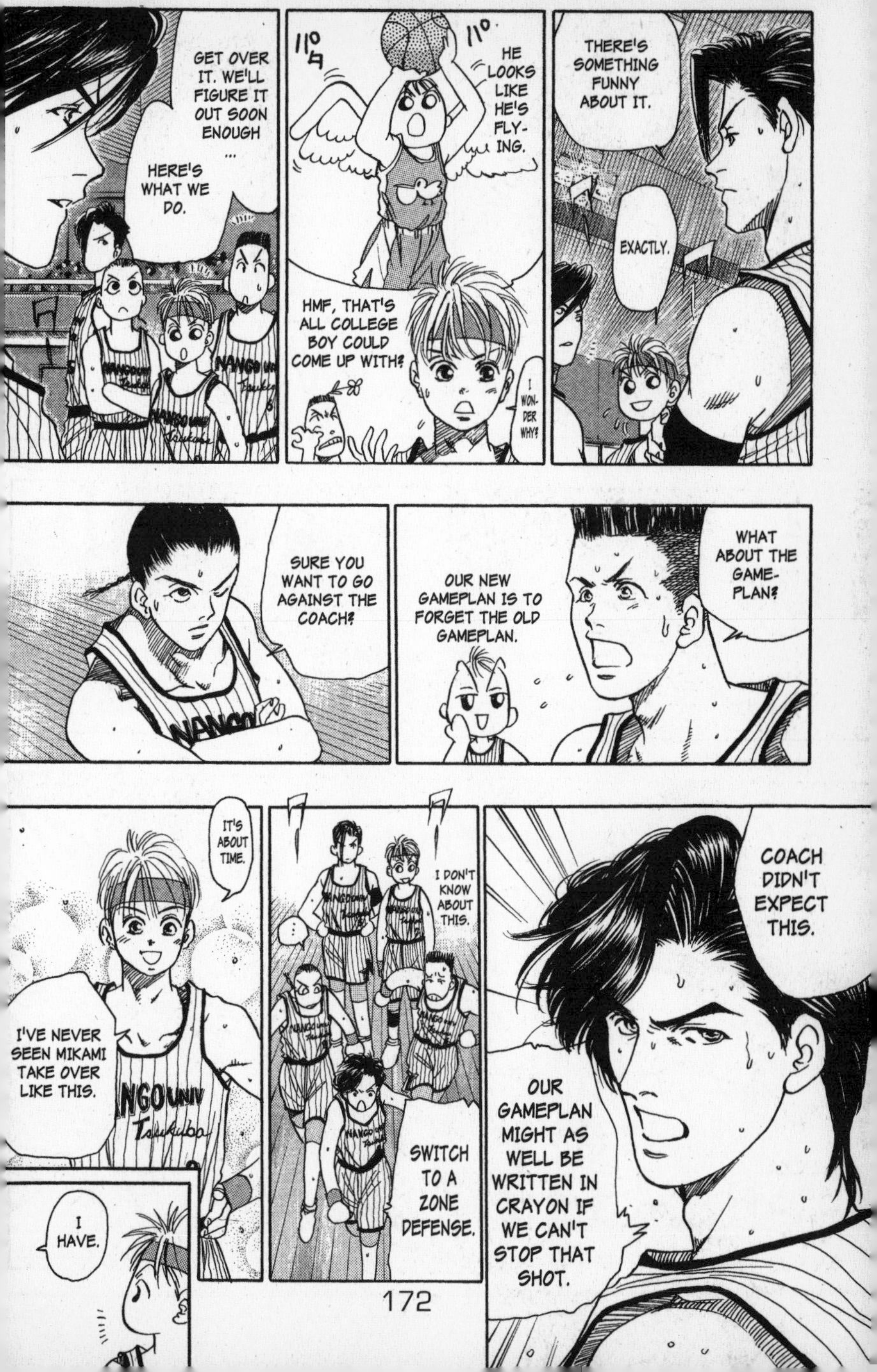
THERE'S SOMETHING FUNNY ABOUT IT.
EXACTLY.
HE LOOKS LIKE HE'S FLY-ING.
HMF, THAT'S ALL COLLEGE BOY COULD COME UP WITH?
I WON-DER WHY?
GET OVER IT. WE'LL FIGURE IT OUT SOON ENOUGH ...
HERE'S WHAT WE DO.
WHAT ABOUT THE GAME-PLAN?
OUR NEW GAMEPLAN IS TO FORGET THE OLD GAMEPLAN.
SURE YOU WANT TO GO AGAINST THE COACH?
COACH DIDN'T EXPECT THIS.
OUR GAMEPLAN MIGHT AS WELL BE WRITTEN IN CRAYON IF WE CAN'T STOP THAT SHOT.
I DON'T KNOW ABOUT THIS.
SWITCH TO A ZONE DEFENSE.
IT'S ABOUT TIME.
I'VE NEVER SEEN MIKAMI TAKE OVER LIKE THIS.
I HAVE.

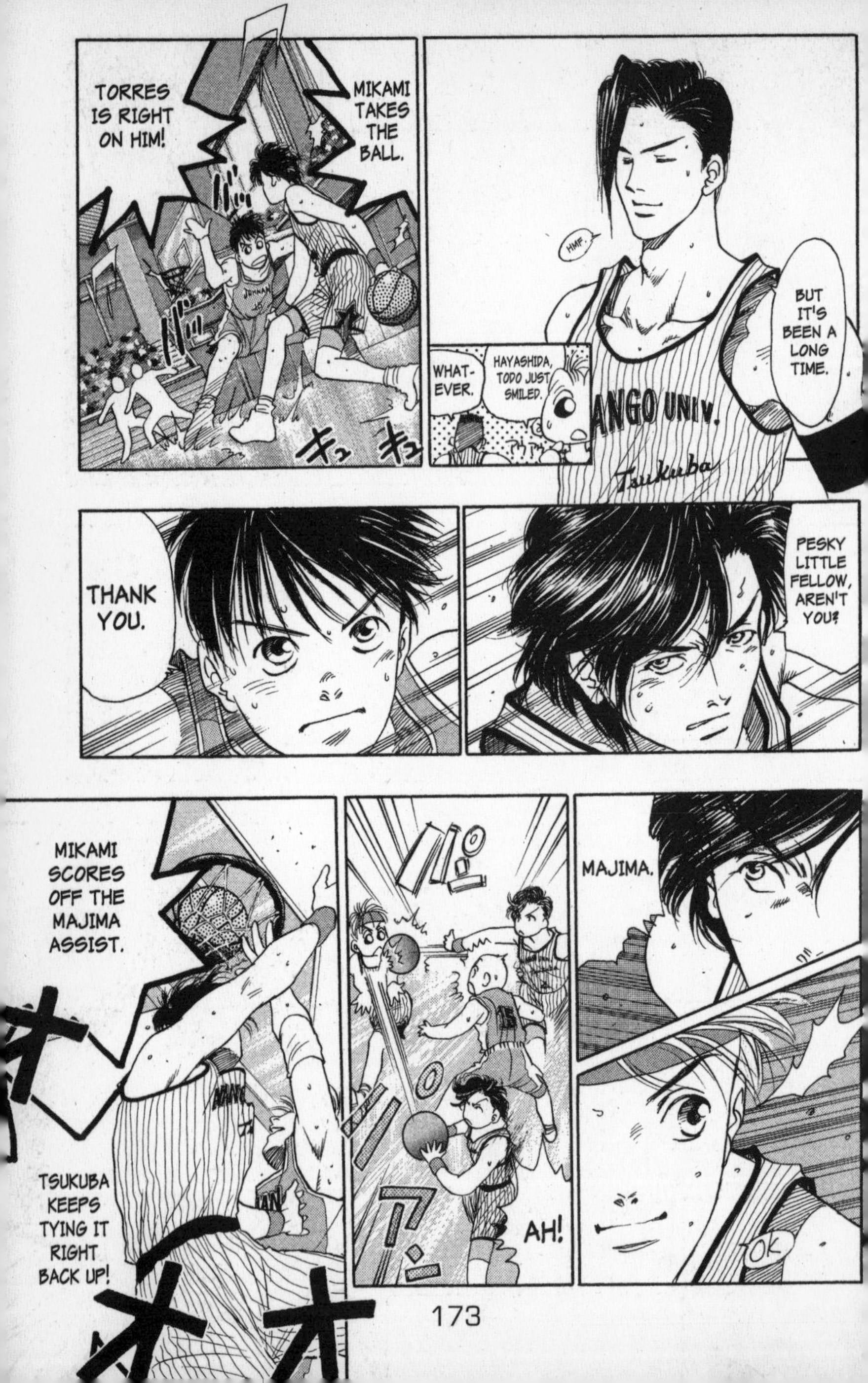
HMF.
BUT IT'S BEEN A LONG TIME.
HAYASHIDA, TODO JUST SMILED.
WHAT-EVER.
MIKAMI TAKES THE BALL.
TORRES IS RIGHT ON HIM!
PESKY LITTLE FELLOW, AREN'T YOU?
THANK YOU.
MAJIMA.
OK
AH!
MIKAMI SCORES OFF THE MAJIMA ASSIST.
TSUKUBA KEEPS TYING IT RIGHT BACK UP!

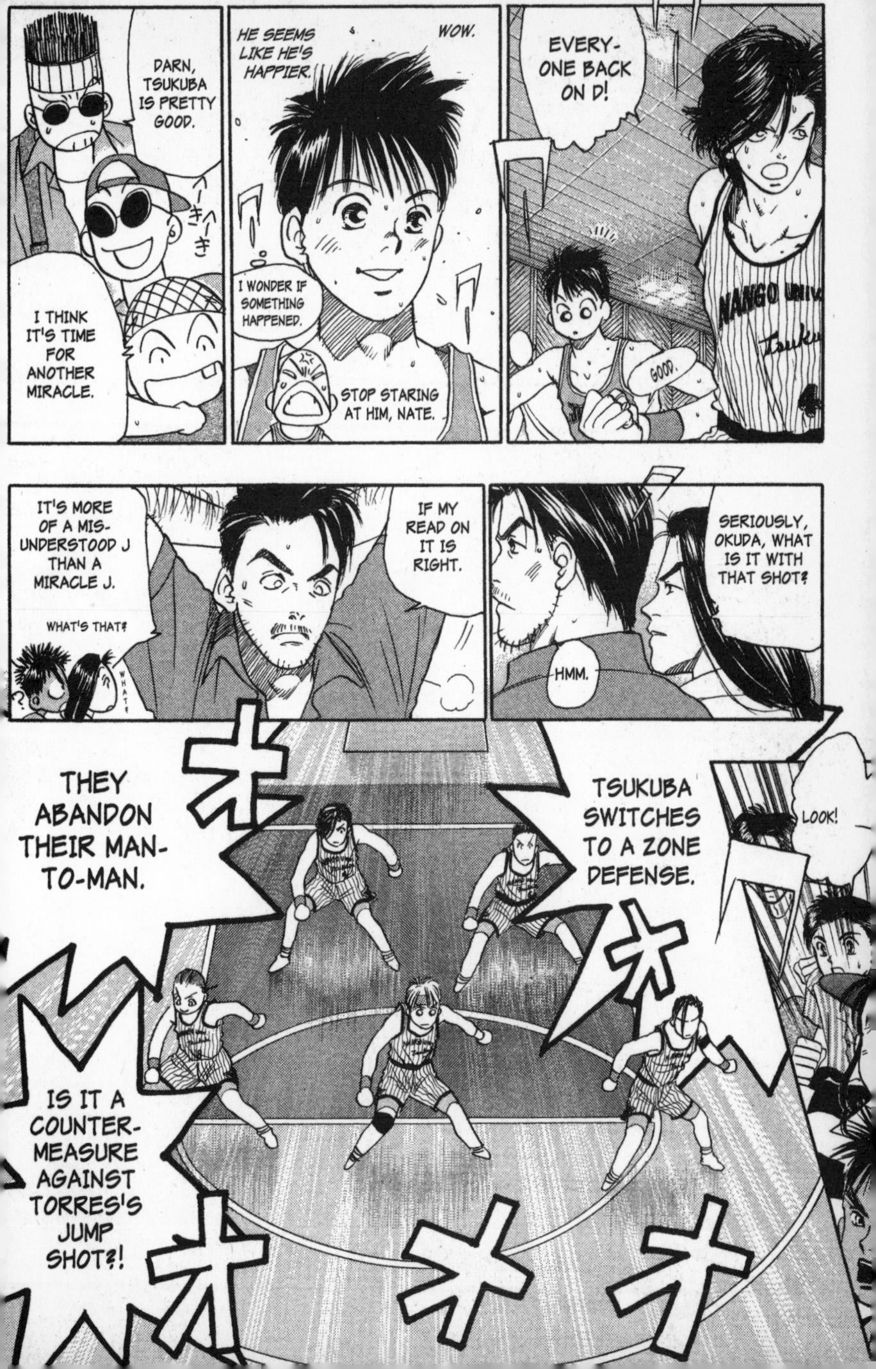
EVERY-ONE BACK ON D!
GOOD.
WOW.
HE SEEMS LIKE HE'S HAPPIER.
I WONDER IF SOMETHING HAPPENED.
STOP STARING AT HIM, NATE.
DARN, TSUKUBA IS PRETTY GOOD.
へーき へーき
I THINK IT'S TIME FOR ANOTHER MIRACLE.
SERIOUSLY, OKUDA, WHAT IS IT WITH THAT SHOT?
HMM.
IF MY READ ON IT IS RIGHT.
IT'S MORE OF A MIS-UNDERSTOOD J THAN A MIRACLE J.
WHAT'S THAT?
WHAT?
?
LOOK!
TSUKUBA SWITCHES TO A ZONE DEFENSE.
THEY ABANDON THEIR MAN-TO-MAN.
IS IT A COUNTER-MEASURE AGAINST TORRES'S JUMP SHOT?!
オ
オ
オ
オ
オ

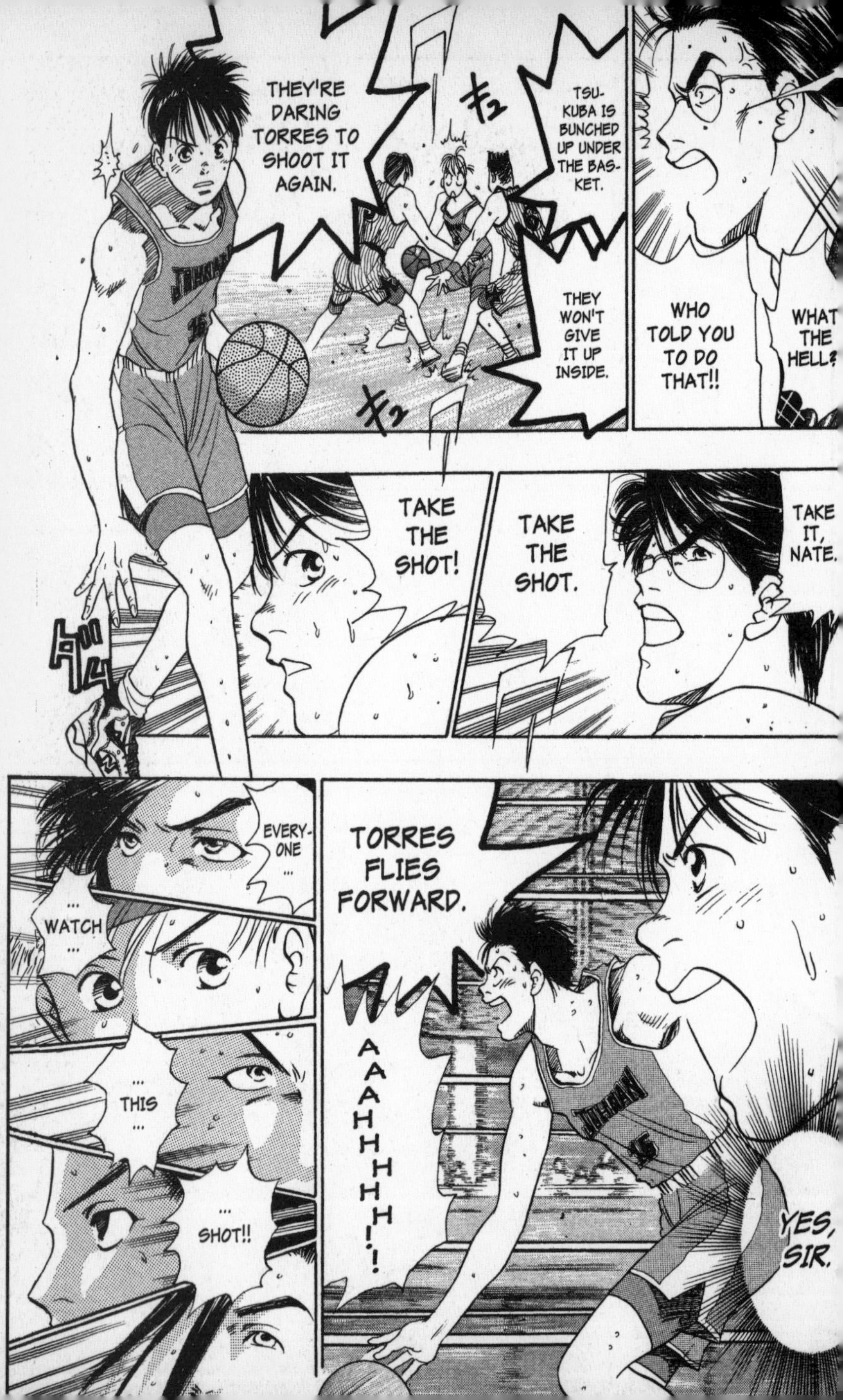
WHAT THE HELL?
WHO TOLD YOU TO DO THAT!!
TSU-KUBA IS BUNCHED UP UNDER THE BAS-KET.
THEY WON'T GIVE IT UP INSIDE.
TAKE IT, NATE.
TAKE THE SHOT.
TAKE THE SHOT!
THEY'RE DARING TORRES TO SHOOT IT AGAIN.
YES, SIR.
TORRES FLIES FORWARD.
AAAHHHHH!!
EVERY-ONE ...
... WATCH ...
... THIS ...
... SHOT!!

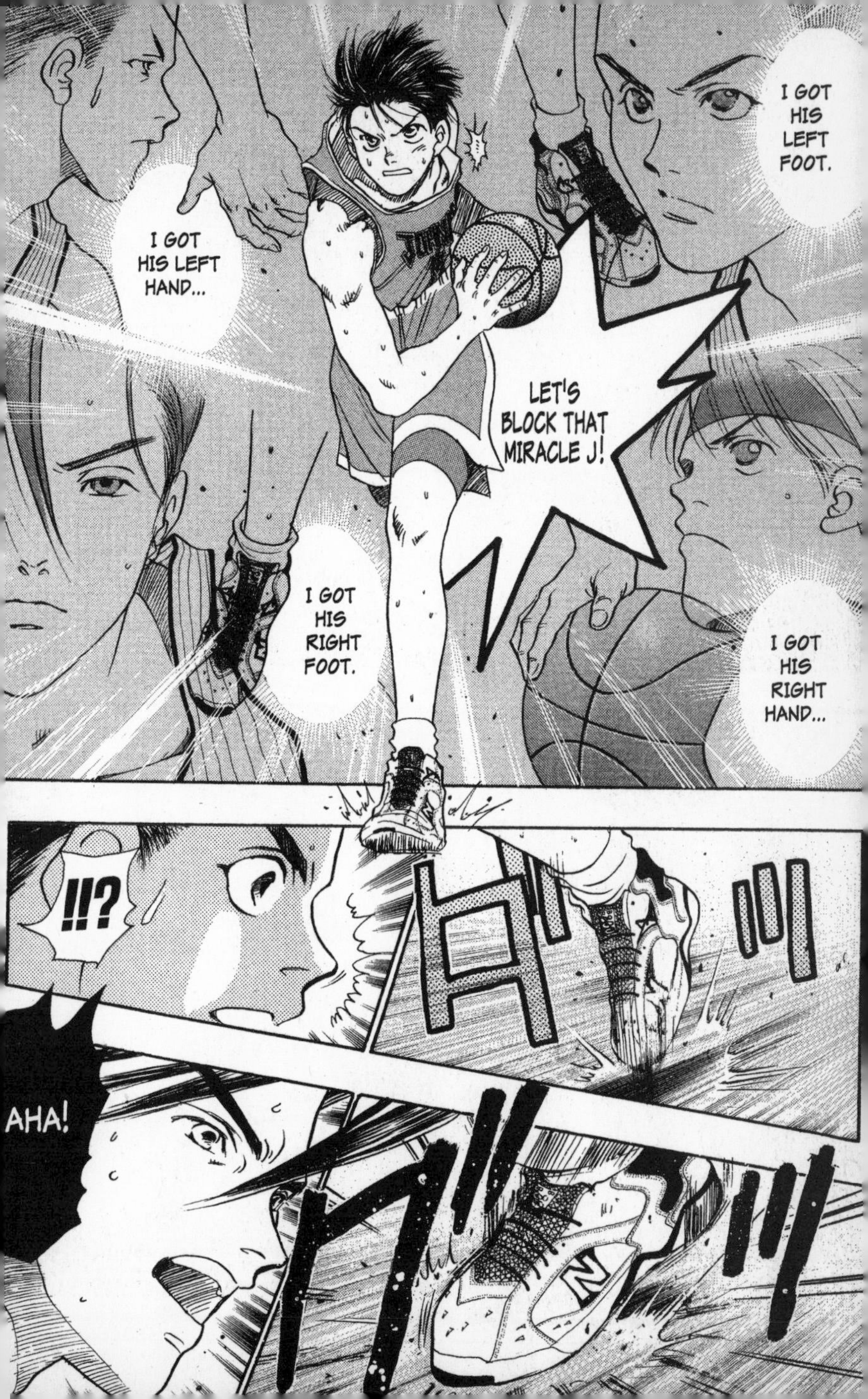

I GOT HIS LEFT FOOT.
I GOT HIS LEFT HAND...
LET'S BLOCK THAT MIRACLE J!
I GOT HIS RIGHT HAND...
I GOT HIS RIGHT FOOT.
!!?
AHA!

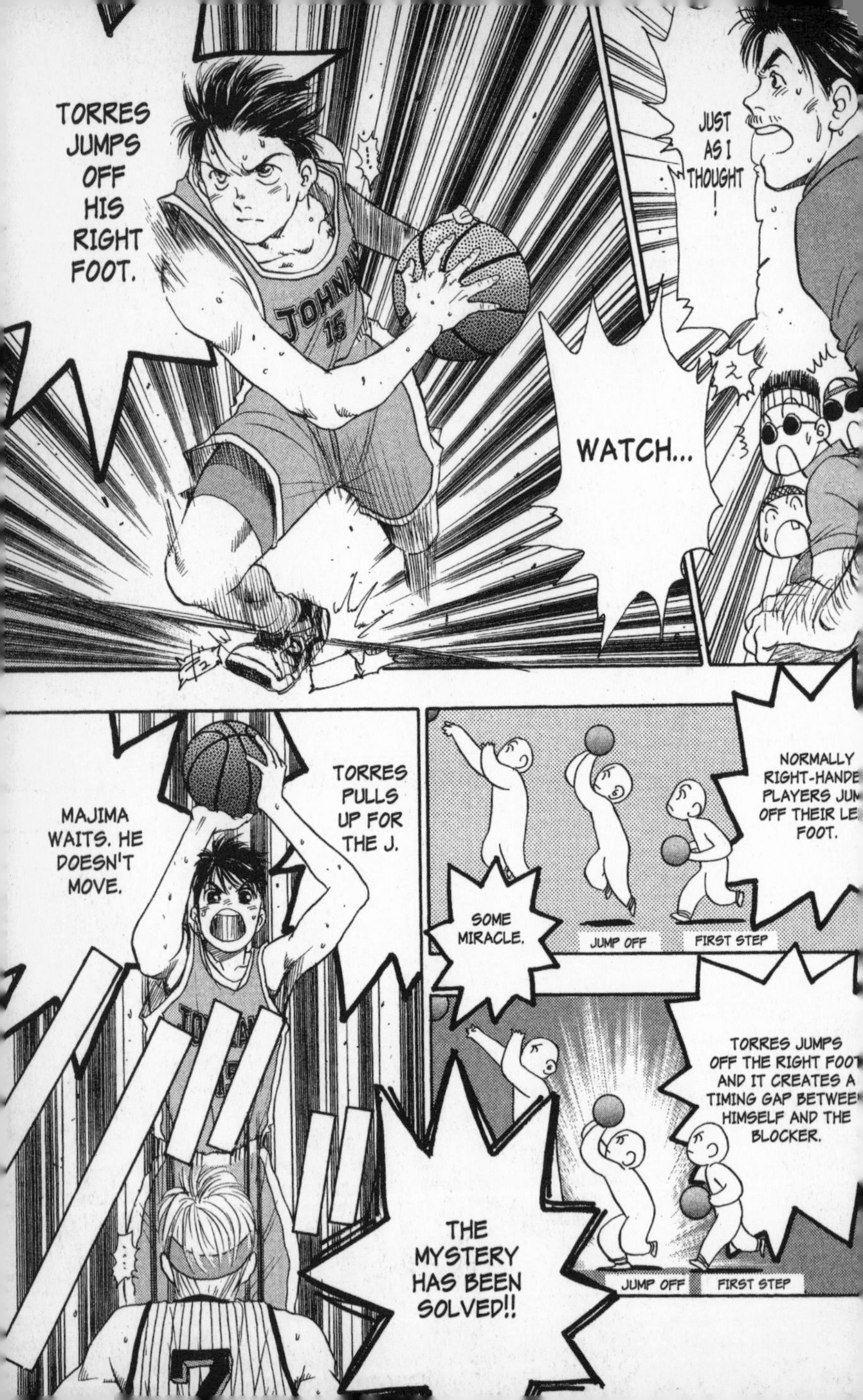

JUST AS I THOUGHT!
え
WATCH...
TORRES JUMPS OFF HIS RIGHT FOOT.
NORMALLY RIGHT-HANDE PLAYERS JUM OFF THEIR LE FOOT.
FIRST STEP
JUMP OFF
SOME MIRACLE.
TORRES JUMPS OFF THE RIGHT FOO AND IT CREATES A TIMING GAP BETWEE HIMSELF AND THE BLOCKER.
FIRST STEP
JUMP OFF
THE MYSTERY HAS BEEN SOLVED!!
TORRES PULLS UP FOR THE J.
MAJIMA WAITS. HE DOESN'T MOVE.

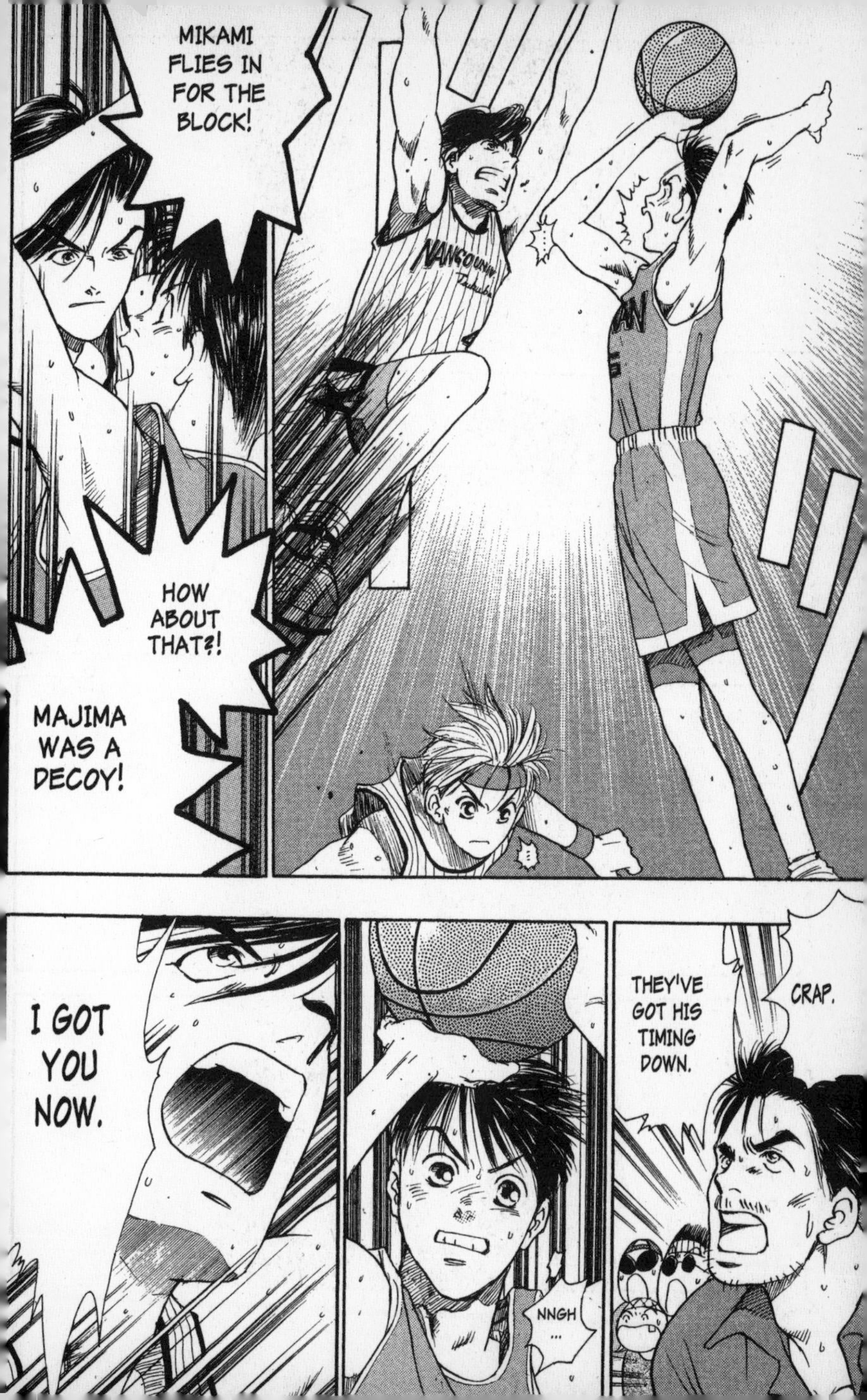
MIKAMI FLIES IN FOR THE BLOCK!
HOW ABOUT THAT?!
MAJIMA WAS A DECOY!
CRAP.
THEY'VE GOT HIS TIMING DOWN.
NNGH ...
I GOT YOU NOW.

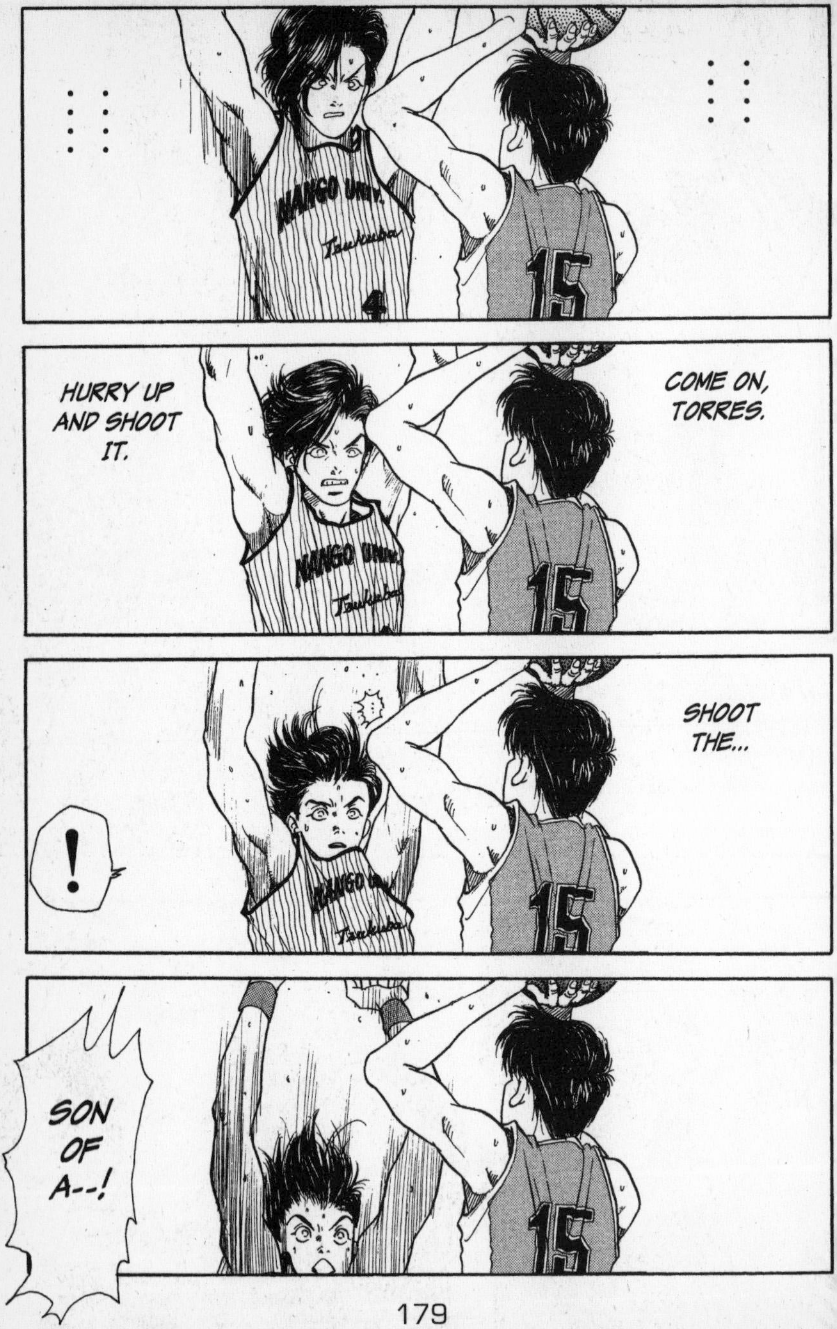
...
...
COME ON, TORRES.
HURRY UP AND SHOOT IT.
SHOOT THE...
!
SON OF A--!

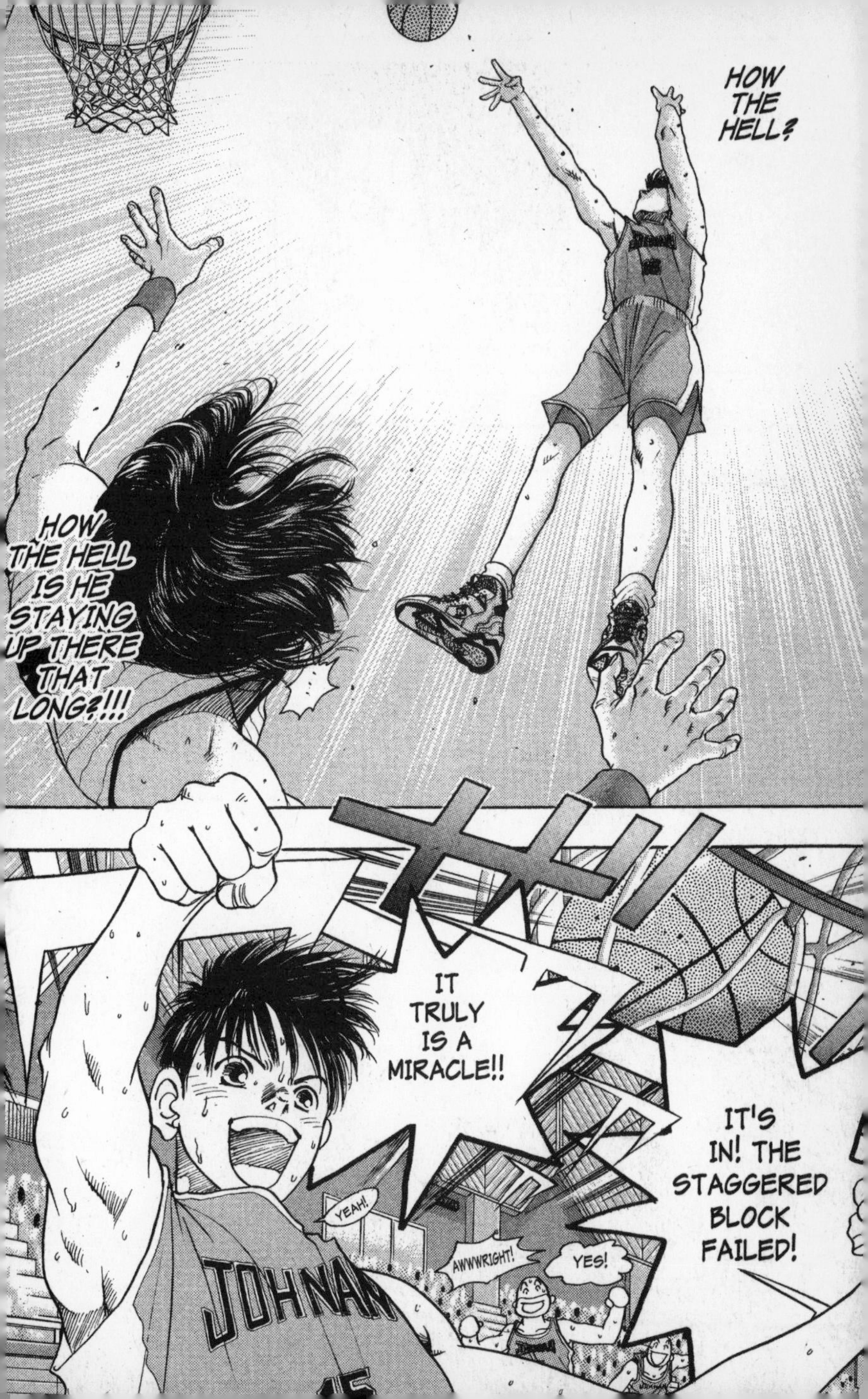
HOW THE HELL?
HOW THE HELL IS HE STAYING UP THERE THAT LONG?!!!
IT'S IN! THE STAGGERED BLOCK FAILED!
IT TRULY IS A MIRACLE!!
YES!
AWWWRIGHT!
YEAH!

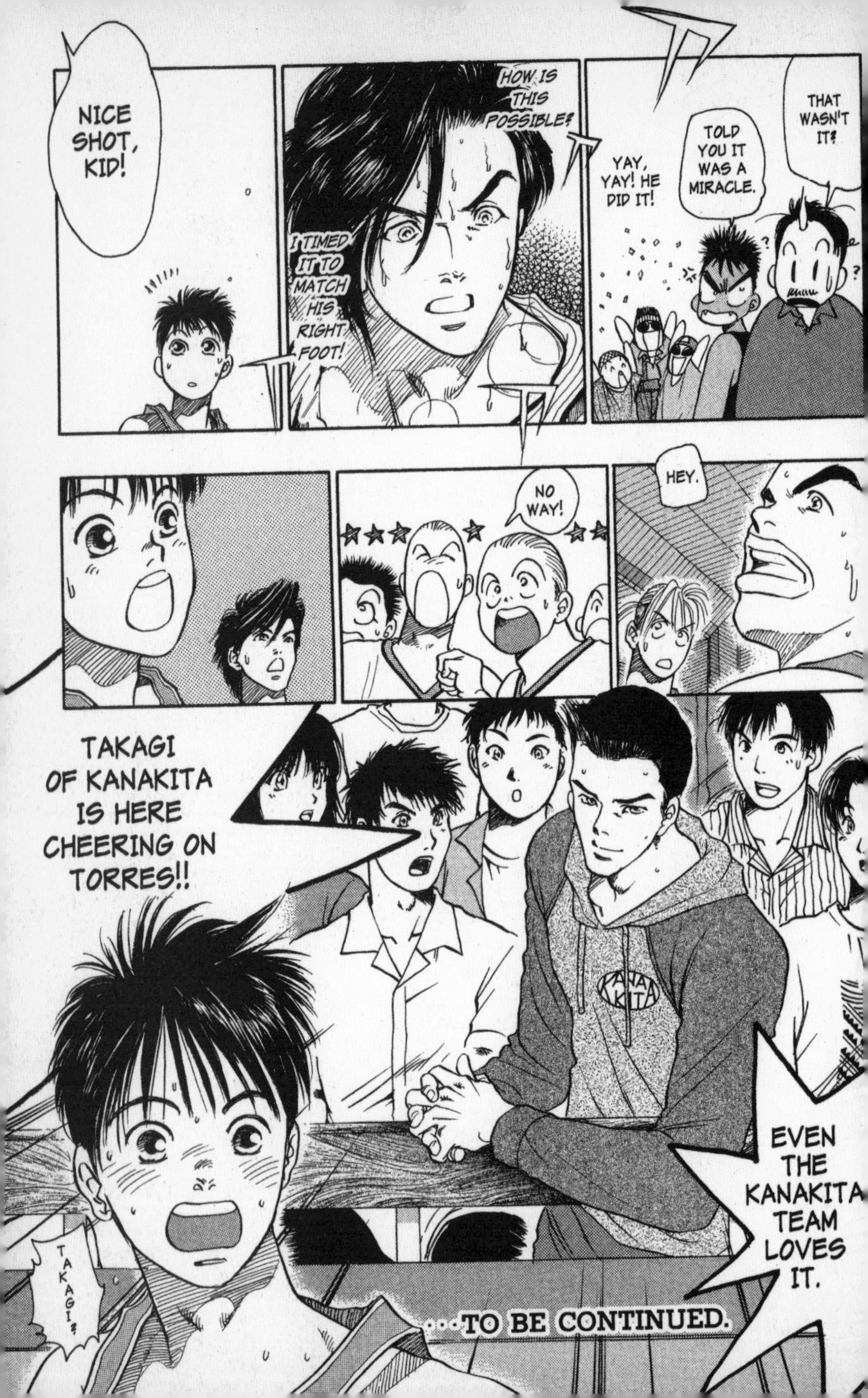
THAT WASN'T IT?
TOLD YOU IT WAS A MIRACLE.
YAY, YAY! HE DID IT!
HOW IS THIS POSSIBLE?
I TIMED IT TO MATCH HIS RIGHT FOOT!
NICE SHOT, KID!
HEY.
NO WAY!
EVEN THE KANAKITA TEAM LOVES IT.
TAKAGI OF KANAKITA IS HERE CHEERING ON TORRES!!
TAKAGI?
...TO BE CONTINUED.

STAY TUNED!!!

We hope you enjoyed your selected manga, *Rebound* Volume 4. Tune in two months from now when the tale continues and Johnan's basketball crew might be in for the basketball blues...

Preview for  Volume 5

Well, Nate may be pulling miracles out of the air, but the game's far from over. The Johnan team is going to need a lot more muscle if they want to take down their archenemies, now under the command of a newly invigorated younger Mikami. But Johnan still has some aces up their sleeve, namely Kyle and Sawamura who are still slothing to the game on a clunky motorbike, which is good because when Shurman's ankle starts acting up, Johnan's going to need more miracles to see them through.

And now, a commercial break...

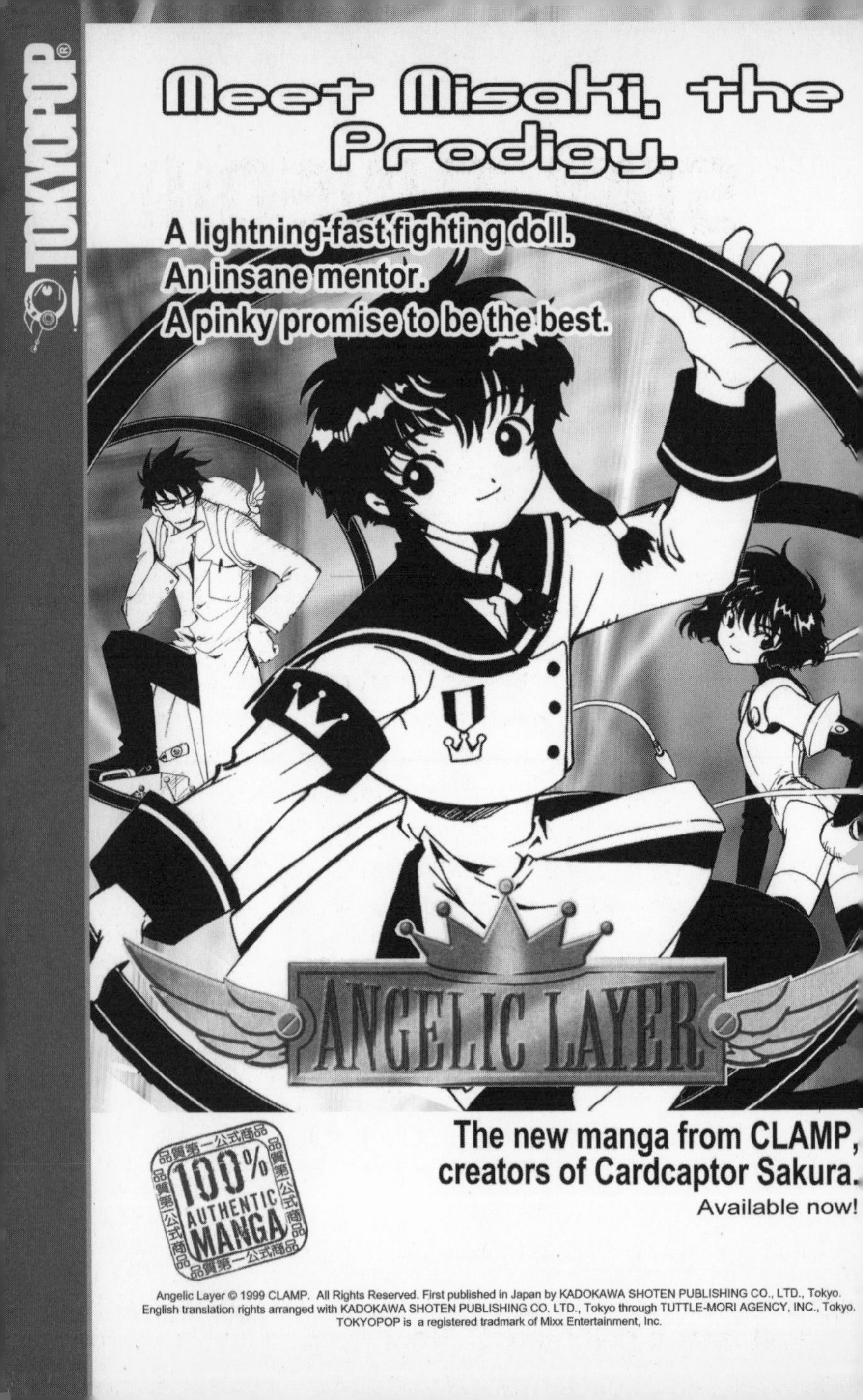
TOKYOPOP®
Meet Misaki, the Prodigy.
A lightning-fast fighting doll.
An insane mentor.
A pinky promise to be the best.
ANGELIC LAYER
100% AUTHENTIC MANGA
品質第一公式商品
The new manga from CLAMP, creators of Cardcaptor Sakura.
Available now!
Angelic Layer © 1999 CLAMP. All Rights Reserved. First published in Japan by KADOKAWA SHOTEN PUBLISHING CO., LTD., Tokyo. English translation rights arranged with KADOKAWA SHOTEN PUBLISHING CO. LTD., Tokyo through TUTTLE-MORI AGENCY, INC., Tokyo. TOKYOPOP is a registered tradmark of Mixx Entertainment, Inc.

TODAY'S HOTTEST MANGA COMES TO AMERICA

KING of HELL

BY RA IN-SOO

ONLY ONE MAN CAN BRIDGE THE RIFT BETWEEN HERE & HELL

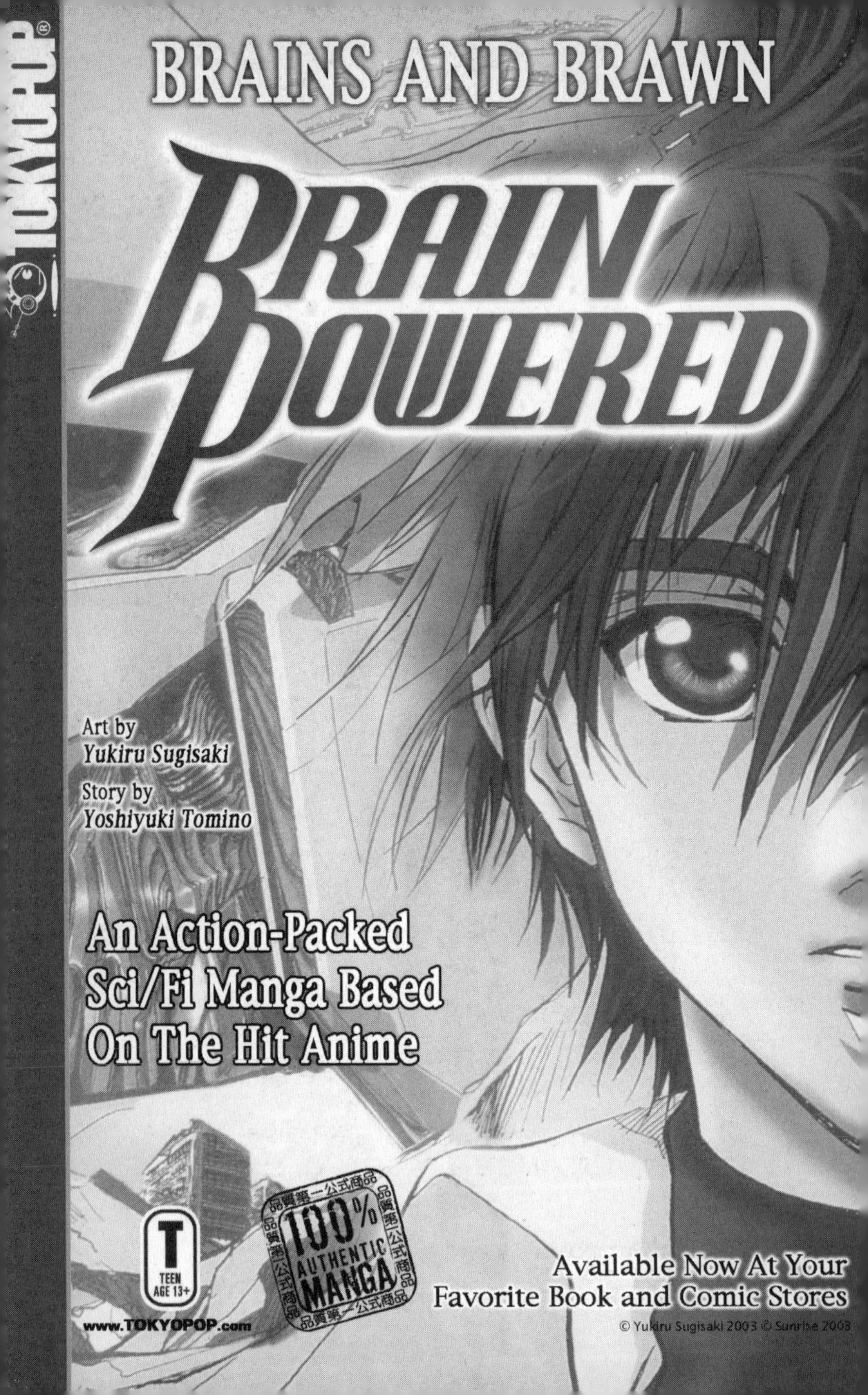
TOKYOPOP
BRAINS AND BRAWN
BRAIN POWERED
Art by
Yukiru Sugisaki
Story by
Yoshiyuki Tomino
An Action-Packed
Sci/Fi Manga Based
On The Hit Anime
T
TEEN
AGE 13+
100%
AUTHENTIC
MANGA
Available Now At Your
Favorite Book and Comic Stores
www.TOKYOPOP.com
© Yukiru Sugisaki 2003 © Sunrise 2003

GATE·KEEPERS
トキーパーズ

By:
Keiji Gotoh

100% AUTHENTIC MANGA

Finding Time to Defend The Earth
Between School & Homework

GET GATEKEEPERS IN YOUR FAVORITE BOOK & COMIC STORES NOW!

Y YOUTH AGE 7+

www.TOKYOPOP.com

TOKYOPOP®

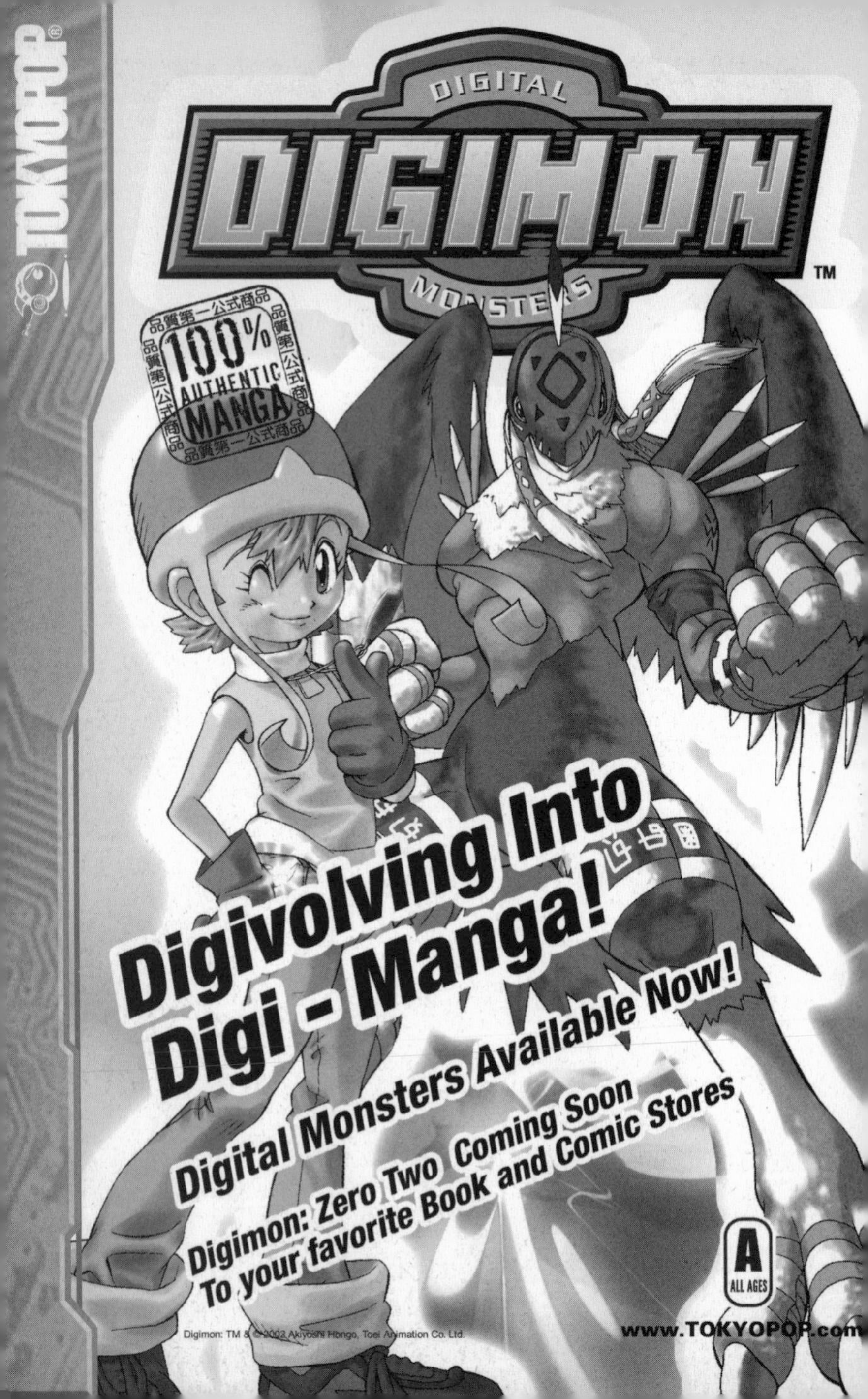
TOKYOPOP
DIGITAL
DIGIMON
MONSTERS
TM
品質第一公式商品
100%
AUTHENTIC
MANGA
Digivolving Into
Digi - Manga!
Digital Monsters Available Now!
Digimon: Zero Two Coming Soon
To your favorite Book and Comic Stores
A
ALL AGES
Digimon: TM & © 2002 Akiyoshi Hongo, Toei Animation Co. Ltd.
www.TOKYOPOP.com

MOBILE SUIT
GUNDAM
THE LAST OUTPOST

TOKYOPOP

ANONTHER EXCITING ADVENTURE
IN THE GUNDAM UNIVERSE

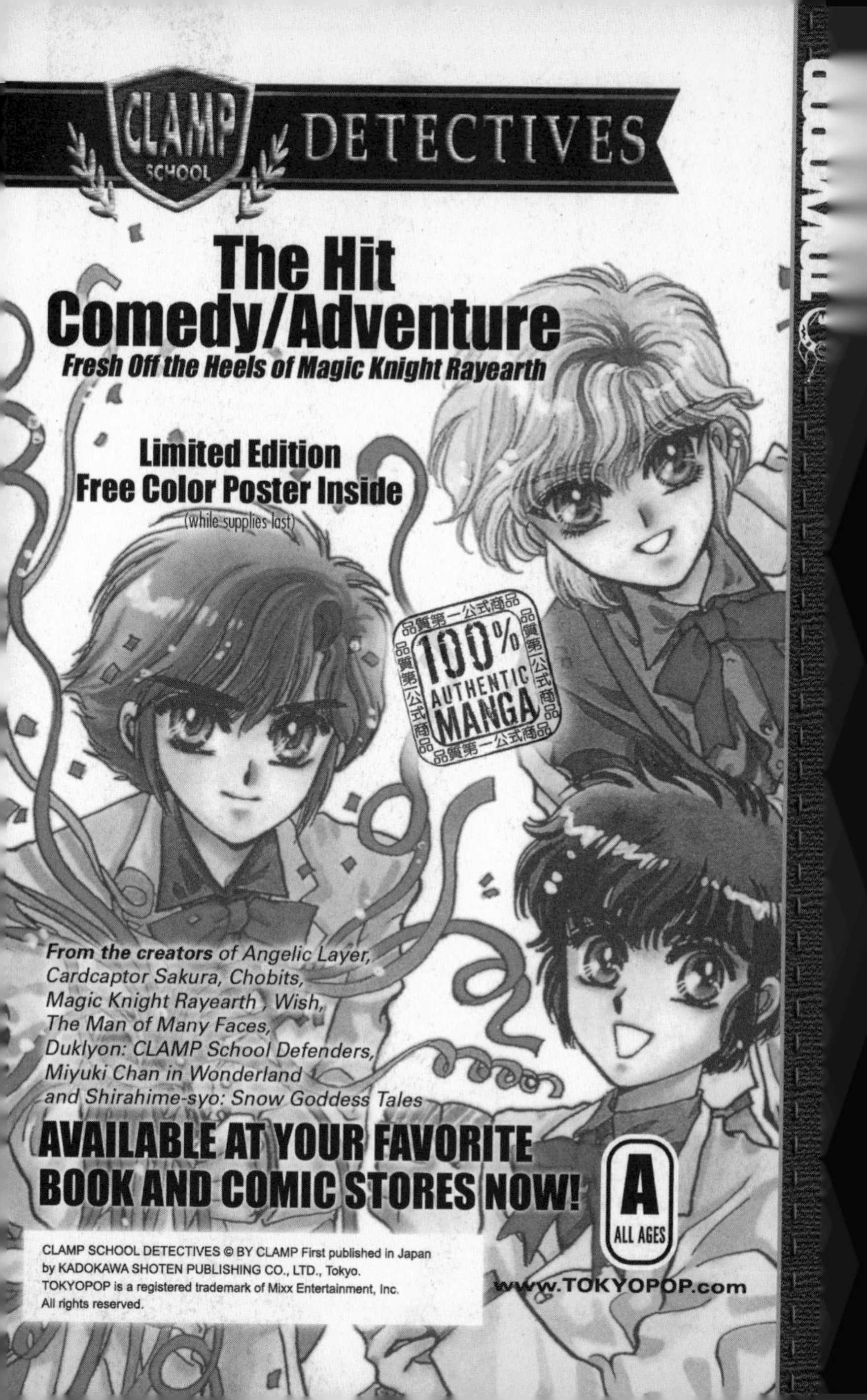
CLAMP SCHOOL
DETECTIVES
The Hit Comedy/Adventure
Fresh Off the Heels of Magic Knight Rayearth
Limited Edition
Free Color Poster Inside
(while supplies last)
品質第一公式商品
100% AUTHENTIC MANGA
From the creators of Angelic Layer, Cardcaptor Sakura, Chobits, Magic Knight Rayearth, Wish, The Man of Many Faces, Duklyon: CLAMP School Defenders, Miyuki Chan in Wonderland and Shirahime-syo: Snow Goddess Tales
AVAILABLE AT YOUR FAVORITE BOOK AND COMIC STORES NOW!
A
ALL AGES
CLAMP SCHOOL DETECTIVES © BY CLAMP First published in Japan by KADOKAWA SHOTEN PUBLISHING CO., LTD., Tokyo. TOKYOPOP is a registered trademark of Mixx Entertainment, Inc. All rights reserved.
www.TOKYOPOP.com
TOKYOPOP

S0-BAW-575

STOP!

This is the back of the book.
You wouldn't want to spoil a great ending!

This book is printed "manga-style," in the authentic Japanese right-to-left format. Since none of the artwork has been flipped or altered, readers get to experience the story just as the creator intended. You've been asking for it, so TOKYOPOP® delivered: authentic, hot-off-the-press, and far more fun!

DIRECTIONS

If this is your first time reading manga-style, here's a quick guide to help you understand how it works.

It's easy... just start in the top right panel and follow the numbers. Have fun, and look for more 100% authentic manga from TOKYOPOP®!